CLASSROOM
ASSESSMENT
TECHNIQUES

CLASSROOM ASSESSMENT TECHNIQUES

A Handbook for College Teachers

SECOND EDITION

Thomas A. Angelo
K. Patricia Cross

 JOSSEY-BASS PUBLISHERS
San Francisco

Published by

JOSSEY-BASS
A Wiley Company
989 Market Street
San Francisco, CA 94103-1741

www.josseybass.com

Jossey-Bass books and products are available through most bookstores. To contact Jossey-Bass directly, call (888) 378-2537, fax to (800) 605-2665, or visit our website at www.josseybass.com.

Substantial discounts on bulk quantities of Jossey-Bass books are available to corporations, professional associations, and other organizations. For details and discount information, contact the special sales department at Jossey-Bass.

We at Jossey-Bass strive to use the most environmentally sensitive paper stocks available to us. Our publications are printed on acid-free recycled stock whenever possible, and our paper always meets or exceeds minimum GPO and EPA requirements.

Library of Congress Cataloging-in-Publication Data

Angelo, Thomas A., date.
    Classroom assessment techniques: a handbook for college teachers
/ Thomas A. Angelo, K. Patricia Cross. – 2nd ed.
      p.   cm. – (The Jossey-Bass higher and adult education series)
    Rev. ed. of: Classroom assessment techniques: a handbook for
faculty, 1988.
    Includes bibliographical references and index.
    ISBN 1-55542-500-3
    1. Educational evaluation – United States – Handbooks, manuals, etc.
    2. College teaching – United States – Handbooks, manuals, etc.
    3. College students – United States – Rating of – Case studies.
    I. Cross, K. Patricia (Kathryn Patricia), date.   II. Title
III. Series.
    LB2822.75.A54   1993
    378.1'25 – dc20   92-33901

SECOND EDITION
HB Printing   20 19 18 17 16 15 14 13

The Jossey-Bass
Higher and Adult Education Series

Contents

Preface

It has been just a decade since *A Nation at Risk* took aim and fired its salvos at the American educational system, initiating an intense reexamination of the quality of teaching and learning at all levels of education. In the 1990s, educational reformers are seeking answers to two fundamental questions: (1) How well are students learning? and (2) How effectively are teachers teaching?

The first question is being addressed primarily by the assessment movement. There is heavy public and political pressure on colleges and universities to explain what they are trying to do and to demonstrate how well they are doing it. Across the country, a majority of the states have mandated some form of assessment for higher education. And most colleges, both public and private, have at least begun to plan ways to assess the effectiveness of their programs. A major problem encountered by the assessment movement, however, is that faculty members are not fully involved in the process, and the results of the institutional assessment are rarely used to make a difference in the classroom.

The second question—How effectively are teachers teaching?—is the subject of continuing debates about the appropriate balance between research and teaching and about how to evaluate and reward good teaching. But across the broad spectrum of higher education, its leaders are calling for more attention to teaching, and there is evidence of increased effort to help faculty members become more effective teachers. Many, if not most, colleges now provide some services to faculty members through offices for instructional improvement, and training for the next generation of college faculty members is gaining momentum through the development of special programs on teaching for graduate teaching assistants.

Classroom Research and Classroom Assessment respond directly to concerns about better learning and more effective teaching. Classroom Research was developed to encourage college teachers to become more systematic and sensitive observers of learning as it takes place every day in their classrooms. Faculty have an exceptional opportunity to use their classrooms as laboratories for the study of learning and through such study to develop a better understanding of the learning process and the impact of their teaching upon it.

Classroom Assessment, a major component of Classroom Research, involves students and teachers in the continuous monitoring of students' learning. It provides faculty with feedback about their effectiveness as teachers, and it gives students a measure of their progress as learners. Most important, because Classroom Assessments are created, administered, and analyzed by teachers themselves on questions of teaching and learning that are important to them, the likelihood that instructors will apply the results of the assessment to their own teaching is greatly enhanced.

AUDIENCE AND BACKGROUND

Classroom Assessment Techniques has been written for college teachers — regardless of their prior training in pedagogy, assessment, or education. It acknowledges the discipline-based orientation of most college faculty members and even documents the fact that teaching goals and priorities are significantly related to the subject matter taught (see Chapter Ten for research findings). This volume is designed as a practical how-to-do-it handbook that college faculty members can use to assess the quality of teaching and learning in their own classrooms. We hope that the detailed and precise instructions provided will help teachers apply their own creativity and knowledge of their discipline to develop assessment measures that meet their particular needs and teaching priorities.

The handbook is a revised and greatly expanded version of *Classroom Assessment Techniques: A Handbook for Faculty* (Cross and Angelo, 1988). A product of our first year of experience with Classroom Research and Assessment, the 1988 handbook contained thirty Classroom Assessment Techniques (CATs) along with suggestions about how to use them. We produced the first book as a "first cut" — a first step toward defining Classroom Assessment and determining its usefulness to classroom teachers. The book was a success, selling thousands of copies, primarily through word of mouth from college teachers who found the Classroom Assessment Techniques stimulating and useful in improving their teaching.

Since 1988, the Classroom Research Project, funded by the Ford Foundation and the Pew Charitable Trusts, has worked to meet the needs of the growing band of college teachers knowledgeable about Classroom Assessment. The project produced two videotapes, exploring the concepts and uses of Classroom Research, and several colleges have since produced their own videotapes for use in staff development activities on their own campuses. Two edited volumes containing teachers' descriptions of their experiences with Classroom Research have been published, along with a number of articles and newsletters. (See Resource E for a bibliography of materials on Classroom Research and Assessment.) In addition, hundreds of workshops have been conducted nationally, regionally, and locally, with staff development specialists and faculty members sharing their knowledge of Classroom Assessment with teaching colleagues on their own campuses.

As the number of teachers interested in Classroom Assessment expands, so does the need for communication and networking. The American Association for Higher Education (AAHE) has established a Classroom Research Community Action Group, which enables Classroom Researchers to meet annually at the AAHE National Conference and sponsors conference sessions concerned with Classroom Research. The Classroom Research Project has also sponsored a series of workshops and conferences at the University of California, Berkeley, where Classroom Researchers can gather to learn and to share experiences and insights.

This new handbook draws on more than five years of experience — our own and that of hundreds of teachers who participated in workshops and campus programs related to the Classroom Research Project. The new volume includes many elements that did not even exist in 1988. For example, it contains a self-scorable version of the Teaching Goals Inventory (TGI), which enables teachers to locate the assessment techniques that are most appropriate for their particular teaching goals. Prior to its publication in this handbook, we used the TGI as an experimental device for clarifying teaching goals during workshops on Classroom Assessment and as a research instrument to inform us about the priorities that college teachers representing a variety of disciplines assigned to the fifty-two teaching goals. (A discussion of the development of the TGI and our research findings is found in Chapters Two and Ten.)

OVERVIEW OF THE CONTENTS

This is a practical handbook, designed for easy reference and for readers with varied levels of experience with Classroom Assessment. Rather than reading it cover to cover, readers may want first to get an overview and an understanding of the purposes and uses of Classroom Assessment; they can then move directly to perusing and exploring the CATs that are most appropriate and interesting for their field of study and their personal teaching goals. To that end, the book is organized into three main parts.

Part One can provide either an introduction to Classroom Assessment or a comprehensive review, depending on the reader's prior experience. The first chapter explains what Classroom Assessment is, how it works, and how to get started using it. Chapters Two and Three introduce the basic tools of Classroom Assessment: the Teaching Goals Inventory and Classroom Assessment Techniques. Chapters Four and Five illustrate the concept in greater depth. Chapter Four describes, step by step, how faculty plan and carry out Classroom Assessment projects, while Chapter Five provides a dozen examples of Classroom Assessment projects carried out in as many different disciplines. These twelve case studies detail the real-life classroom experiences of teachers who adapted and applied some of the Classroom Assessment Techniques described in our initial work.

Part Two is an easy-to-use compendium of fifty different Classroom Assessment Techniques. Chapter Six introduces the CATs and offers readers three indexes to help them find the right "tool" for the right "job." The extensive indexing is new to this handbook — and unique, we believe, to Classroom Assessment. With the alphabetical index, teachers can locate, by name, CATs that they have read about or heard about. The second index groups the CATs under disciplines—highlighting techniques that have proved especially useful to teachers in the various disciplines. The third index groups CATs under six major goal clusters, so that faculty can locate CATs that are most appropriate for assessing their own teaching goals (as determined by their scores on the Teaching Goals Inventory).

The heart of this new volume is contained in Chapters Seven, Eight, and Nine, which present fifty CATs, some completely new and some extensively revised in light of the experience gained from classroom use of the original thirty techniques. These three chapters contain subsets of the CAT collection, with techniques grouped together broadly by what they assess: knowledge and skills (Chapter Seven); attitudes, values, and self-awareness (Chapter Eight); and reactions to instruction (Chapter Nine).

Each CAT follows a basic format that provides the following information: (1) an estimate of the ease of use; (2) a concise description; (3) a definition of the purpose of using the particular technique; (4) a short list of teaching goals (identified by TGI Goal number) that might be assessed by the use of the CAT; (5) suggestions for use; (6) a few actual examples of the ways in which the CAT has been used by instructors from a variety of disciplines; (7) the step-by-step procedures for designing and administering the CAT; (8) some practical advice on how to analyze the data; (9) suggestions for adapting and extending the CAT; (10) pros, (11) cons, and (12) caveats. A brief description of resources and references for further information is also provided for many of the CATs.

In the last two chapters, which constitute Part Three, we look backward and forward. Chapter Ten reviews the lessons we have learned from our experiences to date, and Chapter Eleven suggests promising new directions in Classroom Assessment and Classroom Research. Apart from the bibliography (Resource E) mentioned earlier, the resources (A–D) provide background on the Teaching Goals Inventory.

We believe that this handbook contains all the information, examples, and instructions needed by any instructor wishing to use Classroom Assessment in his or her own classroom. While our intention is to provide a self-contained guide that can be used independently, our experience suggests that Classroom Assessment is more effective, more intellectually engaging, and more fun when the assessment process is shared with colleagues. Comparing teaching goals on the TGI provides fascinating insights into one's own priorities as well as those of colleagues in the same or different disciplines. The process of finding, adapting, and devising CATs that are especially appropriate to a particular class is more rewarding, and probably more productive, when shared with others. The process of interpreting the results of the analysis is usually enriched by the perspectives of colleagues and, of course, by those of students. Thus, we encourage the use of the handbook by individual faculty members, to be sure, but also by groups of teachers—dyads, triads, seminars and study groups, departments and divisions, staff development workshops, and any other groups of teachers interested in learning more about teaching and learning. To that end, Chapter Eleven contains some suggestions for the collaborative and departmental use of Classroom Assessment and Classroom Research.

ACKNOWLEDGMENTS   In developing the concept of Classroom Research and in preparing this handbook of its applications to Classroom Assessment, we have drawn on the ideas and research of scholars through the ages who have sought to improve teaching and learning, and on the experiences and insights of dedicated college teachers who are constantly in search of more effective ways to help students learn. But most immediately, we are indebted to the many classroom teachers from a variety of colleges and teaching disciplines who have helped us clarify our concepts and develop useful and exciting ways to assess learning in classrooms of every description. Through their use of Classroom Assessment and their modifications of the techniques presented in our 1988 handbook, these teachers have inspired us by their dedication to better teaching, informed us about what is practical and realistic, and kept us true to our mission of providing useful assessments of teaching and learning, directed by faculty.

Early work on Classroom Research, from 1986 to 1988, was supported by three organizations that provided resources and staff time to prepare the first version of *Classroom Assessment Techniques* (Cross and Angelo, 1988). The National Center for Research to Improve Postsecondary Teaching and Learning (NCRIPTAL) at the University of Michigan, the Harvard Graduate School of Education, and the Harvard Seminar on Assessment all provided timely support and staff for the literature search, the conceptualization of Classroom Research, and the creation, adaptation, and categorization of the initial thirty Classroom Assessment Techniques. NCRIPTAL also published and distributed the 1988 handbook and sponsored early Classroom Research workshops. For their encouragement and assistance throughout, we extend special thanks to Richard J. Light, director of the Harvard Seminar on Assessment; Joan S. Stark, director of NCRIPTAL; and Wilbert J. McKeachie, associate director of NCRIPTAL.

Beginning in 1988, grants from the Ford Foundation and the Pew Charitable Trusts provided funds for the creation of the Classroom Research Project. The project, initially established at Harvard, moved to the University of California, Berkeley, in the fall of 1988. The Ford and Pew grants provided support for the development and dissemination of workshop materials and the training of more than five thousand college teachers in Classroom Assessment methods, plus extensive work on the construction, administration, and analysis of the Teaching Goals Inventory.

The development of the TGI benefited from the work of many people, whose assistance we gratefully acknowledge. Elizabeth Fideler, a doctoral student at the Harvard Graduate School of Education in 1986 and currently the associate dean for teaching/learning and professional development at Massachusetts Bay Community College, assisted in the review of the literature, the construction of the first set of items, and the pilot surveys at Bradford College and Miami-Dade Community College. Jane Gerloff and Aline Sayer from Harvard and Patricia Busk of the University of San Francisco provided data analysis for the various surveys and cluster analyses. John Losak, director of institutional research at Miami-Dade, selected and engaged the participation of the random sample of Miami-Dade faculty. Michael O'Keefe provided liaison for the participation of the thirteen colleges from the Council for the Advancement of Private Higher Education

(CAPHE) in the spring 1988 administration. Mary Ann Rehnke played a similar valuable role in helping us involve seventeen member institutions from the Council of Independent Colleges (CIC) in the 1990 survey.

In addition, we would like to thank the many faculty and administrative liaisons who assisted in the various administrations of the TGI on their campuses, and the faculty development specialists who helped in the interpretation and revision of items. We are grateful to the thousands of faculty members who contributed their perspectives on teaching priorities through responding to the questionnaire, as well as through contributing valuable insights from their experience with the TGI in workshops and in their own classrooms.

As the Classroom Research Project grew, many other people made valuable contributions to various phases of the project. We would especially like to acknowledge the work of Kate O. Brooks, a physical science professor and faculty development specialist at Los Medanos College in Pittsburg, California, who played an important role in developing the Classroom Assessment Project Cycle and the related guidelines discussed in Chapter Four. Mardee Jenrette and Robert McCabe of Miami-Dade Community College and Lorraine Barry and Nancy Stetson of the College of Marin in California assisted in the development of the early training videotapes in Classroom Research. Kathleen Kirkpatrick of the College of Marin was the producer of the two videotapes developed with support from the Classroom Research Project (see Resource E). Through their hard work, Sue Kahl Smith and Faye Bishop, of the University of California, Berkeley, Extension Division, made the three summer workshops and the 1990 Conference on Classroom Research possible. Micaela Rubalcava, a doctoral candidate in the Graduate School of Education at Berkeley, served as the project's graduate assistant from 1988 through 1990, providing valuable assistance in virtually every aspect of the effort. Several other skilled professionals helped us through various iterations of this project. For their expert word processing, we thank Bobbi Callison, Anne Cullinane, Nancy Dunn (who also proofread many drafts of the manuscript), Jane Gerloff, and Vanessa True.

Finally, a vote of thanks to our respective employers between 1988 and 1992—the Graduate School of Education at the University of California, Berkeley; California State University, Long Beach; and Boston College—all of which have been supportive and helpful along the way.

January 1993

Thomas A. Angelo
Chestnut Hill, Massachusetts

K. Patricia Cross
Berkeley, California

The Authors

Thomas A. Angelo is founding director of the Academic Development Center at Boston College. In 1990–91, he directed the Center for Faculty Development at California State University, Long Beach, where he also taught political science. From 1988 to 1990, Angelo was assistant director of the Classroom Research Project and a lecturer at the Graduate School of Education at the University of California, Berkeley. Before that, he served as assistant director of Harvard University's Seminar on Assessment. Angelo received his B.A. degree (1975) from California State University, Sacramento, in government. He holds two master's degrees from Boston University — an M.A. degree (1977) in political science and an Ed.M. degree (1981) in teaching English as a second language — and has taught a variety of subjects in high school, college, and graduate school settings. Angelo received his Ed.D. degree (1987) from the Harvard Graduate School of Education, where he concentrated on applied linguistics and assessment. He has been a Fulbright Fellow in Italy and a Gulbenkian Foundation Fellow in Portugal and has taught in Malaysia.

Since 1986, Angelo has worked with K. Patricia Cross to develop and disseminate Classroom Research, an effort to bring the benefits of assessment and educational research into the classroom and under the control of faculty members. In the past five years, he has led workshops in Classroom Assessment involving nearly five thousand college teachers and faculty developers across the United States, as well as in Canada and Germany. Angelo coauthored *Classroom Assessment Techniques: A Handbook for Faculty* (1988, with K. P. Cross) and edited *Classroom Research: Early Lessons from Success* (1991), in the Jossey-Bass New Directions for Teaching and Learning series.

K. Patricia Cross, director of the Classroom Research Project, is the Elizabeth and Edward Conner Professor of Higher Education in the Graduate School of Education at the University of California, Berkeley. A social psychologist by training, Cross has had a varied career as university administrator (University of Illinois and Cornell University), researcher (Educational Testing Service and the Center for Research and Development in Higher Education, University of California, Berkeley), and teacher (Harvard Graduate School of Education and Graduate School of Education at the University of California, Berkeley).

Cross received her B.S. degree (1948) from Illinois State University in mathematics and her A.M. (1951) and Ph.D. (1958) degrees from the University of Illinois, in psychology and social psychology, respectively. She is the author of six books — including *Beyond the Open Door* (1971), *Accent on Learning* (1976), and *Adults as Learners* (1981) — and more than 150 articles and chapters.

Cross has been recognized for her scholarship by election to the National Academy of Education and receipt of the E. F. Lindquist Award for research from the American Educational Research Association. Twice elected president of the American Association for Higher Education, she has been awarded many honors for leadership in higher education, among them the 1990 Leadership Award from the American Association of Community and Junior Colleges, the Adult Educator of the Year Award from the Coalition of Adult Education Associations, and an award for "outstanding contributions to the improvement of instruction" by the National Council of Instructional Administrators.

K. Patricia Cross has lectured widely on higher education in the United States, France, Germany, the former Soviet Union, Japan, Australia, and Holland. She serves on the editorial boards of six national and international journals of higher education and is currently continuing her research on the improvement of teaching and learning in higher education.

Getting Started
in Classroom
Assessment

What Is Classroom Assessment?

CHAPTER

1

Through close observation of students in the process of learning, the collection of frequent feedback on students' learning, and the design of modest classroom experiments, classroom teachers can learn much about how students learn and, more specifically, how students respond to particular teaching approaches. Classroom Assessment helps individual college teachers obtain useful feedback on what, how much, and how well their students are learning. Faculty can then use this information to refocus their teaching to help students make their learning more efficient and more effective.

PURPOSE OF CLASSROOM ASSESSMENT

There are more than three thousand colleges and universities in the United States, and the diversity in their missions and students is enormous. Yet all these institutions share one fundamental goal: to produce the highest possible quality of student learning. In other words, the central aim of all colleges is to help students learn more effectively and efficiently than they could on their own.

Learning can and often does take place without the benefit of teaching—and sometimes even in spite of it—but there is no such thing as effective teaching in the absence of learning. Teaching without learning is just talking. College instructors who have assumed that their students were learning what they were trying to teach them are regularly faced with disappointing evidence to the contrary when they grade tests and term papers. Too often, students have not learned as much or as well as was expected. There are gaps, sometimes considerable ones, between what was taught and what has been learned. By the time faculty notice these gaps in knowledge or understanding, it is frequently too late to remedy the problems.

To avoid such unhappy surprises, faculty and students need better ways to monitor learning throughout the semester. Specifically, teachers need a continuous flow of accurate information on student learning. For example, if a teacher's goal is to help students learn points A through Z during the course, then that teacher needs first to know whether all students are really starting at point A and, as the course proceeds, whether they have reached intermediate points B, G, L, R, W, and so on. To ensure high-quality learning, it is not enough to test students when the syllabus has arrived at points M and Z. Classroom Assessment is particularly useful for checking how well students are learning at those initial and intermediate points, and for providing information for improvement when learning is less than satisfactory.

Through practice in Classroom Assessment, faculty become better able to understand and promote learning, and increase their ability to help the students themselves become more effective, self-assessing, self-directed learners. Simply put, the central purpose of Classroom Assessment is to empower both teachers and their students to improve the quality of learning in the classroom.

CHARACTERISTICS OF CLASSROOM ASSESSMENT

Classroom Assessment is an approach designed to help teachers find out what students are learning in the classroom and how well they are learning it. This approach is learner-centered, teacher-directed, mutually beneficial, formative, context-specific, ongoing, and firmly rooted in good practice.

Learner-Centered

Classroom Assessment focuses the primary attention of teachers and students on observing and improving learning, rather than on observing and improving teaching. To improve learning, it may often be more effective to help students change their study habits or develop their metacognitive skills (skills in thinking about their own thinking and learning) than to change the instructor's teaching behavior. In the end, if they are to become independent, lifelong learners, students must learn to take full responsibility for their learning. To achieve that end, both teachers and students will need to make adjustments to improve learning. Classroom Assessment can provide information to guide them in making those adjustments.

Teacher-Directed

A defining characteristic of any profession is that it depends on the wise and effective use of judgment and knowledge. No one can provide teachers with rules that will tell them what to do from moment to moment in the complex and fluid reality of a college classroom. What faculty do depends on their skill, experience, professional knowledge, and insight. Classroom Assessment respects the autonomy, academic freedom, and professional judgment of college faculty. As a result, in this approach, the individual teacher decides what to assess, how to assess, and how to respond to the information gained through the assessment. Furthermore, the teacher is not obliged to share the results of Classroom Assessment with anyone outside the classroom.

Mutually Beneficial

Because it is focused on learning, Classroom Assessment requires the active participation of students. By cooperating in assessment, students reinforce their grasp of the course content and strengthen their own skills at self-assessment. Their motivation is increased when they realize that faculty are interested and invested in their success as learners. When students focus more clearly, participate more actively, and feel more confident that they can succeed, they are likely to do better in their course work.

Faculty also sharpen their teaching focus by continually asking themselves three questions: "What are the essential skills and knowledge I am trying to teach?" "How can I find out whether students are learning them?" "How can I help students learn better?" As teachers work closely with students to answer these questions, they improve their teaching skills and gain new insights.

Formative

Classroom Assessment is a formative rather than a summative approach to assessment. Its purpose is to improve the quality of student learning, not to provide evidence for evaluating or grading students; consequently, many of the concerns that constrain testing do not apply. Good summative assessments—tests and other graded evaluations—must be demonstrably reliable, valid, and free of bias. They must take into account student anxiety, cheating, and issues of fairness. Classroom Assessments, on the other hand, are almost never graded and are almost always anonymous. Their aim is to provide faculty with information on what, how much, and how well students are learning, in order to help them better prepare to succeed—both on the subsequent graded evaluations and in the world beyond the classroom.

Context-Specific

To be most useful, Classroom Assessments have to respond to the particular needs and characteristics of the teachers, students, and disciplines to which they are applied. Any good mechanic or carpenter will tell you, "You need the right tool to do the job right"; similarly, you need the right Classroom Assessment Technique to answer the question right. Therefore, Classroom Assessment is context-specific: what works well in one class will not necessarily work in another.

As all experienced college teachers know, each class has its own particular dynamic, its own collective personality, its own "chemistry." Many of us who have been assigned to teach two sections of the same course in a given semester—using the same syllabus, the same books, the same lecture notes, perhaps even the same room—have discovered that these "parallel" sections quickly become very different classes. Each individual student brings a complex mix of background variables to the course. The student's socioeconomic class, linguistic and cultural background, attitudes and values, level of general academic preparation, learning strategies and skills, and previous knowledge of the specific subject matter can all influence his or her performance in the course. As students interact in the classroom, the mixture of variables that can affect learning becomes vastly more complex. In addition, the instructor, the discipline, the organization of the course, the materials used, and even the time of day the class meets—all have an effect on classroom learning.

As a result of these complex interactions, each class develops its own "microculture." The most successful faculty members are those who recognize and respond to these differences by fitting their teaching to the context of the class, even as they subtly shape that context through their teaching. Classroom Assessment respects and depends on the faculty's professional judgment, the "craft knowledge" that college teachers develop over time. We assume that the most appropriate person to assess student learning is the person who is responsible for promoting student learning: the individual faculty member. That is why the Classroom Assessment Techniques in this handbook are presented as examples and suggestions to be adapted, not as models to be adopted.

Ongoing

Classroom Assessment is an ongoing process, perhaps best thought of as the creation and maintenance of a classroom "feedback loop." By employing a number of simple Classroom Assessment Techniques that are quick and easy to use, teachers get feedback from students on their learning. Faculty then complete the loop by providing students with feedback on the results of the assessment and suggestions for improving learning. To check on the usefulness of their suggestions, faculty use Classroom Assessment again, continuing the "feedback loop." As this approach becomes integrated into everyday classroom activities, the communications loop connecting faculty to students—and teaching to learning—becomes more efficient and more effective.

Rooted in Good Teaching Practice

Most college teachers already collect some feedback on their students' learning and use that feedback to inform their teaching. Classroom Assessment is an attempt to build on existing good practice by making it more systematic, more flexible, and more effective. Teachers ask questions, react to students' questions, monitor body language and facial expressions, read homework and tests, and so on. Classroom Assessment provides a way to integrate assessment systematically and seamlessly into the traditional classroom teaching and learning process.

By taking a few minutes to administer a simple assessment before teaching a particular class session, the teacher can get a clearer idea of where the students are and, thus, where to begin instruction. A quick assessment during the class can reveal how well the students are following the lesson in progress. Classroom Assessment immediately after the class session helps to reinforce the material taught and also uncovers gaps in understanding before they become serious impediments to further learning.

Finally, teaching students techniques for self-assessment that they can use in class or while they are studying helps them integrate classroom learning with learning outside school. Directed practice in self-assessment also gives students the opportunity to develop metacognitive skills; that is, to become skilled in thinking carefully about their own thinking and learning.

NEED FOR CLASSROOM ASSESSMENT   As they are teaching, faculty monitor and react to student questions, comments, body language, and facial expressions in an almost automatic fashion. This "automatic" information gathering and impression formation is, in large part, a subconscious and implicit process. Teachers depend heavily on their impressions of student learning and make important judgments based on them, but they rarely make those informal assessments explicit or check them against the students' own impressions or ability to perform. In the course of teaching, college faculty assume a great deal about their students' learning, but most of their assumptions remain untested.

Even when college teachers routinely gather potentially useful information on student learning through questions, quizzes, homework, and exams, it is often collected too late—at least from the students' perspective—to affect their learning. In practice, it is very difficult to "de-program" students who are used to thinking of anything they have been tested and graded on as being "over and done with." Consequently, the most effective times to assess and provide feedback are before the chapter tests or the midterm and final examinations. Classroom Assessment aims at providing that early feedback.

THE SEVEN BASIC ASSUMPTIONS OF CLASSROOM ASSESSMENT

Our model of Classroom Assessment is based on seven assumptions. They are stated below, along with brief observations about their applicability to the present state of higher education.

ASSUMPTION 1

The quality of student learning is directly, although not exclusively, related to the quality of teaching. Therefore, one of the most promising ways to improve learning is to improve teaching.

The publication of *A Nation at Risk* in 1983 kicked off an intense examination of the quality of education in the United States. Mounting political and economic pressures to improve the quality of education led to widespread interest in developing better indicators of student learning. As institutions sought to meet demands for accountability by determining the outcomes of their programs and documenting their effectiveness, the general lack of information about the effects of college on student learning became painfully clear.

Assessment, a term applied to a wide range of approaches used to measure educational effectiveness, soon became a cornerstone of the reform movement. During the 1980s, assessment usually was undertaken for the purpose of improving effectiveness at system, campus, or program levels. Typically, commercially available, norm-referenced tests and locally developed, criterion-referenced instruments were administered to large numbers of students; and the results of these assessments were used to respond to external reporting requirements for accountability, to guide curriculum revision, or to evaluate the effectiveness of specific programs. In most cases, these macro-level, top-down assessment efforts involved relatively few faculty, and their effects rarely trickled down to the classroom level. The major players during the first few years of the national "assessment movement" were state officials, campus administrators, institutional researchers, and test-and-measurement specialists. At the same time, most of the questions being asked concerned what and how much (or how little) students already knew at point A or had learned between points A and B. Comparatively little attention was paid to assessing how well students were learning or to discovering what factors directly influence the quality of student learning in the classroom.

Yet it is in those thousands of college classrooms across the nation that the fundamental work of higher education—teaching and learning—takes place. If assessment is to improve the quality of student learning, and not just provide greater accountability, both faculty and students must become personally invested and actively involved in the process. One way to involve them is to build a complementary, micro-level, "grass-roots" assessment movement. Classroom Assessment aims to do just that by developing methods to bring the benefits of assessment into individual classrooms and under the control of individual teachers and learners.

ASSUMPTION 2

To improve their effectiveness, teachers need first to make their goals and objectives explicit and then to get specific, comprehensible feedback on the extent to which they are achieving those goals and objectives.

Effective assessment begins with clear goals. Before faculty can assess how well their students are learning, they must identify and clarify what they are trying to teach. This seems straightforward enough. When asked, most faculty can say what it is they are trying to teach. For the purpose of assessment, the difficulty lies in the kinds of answers they give. College teachers tend to define their instructional goals in terms of course content. When asked "What are your teaching goals for this class?" most college faculty at first will say something like "My goal is to teach linear algebra" or "I'm trying to teach the nineteenth-century British novel" or "I teach introductory-level Japanese." It usually takes some hard thinking before teachers can articulate the specific skills and competencies they hope to teach through the course content. After reconsidering the question, they give such answers as these: "I want to help my students learn to define and solve real-world problems in engineering and physics that require the application of linear algebra," or "I want to help my students develop an informed, critical appreciation of nineteenth-century British literature and foster the kind of thoughtful reading that they can enjoy throughout their lives," or "I want my students to learn enough Japanese to carry on simple conversations and read simple texts." Though they remain broadly drawn, these "second-round" goals help faculty recognize what guides their choice of course content, or what ought to. These goals, focusing on the knowledge, skills, and values that students will develop if they succeed in a given course, can be further limited and clarified until they are actually assessable.

One instrument designed to help faculty identify and clarify their instructional goals is the Teaching Goals Inventory, or TGI. A self-scorable version of this instrument, developed by the Classroom Research Project after three years of field testing and research, appears in Chapter Two and as Resource B. The fifty-two goals in the TGI are phrased very broadly, in order to be applicable across disciplines. Nonetheless, these goals can serve as useful starting points for reflection and discussion.

After faculty members identify specific teaching goals they wish to assess, they can better determine what kinds of feedback to collect. At this stage, teachers need ways to collect that feedback. The Classroom Assessment Techniques (CATs) described in this handbook can be thought of as a collection of "tools" faculty can use to get feedback on how well they are achieving their teaching goals. In addition, these techniques can reinforce student learning of the goals being assessed. CATs reinforce student learning in three ways: by focusing student attention on the most important elements of the course; by providing additional practice in valuable learning and thinking skills; and by training students to become more self-aware, self-assessing, independent learners. For these reasons, we think of CATs as both "assessment techniques" and "teaching strategies," and we believe that their dual nature is a strength.

ASSUMPTION 3

To improve their learning, students need to receive appropriate and focused feedback early and often; they also need to learn how to assess their own learning.

Students need opportunities to give and get feedback on their learning before they are evaluated for grades. If they are to become self-directed, lifelong learners, they also need instruction and practice in self-assessment.

ASSUMPTION 4

The type of assessment most likely to improve teaching and learning is that conducted by faculty to answer questions they themselves have formulated in response to issues or problems in their own teaching.

While assessment at the institutional or program level can provide useful information to the faculty as a whole, large-scale assessments are rarely designed to ask questions that are meaningful and useful to individual classroom teachers. For example, it is both legitimate and useful for a college to assess the overall outcomes of general education or what students have learned through studies in the major. The results of such assessments, however, tend to apply more to the structure of the curriculum or the organization of programs and departments than to teaching and learning in particular courses. To best understand their students' learning, faculty need specific and timely information about the particular individuals in their classes, not about the student body in general or all chemistry majors. As a result of these different needs and purposes, there is often a gap between assessment and classroom teaching.

One goal of Classroom Assessment is to reduce the gap between teaching and assessment. Engaging faculty in the design and practice of Classroom Assessment is one way of ensuring that the questions asked by the assessor are meaningful and useful to the teacher. Moreover, as faculty become more involved in carrying out their own assessments of student learning, they also will become more interested in and capable of making use of the generalized findings that result from large-scale assessments.

ASSUMPTION 5

Systematic inquiry and intellectual challenge are powerful sources of motivation, growth, and renewal for college teachers, and Classroom Assessment can provide such challenge.

Since the 1980s, there has been much discussion in higher education about the proper definition of scholarship and about the professional identity of faculty. The implicit assumption that research and publication in the disciplines are the most appropriate measures of professional achievement for all faculty members, and of academic excellence for all postsecondary institutions, has been increasingly called into question. Even in research universities such as Harvard, Stanford, and the University of California, Berkeley, where the mission of the institution is in great part to push back the frontiers of knowledge through disciplinary research, there is an increasing recognition of the importance of teaching. In two- and four-year teaching institutions, there is also a growing awareness that faculty need to seek intellectual challenge throughout their careers. We believe that such challenge may legitimately be found in many activities: through research in the disciplines, through creative and scholarly activities, and through the systematic study of classroom teaching and learning.

Most colleges and universities are teaching institutions, and most faculty—70 percent according to a 1985 Carnegie survey (*Chronicles of Higher Education*, December 18, 1985)—say they are more interested in teaching than in research. Given these facts, it makes sense to encourage faculty to seek professional identity and intellectual challenge through disciplined inquiry into teaching and learning in their classrooms. In this way, faculty can continue to enhance their ability to achieve high levels of competence in their chosen profession—teaching—as they deepen their understanding of learning in their particular disciplines. Classroom Assessment is an effort to encourage and assist those faculty who wish to become more knowledgeable, involved, and successful as college teachers.

ASSUMPTION 6

Classroom Assessment does not require specialized training; it can be carried out by dedicated teachers from all disciplines.

As we have seen, the goals of Classroom Assessment differ from those of large-scale assessment efforts. Those carrying out assessment at the institutional and program levels need to be trained in research design, sampling theory, the collection and management of large pools of data, sophisticated statistical analysis, or the increasingly specialized methods of qualitative research. Faculty members engaged in Classroom Assessment usually do not need these specialized research methods, because they are not required to establish publicly defensible, replicable results. Instead, they are interested in uncovering trends and indications, often of an informal nature, that can inform and improve teaching. To succeed in Classroom Assessment, they need only a detailed knowledge of the discipline, dedication to teaching, and the motivation to improve.

Classroom Assessment can play an important role in the larger "assessment movement" that has swept U.S. higher education in the last few years, but it requires procedures and criteria consistent with its scope and aims. At the same time, Classroom Assessment needs tools and methods to fit its purposes, and those will not be the same standardized tests and large-scale survey instruments needed for institutional assessment. To borrow a phrase from the late E. F. Schumacher, best known as the author of *Small Is Beautiful* (1975), Classroom Assessment requires the development of its own "appropriate technology" — simple tools designed for the task at hand: the understanding and improvement of learning.

ASSUMPTION 7

By collaborating with colleagues and actively involving students in Classroom Assessment efforts, faculty (and students) enhance learning and personal satisfaction.

This last assumption reflects our experiences over the last several years, working with hundreds of faculty members engaged in Classroom Assessment. It also represents significant learning on our part, since our original assumption was just the contrary. That is, we originally assumed that faculty would find this approach attractive in large part because it allowed them to work alone and in the privacy of their own classrooms, without the approval or involvement of others. We have observed, however, that Classroom Assessment is a highly social activity for most participants.

Most faculty are not hesitant to share their results. Indeed, one of the major attractions of Classroom Assessment, mentioned by faculty as its primary advantage, is that it gives them opportunities and stimulus for talking about teaching and learning and for sharing their assessment project designs, techniques, and experiences with colleagues. Faculty also mention the value of discussing their plans and findings with their students, and of involving students in all phases of the work. One of the unanticipated benefits of Classroom Assessment is the appreciation shown by students. Over and over again, faculty report that their students are genuinely appreciative of their interest in improving teaching and learning. By using Classroom Assessment Techniques, instructors demonstrate their concern and interest in practical, visible ways.

When faculty collaborate with other teachers or with students in assessing student learning, they often experience synergy. That is, by working together, all parties achieve results of greater value than those they can achieve by working separately. Participating teachers often remark on the personal satisfaction they feel in working with colleagues and students toward the shared goal of improving learning.

The Teaching Goals Inventory

2

Goals are ends we work toward, destinations we set out for, results we strive to achieve. But goals are far more than terminal points. They are also reference points that we use to measure our progress and to determine whether we are headed in the right direction. Without clear goals, we cannot readily assess the effectiveness of our efforts or realize when we are off course, how far off we are, and how to get back on the right track. For these reasons, assessment efforts of all kinds typically begin with goal-setting or goal-clarifying exercises.

Classroom Assessment is no exception. To assess and improve instruction, faculty must first clarify exactly what they want students in their courses to learn. Once teachers know what their instructional goals are, and have determined the relative importance of those goals, they can begin to assess how well students are learning what they are trying to teach. This chapter provides individual college teachers with a simple, effective tool for identifying and clarifying their teaching goals, the first step in Classroom Assessment. We call this tool the Teaching Goals Inventory, or TGI. The self-scorable version of the TGI (the version presented here) was shaped by the participation of nearly five thousand college teachers who took part in three separate TGI survey administrations. From 1987 through 1990, the self-scorable inventory form was also field-tested in dozens of Classroom Assessment faculty-training workshops and was repeatedly revised and improved in response to feedback from workshop participants.

BACKGROUND: DEVELOPMENT OF THE TEACHING GOALS INVENTORY

(*Note:* Readers who are particularly eager to get started with Classroom Assessment may wish to skip ahead to the section headed "The Teaching Goals Inventory" on p. 18 and read this background information at another time.)

In 1986, as a first step in Classroom Assessment, we began constructing the Teaching Goals Inventory (TGI), a questionnaire intended to help faculty identify and rank the relative importance of their teaching goals.

Over the next four years, with support first from the Harvard Graduate School of Education and the Harvard Seminars on Assessment and later from the Ford Foundation and the Pew Charitable Trusts, the Classroom Research Project continued to field-test and refine the instrument. The development of the Teaching Goals Inventory has been a complex process involving a literature search, several cycles of data collection and analysis, review and critique by expert judges, and field tests with hundreds of classroom teachers.

Our literature search was aimed at discovering what had been learned from past efforts to study instructional goals. We found that surprisingly few researchers had asked college faculty what they were trying to teach. There is considerable research on what does happen to students as a result of their overall college experience (outcomes), but relatively little about what educators think should happen (goals). Therefore, we created the TGI to find out what faculty think students should learn in their classrooms.

Notwithstanding the relative lack of prior research on faculty teaching goals, our work on the TGI benefited from the research and writing of many scholars. Bayer's (1975) national survey of faculty was one of the few studies that included a brief set of items about teaching goals. Bowen's (1977) excellent review of the research and his subsequent analysis and classification of the intended outcomes of higher education provided a comprehensive map for the scope of the TGI. The landmark *Taxonomy of Educational Objectives* by Benjamin Bloom and his colleagues (1956) also proved invaluable in helping us ensure that the TGI did not overlook any major dimension of the intended outcomes of education. In addition, we drew from Feldman and Newcomb's (1969) comprehensive two-volume compilation, *The Impact of College on Students*; Chickering's (1969) vectors of student development; and Astin's work on college outcomes (Astin, 1977; Astin and Panos, 1969).

We also reviewed past research on students' reactions to instruction (Center for Faculty Evaluation and Development in Higher Education, 1975; Kulik, 1976) and the statements by professional groups that have identified the competencies expected of college-educated persons (Association of American Colleges, 1985; College Board, 1983). The design of the TGI was influenced by the work of researchers at the Educational Testing Service who developed the Community College Goals Inventory (CCGI), an instrument used by community colleges to assess institutional goals. All this work, reported in the literature over the past thirty-five years, helped provide a foundation for the content of the TGI and determined the depth and scope of its coverage.

The initial version of the TGI was completed in the winter of 1986. In April 1987, after a small-scale pilot survey conducted with faculty from Bradford College in Massachusetts, the original forty-eight-item TGI was administered to 200 randomly selected full-time and part-time instructors at Miami-Dade Community College. (*Note:* the term *item* will be used throughout to refer to individual teaching-goal statements on the TGI.) A total of 139 Miami-Dade instructors, or 70 percent of the sample, responded. We chose Miami-Dade for the study because it is one of the largest and most diverse community colleges in the United States and is considered by many observers to be one of the best. Despite the relatively small sample size, we obtained a representative pool of respondents through careful implementation of the random-selection procedure and as a result of the high response rate.

The results of this first TGI survey are discussed in detail in an article by Cross and Fideler (1988). Here it is enough to note that the strength and breadth of the survey response gave us confidence that the data collected at Miami-Dade could help us validate the instrument for use in a variety of institutional settings. Consequently, after descriptive and cluster analyses of the results from the 1987 Miami-Dade survey, we revised the TGI in preparation for a second, more ambitious administration. The revised TGI survey still contained a total of forty-eight goals, but they were not identical to those included in the first form; some items were added, others were dropped, and many were rewritten for greater clarity.

The second TGI administration took place in spring 1988 and involved a selected sample of twenty-nine colleges nationwide: thirteen private four-year liberal arts colleges, all member institutions of the Council for the Advancement of Private Higher Education (CAPHE); three public four-year colleges in Vermont; and four community college districts consisting of thirteen colleges or centers in Arizona, Massachusetts, Vermont, and California. All in all, 1,856 faculty members (1,100 from four-year colleges and 756 from community colleges) responded to the revised TGI. The response rate was 62 percent for four-year colleges and 36 percent for community colleges.

This second major step in the development of the TGI gave us insights into the structure of the instrument, its coverage, and its general usefulness as a tool for articulating the teaching goals of college faculty members. We conducted extensive item analyses on the spring 1988 survey results, as well as cluster analysis and factor analysis, designed to reveal how items related to one another empirically. The six clusters identified in this empirical analysis were encouraging but somewhat ragged, ranging from four to thirteen items per cluster. Identification of the goal clusters, however, enabled us to rewrite some items for greater clarity, to construct new items targeted to the central theme of each cluster, and to study the face validity of the TGI in campus workshops.

After completing our analysis of results from the second administration, we decided that one more study was desirable before we developed a final version of the TGI. Therefore, during the summer of 1989, we began the process of revising the TGI once again. The purpose of this third revision was to come up with the most valid and comprehensive list of teaching goals and clusters possible for the final questionnaire.

Goal Clusters of the TGI

Throughout the development of the TGI, we sought to identify sets or clusters of items that seemed to "go together" in the minds of teachers. We approached this task from three rather different perspectives. First, we wrote items related to the broad-based goals found in the literature. For example, one of Bowen's cognitive goals is "rationality," which consists of the "disposition to think logically. . . . Capacity to see facts and events objectively. . . . Disposition to weigh evidence. . . . Ability to analyze and synthesize," and the like (Bowen, 1977, p. 55). While these characteristics taken together define "rationality" for Bowen, college teachers might bring different perceptions to bear. Initially, we wanted to break complex goals—such as Bowen's "rationality"—into items that were as specific and unambiguous as possible, and then to determine empirically which items went together in the minds of teachers.

The task of discovering goal clusters was accomplished via cluster analysis, "a classification technique for forming homogeneous groups within complex data sets" (Borgen and Barnett, 1987, p. 456). Basically, this empirical analysis consists of administering the TGI to a large number of people and then correlating every item with every other item to see which items "cluster" together. Through cluster analysis, for example, one can determine whether teachers who rate synthesis as "essential" tend to rate analysis high also. Once items are grouped together on the basis of their intercorrelations, there is the task of identifying a common dimension that runs through all the items in that cluster. This is the process of "naming" the cluster. In our analysis, for example, the items shown in Cluster I of the self-scorable TGI suggested a set of goals that all had to do with teachers' desires to develop the higher-order thinking skills of their students. As a result, we named that cluster "Higher-Order Thinking Skills."

The problem with using the empirical derivation of clusters alone is that the resulting clusters are sometimes quite ragged and difficult to interpret. This means that clusters derived solely by statistical means can lack face validity. At the same time, the number of items in the clusters tends to range widely (from four to thirteen items per cluster in our initial administrations, for example), thus oversampling some dimensions of teaching goals and underrepresenting others. For those reasons, we conducted a third type of clustering analysis, known as Q sorting, to determine how well a group of expert judges could agree on which items belong in which clusters (Mueller, 1986). In our Q-sorting effort, we sent the revised TGI to a selected sample of eighty-five faculty development experts from across the country. These educators, all of whom had wide experience working with faculty on matters related to teaching and learning, were asked to create their own ideal goal clusters for the TGI by sorting the forty-eight goals into a limited number of clusters. We then asked the expert judges to indicate any goals they felt should be deleted from the inventory, and to propose new goals for inclusion in the final version of the TGI. To ensure that all respondents were working from the same procedural assumptions, we asked the expert "sorters" to observe the following guidelines:

1. Create no fewer than five and no more than eight clusters.

2. Create clusters that include more or less equal numbers of goals.

3. Include each of the forty-eight goals in one and only one cluster.

4. Give each cluster a short descriptive title.

5. List any goals that should be dropped.

6. Identify any additional goals that should be included.

Fifty-two of the eight-five faculty development professionals returned responses that were useful for all phases of the analysis, for an overall response rate of 61 percent. Guided by the results of the Q-sort procedure, a cluster analysis of the Q-sort results, and experience gained from using the earlier self-scorable version of the TGI, we dropped fourteen goals from the original forty-eight, added eighteen new items, and rephrased all goals to make their wording parallel and as clear as possible. This newly revised set of fifty-two goals formed the basis of the survey form used in the 1990 TGI administration, the results of which are discussed in Chapter Ten. In the final self-scorable version of the TGI, the clusters of items are grouped together for convenience in scoring. In all the experimental administrations of the TGI, however, items that ultimately clustered together were distributed throughout the form, so that respondents would have no way of knowing which items formed a "cluster."

After all this work on refining the clusters, in 1990 we administered the revised TGI to a sample of 2,824 faculty members (see below), and computed coefficient alpha reliabilities for each of the clusters. Coefficient alpha—often referred to as Cronbach's alpha, in honor of the developer of the procedure (Cronbach, 1951)—is an estimate of the internal consistency of, in this case, the individual goal clusters that make up the TGI. The alpha coefficients, which were very satisfactory, are shown in Table 2.1.

Table 2.1. Coefficient Alpha Reliabilities for Final TGI Clusters.

Cluster Number	Cluster Name	Alpha Coefficient
I	Higher-Order Thinking Skills	(.77)
II	Basic Academic Success Skills	(.79)
III	Discipline-Specific Knowledge and Skills	(.71)
IV	Liberal Arts and Academic Values	(.84)
V	Work and Career Preparation	(.85)
VI	Personal Development	(.86)

The 1990 TGI Administration

In the spring of 1990, we invited seventeen private four-year colleges and fifteen public community colleges to participate in an administration of the fifty-two item survey form of the TGI. A diverse but not necessarily representative sample, these were colleges where faculty members had shown an interest in Classroom Assessment. We hoped to capitalize on that interest to get broad, campuswide participation in this final administration. The Classroom Research Project agreed to provide each participating college with TGI forms, data analysis, and a detailed report of results. In return, we asked the administrators acting as campus liaisons to try to obtain at least a 65 percent response rate from their full-time faculty. Although we encouraged the participation of part-time faculty and included them in the analyses, they were not counted in the return rate.

Overall, 2,070 full-time and 754 part-time faculty returned the completed TGIs by the deadline date (total $N = 2,824$). Thanks to the diligence of campus liaisons and the cooperation of faculty, the overall response rate for full-time faculty was 65 percent. (The response rate equals the percentage of members in a given group who participate in the study.) For four-year colleges, the response rate of full-time faculty was 74 percent ($N = 951$). For community colleges, the response rate was 61 percent ($N = 1,873$). Resource A lists the thirty-two colleges that participated in the spring 1990 study.

Our primary interest in this third and final TGI administration was to obtain high-quality comparative data from a fairly large and reasonably diverse sample of college teachers. Our purpose in collecting this survey data was to provide both institutions and individual teachers with some basis for comparison of their teaching-goal priorities. Given the variety of colleges and faculty who took part, and the high response rate overall, the final TGI administration succeeded in creating a new and potentially useful information base on faculty teaching goals.

THE TEACHING GOALS INVENTORY: SELF-SCORABLE VERSION AND SELF-SCORING WORKSHEET

On the pages that follow, you will find a copy of the self-scorable Teaching Goals Inventory (Exhibit 2.1), along with a Self-Scoring Worksheet (Exhibit 2.2). The self-scorable version of the TGI contains the same fifty-two goal statements used in the 1990 survey version, but the goals are organized into the six goal clusters for ease of scoring. The 1990 TGI survey form also contained a number of background questions that were not relevant to the self-scorable form. The final question on the self-scorable form—Item 52, concerning "your primary role as teacher" in the focus class—was included on the 1990 survey form. Faculty responses to Item 52 are discussed in some detail in Chapter Ten. (For your convenience, a second copy of the TGI and the Self-Scoring Worksheet is provided in Resource B.) You may reproduce both for personal use.

SCORING THE TGI: ITEMS AND CLUSTERS

The Self-Scoring Worksheet provides a simple way to turn data from the TGI into useful information and to help you discover patterns in your responses. The first information this worksheet elicits is the total number of teaching goals you consider "essential" in the course on which you focused. Many of the college teachers we worked with were surprised by the number of "essential" goals they identified in scoring their TGI responses. Some wondered, for example, whether eighteen "essential" goals are too many to accomplish in a fifteen-week semester; others asked themselves whether three might be too modest a target.

In our experience, such large contrasts in total numbers of course goals often occurred within departments, and even among faculty teaching parallel sections of the same course. The process of taking and scoring the TGI does not create such differences, of course, but it often makes them explicit to faculty for the first time. More interesting than the sheer quantity of "essential" teaching goals is their distribution across clusters—and the teaching priorities reflected by that distribution. The quickest way to obtain scores indicative of your teaching priorities is simply to count the number of items marked "essential" in each cluster. Record this number on your Self-Scoring Worksheet. By ranking the clusters in order of the number of "essential" items they contain, you will have a rough profile of your teaching priorities for one course. You can compare these priorities, if you wish, with the priorities of other community college or four-year college faculty members, as shown in Resource C and Resource D. The data of most interest to you may be the percentages of faculty members marking each item "essential" (shown in the last column). For example, Resource C shows that 62 percent of the 1,873 community college faculty taking the TGI in 1990 marked Goal 1 "essential." The other columns show the means and standard deviations for each goal, as well as the means for each cluster. If you are interested in doing so, you can compare your rating for a given item (goal) with the mean rating for that item. More to the point, perhaps, you can also compare your mean ratings for each goal cluster with those shown in Resources C and D. Data in Resources C and D will be of special interest to departments and colleges that wish to analyze group responses to the TGI.

Another way to gain insights into your teaching goals is to gauge the fit between your teaching priorities — as represented by your relative ranking of the goal clusters — and the primary teaching role you selected in response to Item 52. If your primary teaching role and your highest-ranked goal cluster are not one and the same, you may want to take a second look.

Since our studies show that there are large, statistically significant differences in the ratings given to the teaching goals by teachers of different subjects (see Chapter Ten), we encourage colleges, and especially departments and divisions, to do their own analyses of TGI responses. In some cases, departments may have targeted a small number of goals on which they are striving for high agreement among faculty members. In other cases, members of a department may decide that they want to expose students to a wide variety of teaching goals; thus, they may look for and encourage a diversity of teaching priorities.

Chapter Ten provides a more detailed analysis of our findings, plus an account of lessons we have learned from the experiences of faculty using Classroom Assessment in their classrooms. In Chapter Eleven, we speculate on the future of Classroom Research, a topic we hope will be of special interest to advanced practitioners of Classroom Assessment looking for ideas on next steps.

USING YOUR TGI RESPONSES TO DIRECT CLASSROOM ASSESSMENTS Completing and analyzing the TGI can be an interesting exercise in its own right, but the main reason for including the inventory in this volume is to help teachers link their Classroom Assessment efforts to their teaching goals. The advantages of starting your assessments with goals are discussed at length in Chapter Four. Chapter Four also offers a step-by-step process for transforming the very general goal statements of the TGI into course-specific questions and provides examples of this goal-specifying process in several disciplines.

A second way to use the results of the Teaching Goals Inventory to help you get started in Classroom Assessment is simply to use the indexes (Tables 6.1, 6.2, and 6.3) in Chapter Six. In Table 6.3, the six goal clusters are indexed to specific Classroom Assessment Techniques. Once you have used the Self-Scoring Worksheet to determine your highest-ranked goal cluster, you can use the table to locate the CATs that are likely to be most useful for assessing those particular goals.

Exhibit 2.1. Teaching Goals Inventory, Self-Scorable Version.

Purpose: The Teaching Goals Inventory (TGI) is a self-assessment of instructional goals. Its purpose is threefold: (1) to help college teachers become more aware of what they want to accomplish in individual courses; (2) to help faculty locate Classroom Assessment Techniques they can adapt and use to assess how well they are achieving their teaching and learning goals; and (3) to provide a starting point for discussions of teaching and learning goals among colleagues.

Directions: Please select ONE course you are currently teaching. Respond to each item on the inventory in relation to that particular course. (Your responses might be quite different if you were asked about your overall teaching and learning goals, for example, or the appropriate instructional goals for your discipline.)

Please print the title of the specific course you are focusing on:

_____

Please rate the importance of each of the fifty-two goals listed below to the specific course you have selected. Assess each goal's importance to what you deliberately aim to have your students accomplish, rather than the goal's general worthiness or overall importance to your institution's mission. There are no "right" or "wrong" answers; only personally more or less accurate ones.

For each goal, circle only one response on the 1-to-5 rating scale. You may want to read quickly through all fifty-two goals before rating their relative importance.

In relation to the course you are focusing on, indicate whether each goal you rate is:

(5)	Essential	a goal you always/nearly always try to achieve
(4)	Very important	a goal you often try to achieve
(3)	Important	a goal you sometimes try to achieve
(2)	Unimportant	a goal you rarely try to achieve
(1)	Not applicable	a goal you never try to achieve

Rate the importance of each goal to what you aim to have students accomplish in your course.

	Essential	Very Important	Important	Unimportant	Not Applicable
1. Develop ability to apply principles and generalizations already learned to new problems and situations	5	4	3	2	1
2. Develop analytic skills	5	4	3	2	1
3. Develop problem-solving skills	5	4	3	2	1
4. Develop ability to draw reasonable inferences from observations	5	4	3	2	1
5. Develop ability to synthesize and integrate information and ideas	5	4	3	2	1
6. Develop ability to think holistically: to see the whole as well as the parts	5	4	3	2	1
7. Develop ability to think creatively	5	4	3	2	1
8. Develop ability to distinguish between fact and opinion	5	4	3	2	1
9. Improve skill at paying attention	5	4	3	2	1
10. Develop ability to concentrate	5	4	3	2	1
11. Improve memory skills	5	4	3	2	1
12. Improve listening skills	5	4	3	2	1
13. Improve speaking skills	5	4	3	2	1
14. Improve reading skills	5	4	3	2	1
15. Improve writing skills	5	4	3	2	1
16. Develop appropriate study skills, strategies, and habits	5	4	3	2	1
17. Improve mathematical skills	5	4	3	2	1
18. Learn terms and facts of this subject	5	4	3	2	1
19. Learn concepts and theories in this subject	5	4	3	2	1
20. Develop skill in using materials, tools, and/or technology central to this subject	5	4	3	2	1
21. Learn to understand perspectives and values of this subject	5	4	3	2	1

Exhibit 2.1. Teaching Goals Inventory, Self-Scorable Version, Cont'd.

Rate the importance of each goal to what you aim to have students accomplish in your course.

	Essential	Very Important	Important	Unimportant	Not Applicable
22 Prepare for transfer or graduate study	5	4	3	2	1
23. Learn techniques and methods used to gain new knowledge in this subject	5	4	3	2	1
24. Learn to evaluate methods and materials in this subject	5	4	3	2	1
25. Learn to appreciate important contributions to this subject	5	4	3	2	1
26. Develop an appreciation of the liberal arts and sciences	5	4	3	2	1
27. Develop an openness to new ideas	5	4	3	2	1
28. Develop an informed concern about contemporary social issues	5	4	3	2	1
29. Develop a commitment to exercise the rights and responsibilities of citizenship	5	4	3	2	1
30. Develop a lifelong love of learning	5	4	3	2	1
31. Develop aesthetic appreciations	5	4	3	2	1
32. Develop an informed historical perspective	5	4	3	2	1
33. Develop an informed understanding of the role of science and technology	5	4	3	2	1
34. Develop an informed appreciation of other cultures	5	4	3	2	1
35. Develop capacity to make informed ethical choices	5	4	3	2	1
36. Develop ability to work productively with others	5	4	3	2	1
37. Develop management skills	5	4	3	2	1
38. Develop leadership skills	5	4	3	2	1
39. Develop a commitment to accurate work	5	4	3	2	1
40. Improve ability to follow directions, instructions, and plans	5	4	3	2	1
41. Improve ability to organize and use time effectively	5	4	3	2	1
42. Develop a commitment to personal achievement	5	4	3	2	1
43. Develop ability to perform skillfully	5	4	3	2	1
44. Cultivate a sense of responsibility for one's own behavior	5	4	3	2	1
45. Improve self-esteem/self-confidence	5	4	3	2	1
46. Develop a commitment to one's own values	5	4	3	2	1
47. Develop respect for others	5	4	3	2	1
48. Cultivate emotional health and well-being	5	4	3	2	1
49. Cultivate an active commitment to honesty	5	4	3	2	1
50. Develop capacity to think for one's self	5	4	3	2	1
51. Develop capacity to make wise decisions	5	4	3	2	1

52. In general, how do you see your primary role as a teacher?
     (Although more than one statement may apply, please circle only one.)

   1 Teaching students facts and principles of the subject matter

   2 Providing a role model for students

   3 Helping students develop higher-order thinking skills

   4 Preparing students for jobs/careers

   5 Fostering student development and personal growth

   6 Helping students develop basic learning skills

Exhibit 2.2. Teaching Goals Inventory, Self-Scoring Worksheet.

1. In all, how many of the fifty-two goals did you rate as "essential"? _____

2. How many "essential" goals did you have in each of the six clusters listed below?

Cluster Number and Name	Goals Included in Cluster	Total Number of "Essential" Goals in Each Cluster	Clusters Ranked—from 1st to 6th—by Number of "Essential" Goals
I Higher-Order Thinking Skills	1–8	_____	_____
II Basic Academic Success Skills	9–17	_____	_____
III Discipline-Specific Knowledge and Skills	18–25	_____	_____
IV Liberal Arts and Academic Values	26–35	_____	_____
V Work and Career Preparation	36–43	_____	_____
VI Personal Development	44–52	_____	_____

3. Compute your cluster scores (average item ratings by cluster) using the following worksheet.

A	B	C	D	E
Cluster Number and Name	Goals Included	Sum of Ratings Given to Goals in That Cluster	Divide C by This Number	Your Cluster Scores
I Higher-Order Thinking Skills	1–8	_____	8	_____
II Basic Academic Success Skills	9–17	_____	9	_____
III Discipline-Specific Knowledge and Skills	18–25	_____	8	_____
IV Liberal Arts and Academic Values	26–35	_____	10	_____
V Work and Career Preparation	36–43	_____	8	_____
VI Personal Development	44–52	_____	9	_____

Source: Classroom Assessment Techniques, by Thomas A. Angelo and K. Patricia Cross. Copyright © 1993. Permission to reproduce is hereby granted.

If you are just beginning to experiment with Classroom Assessment, it is not necessary, or productive, to worry too much about linking goals to assessment tools. Many faculty start out by trying a few simple Classroom

Assessment Techniques. After they gain some experience with the process, they can more easily connect teaching priorities and assessment techniques. For the relatively inexperienced Classroom Researcher, Chapter Three offers simple first steps. Those readers who have already experimented with simple CATs may wish to skip ahead to Chapter Four.

CHAPTER 3

First Steps

Effective teachers use a variety of means, some formal and others informal, to determine how much and how well their students are learning. For example, to evaluate student learning formally, most college teachers use techniques such as quizzes, tests, or examinations; many instructors also use assignments such as term papers, lab reports, and homework. These techniques and assignments are the "tools" of formal classroom evaluation. Instructors use these evaluations to make judgments about individual student achievement and assign grades. As we noted earlier, evaluations used to assign grades are known as "summative" evaluations and typically occur at the end of lessons, units, and courses.

To evaluate classroom learning informally, most faculty also have a repertoire of techniques. College teachers pose questions, listen carefully to student questions and comments, and monitor body language and facial expressions. These informal, often implicit evaluations allow instructors to make quick adjustments in their teaching: to slow down or review material in response to questions, confusion, and misunderstandings; or to move on because students have understood a particular concept well. As noted in Chapter One, evaluations used primarily to inform teaching and improve learning, rather than to assign grades, are referred to as "formative."

Classroom Assessment is a systematic approach to formative evaluation, and Classroom Assessment Techniques (CATs) are simple tools for collecting data on student learning in order to improve it. CATs are "feedback devices," instruments that faculty can use to find out how much, how well, and even how students are learning what they are trying to teach. Each Classroom Assessment Technique is a specific procedure or activity designed to help faculty get immediate and useful answers to very focused questions about student learning.

Classroom Assessment Techniques are not meant to take the place of more traditional forms of classroom evaluation. Rather, these formative assessment tools are meant to give teachers and students information on learning before and between tests and examinations; therefore, they supplement and complement formal evaluations of learning. Used effectively, CATs can reduce the uncertainty that faculty and students feel as they face midterms, final examinations, and the calculation of course grades. When teachers and learners both receive regular feedback on student learning throughout the course, there are likely to be fewer surprises at semester's end.

At the same time, Classroom Assessment Techniques can complement the informal evaluation techniques that faculty already use to inform their teaching. First, CATs can help teachers make informal evaluation more focused and systematic, thereby improving the quality and usefulness of the data collected. Second, most CATs result in some record of student feedback, a record that both faculty and students can refer to and learn from. Typically, when teachers ask questions or hold discussions, they pay careful attention to students' answers, expressions, and body language. After class, instructors must rely on their memories to guide them as they prepare for the next session. But memory is imperfect and often fleeting, and many important details can be lost between the moment one class session ends and the next begins. The feedback collected through CATs can serve as a check on and an enhancement of the teacher's memory.

Perhaps a nautical metaphor will help define Classroom Assessment Techniques. Imagine the college course as a sea voyage, back in the days before sophisticated radar and satellite technology. And think of the tests and exams as ports of call along the way. In this metaphor, doing Classroom Assessment can be likened to navigating. The various Classroom Assessment Techniques represent the range of procedures and simple devices the navigator could use to determine and double-check the ship's position at sea. These position checks allow the captain to keep the vessel on course, or to tell how far off course it is and how best to return to the correct route. In a similar fashion, CATs give teachers information to "navigate by," feedback to guide the continual small adjustments and corrections needed to keep student learning "on course."

The CATs presented in this handbook have three basic sources. Some were culled through an extensive review of the literature on teaching methods in both postsecondary and secondary education. Others came from our own teaching repertoires. Still others were developed by college faculty who participated in Classroom Research and Classroom Assessment programs on campuses across the country. A few basic criteria guided our search for and selection of Classroom Assessment Techniques to include in this volume. As we reviewed each potential CAT, we asked the following questions based on those selection criteria:

1. Is it context-sensitive? Will the assessment technique provide useful information on what a specific group of students is or is not learning about a clearly defined topic at a given moment in a particular classroom?

2. Is it flexible? Can faculty from a range of disciplines easily adapt the technique for use in a variety of courses and contexts?

3. Is it likely to make a difference? Does the technique focus on "alterable variables"? In other words, does it assess aspects of teacher or student behavior that could be changed to promote better learning within the limits of time and energy available in a semester?

4. Is it mutually beneficial? Will it give both teachers and students the kind of information they need to make mid-course changes and corrections in order to improve teaching and learning?

5. Is it easy to administer? Is the assessment technique relatively simple and quick to prepare and use?

6. Is it easy to respond to? Is the feedback that results from the use of the technology relatively easy to organize and analyze?

7. Is it educationally valid? Does it reinforce and enhance learning of the specific content or skills being assessed?

A positive answer to all seven questions meant that the technique was worth considering for inclusion. However, none of the questions could be answered with a simple "yes" or "no," since each allows for a range of responses. Therefore, the reader will soon note that some CATs are more flexible, or easier to administer, or easier to respond to than others. Because we recognize that college faculty have a wide range of instructional goals, teaching styles, intellectual interests, and types of students, we have included a broad variety of assessment techniques and a range of complexity. As we assembled the collection, we looked for feedback devices that could provide quantitative or qualitative data, written or oral feedback, and information on individual students, small groups, or entire classes.

Our experiences in the Classroom Research Project convinced us of the importance of providing options in assessment techniques. In the first administration of the Teaching Goals Inventory (TGI) in 1988, we found that every one of the forty-eight instructional goals included in the TGI received the full range of responses. For example, a goal that some teachers rated "essential" was rated "irrelevant" by some of their colleagues at the same institution (Cross and Fideler, 1988). When we administered a revised version of the TGI in 1990, the same pattern of responses emerged in response to the fifty-two goals on that inventory. Individual faculty members do not think in the aggregate, of course, and their goals are often quite different one from the other. Even two instructors of the same sex and age group, teaching in the same department at the same college, may legitimately have different instructional goals for the same course. We reasoned that since faculty teaching goals differ, so too must the devices teachers use to assess how well they are achieving them. We also recognized that instructors would need to modify and adapt these "feedback devices" to fit the specific demands of their courses and the characteristics of their students. To accommodate those needs, we included a range of techniques—from simple "ready-made" devices designed for immediate application, to open-ended "do-it-yourself" designs that offer flexible frameworks for teachers to adapt.

Because of the enormous variation in faculty goals and interests, we expect that a given college teacher will find certain of the Classroom Assessment Techniques included here germane and useful, while another instructor will reject the same techniques as inappropriate and irrelevant. Our hope is that each reader will find at least one or two simple Classroom Assessment Techniques that can be successfully used "off the shelf," and several more that can be adapted or recast to fit that faculty member's particular requirements.

THE VALUE OF STARTING SMALL: A THREE-STEP PROCESS

If you are not already familiar with Classroom Assessment, we recommend that you "get your feet wet" by trying out one or two of the simplest Classroom Assessment Techniques in one of your classes. By starting with CATs that require very little planning or preparation, you risk very little of your own—and your students'—time and energy. In most cases, trying out a simple Classroom Assessment Technique will require only five to ten minutes of class time and less than an hour of your time out of class. After trying one or two quick assessments, you can decide whether this approach is worth further investments of time and energy.

Chapter Four presents a systematic and detailed process for carrying out Classroom Assessment. While that nine-step process has been useful to many faculty who practice Classroom Assessment, most of them actually began with much simpler first steps. Below, we offer a streamlined, three-step process designed to minimize time and energy required and maximize the likelihood of success for first-time Classroom Assessment efforts. The suggestions are based on our own Classroom Assessment experiences and on our observations of many other instructors as they began experimenting with this approach.

Step 1: Planning

Start by selecting one, and only one, of your classes in which to try out the Classroom Assessment. We recommend focusing your first assessments on a course that you know well and are comfortable with. Your "focus class" should also be one that you are confident is going well, one in which most students are succeeding and relatively satisfied. Although this may seem an odd suggestion, it is best not to use Classroom Assessment to gather data on a problematic or difficult situation until you become experienced in the approach. In other words, it is best to minimize risks while you develop confidence and skill.

Once you have chosen the "focus class," decide on the class meeting during which you will use the Classroom Assessment Technique. Make sure to reserve a few minutes of that class session for the assessment. At this point, you need to select a CAT. The five techniques listed below are all flexible and easily adaptable to many situations, and simple and quick to apply. They also generate data that are easy to analyze. For those reasons, they make excellent introductory CATs and have been widely used by faculty from many disciplines.

Five Useful "Introductory" CATs

The Minute Paper (CAT 6)
The Muddiest Point (CAT 7)
The One-Sentence Summary (CAT 13)
Directed Paraphrasing (CAT 23)
Applications Cards (CAT 24)

Although each of these CATs is described in detail in Chapter Seven, they can be quickly summarized here. The Minute Paper asks students to respond to two questions: (1) What was the most important thing you learned today? (2) What questions remain uppermost in your mind as we conclude this class session? The Muddiest Point is an adaptation of the Minute Paper and is used to find out what students are unclear about. At the end of a lecture or class session, students are asked to write brief answers to the following question: What was the muddiest point in my lecture today?

The One-Sentence Summary assesses students' skill at summarizing a large amount of information within a highly structured, compact format. Given a topic, students respond to the following prompt: Who did what to/ for whom, when, where, how, and why? In a course on U.S. government or American history, for example, this CAT could be used to assess students' understanding of the Constitutional Convention.

Directed Paraphrasing assesses students' understanding of a concept or procedure by asking them to paraphrase it in two or three sentences for a specific audience. For example, if you were in a class at this moment, you might be asked to paraphrase "Classroom Assessment" in a way that would be meaningful to your colleagues. Applications Cards assess learners' skill at transference by eliciting possible applications of lessons learned in class to real life or to other specific areas. In an economics course, for instance, the instructor might ask students to come up with applications of "satisficing" in everyday, nontextbook settings. If one of these five simple CATs appeals to you, we suggest that you read through its complete description in Chapter Seven before using it in your classroom.

Step 2: Implementing

Once you have chosen a focus course and selected a simple CAT to use in it, let students know beforehand (at the beginning of the class period or at the prior class meeting) what you are going to do. Whenever you announce your plans, be sure to tell the students why you are asking them for information. Assure them that you will be assessing their learning in order to help them improve, and not to grade them. In most cases, it is best to ask for anonymous responses.

When it comes time to use the Classroom Assessment Technique, make sure that the students clearly understand the procedure. You may need to write directions for the CAT on the chalkboard or project them using an overhead projector and transparency. Let students know how much time they will have to complete the assessment. The first time you use a particular CAT, it is helpful to allow a little extra time for responses.

After the students have finished, collect their responses and read through them quickly as soon as you can. If you have time to read and analyze the responses fully immediately after class, so much the better. However, if you must put the CAT responses aside for a while, this fast "read-through" will help you recall exactly what students were responding to when you later read their answers more carefully.

As a rough technique for estimating time required, you can expect to spend one to two minutes per response analyzing the feedback. For example, if you were to use the Muddiest Point technique in a class of thirty students, you would need to budget at least thirty minutes—one minute per response—of your out-of-class time to analyze the feedback; for the Minute Paper, which poses two questions, you would estimate sixty minutes; for the One-Sentence Summary, which requires more complex feedback from students, you would probably need slightly more than an hour. The good news is that, with practice, teachers get faster at "processing" the data from Classroom Assessments.

Even a cursory reading of the five CATs can provide useful information. In analyzing feedback from the Muddiest Point technique, for example, you can simply note how many and which "muddy points" are mentioned and how many times the same "muddy points" come up. The same method can be used to analyze feedback from the Minute Paper or any other CAT that elicits student opinions or questions. Other techniques, such as Directed Paraphrasing, the One-Sentence Summary, or Applications Cards, prompt responses that can be judged more or less correct, or more or less complete. Student response to this type of CAT can be quickly sorted into three piles: correct / complete (or "on-target") responses, somewhat correct / complete (or "close") responses, and incorrect / incomplete ("off-target") responses. Then the number of responses in each pile can be counted, and the approximate percentage of the total class each represents can be calculated. Teachers also can look for particularly revealing or thoughtful responses among the on- and off-target groups.

Step 3: Responding

To capitalize on time spent assessing, and to motivate students to become actively involved, you will need to "close the feedback loop" by letting them know what you learned from the CAT exercise and what difference that information will make. Take a few moments to think through what, how, and when you will tell your students about their responses. Responding can take the form of simply telling the class, "Forty percent of you thought that X was the 'muddiest' point, and about one-third each mentioned Y or Z. Let's go over all three points in that order." In other cases, a handout may allow for a more effective and complete response. However you respond, let the class know what adjustments, if any, you are making in your teaching as a result of the information they have provided. Just as important, inform students of adjustments they could make in their behavior, in response to the CAT feedback, in order to improve learning. In other words, let students know that their participation in the Classroom Assessment can make a difference in your teaching and their learning.

FIVE SUGGESTIONS FOR A SUCCESSFUL START

Chapter Four offers a number of specific suggestions to increase success in Classroom Assessment. For readers who are just getting started, however, the five broad suggestions below are the most important—and enough to keep in mind at first.

▶ *1. If a Classroom Assessment Technique does not appeal to your intuition and professional judgment as a teacher, don't use it.*

All the techniques presented in this handbook are meant to be suggestions and should be taken as such. We believe that individual college teachers are the most reliable authorities about what is and what is not likely to help them improve teaching and learning in their classrooms.

▶ *2. Don't make Classroom Assessment into a self-inflicted chore or burden.*

This second suggestion stems from our faith in ongoing, incremental improvement. We believe that it is more effective and satisfying to try one or two of these techniques in a semester—and fully and thoughtfully work through the process—than to try out several CATs, only to become overwhelmed and discouraged. We therefore recommend that you start simple, with quick and easy Classroom Assessment Techniques, and stay simple for some time, building skill and confidence.

▶ *3. Don't ask your students to use any Classroom Assessment Technique you haven't previously tried on yourself.*

By trying out the assessment techniques on yourself first, you can find out whether the techniques are really appropriate, where problems are likely to occur, whether any modifications are necessary, and how long it takes to go through them. In assessment, as in teaching, thoughtful preparation and rehearsal are major parts of successful performance.

▶ *4. Allow for more time than you think you will need to carry out and respond to the assessment.*

Be forewarned that administering a Classroom Assessment Technique and analyzing the feedback, particularly the first few times, are likely to take at least twice as much time to complete as you first estimate. This is yet another reason to begin with the simplest possible assessments.

▶ *5. Make sure to "close the loop." Let students know what you learn from their feedback and how you and they can use that information to improve learning.*

Although many teachers already assess student learning informally, relatively few let students know the outcomes of their assessments. Students are unlikely to realize the value of assessment, or of self-assessment, unless faculty make them explicitly aware of it through instruction and modeling. When students are helped to see the useful ways that Classroom Assessment can inform teaching and learning, they are much more likely to participate fully and positively.

NEXT STEPS If you have not yet tried a Classroom Assessment Technique in one of your classes, we recommend that you do so before going on to Chapter Four. Experience has shown us that faculty who start small and simple and stay at that level for several weeks or months are more likely to succeed and persist in Classroom Assessment than those who begin with very ambitious first attempts. Many instructors experiment with simple Classroom Assessment Techniques for one or even two semesters before engaging in more systematic assessment efforts, which we call Classroom Assessment Projects. Once you have gained experience and confidence in using simple Classroom Assessment Techniques, you may want to link assessment more directly to your instructional goals. Chapter Four presents a step-by-step method for more fully integrating Classroom Assessment into your courses.

Planning and Implementing Classroom Assessment Projects

In working with faculty groups on several campuses, we found that many teachers experiment informally with simple Classroom Assessment Techniques for one or more semesters. If and when such informal use convinces them of the value of Classroom Assessment — and it often does — faculty look for ways to incorporate the approach more fully into their teaching. These instructors are motivated to move beyond using Classroom Assessment Techniques as "add-ons." They want to build assessment into their everyday classroom routines. When Classroom Assessment is fully integrated into a course, ongoing assessment becomes part of the faculty member's overall plan for instruction. In such courses, Classroom Assessment is an important element of the syllabus, along with classwork, homework assignments, and tests. We refer to the carefully planned use of a Classroom Assessment Technique that is well integrated into the course syllabus as a Classroom Assessment Project. Classroom Assessment Projects differ from simple Classroom Assessments in much the same way that a carefully planned, scheduled examination differs from a spur-of-the-moment, unannounced "pop quiz." While "pop quizzes" may serve a useful function, they cannot take the place of well-constructed exams. Similarly, simple, spur-of-the-moment Classroom Assessments are often helpful and informative, but they cannot substitute for carefully planned Classroom Assessment Projects.

This chapter presents, in some detail, a process for successfully planning and carrying out Classroom Assessment Projects, as well as for responding to the feedback these assessments generate. This step-by-step process, called the Classroom Assessment Project Cycle (or, simply, the Project Cycle), was developed and refined through field testing at several colleges over a three-year period. Many faculty have found it to be a useful framework, one that helped them structure and organize their Classroom Assessment Projects more effectively. And on those campuses where groups of faculty have collaborated in Classroom Assessment and Classroom Research programs, the Project Cycle has served as a shared experience and a common point of reference.

As faculty gain experience in Classroom Assessment, they often revise the Project Cycle to fit their own needs and preferences. Individual faculty and campus groups have come up with various process models, some simpler and others rather more complex than the one presented below. From our viewpoint, that is exactly how it should be. The process described in this chapter is meant to serve as a starting point, an outline that can and should be adapted to fit the specific circumstances, disciplines, and particular teaching styles of individual instructors.

AN INTRODUCTION TO THE CLASSROOM ASSESSMENT PROJECT CYCLE

The Classroom Assessment Project Cycle has three main phases, and each phase consists of three steps. As you will note, the three phases of the Project Cycle correspond to the three simple steps outlined in Chapter Three.

Phase I   Planning a Classroom Assessment Project
- Step 1: Choosing the class in which to carry out the Classroom Assessment Project
- Step 2: Focusing on an "assessable question" about student learning
- Step 3: Designing a Classroom Assessment Project to answer that "assessable question"

Phase II   Implementing the Classroom Assessment Project
- Step 4: Teaching the "target" lesson related to the question being assessed
- Step 5: Assessing learning by collecting feedback on that assessable question
- Step 6: Analyzing the feedback and turning data into usable information

Phase III   Responding to the results of the Classroom Assessment
- Step 7: Interpreting the results and formulating an appropriate response to improve learning
- Step 8: Communicating the results to students and trying out the response
- Step 9: Evaluating the Classroom Assessment Project's effect(s) on teaching and learning

Although there are nine steps in a single Classroom Assessment Project Cycle, a tenth step is included in Figure 4.1. In that graphic representation of a Project Cycle, Step 10 represents the beginning of a new but closely related Classroom Assessment Project. Successful projects often spawn new questions; so the beginning of a new project is a natural and often desirable outcome.

In the first or Planning phase of a Classroom Assessment Project, the faculty member comes up with a project idea and then designs a simple plan for carrying it out. After choosing a specific class in which to carry out the project, the instructor focuses on one important teaching goal for the course or on one specific question about student learning in that course.

Figure 4.1. Map of a Classroom Assessment Project Cycle.

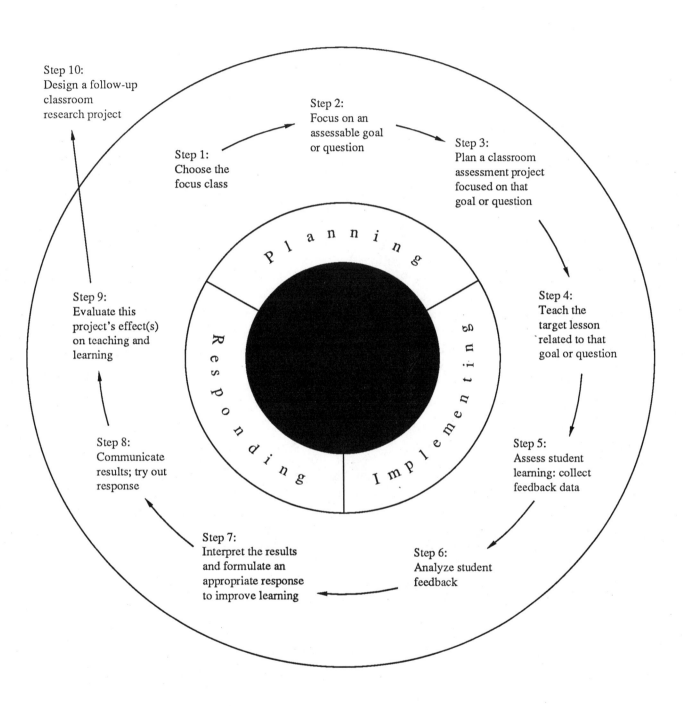

Step 10: Design a follow-up classroom research project

Step 1: Choose the focus class

Step 2: Focus on an assessable goal or question

Step 3: Plan a classroom assessment project focused on that goal or question

Step 4: Teach the target lesson related to that goal or question

Step 5: Assess student learning: collect feedback data

Step 6: Analyze student feedback

Step 7: Interpret the results and formulate an appropriate response to improve learning

Step 8: Communicate results; try out response

Step 9: Evaluate this project's effect(s) on teaching and learning

Planning

Implementing

Responding

The primary purpose of a Classroom Assessment Project is to assess the degree to which the teacher's "focus goal" is being accomplished or to answer the "focus question" about student learning as fully as possible. In order to accomplish either end, the teacher must formulate an "assessable" question, a question that is so well focused and limited in scope that it can be answered, in most cases, through the use of one Classroom Assessment Technique. To formulate such a question, the teacher usually must narrow the Classroom Assessment Project to focus on only one "target" lesson, or even on a single part of one lesson.

Once the instructor has selected the specific course, teaching goal, and lesson to assess, he or she develops a simple plan for carrying out the rest of the project. This design step involves deciding what kind of feedback to collect to answer the "assessable" question, and then selecting or devising a Classroom Assessment Technique with which to collect that feedback.

In the second phase, Implementing, the instructor teaches the "target" lesson, administers the Classroom Assessment Technique during that lesson, and then collects and analyzes the feedback. The analysis should be no more complicated than is necessary to turn data into information that can be used to improve learning.

In the Responding phase, the instructor interprets the results of the assessment and, on the basis of that interpretation, prepares and presents an appropriate response to the students. In essence, teachers respond to Classroom Assessments by telling their students what they learned from the feedback and what, if anything, they plan to do differently as a result. After the instructor has responded to the students and made any planned adjustments, it is useful to take stock, to evaluate the effects of the Classroom Assessment Project on teaching and learning.

STARTING WITH TEACHING GOALS

The Classroom Research Project encouraged faculty to begin their experiments with Classroom Assessment by first identifying and clarifying their teaching goals, since it is difficult to carry out meaningful assessment without clearly articulated goals. Starting with teaching goals allows faculty to take a serious look at what they believe is most important to teach, and what they really want students to learn. From our observations, it appears that instructional goals, which one might expect college teachers to reconsider regularly, are in fact rarely discussed explicitly. This is not to imply that most faculty do not have teaching goals. They clearly do. Nonetheless, many teachers find it difficult at first to articulate their specific instructional goals for particular classes. We therefore developed a survey questionnaire known as the Teaching Goals Inventory, or TGI. (For information on the development of the TGI, see Chapter Two.) This handbook contains the newest self-scorable version of the Inventory (see Exhibit 2.1 in Chapter Two).

To use this new version of the Teaching Goals Inventory, the instructor first chooses a single class to focus on. He or she rates each of the goals on the TGI according to how important its achievement is in that particular class. Each teaching goal is rated as "essential," "very important," "important," "unimportant," or "not applicable." By using the TGI Self-Scoring Worksheet (see Exhibit 2.2 in Chapter Two), faculty can quickly analyze their own results to determine how many "essential" goals they have and which of six goal clusters—such as Higher-Order Thinking Skills, Discipline-Specific Skills and Knowledge, or Work and Career Preparation—they tend to emphasize most in teaching that course. Finally, from among the essential goals, the instructor chooses a single goal on which to focus the Classroom Assessment Project. In order to start with success, we recommend that faculty focus their first Classroom Assessment Projects on instructional goals they feel relatively confident they are achieving. Not all faculty choose to do so, however. In fact, many wish to look first at the goals they feel they teach least effectively. While it is easy to understand a college teacher's desire to focus first on problem areas in hopes of remedying them, this can be a confusing and sometimes counterproductive way to begin using Classroom Assessment. The "problem-first" approach has proven less than satisfactory for many faculty because, in general, their informal judgments about what is not working are quite accurate. As a result, when teachers begin by assessing a topic that they suspect students are not learning well, they often find their suspicions overwhelmingly confirmed. A pair of contrasting examples may help illustrate the possible pitfalls in starting with problems.

☞ CASE IN POINT

Two women's studies instructors, Professors Alpha and Beta, decided to carry out their initial Classroom Assessment Projects in their required, introductory-level, general education courses. Professor Alpha had long felt that many of her students, although they were passing the course, were failing to develop an informed concern about the contemporary social issues on which the course focused (Goal 28). Since Professor Alpha viewed the development of an informed concern with issues such as sexism, sexual harassment and abuse, and gender bias in the workplace as an essential teaching goal, she wanted to know why she and her students had failed to achieve that aim. She therefore asked her students to indicate, before and after the relevant unit of instruction, how important a number of these issues were to their personal lives. Before studying these issues, virtually all the students, men and women, indicated that they considered these social problems of little personal relevance. At the conclusion of the month-long unit, she administered the same short questionnaire. To her dismay, the results showed negligible change. Through her Classroom Assessment Project, Professor Alpha confirmed what she already had informally observed: that many of her students were not learning to make connections between their study of social problems and their own experiences.

Even though the assessment confirmed her informal hypothesis, she was disheartened by the lack of change in the students' reactions before and after instruction. In other words, although it was no surprise, the actual situation was even worse than she had suspected. Her problem-centered Classroom Assessment Project failed to provide her with any possible solutions or next steps. As a result, the students' feedback merely served to make the instructor question the possibility of achieving her goal, as well as its value. After this initial, negative experience, Professor Alpha had little interest in experimenting further with Classroom Assessment for the next several months.

Her colleague, Professor Beta, felt many similar frustrations in teaching her sections of the same course, but she decided to take the campus Classroom Assessment group leader's advice and focus first on a teaching goal she felt she was achieving. While she agreed with Alpha that students were not connecting the issues to their own lives, Beta saw indications that her students were developing a clearer awareness of the issues. Since Professor Beta believed that students should learn the fundamental concepts and theories of her field (Goal 19), she decided to focus her project on assessing that goal. Specifically, she asked students to define and give one example of three key concepts—sexual harassment, gender bias in the workplace, and sexism—before and after the month-long unit in which they studied and discussed these issues. The responses were strictly anonymous, but students were asked to indicate their gender.

By comparing "before and after" responses, Professor Beta not only saw evidence of change in the students' awareness but also gained insights into ways to strengthen that learning. For example, although only a few students could adequately define the three terms before they had studied the material, nearly all could do so afterward; more significantly, nearly all the women in the class gave a variety of convincing, real-life examples, whereas those men who gave examples—only about half of them—generally repeated ones taken from the readings or from her lectures. When Professor Beta reported these results to her class, she asked the students what might account for the observed differences. Women students quickly pointed out that they had often heard about such problems first-hand from other women—usually relatives, friends, or co-workers—whereas the men said they had not. As a result, Beta decided to assign all her students to interview women friends and relatives about some of the less painful, more common problems they had encountered. She suggested that students might ask their mothers, sisters, aunts, and women friends about experiences with job discrimination or verbal harassment.

The interviewing assignment had a powerful impact on many of the students, particularly the men. Many of the men openly admitted that they had been shocked and angered to find out that women friends and family members had suffered sexual discrimination, harassment, or even abuse. After those interviews were completed, Beta asked for definitions and examples a third time, and observed that the quality of both increased markedly. Overall, the feedback from male students had improved dramatically, with definitions and examples written in more detail and in more convincingly personal language.

At that point, Professor Beta took her Classroom Assessment Project a step further. She asked students to create hypothetical examples of ways in which each of these social problems might touch their own personal lives. Most of the students were willing and able to generate possible examples, an indication of their developing ability to connect the course content to their lives outside of class. She shared a number of the best "hypotheticals" with the class, sparking a lively discussion about how realistic the examples were. Buoyed by these successful experiences, Professor Beta began to revise her syllabus and plan new assessments for the following semester.

By starting with a related goal that she believed she was achieving, Professor Beta found her way to the more challenging, problematic goal that Alpha had attempted to assess "head on." At the same time, by starting with a Classroom Assessment Project likely to reap some initial positive feedback, Beta increased its likelihood of being both useful and motivating.

The example above is not meant to dissuade teachers from focusing Classroom Assessment on tough teaching and learning problems. To the contrary, this approach is designed to help faculty and students understand and improve their achievement of the most challenging and essential instructional goals. The question here is where and how to begin, and how best to become skilled in the process of Classroom Assessment. Experience has shown us that beginning with success—by assessing teaching goals that are being achieved to some degree—more often leads to success.

Advantages of Starting with Goals

Starting with goals has at least five advantages. The first three advantages can benefit any teacher using this approach, whether working alone or as part of a group project. The last two advantages affect only those faculty working with colleagues. The first advantage of beginning with goals is that it encourages faculty to engage in a deep level of self-assessment about their teaching aims. Second, it enhances motivation and teacher ownership of the process by tying assessment directly to the instructional goals that individual classroom teachers value most. Third, it promotes good instructional practice by ensuring that faculty are assessing what they are teaching and teaching what they are assessing. A fourth advantage, one that is available to faculty working in groups, is that beginning with goals creates the basis for a shared vocabulary, which teachers from different disciplines can use in discussing their Classroom Assessment Projects. Once created, this shared vocabulary can benefit subsequent instructional improvement efforts. Fifth, as Classroom Assessment continues to evolve, the goal-based approach offers a natural, effective way to structure future networks of participants. For example, faculty focusing on goals related to "critical thinking" could form disciplinary and interdisciplinary networks for sharing the results of their assessments within and between colleges. (See Chapter Eleven for more about collaboration in Classroom Assessment.)

Disadvantages of Starting with Goals

Starting a Classroom Assessment Project with goals can also have some disadvantages. First, it can initially appear somewhat complex and time-consuming. The second disadvantage is that, for some teachers, the process of identifying and clarifying goals can seem overwhelming and even a bit threatening. Third, using the Teaching Goals Inventory can keep the process at an abstract level longer than is comfortable for some faculty. Because the goals of the TGI are necessarily too broad to apply to any particular course, faculty must revise and specify the TGI goals to fit their syllabi and teaching styles.

For many faculty, there is a wide gulf between stating a general instructional goal and knowing exactly how to assess that goal in a particular classroom. For example, although most faculty in most disciplines place a high value on teaching students to think clearly and critically, few instructors are able at first to point out exactly where and how they teach — or assess — clear thinking or critical reasoning in their courses.

Our impression is that college courses are more often "content-driven" than "goal-directed." As a result, although most courses probably address goals beyond simply "covering the content" — the learning of facts and principles — those higher-order goals may be woven throughout the course in a subtle and sporadic manner and therefore may be difficult to assess, even for those faculty who are clear in general about what their goals are and how they address them.

☞ **CASE IN POINT**

For years, in discussions with colleagues in his department and across the campus, a math instructor had argued the importance of teaching problem solving (Goal 3) and metacognition — the awareness and management of one's thought processes (Goal 16). In planning his first Classroom Assessment Project, however, he came to the surprising realization that he could not identify where he was teaching those skills in the algebra course he was focusing on. At that point, he decided to devise new lessons to help students develop those skills. In other words, he had to make sure he was teaching to the goal before he could reasonably assess how well students were learning it.

Another problem can arise when teachers reframe a large, often idealistic, goal in the form of a small, specific, assessable question, which, by comparison, may seem trivial. As teachers think about what to assess, they may dismiss many possible first projects as not significant enough. Behind this reaction lies a powerful assumption, if not a fallacy, that bigger is necessarily better. Experience in Classroom Assessment often convinces faculty that seemingly insignificant, small-scale assessment questions can in fact produce a wealth of meaningful and useful responses from students.

☞ **CASE IN POINT**

A music history instructor wanted to assess his goal of helping students learn the central concepts and theories of the discipline (Goal 19). In particular, he wanted to assess students' conceptual understanding of the European Renaissance. After considering a number of complicated assessments focusing on students' overall understanding, he was persuaded to start by simply assessing what students retained, one week later, from two lectures on the Renaissance. Since he believed that conceptual understanding depends on prior understanding of key facts and principles, this seemed a reasonable starting point.

He therefore asked the students to list the most important facts and topics that they could recall from his lectures on the musical history of the Renaissance. Students first made individual lists and then created a composite class list. He was amazed to see how good the class's collective memory was and, by contrast, how dismal many of the individual students' memories were. The information he gleaned from this brief exercise helped him decide what to review in the next class session and how to help the students move toward a more conceptual understanding of the Renaissance in the larger context of Western musical history. This first Classroom Assessment Project convinced him that even the simplest CATs, such as the Focused Listing technique he used (CAT 2, discussed in Chapter Seven), could yield useful information on student learning.

To provide you with an idea of how college teachers get from broad teaching goals to specific, assessable questions, we have included three detailed examples. In each example, the faculty member started with an "essential" goal selected from the Teaching Goals Inventory. The teacher then personalized and contextualized that goal, making it fit his or her course. Next, the instructor generated specific, assessable questions related to the course-specific goal. Each of those assessable questions became a possible starting point for a single Classroom Assessment Project.

In all three examples, the simple framework used in transforming the broad TGI goal into a more meaningful, course-specific one is a Classroom Assessment Technique called the One-Sentence Summary (CAT 13, discussed in Chapter Seven). This simple CAT encourages the instructor to state the teaching goal more exactly and fully by prompting answers to a series of simple questions: Who does what to/for whom, when, where, how, and why? The brief answers to those questions are then cobbled together into one summary sentence, hence the CAT's name. Although the initial summary sentence that results is usually too long and inelegant, its content provides a useful first-draft teaching goal. Once all the "pieces" of the goal have been generated, the summary sentence can be revised and rewritten. Many times, these rewritten goal summaries end up being included in the instructor's syllabi.

If you use the One-Sentence Summary as a tool to help you elaborate and specify your teaching goals, don't feel bound to answer each and every question, or to answer the questions in the order given below. The point of this exercise is to state a teaching goal in as much relevant detail as possible, not to adhere rigidly to the format of the technique.

The three examples shown here are linked, respectively, to Examples 1, 4, and 8 in Chapter Five. You may find it useful to skim those three extended examples after reading the examples in this section.

Example 1

Course: INTRODUCTION TO CULTURAL ANTHROPOLOGY

TGI Goal: To help students develop an informed historical perspective (Goal 32)

▶ **Using the One-Sentence Summary to develop a course-specific goal:**

Who: I (the anthropology instructor)

Does what: aim to help my students develop an awareness of and familiarity with key people, places, and events in twentieth-century history

To/for whom: (my students)

When: early in the semester

Where: in my cultural anthropology course

How: by helping them become aware of how much of this information they already do know and where to find out what they do not know

Why: because I believe they need to know this information in order to fully understand the course lectures and readings.

Course-specific teaching goal in sentence form: I (the anthropology instructor) aim to help my students develop an awareness of and familiarity with key people, places, and events in twentieth-century history, early in the semester in my cultural anthropology class, by helping them become aware of how much of this information they already do know and where to find out what they do not know, because I believe they need to know this information in order to fully understand the course lectures and readings.

▶ **Focused assessable questions related to the course-specific goal:**

How many of the people, places, and events that I have identified as critical background information do my students believe they know?

How much do my students know about each of the people, places, and events that I have identified as critical background information?

How well can students who know a given item explain it to those who do not?

▶ **Possible Classroom Assessment Projects to answer the questions above:**

Develop a questionnaire that allows students to indicate their degree of familiarity with each of the critical items, ranging from no knowledge to complete knowledge. Tally the responses and report back to the class. Encourage students to review those items with which they were least familiar. Repeat the assessment within a few days or weeks to measure progress.

Create a simple questionnaire that requires students to define or explain each critical term in their own words. Tally answers into three categories—correct, partially correct, or incorrect—and report the outcome to the students. Provide the class with contrasting examples of good and poor responses. As above, encourage students to review. Repeat the assessment later to measure progress.

Example 2

Course: SECOND-SEMESTER CALCULUS

TGI Goal: To help students develop effective problem-solving skills (Goal 3)

▶ **Using the One-Sentence Summary to develop a course-specific goal:**

Who: I (the calculus teacher)

Does what: want to develop my students' skill at figuring out which questions to ask next

To/for whom: (my students)

When: when they don't know how to solve a problem

Where: in their homework assignments

How: by teaching them a variety of techniques for getting "unstuck,"

Why: so that they can become more effective, independent problem solvers.

Course-specific goal in sentence form: I (the instructor) want to develop my students' skill at figuring out what questions to ask next when they don't know how to solve a problem in their homework assignments by teaching them a variety of techniques for getting "unstuck," so they can become more effective, independent problem solvers.

▶ **Focused assessable questions related to the course-specific goal:**

How accurately can my students now determine when, where, and why they have gotten "stuck" when they cannot solve a given problem?

What kinds of questions do my students ask themselves when they feel stuck?

What techniques do they use now to get "unstuck" when they don't know how to solve a particular problem?

▶ **Possible Classroom Assessment Projects to answer the questions above:**

Prepare three or four problems of increasing difficulty, ranging from one that I expect all students to be able to solve to one that I expect no students to succeed in solving. Give students the problem set, along with instructions to indicate when and where, and explain why they have become "stuck" when they cannot solve one of the problems. Read through the responses and look for patterns, as well as for particularly good explanations to share with the class as examples of problem-solving reasoning.

Provide students with a problem set, as above, but ask them to explain—step-by-step, in writing—how they successfully solved one of the "easy" problems. Look for particularly clear explanations to share with the class, as well as for patterns in the problem-solving approaches used.

Give the students one or two quite difficult problems, letting them know that I realize they may not be able to solve them. Ask the students to work the problems as completely as possible and, if and when they get stuck, to write down the questions they ask themselves as they try to get "unstuck." Present some of the most illuminating questions to the class and help them see when and how to ask themselves questions that will serve as problem-solving "levers."

Example 3

Course: **CLINICAL NURSING PRACTICUM**

TGI Goal: To help students improve their self-esteem and self-confidence (Goal 45)

▶ **Using the One-Sentence Summary to develop a course-specific goal:**

Who: I (the nursing instructor)

Does what: aim to help improve the self-confidence and self-esteem

To/for whom: my nursing students

When: demonstrate during supervised work with patients

Where: in their hospital placements

How: by explicitly teaching them how to actively build self-confidence and self-esteem

Why: because I believe that positive self-regard is critical to successful nursing performance.

Course-specific teaching goal in sentence form: I (the instructor) aim to help improve the self-confidence and self-esteem my nursing students demonstrate during supervised work with patients in their hospital placements by explicitly teaching them how to actively build self-confidence and self-esteem, because I believe that positive self-regard is critical to successful nursing performance.

▶ **Focused assessable questions related to the course-specific goal:**

What, specifically, do my students think is causing them to lack confidence in their work at the placement site?

Will my students' self-confidence and self-esteem improve if I provide them with more and more frequent feedback on their learning successes?

Will their self-confidence and self-esteem improve if the students practice positive "self-talk" at the placement?

▶ **Possible Classroom Assessment Projects to answer the questions above:**

Create a simple questionnaire and ask students what they think causes them to lack confidence and self-esteem in the placement.

Find a way to measure, however informally, students' self-confidence in the placement. Get a first measure before providing students with more and more frequent feedback on their learning successes. After a few weeks, take a second measure of the students' self-confidence. Compare the two sets of measurements, looking for evidence of change. Report results to the students and ask them to explain change or lack of change.

After measuring students' self-confidence, ask students to keep a log of the things they "say" to themselves, in their minds, as they prepare to confront stressful situations in the clinic. Collect and categorize these examples of "self-talk" as likely to be helpful, irrelevant, or detrimental. Encourage each student to prepare several positive, helpful messages to use as self-talk in the clinical setting. After students have practiced positive self-talk for a reasonable period, measure self-confidence a second time and discuss the outcomes with students.

AN ALTERNATE ROUTE: STARTING WITH QUESTIONS

For some college teachers, beginning a Classroom Assessment Project by identifying and clarifying teaching goals does not work well. Faculty who are uncomfortable with this approach, or who do not find it helpful, may get off to a better start by simply listing some specific questions they have about their students' learning in the focus course.

☛ CASE IN POINT

Instead of starting by analyzing her teaching goals, another clinical nursing instructor began her first Classroom Assessment Project with this simple question: "What goals do my students have for their first day at their field placement sites?" At the class meeting before students entered their field placements, she handed out index cards and asked the nurses-in-training to list three important goals they had for the upcoming experience. To the instructor's surprise, the most frequently listed goals had to do with "feeling comfortable, safe, and confident in that setting," rather than with applying specific nursing procedures or techniques. In response to their feedback to her "assessable question," the instructor decided to hold a class discussion on how to prepare oneself emotionally — as well as intellectually — to begin practicing nursing in a new and unfamiliar environment.

The primary advantage of starting with questions is that this approach is simpler and more immediately familiar than a goal-based approach. College teachers are characteristically motivated to generate and follow up questions and hypotheses in their disciplines. When they are encouraged to pose and pursue questions in relation to student learning in their disciplines, faculty bring formidable intellectual skills and experience to bear.

The primary disadvantage of starting with questions, on the other hand, is that the assessment effort can easily become disconnected from the larger instructional picture. When faculty start with course goals and move to assessable questions, their individual assessment projects are likely to have some connection to their overall teaching goals. In contrast, starting with assessable questions does not always lead back to goals and can result in a scattershot series of inquiries that fail to add up to a sum greater than the parts. There are, after all, a great many interesting questions one might try to answer about student learning, but only a small number of those questions will be of direct, practical relevance to improving that learning.

No matter which approach faculty take to "get into" Classroom Assessment, they must eventually frame the single questions they want to answer in their Classroom Assessment Projects. Many faculty, especially the most ambitious and enthusiastic ones, are reluctant to narrow the effort to something that seems less meaningful than what they originally set out to achieve. Nonetheless, limiting the size and scope of the Classroom Assessment Project goal or question is analogous to the adjustments many teachers make in response to feedback from Classroom Assessments. That is, to help students learn, faculty often must break down and reorganize ambitious learning tasks into manageable, incremental steps. Similarly, to gain useful information on student learning, teachers often must break a broad question into a number of smaller, more easily assessable questions.

☞ *CASE IN POINT*

An English composition instructor began her first Classroom Assessment Project with this "focus goal": "enabling students to synthesize and integrate information and ideas from different sources, including personal experience, reading, and class discussion." She wanted to answer eight related questions (with accompanying subtopics), among them the following: "Where does goal attainment break down?" "Do students agree with departmental goals?" "Can students learn the various functions in essay writing?" "Can they integrate them?" "If not, how can the instructor help enable them to do so?"

Her project idea was extremely ambitious and worthy of a multi-semester research effort. Even though this particular instructor had boundless enthusiasm, energy, and a considerable amount of time to invest in a major effort, the other faculty in her Classroom Research group strongly encouraged her to reduce the project to a smaller, more manageable size by trying to answer only one question at first.

By the end of her second month on the project, she was convinced. She narrowed the focus to one question: "How well do students integrate the ideas of other writers into their own essays?" To help students learn this type of synthesis, she broke the teaching process into three sequential lessons. Although she still was not sure that she had developed the best possible method for teaching students to make the "quantum leap" from following "paint-by-numbers" steps to synthesizing on their own, the feedback on her assessments showed her that many were making observable progress.

THE CLASSROOM ASSESSMENT PROJECT CYCLE: A DETAILED LOOK

The following guidelines are based on our own experiences and those of many faculty with whom we worked.

Phase I: Planning a Classroom Assessment Project _____

Step 1: Choosing a Class to Focus on. In your initial Classroom Assessment Projects, focus on only one class each term. Choose a class that you have taught recently and will teach again soon, one that goes well overall, and one that you are willing and able to experiment with. A typical problem for many first-time Classroom Assessors is thinking too big. Trying to conduct assessments in more than one course is virtually guaranteed to make the first round overcomplicated and burdensome. Most teachers have little trouble selecting a focus course, but for those who find it difficult at first, the following questions may help clarify the choice.

Have you taught this course before?

Will you be teaching this course again soon?

Overall, do you feel that this course goes well?

Is there some specific, reasonably limited element of the course that you would like to improve?

Will you have the time, energy, and opportunity to carry out an assessment and take appropriate follow-up measures in this course?

If the answer to any of the five questions above is "no," then the course is probably not a promising candidate for an initial Classroom Assessment Project. You may then wish to apply these questions to another class, to determine whether it is a more likely candidate for a first project.

Step 2: Focusing on an Assessable Teaching Goal or Question. Identify a single teaching and learning goal, or a single question about your students' learning, that you can begin to assess through one limited project. Choose a goal or question that focuses on teaching and learning behaviors that can be changed and that you are willing to change if need be.

This second step is the point at which many teachers really begin to find their "way into" the Classroom Assessment Project. In this step, you select a teaching goal or question about some aspect of your teaching and formulate a single, "assessable" question. For some participants, identifying an assessable question is the most challenging step in the entire cycle.

Step 3: Designing a Classroom Assessment Project. Start by imagining what a successful outcome would be. Decide what kind of feedback to collect, and when and how you will collect it. Clearly distinguish the Classroom Assessment from your usual teaching and testing activities. Finally, estimate the amount of time and energy your planned project will require.

In this step, you map out the path by which you will seek an answer to the assessable question and choose the tools that will help you get that answer. After identifying the teaching goal for the lesson or activity you plan to assess, you then examine what you actually do to teach to that goal and what the students are required to do to reach it. In addition, to plan effectively, you should determine what kind of feedback to collect and what kind of strategy or technique might get you that feedback. By the end of this step, you should be able to identify the particular class session in which the assessment will occur and the desired outcomes. Finally, you should be able to clarify what you, as teacher, and your students stand to gain from carrying out the assessment.

To begin with, you need to imagine what a successful project would look like. How will you know whether you have succeeded? What kinds of data will qualify as useful? At this stage, many of the questions teachers raise stem from uncertainty about the differences between Classroom Assessment and the kinds of assessment they normally do through testing. To some faculty, Classroom Assessment appears to be just another name, perhaps simply jargon, to describe procedures they use all the time in classroom teaching. A central and defining feature of Classroom Assessment is that, in this approach, assessment occurs before students receive evaluation of learning on a test or exam, while there is still time to do something about teaching and learning difficulties.

☞ CASE IN POINT

An English composition instructor identified as one of his essential goals "teaching students to successfully and ethically integrate the ideas of others into their own writing." To achieve this goal, he lectures on the topic and gives examples of successful and unsuccessful syntheses. During class discussions, he uses questions, both his own and those that students ask, to assess the students' understanding. He then gives a writing assignment and grades the students' papers, assessing the degree to which they have succeeded at integrating the ideas of others to support their own arguments. His question was "Isn't what I am doing already really the same thing as Classroom Assessment, minus the jargon?"

And the answer was "Yes, but only to a point." As the instructor was lecturing and leading discussion, he was certainly assessing student learning. But that assessment was at best partial, since not every student participated, and unsystematic, since it was not planned. It also left few traces that could be reexamined later. The assigned essays, on the other hand, were evaluated systematically and completely. All the students turned their essays in; so there was feedback on each individual's learning. Once the essays were written and graded, however, there was little opportunity to "recycle" them in the learning process. The instructor had often noticed that students failed to incorporate his comments into subject essays.

A Classroom Assessment Project could fit naturally between these two assessment moments: between the sporadic and evanescent attention to feedback during the lecture and discussion and the careful summative evaluation of the essays. In this case, Classroom Assessment might entail giving the students a short, ungraded practice exercise soon after the lecture/discussion but before the graded essay. Such an assessment would require them to demonstrate their skill in synthesizing. The Classroom Assessment Technique should reinforce the lecture and foreshadow the essay assignment. It should serve as an early check on student learning of the skill, providing information that the teacher and the students can use to make some mid-course corrections.

Confusion about the appropriate scope of the project is another problem during the planning phase. Faculty often are interested in learning something that cannot be gleaned from a single assessment carried out during a single class session. As professionals and adult learners, faculty should set and follow their own agendas. Nevertheless, we have become convinced that it is advisable to begin by going through the whole cycle with a single, simple assessment first, then branching out to plan a more comprehensive project. It is important to experience both the positive outcomes and the possible difficulties of each phase.

In summary, when you create the plan for your Classroom Assessment Project, you should describe the assessment strategy you plan to use, making sure that your description answers the following questions:

1. What "assessable" question are you trying to answer?

2. What specific Classroom Assessment Technique or instrument(s) will you use to collect data?

3. How will you introduce the assessment activity to students?

4. How will you integrate it into ongoing classroom activities?

5. What technique will you use to collect feedback?

6. Realistically, how much time can you devote to this project?

7. Will that be enough time to accomplish what you are planning?

8. What will a successful outcome look like?

9. What is the minimum outcome that you would consider worthwhile?

10. What steps can you take to "build in" success?

Phase II: Implementing the Assessment _____

Step 4: Teaching the Target Lesson Related to the Goal or Question Being Assessed. Plan to integrate the Classroom Assessment activity into your regular class activities as smoothly as possible.

In principle, teaching the target lesson should involve nothing more than conducting a particular class session in the usual way and then assessing its effects. However, faculty who have become involved in Classroom Assessment often revise their lesson plans or devise new ones in order to teach the focus goal more explicitly than before. Although a new teaching approach can be an additional barrier to getting started with a Classroom Assessment Project, that should not discourage you from making changes. Improving teaching is, after all, a primary goal of this approach. Many faculty have lists in the back of their minds of "ideas they would like to try someday" to make their lessons better. Carrying out a Classroom Assessment Project can provide the impetus for putting these ideas into practice.

One aspect you might think through and talk over with peers is how you will introduce and conduct the assessment and where it will fit in the lesson. Many of the simpler Classroom Assessment Techniques in the handbook can easily be completed in a few minutes at the beginning or end of class. Other techniques may be assigned in class but completed at home. In any case, the ideal Classroom Assessment Technique fits seamlessly into the flow of learning activities. An awkwardly placed or hurried assessment, or one in which anonymity is important but not ensured, can lead to student frustration and confusion. If an assessment interrupts the flow of a lesson, it will yield less useful feedback and may actually hamper learning.

Step 5: Assessing Student Learning by Collecting Feedback. Choose a simple Classroom Assessment Technique. Introduce the technique positively and explain it carefully. Make sure to ensure anonymity if responding to the assessment poses any risks—real or perceived—to the student.

The assessment tool can vary from a simple list or one-sentence summary to an elaborate survey with multiple-choice, scaled-response, and/or open-ended questions. To avoid being overwhelmed by more data than you have time to analyze, start with a simple technique and develop a sense of how much information you can glean from a single question or two. Later, if necessary, you can expand a short and simple technique into a longer, more complex one. You will also find it easier to respond and adjust your teaching if the messages that come back from students address only one or two issues at a time.

☞ CASE IN POINT

An English instructor, on his first go-round with Classroom Assessment, decided to solicit feedback from students regarding his comments on their essays in a college composition class. He asked one simple question: "How could my comments on your essays be more helpful?" He got back two very important messages. First, many of the students could not read his handwritten comments; second, many wished for more guidance on how to correct the deficiencies he pointed out in their writing.

The design of the assessment tool is crucial. Multiple-choice or scaled-response items are easier to tally, but they allow students less freedom of expression than written responses. Open-ended questions, while more difficult to summarize, encourage students to bring up issues or mention problems that teachers might never suspect exist. For that reason, you may often be better off using one or two open-ended questions rather than a set of multiple-choice items. The wording of questions on Classroom Assessments, as on tests, must be extremely clear. Confusing or ambiguous questions will elicit confusing and ambiguous responses, clouding your analysis and interpretation. To ensure that your questions are clear, you might want to do a trial run of the technique on a fellow instructor or a student assistant.

Introducing the assessment to students is an important step in the process. Students usually are pleased that an instructor might want to evaluate their learning for some other reason than to assign a grade. By announcing to your class that you want to assess how much and how well they are learning so that you can help them learn better, you can lower barriers to effective learning set up by the grading system and power structure of the classroom. By including students in Classroom Assessment Projects, you suggest that everyone is really pursuing the same ultimate goal—better learning.

Before using Classroom Assessment Techniques, you will want to consider the possible need for anonymity. Where student mastery of content or a skill is being assessed, you may want to know who gave which responses, and students may not feel threatened or hesitant about providing names. However, when students are being asked to give evaluative comments about the class, the materials, or the instructor, they should be directed to give anonymous responses. Students' anonymity also must be safeguarded whenever they are being asked questions that concern their attitudes, opinions, values, or personal histories. Even when the questions concern facts and principles, however, asking for anonymous responses can mean the difference between finding out what students think is the "right" answer and finding out what students really think.

☛ *CASE IN POINT*

When an astronomy instructor asked students to classify a list of statements according to whether they were "descriptive and factual" or "interpretive and theoretical," she found it helpful to have names on the responses. She followed up puzzling responses by asking a few students why they had made certain selections. In so doing, she gained significant new insights into why her students had difficulty in making the distinction between facts and theories in astronomy. These insights allowed her to develop more explicit and effective ways to illustrate and teach the contrast. Later, however, when she asked students to rate the value of the course to their lives, she insisted on anonymity in order to encourage honesty and protect students.

Step 6: *Analyzing Student Feedback.* Prepare yourself for surprising feedback. Look carefully at both positive and negative results. Carry out only as much analysis as is useful and reasonable, given the time and energy available.

This step in the Classroom Assessment Project Cycle often has the greatest impact on instructors, because here the faculty member's assumptions about what students are actually learning, thinking, or feeling in a particular class come into direct contact with information from the students. Many teachers are, of course, already in touch with and aware of student reactions, but few go through a Classroom Assessment Project without uncovering at least one or two surprises.

For many teachers, analysis is the first step in refocusing their efforts on student learning, in moving from a teacher-centered toward a learner-centered approach to teaching. The awareness of student needs and perceptions suddenly thrust upon them can stimulate or fortify a resolve to improve the quality of learning. The meaning of "doing a better job" in the classroom begins to change from "performing better as a teacher" to "promoting better learning in students." Although most teachers are dedicated in principle to this idea, Classroom Assessment can help them put it into practice.

When you begin to analyze the data from a Classroom Assessment, remember to look at the whole range of student responses. Some responses, especially negative ones, may strike sensitive chords and have a selectively greater impact than others. However, a balanced picture of the feedback will be more truthful and, in the end, more helpful to you and students alike.

General Comments on Analyzing the Data You Collect. Nearly all the techniques presented in this handbook generate data that can be analyzed and assessed quantitatively, qualitatively, or by a combination of the two approaches. Given the formative nature of Classroom Assessment, an approach that combines numbers and narrative is often the most enlightening and useful.

Before deciding how to analyze the data that you have collected through the use of assessment techniques, you will need to clarify why you are analyzing these data. Your original purpose for assessing learning in your classroom—to assess your students' knowledge of a particular concept or their reactions to a lesson, for example—should determine how you analyze the data.

All quantitative data analysis is based on measuring, counting, categorizing, and comparing amounts, numbers, and proportions of items. At the simplest level, we use quantitative analyses to answer the questions "how much" or "how many." A quantitative analysis of student responses to Classroom Assessment Techniques can be as simple as counting the total number of relevant items listed or mentioned. One easy way to analyze such lists is "vote counting," tallying the number of responses on the students' lists that match those on a master list. This is basically what happens when teachers score multiple-choice tests. Qualitative analysis, on the other hand, provides answers to questions such as "what kind," "how well," and "in what ways." A simple and familiar example of qualitative analysis occurs when teachers read and evaluate essay exams or term papers. In Classroom Assessment, to report the results of qualitative data analysis, we depend on narrating, explaining, and giving examples.

The skills required to analyze data collected through Classroom Assessment Techniques are familiar to most teachers and, as noted above, can be as simple as those used to evaluate and score tests and term papers. However, the task of analyzing data for Classroom Assessment differs in three important ways from the normal evaluation of student learning that takes place in classrooms. These differences concern purpose, unit of analysis, and the criteria on which the analysis is based.

When teachers analyze and assess tests and major assignments, they often have multiple and sometimes even conflicting purposes. One purpose is usually to give students feedback on how much and how well they are learning. At the same time, teachers almost always have to grade the students' work for administrative purposes. In the end, the extrinsic, institutional demand for grades is often the most powerful motivator for the evaluation of student learning. The data collected through use of Classroom Assessment Techniques, in contrast, should not be analyzed for grading purposes. The motivation for analyzing data collected through Classroom Assessment is intrinsic and personal. The analysis is driven by the teacher's desire to learn more about student learning in order to improve it.

The second major difference concerns the unit of analysis. In traditional classroom evaluations of student work, the primary unit of analysis is the individual student. It is the individual student's work that is evaluated, rated, ranked, and graded. Even when class averages are computed and students are graded on the curve, the real focus is on the individual student's performance. Classroom Assessment, on the other hand, focuses on the whole class, or groups within the class, as the primary unit of analysis. While results of this aggregate analysis may subsequently lead the teacher to focus on individual students, that is not its principal function. Classroom Assessment Techniques are aimed at collecting data on the class as a "learning community."

The third difference concerns the criteria used and the explicitness with which teachers must define these criteria in their analyses. In traditional classroom evaluation, the criteria for assessing student work are intimately linked to grading. Such criteria are sometimes binary: right or wrong, acceptable or not, pass or fail. More often, they are scalar, as represented by the letter grades A through F or the numbers 1 through 100. In either case, the criteria may be linked to an external standard, such as a national norm, or an internal standard, such as the class average. All such criteria are useful insofar as they make it possible to indicate, with one letter or a single number, the level of performance that the student has demonstrated. As such, they are primarily criteria for rating the products or outcomes of learning. In teacher-directed Classroom Assessment, the criteria used in analyzing the students' responses depend a great deal on the individual teacher's purpose for assessing and very little on institutional needs. The teacher is responsible for choosing or developing criteria to fit that purpose. We suspect that many teachers find it easier to judge an answer right or wrong than to analyze and assess a written record of the process that led to the answer. Nonetheless, the most useful criteria in Classroom Assessment are often those that can be used to analyze processes and intermediate outcomes of learning — rather than the final products.

Perhaps the simplest way to sum up the difference between classroom evaluation used to grade individual students and Classroom Assessment is to note that the primary purpose of evaluation is to classify students, whereas the primary purpose of assessment is to understand and improve learning.

Suggestions for Analyzing the Data You Collect. What specific kinds of analysis do you need to transform raw data into information that will help you make instructional decisions? One way to begin to answer that question is to consider several possible general questions about student learning that you might want to answer through Classroom Assessment.

Questions About Your Students

How many students are learning well and how many are not?

Which students are learning well and which are not?

What do successful learners do that other learners don't do, or don't do as well?

What do less successful students do that might account for their failures?

Questions About Course Content

How much of the course content are students learning?

Which elements of the course content are students learning?

How well are students learning the various elements of the course content?

How well are students integrating the various elements of the course content?

Questions About Teaching

How does my teaching affect student learning, positively and negatively?

What, specifically, could I change about my teaching to improve learning inside the classroom?

What, specifically, could I change about my teaching to improve learning outside the classroom?

Phase III: Responding to the Results

Step 7: Interpreting the Results and Formulating an Appropriate Response. Try to understand why students gave the feedback they did. Think through how you can respond to their feedback in ways that will help the students improve their own learning.

Assessment often generates more questions than it answers, and Classroom Assessment is no exception. The first questions that follow the receipt of feedback are "why" questions: Why did the students respond the way they did? Why did fewer of them succeed in the assessed learning task than you had hoped? In the interpretation step, you seek answers to these questions. Separating analysis from interpretation encourages faculty to look carefully at the total picture of the feedback they receive before jumping to conclusions or overinterpreting. Although you probably cannot help having interpretive thoughts while analyzing data, it is nevertheless good discipline to try to develop an objective picture of the total response before deciding what it means.

Some feedback instruments include the question "why" in the response items, so that instructors can consider students' own reasons for their responses. In other cases, you will have to infer or collect additional feedback in order to interpret the data. You can get more feedback through a second survey or through follow-up discussions with small groups or individual students. Discussing results with colleagues is an invaluable aid in arriving at a full and balanced interpretation. Colleagues often see results in a very different light and offer fresh perspectives.

☛ CASE IN POINT

In a Classroom Assessment Project mentioned earlier, a nursing instructor asked students to state their most important personal goals in taking her course. She had hoped to find that they were primarily interested in learning certain content knowledge and skills. Instead, she found that the students were most interested in feeling comfortable and secure in the clinical setting and valued most highly the personal contact with her. At first, she felt that the assessment had failed and that she had erred in giving it on the first day the students were in the clinic. When she shared the results with a colleague, however, he heard another message, one that the nursing instructor was perhaps undervaluing. He interpreted the results as evidence of the students' dependence on her as their source of security in a new and unsettling environment.

Formulating a response is often part and parcel of interpreting the data. As questions emerge from looking at student feedback, so do possible instructional responses.

☞ *CASE IN POINT*

A physical education instructor who had asked students to state and rank their goals in taking her elective aerobics class was surprised to learn that many students were not most interested in losing weight or getting a good cardiovascular workout. Instead, these students—particularly the adult women—wanted to improve their self-esteem and to relieve depression and personal and academic stress. In response, the instructor decided to teach and have students practice stress reduction exercises. She also incorporated information and activities that explored the relation of body image and fitness to self-esteem. By assessing the students' goals, she was better able to serve their goals. As a result, students were more motivated to share and meet her goals.

Much of the potential value of Classroom Assessment can be lost if you end the analysis and interpretation of feedback with your first reactions. To understand what the student feedback really means and how you should best respond to it, you might ask yourself the following questions before you discuss the results with your class:

1. Do your data indicate how well (or poorly) students achieved the teaching/learning goal or task?

2. Can you interpret why you got the results you did—why students did or did not achieve the learning goal? For example, if students did poorly, what was responsible for their lack of success: instructional methods, teaching style, or poor learning skills?

3. What follow-up questions might you pose to understand the results more deeply?

4. How might you best respond and make use of your findings to improve student learning? (Revise your teaching? Give a new assessment? Obtain additional feedback to understand why students responded as they did?)

Step 8: Communicating Results and Trying Out a Response. Maximize the possible positive impact of Classroom Assessment by letting students know what the assessment results were, how you interpreted them, and what you intend to do in response. Faculty responses to assessment results can range from simply sharing the feedback with students to restructuring lessons or entire courses. Not all assessments point out the need for change. At times, the results of a Classroom Assessment serve to validate successful practices. In these cases, simply giving students information on their feedback is often sufficient.

☞ *CASE IN POINT*

A humanities instructor used a small-group discussion exercise to teach the application of Lawrence Kohlberg's (1984) stages of moral growth to real-life ethical dilemmas. After assessing student reactions to the exercise, he simply shared the positive student feedback regarding the small-group method and students' estimates of the value of the exercise. He felt that letting the individual students know how highly their classmates valued the lesson was sufficient to encourage their continued participation. Since most of the students had reacted very favorably, he saw no reason to change the lesson.

In other cases, faculty may revise their teaching in response to the results of Classroom Assessments.

☞ *CASE IN POINT*

A physics instructor noticed from an initial assessment that his students' approach to visualizing problems seemed to be modeled closely on his demonstrations in class. The students tended to use only the points of view he demonstrated. In order to teach students to visualize more effectively, he explicitly modeled several different approaches to visualization in class sessions. Just as important as modeling the different approaches was the fact that he explained to the students what he was doing and why (Nakaji, 1991).

As you complete this step, you might ask yourself the questions listed below and, if possible, discuss them with one colleague or in a small group. They are meant to help you think through your response to the feedback from your Classroom Assessment Project before you present the results and your interpretation of them to the class.

1. How will you communicate the results of the assessment to your students?

2. How will you obtain their reactions to the results?

3. What do you expect their reactions to be?

4. What will you do or say to respond to the results?

5. What impact should your response have — on students and on their learning?

6. How will you determine the impact?

7. How can you help students make the best use of your results to improve their learning?

Step 9: *Evaluating This Project's Effect(s) on Teaching and Learning.* Assess the outcomes of your Classroom Assessment Project. How well did it achieve its goals? Were there any unexpected results? How did it affect your teaching? And what impact, if any, did it have on student learning?

Although you have now reached the end of the Project Cycle, your project still may not seem "finished" to you, since each completed assessment bears the seeds of many possible future responses and investigations. You may simply want to ask one or two additional questions to clarify the results, or you may want to plan a major course revision. From our point of view, this "open-endedness" is both a natural and a highly desirable aspect of Classroom Assessment.

The following questions may help you begin to evaluate the effects of your Classroom Assessment Projects on teaching and learning. Discussing your responses with colleagues who are engaged in the same process will add to your insights and understanding.

1. In what ways has your project affected your teaching in the class you focused on? (Please give specific examples.)

2. In what ways has it affected your students' learning in that class? (Please give specific examples.)

3. What surprised you most in doing the project?

4. What have been the most enjoyable aspects of the project?

5. What have been the least enjoyable aspects?

6. Summing up: What would you do differently next time?

Step 10: *Developing a Comprehensive Classroom Research Project.* After experimenting with simple Classroom Assessment Projects, many faculty are eager to tackle larger issues than can be dealt with in a single assessment cycle. Discussing teaching goals, significant questions, and thorny problems at the beginning of the Project Cycle often encourages this tendency. It is little wonder, therefore, that initial small-scale, short-term assessments often expand into large-scale studies conducted for an entire semester or school year. In these ongoing inquiries, teachers tend to go through cycles of assessing learning, revising teaching methods, and assessing the effects of those changes on learning.

At this stage, individual Classroom Assessment Projects are likely to become elements within larger Classroom Research efforts. The projects described in Chapter Five illustrate a range of inquiries from very simple Classroom Assessments to efforts verging on full-fledged Classroom Research.

TEN GUIDELINES FOR SUCCESS AND A CHECKLIST FOR AVOIDING PROBLEMS

The guidelines below sum up our best advice, based on six years of experience with Classroom Assessment. We hope they will serve you well as guiding principles to consider in structuring your Classroom Assessment Projects.

1. Start with assessable goals.

2. Focus on alterable variables.

3. Build in success.

4. Start small.

5. Get students actively involved.

6. Set limits on the time and effort you will invest.

7. Be flexible and willing to change.

8. Work with other teachers who share your interests.

9. Remember that students must first learn to give useful feedback—and then must practice doing so.

10. Enjoy experimentation and risk-taking, not just success.

The checklist shown as Exhibit 4.1 captures the essential elements of the Classroom Assessment Project Cycle. It is designed, as its name implies, to help you avoid common problems. If you are able to answer "yes" to the appropriate checklist questions in each phase of your project, chances are very good that both you and your students will benefit from the assessment.

Exhibit 4.1. A Checklist for Avoiding Problems with Classroom Assessment Projects.

	Yes	No
Choosing a Goal		
Is it the right size?	☐	☐
Is it precisely stated?	☐	☐
Is it relatively easy to assess?	☐	☐
Is it worth assessing?	☐	☐
Is it actually taught in class?	☐	☐
Choosing an Assessment Technique		
Is it appropriate to your goal?	☐	☐
Can you integrate it into your usual class activity?	☐	☐
Is it reasonably simple?	☐	☐
Will it contribute to learning?	☐	☐
Applying the Assessment Technique		
Have you tried it yourself?	☐	☐
Have you done a run-through with a colleague?	☐	☐
Have you made the *purpose* clear to students?	☐	☐
Have you made the *process* clear to students?	☐	☐
Did you provide the necessary *practice* to students?	☐	☐
Have you allowed enough time to apply the technique?	☐	☐
Analyzing the Data		
Did you plan how you are going to analyze the data?	☐	☐
Have you collected a reasonable amount of data (not too much)?	☐	☐
Is your analysis reasonably simple?	☐	☐
Have you allowed enough time to do the analysis?	☐	☐
Responding to the Results		
Have you planned your response?	☐	☐
Have you made your feedback explicit to students?	☐	☐
Have you presented your response appropriately?	☐	☐
Does your response fit into what you have planned for the class?	☐	☐
Have you presented the good *and* the bad news?	☐	☐
Have you tried to accomplish a reasonable change?	☐	☐
Have you allowed time to respond adequately?	☐	☐

Twelve Examples
of Successful
Projects

The twelve successful Classroom Assessment Projects presented in this chapter illustrate the variety and range of activities referred to as Classroom Assessment. Carried out by faculty in a dozen different disciplines, the projects assess different teaching and learning goals, vary in complexity and scope, and make use of different Classroom Assessment Techniques (CATs).

These twelve examples are based on the actual experiences and Classroom Assessment Projects of nearly twenty faculty with whom we worked during the Classroom Research Project. Since many faculty carried out similar or parallel projects, several of the examples that follow draw on more than one source. Other examples represent the work of only one instructor but are drawn from several different experiences with the same Classroom Assessment Technique. They are, therefore, mainly composite examples. Because the purpose of these examples is to illustrate this approach to faculty from many fields, the extremely discipline-specific contents of the original assessments were sometimes made more general to be of use to a wider audience. In other instances, the best features of several actual projects were combined for the sake of economy into one exemplary model. Like many of the best case studies, these examples are meant to be true to life.

To be included in this section as the raw material for these examples of successful Classroom Assessment, faculty projects had to meet three criteria. First, the projects had to demonstrate faculty creativity and initiative. They had to show how faculty "customize" Classroom Assessment Techniques to fit the specific needs of their students and the particular requirements of their disciplines. The faculty involved did not just adopt assessment techniques; they adapted them. Second, the projects selected illustrate how Classroom Assessment helps faculty gain new and useful insights into student learning. Third, the examples demonstrate how teachers apply what they learn from assessments to make changes in their teaching and to improve the quality of their students' learning.

These examples also show how instructors can "close the feedback loop," by giving students feedback on the assessments and explaining the changes they plan to make in response. By getting feedback from their instructors, students learn that their responses have been heard and that they do indeed make a difference. "Closing the loop," then, is a way to acknowledge and reward students' investment of time and energy in the assessments and to encourage their continued involvement.

These projects also possess the characteristics of Classroom Assessment discussed in Chapter One: they are learner-centered, teacher-directed, mutually beneficial, formative, context-specific, and well integrated into the teaching and learning process. Many of them were part of ongoing assessment plans, as instructors designed follow-up projects to find out whether the changes they made in their teaching in response to Classroom Assessment were having any effect on student learning.

As you read these examples of successful Classroom Assessment, you will also soon deduce what "success" does not mean in this context. It does not necessarily mean that you have found out exactly what you set out to discover, or that you have received an absolutely clear-cut answer to the question you posed, or that all your students demonstrated that they had learned well what you set out to teach them. On the other hand, you can consider your assessment successful if it enables you to discover why your students have not learned as well as you had hoped, or if it confirms an assumption about your students' learning, or provides you with a new insight into an ongoing problem, or gives you enough information so that you can ask a more focused question the next time around. Success in Classroom Assessment is usually approximate, incremental, and relative. If you and your students gain insights that can help improve their learning, the assessment activity has been relatively successful. The faculty who have used Classroom Assessment to greatest advantage are those who have learned to recognize, enjoy, and capitalize on these small successes.

Finally, it is important to note that these projects do not represent first attempts. Faculty nearly always begin by trying out several of the simplest CATs, such as the Minute Paper, the Muddiest Point, or RSQC2. These simple techniques do not require much planning, preparation, or class time. They work well as Classroom Assessment "warm-up exercises," allowing faculty to build skill and confidence at low risk and low cost in time and energy. These twelve projects are examples of what can happen after faculty get "warmed up."

The examples that follow are organized under the same general headings as are the Classroom Assessment Techniques in Chapters Seven, Eight, and Nine. Those headings are shown in the following outline:

Areas for Assessment

I. Course-Related Knowledge and Skills
    A. Prior Knowledge, Recall, and Understanding
    B. Skill in Analysis and Critical Thinking
    C. Skill in Synthesis and Creative Thinking
    D. Skill in Problem Solving
    E. Skill in Application and Performance

II. Learner Attitudes, Values, and Self-Awareness
   A. Students' Awareness of Their Attitudes and Values
   B. Students' Self-Awareness as Learners
   C. Course-Related Learning and Study Skills, Strategies, and Behaviors

III. Learner Reactions to Instruction
   A. Learner Reactions to Teachers and Teaching
   B. Learner Reactions to Class Activities, Assignments, and Materials

To make it easier to connect the examples to other segments of the handbook, we have specified the related goals from the Teaching Goals Inventory (TGI) (shown in Chapter Two) and the Classroom Assessment Techniques (CATs) used to assess those goals. In the "CAT used" column, cross-reference is made to the extended discussion of the techniques in Chapters Seven, Eight, or Nine.

ANTHROPOLOGY: ASSESSING PRIOR KNOWLEDGE, RECALL, AND UNDERSTANDING

Example 1: Assessing Students' Prior Knowledge

Discipline:	Anthropology
Course:	Introduction to Cultural Anthropology
Teaching goal:	To help students develop an informed historical perspective (TGI Goal 32)
Teacher's question:	How familiar are students with the important names, events, and places in twentieth-century history that they will need to know as background in order to understand the lectures and readings in this course?
CAT used:	Background Knowledge Probe (CAT 1, Chap. 7)

Background. Increasingly, we hear complaints that today's students enter college with little historical and geographical awareness. Many faculty believe that this lack of basic "world knowledge" limits students' ability to benefit from the traditional curriculum in the arts and sciences. From his own past experience, this anthropology professor suspected that many students in his class lacked an awareness of and familiarity with twentieth-century history sufficient to understand and learn from the examples, analogies, and allusions that permeated his lectures and the required readings. Rather than assuming, however, he decided to ask.

To find out just how familiar his students were with critical people, places, and dates, he first had to decide exactly which knowledge was most important to his course. He set about compiling a list of essential background information. He began by reviewing the readings and his lecture notes and then asked colleagues who taught prerequisite and lower-level

Exhibit 5.1. A Background Knowledge Probe.

The Weimar Republic

(1) Have never heard of this
(2) Have heard of it but don't really know what it means
(3) Have some idea what this means, but not too clear
(4) Have a clear idea what this means and can explain it

Senator Joseph McCarthy

(1) Have never heard of this person
(2) Have heard of him but don't really know who he was
(3) Have some idea who he was, but not too clear
(4) Have a clear idea who he was can explain

The Golden Triangle

(1) Have never heard of this place
(2) Have heard of it but don't really know where it is
(3) Have some idea where this is, but not too clear
(4) Have a clear idea where this is and can explain

courses in anthropology, political science, and history to suggest other important basic knowledge. This process resulted in a preliminary list of ninety items, which he then pared down to fifty items he felt were most critical to understanding his course material. The instructor then did some library research to verify his knowledge of each item and prepared an answer key, complete with references.

Assessment Technique. Once the list was complete, he designed a Background Knowledge Probe, a simple questionnaire to measure students' familiarity with the fifty historical, cultural, and geographical items. In response to each item, the probe directed students to indicate their degree of familiarity. To illustrate, we have included (as Exhibit 5.1) three items from the instructor's Background Knowledge Probe and the possible responses.

On the first day of class, before giving the Background Knowledge Probe to his students, the instructor emphasized that this was not a test and would not be graded, but that he would use the answers to help them learn during the semester. To underscore this point, students were told not to write their names on the probes. They were given fifteen minutes to complete the assessment.

Results. As he was collecting the completed Background Knowledge Probes, the anthropology professor reports that many students expressed surprise and embarrassment that they could recall so little from previous general education courses. After reassuring the students that it is never too late to learn, he let them know that they would discuss the results during the following class. After class, he quickly tabulated the frequency of each of the four possible responses for every item and used his calculator to come up with mean ratings for each of the fifty.

As you might guess, the individual responses were generally dismal, even worse than he had expected. In retrospect, he could understand the students' dismay as they looked over the items, since most of the students had "some idea" or "a clear idea" about only a few items. He did note, though, that for each item there was at least one and often a handful of students who claimed to be able to explain it.

Response. The instructor decided to capitalize on the "group memory" and planned a structured group activity, using the technique referred to as "jigsaw learning," for the following class session. Before class, he divided the list of thirty students into five groups of six, and he assigned each group ten of the fifty items to define or explain. From his quick analysis of the data, he knew which items were relatively familiar and which were virtually unknown. Using this knowledge, he made sure that each group's list began with at least two familiar items, in order to help them start off with some success.

After he had explained the task, broken the class up into small groups, and handed out the ten-item group lists, he gave the groups thirty minutes to get ready to identify and explain the items on their lists to the rest of the class. By the time thirty minutes was up, each group member was expected to be prepared to explain any or all of the items. This meant, in effect, that the members of the group had to explain the items to one another.

At the end of the animated half-hour group-work session, the professor called the class back together and asked each group in turn to explain two items—one "easy" and one "hard"—that he knew would come up in the next few classes. As usually happens, the groups did better than most of the individuals would have in explaining the items. The instructor nonetheless had to do some correcting and refining as they went along.

Just before the class ended, he handed out the brief answer key with relevant references. He asked the class to look for the important items in their readings, to listen for them during lectures and discussions, and to let the whole class know whenever they noticed a reference to any of the fifty key items. Finally, he explained that recognizing and remembering these people, places, and events constituted only the necessary first step toward a deeper knowledge of cultural anthropology.

ASTRONOMY: ASSESSING SKILL IN ANALYSIS AND CRITICAL THINKING

Example 2: Assessing Student's Skill in Categorizing

Discipline:	Astronomy
Course:	Introduction to Astronomy
Teaching goal:	To help students develop an ability to distinguish between facts and opinions (TGI Goal 8)
Teacher's question:	How well can students distinguish facts from opinions in examples taken from course material on astronomy, and in examples taken from everyday life?
CAT used:	Categorizing Grid (CAT 8, Chap. 7)

Background. The ability to distinguish observable, verifiable facts from opinions or untested theories is critical to the scientific method, and also to

Exhibit 5.2. A Categorizing Grid.

Directions: On the grid below, indicate whether each sentence makes a descriptive statement or an interpretative statement by putting a check mark in the appropriate box.

	Descriptive (facts)	Interpretative (theories/opinions)
The full moon causes some people to commit criminal acts.		X
Brighter stars are generally hotter ones.	X	
A greater percentage of Asian students graduate from high school and college, overall, than do students of any other racial or ethnic group.	X	
Women don't have the same natural ability to succeed in math that men have.		X
Statistics show that certain crimes are more likely to occur during a full moon.	X	
Stars shine by "burning" hydrogen through nuclear fusion that takes places in their cores.		X
On the Scholastic Aptitude Test (SAT), men entering this college scored, on average, thirty points higher than women.	X	
If there are Asian students in a class, they will get the highest grades.		X

virtually all methods of inquiry practiced in the academic disciplines. Developing and refining this ability is often a key goal of the liberal arts and of general education courses. In this general education course in astronomy, the instructor wanted to assess how well students could make distinctions between facts and theories in astronomy and between facts and opinions in everyday life.

Assessment Technique. The astronomy instructor began by developing eight pairs of statements, sixteen sentences in all, to be categorized as either "descriptive" (facts) or "interpretive" (theories or opinions). One sentence in each related pair was a statement of fact; the other, a statement of opinion or theory. In addition to four pairs of sentences directly related to astronomy, four other pairs focused on "everyday knowledge" about crime, medicine, ethnicity, and gender differences.

She then made up a one-page form, splitting the pairs and scrambling the order of sentences. Students were given the form and told to categorize each sentence as factual or theoretical by checking the appropriate box in the Categorizing Grid. Four of the eight pairs are reproduced as Exhibit 5.2. The correct answers are indicated by X's.

Results. To the instructor, the most interesting result was that her students miscategorized statements related to astronomy 30 to 40 percent of the time, more frequently than they miscategorized any of the other statements. Between 20 and 30 percent of the students miscategorized the statements about gender and ethnicity, whereas a smaller proportion missed statements on crime or sports. In sum, students showed the least skill at categorizing information they had been exposed to in the astronomy course.

This finding disconfirmed the instructor's prediction that the statements on gender and ethnicity would be most often miscategorized.

Follow-up interviews with students revealed that negative or highly skeptical attitudes toward science were responsible for incorrect responses from some of the brightest students. For example, several A and B students told her that they simply did not believe that astronomers could judge the temperature of a star from its brightness, even though they knew that the statement "Brighter stars are generally hotter ones" is considered in astronomy to be a fact.

Such responses were quite revealing to the instructor. She saw clearly that students could do well in her class on most objective measures, and could succeed in distinguishing facts from theories, without necessarily accepting the general premises or fundamental values of the discipline. In other words, they could play the game without believing in it.

Response. The results of this Classroom Assessment convinced the astronomy professor to devote more class time to making explicit the similarities — and differences — between distinguishing facts from opinions in "everyday" settings and the more explicit and rigorous rules used by scientists. She also used the outcomes of this experiment to convince other general education instructors to work on explicitly teaching students how to distinguish facts from opinions in questions about race, ethnicity, gender, and the like.

PSYCHOLOGY: ASSESSING SKILL IN APPLICATION AND PERFORMANCE

Example 3: Assessing Students' Skill in Applying What They Have Learned

Discipline:	Psychology
Course:	Introduction to Psychology
Teaching goal:	To help students develop an ability to apply principles and generalizations already learned to new problems and situations (TGI Goal 1)
Teacher's question:	Have/how have students applied knowledge and skills learned in this class to situations in their own lives?
CAT used:	Applications Cards (CAT 24, Chap. 7)

Background. Regardless of the discipline or level of the courses they teach, most faculty aim to help students use what they have learned to further their academic, professional, or personal goals. In assessing his introductory survey course, a veteran psychology instructor focused on the goal of application of skills and knowledge. He wondered to what extent his students were applying what they were learning in psychology to their lives. In designing this assessment, this professor gained insight into a question he claimed he had wanted to ask throughout twenty years of college teaching.

Assessment Technique. The psychology professor decided to ask students directly whether they had applied lessons learned in the survey course to their

Exhibit 5.3. An Applications Card.

Have you tried to apply anything you learned in this unit
on human learning to your own life?

Yes   No

If "yes," please give as many specific, detailed examples
of your applications as possible.
If "no," please explain briefly why you have not tried to
apply what you learned in this unit.

lives. In addition, to encourage honest self-reporting, he decided to ask for specific examples of their applications. Realizing that some of the course content was more likely to be applied than others, he chose to assess a unit on human learning, a part of the course that he felt had clear relevance to students' everyday lives and experience.

As soon as the class had completed a three-week unit on "human learning," the instructor wrote his assessment question on the chalkboard and asked students to copy it (see Exhibit 5.3). He told the class that this assessment would be their homework assignment for that evening. He also announced that they would receive credit for completing the assessment but that it would be ungraded. To ensure anonymity, he asked students not to write their names on the cards and encouraged them to type their responses. He explained why he wanted their responses and promised to discuss the results in class after he had carefully read them.

Results. At the beginning of the following class, the instructor assigned one student at random to collect the cards and check off the names of students who had handed them in, so that they would receive credit. That night, the psychology professor took the applications cards home and read through them, tallying positive and negative responses and categorizing the types of applications reported.

To his astonishment, twenty-two of the thirty-five students in the survey course not only said "yes," that they had applied something they learned about learning to their own lives, but also were able to give convincing examples. Several students gave examples of ways in which they had altered their study or test-taking behaviors as a result of what they had learned about their own learning. Not surprisingly, many of the applications were attempts to improve learning by using mnemonics, applying specific learning strategies, or lowering stress. A handful of students who were parents mentioned ideas or techniques from class that they had applied to help their young children learn.

On the other hand, several of the thirteen students who said "no" responded that they had never before been asked to apply things learned in school to their lives, and so they had not tried to do so. Some pointed out, quite correctly, that the instructor had never assigned them to find applications as they were studying the unit. A few students wrote that the question was not relevant, since they were not psychology majors. The instructor reported that the responses of those who had not tried to apply course learning were at least as valuable to him as the positive responses.

Response. During the following class meeting, the psychology professor summarized the results and asked students to share their applications with the class. He made a list of their examples on the board and then challenged each student to think of one other possible application that no one had mentioned. To his surprise, the class had little difficulty coming up with another, longer list of possible applications. The class discussion was one of the liveliest he had witnessed in years, and students indicated that they found it very useful to consider applications.

As a result of his assessment, this instructor made it a point to include discussions of possible applications in each subsequent unit. He found that class participation increased noticeably and that students improved their ability to propose reasonable applications based on psychological theories and research findings. From the first week of class, his students now know that they will be expected to propose applications, even if they choose not to experiment with them in their lives.

MATHEMATICS: ASSESSING SKILL IN PROBLEM SOLVING

Example 4: Assessing Students' Problem-Solving Skills

Discipline:	Mathematics
Course:	Second-Semester Calculus
Teaching goal:	To help students develop problem-solving skills (TGI Goal 3)
Teacher's questions:	To what extent are students aware of the steps they go through in solving calculus problems and how well can they explain their problem-solving steps?
CAT used:	Documented Problem Solutions (CAT 21, Chap. 7)

Background. In mathematics and the sciences, it is common to find students who can solve neat textbook problems but who cannot solve similar but messy real-world problems. One reason for this failure to transfer problem-solving skills may be that few students develop an explicit awareness of the ways they solve problems and, therefore, cannot easily adjust their approaches to new situations. To improve their problem-solving skills, students need to develop metacognitive skills—ways of thinking about how they think.

This calculus instructor was frustrated by his students' seeming inability to analyze and discuss their own problem-solving processes. Although these students were successful math, science, and engineering majors, they found it nearly impossible to explain how, why, or where they were stuck when they could not solve a particular homework or quiz problem. As a result, class discussions almost always degenerated into lecture-demonstrations in which the teacher would show students how to solve the problems they had failed to solve. The instructor suspected that most of his students solved problems by memorizing formulas and plugging familiar-looking problems into them, a strategy that he recognized as necessary but far from sufficient for success in mathematics.

Exhibit 5.4. A Documented Problem Solution.

5. Look over the four problems above. Choose one and write out your solution to it step by step. Draw a line down the middle of a piece of paper. On the left side of the paper, show each step in the math; on the right side, explain in words what you were doing in each step. Write as though you were explaining the steps to a first-semester calculus student who had never solved this type of problem. Be prepared to talk through your solution in the next class meeting.

Since the instructor was convinced that to become competent mathematicians students needed to become self-aware and self-critical problem solvers, he decided to assess his students' skills in order to find ways to improve them.

Assessment Technique. This calculus teacher regularly assigned five homework problems each night, to be discussed the next day in class. To assess students' problem-solving skills without increasing the overall workload, he dropped the number of homework problems to four, eliminating the easiest problem in each set. The new, fifth homework "problem" was the assessment technique itself (see Exhibit 5.4).

After solving the four calculus problems — or going as far as they could go in trying to solve them — the students were directed to select one of these problems and explain, step by step in complete sentences, how they had solved it. In other words, they were to document their solutions.

Results. The instructor met with a lot of resistance at first. Several students, including a few of the best, handed in perfunctory and inadequately documented solutions. Students complained about the fifth "problem" and argued that they should not be required to explain how they solved problems, only to learn to solve them. The instructor was initially taken aback by the vehemence of his students' protests. And he was particularly surprised that the most able students seemed to be leading the charge.

After two weeks of struggling to implement this technique, with minimal success, he asked students point-blank why they objected to the assessment. They gave two different sorts of answers. First, nearly all argued that the process of writing out their problem-solving steps was very time-consuming and that they considered the time wasted. The instructor had initially required the fifth problem but had not graded it or given any credit for its completion. "Why bother doing it," several students asked, "if it isn't going to count?"

The second type of objection related to students' conceptions of mathematics. As mentioned in the previous paragraph, most of the students viewed getting the right answer as the only means of success. They felt strongly that it did not matter how they got the right answer, or whether they understood how they got it, as long as they got it right and received full credit. The most successful students, by definition, already got the right answers most of the time. All the students agreed that no previous math teacher had ever asked them to "document" their problem-solving steps in writing. Why was he inflicting this hardship on them? What could they possibly gain from this exercise?

In discussing the students' responses with his colleagues in the campus Classroom Research group, the calculus teacher admitted his frustration and disappointment. Although he had held his tongue and temper in class, he complained to the faculty group that his students were acting like "grade grubbers," unwilling to learn anything unless they were rewarded or punished with grades. He was particularly puzzled by their insistence that since their previous mathematics teachers had not asked them to focus on problem solving, he had no right to do so.

Most of his colleagues had also come up against student resistance to innovation at one time or another; so his reaction was one that the faculty Classroom Research group could easily empathize with. Several faculty pointed out that the students' reactions were understandable and even rational, however, given their prior "conditioning" in mathematics. Many of his students had no doubt learned to equate success very simplistically with getting the right answers. A colleague suggested that the calculus teacher consider offering the students some incentives for changing their behavior. She argued that his students might be more willing to cooperate if they received some credit for what was clearly hard work and if they clearly saw the value of the task.

Response. The calculus instructor saw the merit in his colleague's suggestion and decided to give the procedure one last try. During the following week, he announced that he had listened carefully to the students' concerns and that, as a result, he would begin giving credit for the fifth problem, but not a grade. If students made a serious, good-faith effort at documenting the steps taken in solving one of the first four problems, they would receive full credit; if not, no credit. In effect, then, the fifth problem was worth 20 percent of the homework grade. If they failed to document a problem solution, the best they could hope for was 80 percent.

It became apparent during the following class discussion that offering credit for the assessment had provided the missing extrinsic motivation. The calculus teacher then took on the second and greater challenge: convincing students of the intrinsic value of becoming explicitly self-aware problem solvers in calculus. In class and through comments on their homework papers, he praised their attempts at explanation. He also began to ask individual students to go to the board and demonstrate their solutions, and he then encouraged others in the class to show how they had solved the same problems in different ways. The instructor brought in parallel but "messier" problems and asked the students to outline in words the steps they would take to solve them. The students then worked in groups for a few minutes to compare their planned approaches.

After only a few more applications of this technique, the class recognized the improvement in their understanding and in the level of class discussion. All the students seemed to benefit from focusing on problem solving, but the weaker students improved dramatically. Many students had begun with virtually no capacity to explain their work, but they had learned from their peers — through group work and board work — to articulate their steps. Their instructor remained convinced throughout that students could gain more control over problem solving when they understood the process.

At the end of the semester, the calculus teacher reported that the percentage of students receiving A's and B's was much higher than usual, reflecting much higher average midterm and final examination scores. For the first time in nearly thirty years of teaching calculus, he did not fail a single student in his calculus course. His midterm and final exams were drawn from the same item bank he had used in the past; so it was unlikely that the exams were easier than in previous years. His cautious explanation was that students had simply learned the calculus better and more deeply by focusing on problem solving and that the information provided by their documented problem sets had allowed him to teach more effectively. He also speculated that his renewed enthusiasm for discussing the "how" of calculus might have boosted student interest.

POLITICAL SCIENCE: ASSESSING SKILL IN SYNTHESIS AND CREATIVE THINKING

Example 5: Assessing Students' Skill in Synthesizing and Summarizing Information

Discipline:	Political science
Course:	Introduction to United States Government
Teaching goal:	To help students develop an ability to synthesize and integrate information and ideas (TGI Goal 5)
Teacher's questions:	How well can students distinguish peripheral material from key points in lectures and how well can they integrate those key points into a coherent summary?
CAT used:	The One-Sentence Summary (CAT 13, Chap. 7)

Background. To learn from a lecture, class presentation, or reading assignment, students must differentiate between relevant and irrelevant information. They must distinguish the few key points from the many supporting details. And to retain what they learn, students must actively integrate and summarize new information.

This political science instructor wondered how well his students were coping with his information-rich lectures on United States government. He was concerned that they might be paying too much attention to taking notes on details and too little on synthesizing those details into a bigger picture. Therefore, he decided to assess how well he was achieving his goal of helping students synthesize and integrate new information.

Assessment Technique. To get feedback on how he could help students achieve the goal, the instructor selected the One-Sentence Summary, a technique in which the learner tries to summarize a specific amount of material by answering the questions "Who does/did what to whom, when, where, how and why?" He chose to focus the assessment on a class session devoted to presidential elections. As he prepared for class, he identified the key concepts that he would discuss in the lecture; and then, working from his notes, he wrote his own One-Sentence Summary. The process of summarizing his own lecture caused him to rethink and rewrite his notes, placing more emphasis on the central points.

Because he doubted that his students had ever been asked to create this type of summary, he decided to teach them how to do the assessment before applying it. At the beginning of the ninety-minute U.S. government class, he explained the One-Sentence Summary technique and worked through an example with the students. The example focused on presidential primary elections, the topic of the previous class session. He asked students to summarize presidential primaries by answering the question "Who does what to whom, when, where, how, and why?" After giving them a few minutes to write a response, he elicited answers to the individual subquestions from volunteers and from their answers constructed an ideal One-Sentence Summary on the chalkboard.

This demonstration took fifteen minutes of class time, but participation was high and the composite summary sentence was really quite good, so he considered the time well spent. Before beginning the day's lecture on presidential elections, he told the students that they would be using the same technique to summarize that topic at the end of class. He announced that he would collect the summaries and use them to see how well the students had understood the lecture, but that the summaries would not be graded.

After almost forty minutes, the instructor concluded his lecture, wrote the summary questions on the chalkboard, and passed out index cards for students to write on. He asked them to summarize what they had learned about presidential elections by answering each of the questions and then combining their answers—in the order requested—into one long, but meaningful and grammatical, sentence. He gave them ten minutes to complete the assessment and then asked them to put their names on the cards and hand them in as they left. He promised to discuss the results with them during the next class. (The professor's model response is shown as Exhibit 5.5.)

Results. The political science instructor first read through the students' One-Sentence Summaries quickly, categorizing each of the responses—as either "excellent," "adequate," or "poor"—by sorting the index cards into three piles. He then read the "adequate" and "poor" responses again more carefully, noting the subquestions that students had found most difficult to answer and the common confusions.

In contrast to the successful summary created by the whole class, the individual students did relatively poorly. The teacher concluded that only about one-third of the class had demonstrated the necessary minimal ability to summarize. In other words, two-thirds of the summaries were in the "poor" pile. He also found that most students could adequately answer the "who" and "what" questions, but not the "how" or "why." Many students left out parts of the summary, some students got basic facts wrong, and very few mentioned the Electoral College, even though the teacher had repeatedly emphasized its role in presidential elections.

Exhibit 5.5. A One-Sentence Summary.

Step 1: Answer each of the seven questions below fully but briefly.

In a U. S. presidential election —

Who:	registered voters
Does what:	cast their votes
To/for whom:	for the one candidate of their choice
When:	on the first Tuesday in November of every fourth year
Where:	in thousands of official neighborhood polling places (or by mail-in absentee ballot)
How:	by indicating their choice on a secret ballot
Why:	in hopes that their preferred candidate will win the majority of votes in their states, be awarded the state's Electoral College votes as a result, and, similarly, win the national election, thereby becoming President.

Step 2: Now create one meaningful and grammatical summary sentence out of the seven individual answers you gave above.

Model response: In a U. S. presidential election, registered voters cast their votes for the one candidate of their choice on the first Tuesday in November of every fourth year, in thousands of official neighborhood polling places (or by mail-in absentee ballot), by indicating their choice on a secret ballot, in hopes that their preferred candidate will win the majority of votes in their states, be awarded the state's Electoral College votes as a result, and, similarly, win the national election, thereby becoming President.

On the positive side, the handful of "excellent" and "adequate" summaries surprised him with their range of approaches to the information. A few students came up with reasonable summaries that never would have occurred to the instructor. There was variety even in the choice of sentence subjects (the "who" question), with good summaries starting with the electorate, the Electoral College, the political parties, and even the media.

Response. Although he was disappointed that few students were able to summarize the lecture adequately, the instructor decided to focus on the best responses. He prepared a handout with five different summaries, ranging in quality from excellent to abysmal. To avoid embarrassing students who had done poorly, he concocted the two worst summaries himself, creating composite sentences based loosely on several student summaries. He gave the handout to the students at the beginning of the next class, asked them to read the five summaries carefully, and then directed them to take ten minutes to rank the five sentences from best to worst.

After they had ranked the five summaries, the instructor allowed students a couple of minutes to indicate what specific qualities about their first choices made it the best summary. He asked volunteers to explain their first choices and encouraged the class to question, support, or disagree with their reasoning. With some help from the instructor, the students came up with a list of qualities necessary for an excellent One-Sentence Summary.

As a part of their homework, he directed the students to rewrite the two sentences they had ranked lowest, turning them into excellent summaries.

This first Classroom Assessment convinced the instructor that most of his students could not summarize a fifty-minute lecture in any useful, meaningful way. Since he regarded the ability to summarize as a fundamental learning skill, he decided to spend class time on improving their performance. With that in mind, he began stopping regularly after each fifteen to twenty minutes of lecture and asking students to summarize quickly. Throughout the semester, he introduced various other summary techniques and found that most students improved their skills noticeably. He was particularly happy to hear from several students that they were using the One-Sentence Summary and the other techniques in other classes.

Example 6: Assessing Students' Awareness of Their Own Values

Discipline:	Criminal justice
Course:	Issues and Ethics in Law Enforcement
Teaching goal:	To help students develop their capacity to make informed ethical choices (TGI Goal 35)
Teacher's questions:	How well can the students reason about everyday ethical dilemmas in law enforcement? How clearly can they articulate the difference between knowing which choice one is supposed to make and knowing why it is the right choice to make?
CAT used:	Everyday Ethical Dilemmas (CAT 31, Chap. 8)

Background. One of this professor's most important goals in her undergraduate law enforcement course was to get students personally engaged in the ethical questions they were reading about and discussing. Far too often, in her experience, the aspiring law officers in her night class would simply recite the right answer, the textbook's answer, when confronted with difficult questions of professional ethics. The students appeared reluctant to engage in any honest introspection. As a result, discussions of ethics were turned immediately into discussions of legality, and the instructor could not discern whether her students had any authentic opinions at all about ethical issues.

Assessment Technique. She decided to try to uncover the students' personal values by posing the questions in a context less threatening than a class discussion. To get honest answers, she knew that she would have to ensure total anonymity. To get meaningful answers, she would have to pose a problem that was not too controversial, unfamiliar, or abstract. And to avoid getting "canned" responses, she would have to select a dilemma for which the text did not provide a simple answer.

The instructor decided to begin with an assessment that would respect students' need to give the "right" answers but would also invite them to give

Exhibit 5.6. An Everyday Ethical Dilemma.

Directions: Read the dilemma below quickly; then, in a concise manner, answer the questions that follow. Be honest and blunt. Please print your answers on the attached sheet but do not write your name on it. You have twenty minutes to complete this exercise.

The Dilemma. Paul had been a member of the Loma Prieta police force for almost ten years. For three of those years, Dave had been his partner in the patrol car. The two of them worked well together and got along well, and they both valued their partnership highly.

In the last year, however, Paul had noticed serious, negative changes in his partner's behavior. About a year before, Dave and his wife had been divorced. And though it had seemed to Paul a relatively "friendly" divorce, Dave clearly took it hard. He became withdrawn and moody.

Paul knew that Dave drank quite a bit from the start, but the drinking had always been on his own time and under control. During the past year, however, Dave's drinking had become much heavier, and Paul knew it had begun to interfere with his performance as a cop.

Paul had tried several times to talk with Dave about it and had been rebuffed. The last time he suggested that Dave should talk with a professional about the drinking, Dave had accused him of being "out to get me, like everybody else seems to be." Paul knew that Dave was slipping and that he needed help. At the same time, he did not want to jeopardize their partnership or add to Dave's already heavy burden of personal problems. So he waited.

But he was constantly worried. He worried when Dave was at the wheel. He worried when they got out of the car to check things out. And he worried about getting into a tight spot where clear, split-second judgments matter. Dave's problem was becoming his problem, too.

The Questions. Imagine that you are Paul. Put yourself in his place and respond.

1. You know police procedures and policy well enough. Explain what you should do—by the book—in this situation and why.
2. You also know real life and what you think is right and reasonable. Explain what you really would do—if you were Paul—and why.

---

their own answers. It would focus on an ethical dilemma familiar to all of them: a conflict between personal loyalty and professional duty. Since this dilemma came up all too often in law enforcement, she believed it was just the kind of issue that these young students ought to think through and talk about in class before they faced it themselves on the street. She sat down and, in less than an hour, wrote the assessment that appears as Exhibit 5.6.

As the next class meeting entered its final half-hour, the instructor announced that she had a special exercise for the class: an assessment of their ability to respond quickly to a difficult problem. She outlined the procedure, emphasized the importance of anonymity and honesty, and told the students that she would read their responses carefully and summarize them for the next class meeting. At that time, she would share the summary with them, and they would discuss the dilemma in depth. She asked them to do their best work in the remaining twenty minutes and to leave their responses on the desk by the door as they left. At that point, she handed out the dilemmas and returned to her desk at the front of the room.

Although the students did not seem particularly excited by the task when she introduced it, she noticed a change in their postures and expressions as they began to read the handout. Within five minutes, virtually all the students were hunched over their too-small desks, writing at full speed. When the twenty minutes had elapsed, most of the students were still writing. Several asked for more time, so she granted an extra five minutes. She found the situation rather ironic, since, in her experience, it was a rare moment when "night school" students asked permission to stay late. Normally, they bolted for the door.

Results. After watching her usually passive students so obviously engaged, the criminal justice instructor couldn't wait to read their responses. She remained in the classroom for another hour as she skimmed the twenty-five papers. From that first quick reading, she could see that almost all the students knew the correct police procedures that Paul was supposed to follow. She had expected that. More than half of them, on the other hand, didn't seem to know the rationale behind those procedures. This information gave her a clear sense of where to start in the next class. Whether they agreed with them or not, students needed to understand that there were principles and values being expressed in even the most mundane of regulations and procedures.

What she had not expected was the wide range of answers to the second question, which asked what they would do in Paul's place. Their responses to that question, and the reasoning behind those responses, revealed differences in values, approaches, and levels of moral and intellectual development that had been hidden from her before. As she read the papers more carefully later, she laughed at herself for wondering whether these students had opinions about ethical dilemmas.

Their responses to the Classroom Assessment proved that they did have opinions, strong ones, and that there were many conflicting views on how Paul should proceed. For example, one student thought that Paul should ask Dave's ex-wife to intervene, since it was "clearly all her fault." Another suggested that Paul set Dave up to get caught drinking on duty, but that he do so in such a way that Dave would never find out. A third student wrote that, without implicating his partner, Paul should ask for a new partner. Three students thought that Paul should simply continue waiting, hoping the situation would resolve itself somehow; and six students were convinced that Paul should turn Dave in to his superiors before the situation resolved itself.

The instructor was taken aback by this diversity of opinions and underlying values, but she also saw the opportunities for teaching and learning it presented. After her second reading, she abstracted basic categories of responses and tallied the students' answers to the second prompt accordingly. She ended up with seven basic categories. The categories and the number of responses in each were as follows:

What I would do if I were Paul.

6   Turn Dave in, as per police procedures.

5   Keep trying to talk Dave into getting help.

4   Find a recovered alcoholic on the police force to convince Dave.

4   Get out of the situation entirely.

3   Do nothing yet; wait and see.

2   Talk with Dave's ex-wife and/or family.

1   Set Dave up to get busted "for his own good."

She decided against trying to tally the related reasons students gave, however, since they were almost all tautologies—examples of circular reasoning. Over and over again, students justified their answers by writing "because it's the right thing to do," or "because that's what the law requires." Their manner of reasoning gave her a clear message, once again, that they were not used to thinking about the reasons or values behind choices. She now knew what the students needed to learn. The question was how best to teach it.

Response. The instructor began the following class by praising and thanking students for their good work on the assessment exercise. She let them know that she had read their responses several times and was ready to share her summary of the results. She told them that their answers to the Everyday Ethical Dilemma would form the basis for that night's discussion.

She began by reporting the area of greatest agreement and success, taking a few minutes to clarify the administratively and legally correct procedures that Paul was supposed to follow. She then asked students what reasons were behind those procedures, what they were supposed to accomplish. Many students volunteered answers, and most of them were acceptable ones. She wrote several reasons on the chalkboard. At that point, she began to move the class into deeper waters by asking what the values were behind the reasons they had given. It took some explaining before students understood the question. When they did understand it, several students were willing to contribute.

They recognized, correctly, that the procedures requiring Paul to report Dave's drinking problem expressed deeply, though not universally, held values in the law enforcement community: values that placed the welfare of the many over the rights of the few, the safety of the community over the privacy of the individual, and the protection of the integrity of the police force over one's loyalty to a fellow officer.

The instructor praised the class and reviewed the clarifying process they had just completed. She summarized the steps in this way: "First, look at the various options. Second, ask what the reasons are for each option. Third, look for the values behind those reasons." Building on that discussion, the students applied this process to the seven options they had suggested for Paul. To minimize defensiveness, the criminal justice teacher made it clear that these were possible courses of action, all worthy of discussion. She asked students not to try to prove which option was the best but, rather, to explore each with open minds.

A difficult, messy, but very exciting discussion followed, with the instructor several times reminding students that these positions were not, at least for the moment, the personal property of anyone. After they had discussed reasons and values, the instructor bowed to popular pressure and let them briefly discuss the feasibility, likelihood of success, and costs and benefits of each option. Although she was not certain exactly what the students had learned, she knew that this had been the first authentic discussion that term.

Fifteen minutes before the end of the class, the instructor had a sudden flash of inspiration. She asked the students whether they would quickly respond once again, anonymously, to Paul's dilemma. In the light of their discussion, what would they now do if they were in his shoes and why? She wrote the question on the board, handed out scrap paper, and asked them to write quickly. Although the students were clearly tired, no one objected to the unplanned assessment.

Later that night, as she read the twenty-five responses at home, she quickly tallied them, using the previous categories. The results of that follow-up assessment are shown below; numbers in parentheses are totals from the first tally, for purposes of comparison.

What I would do if I were Paul.

10 (6) Turn Dave in, as per police procedures.

7 (5) Keep trying to talk Dave into getting help.

5 (4) Find a recovered alcoholic on the police force to convince Dave.

1 (4) Get out of the situation entirely.

2 (3) Do nothing yet; wait and see.

0 (2) Talk with Dave's ex-wife and/or family.

0 (1) Set Dave up to get busted "for his own good."

These results suggested strongly that some of the students had reconsidered their positions and changed their minds, though she had no way of tracking who had moved from one given position to another. She characterized the shift as movement toward accepting more personal responsibility. Much more interesting, from the instructor's point of view, was the change in the reasons that students gave for their choices. More than half of the reasons given were now expressed in terms that referred to underlying values. Although the discussion probably had not changed the students' underlying values, it had certainly improved their awareness of and ability to express those values.

PHYSICAL EDUCATION: ASSESSING STUDENTS' SELF-AWARENESS AS LEARNERS

Example 7: Assessing Students' Awareness of Learning Goals

Discipline: Physical education

Course: Aerobics for Fitness and Fun

Teaching goal: To help students develop a commitment to their own values (TGI Goal 46)

Teacher's questions: How aware are students of the learning goals they have for my course? How well do their learning goals match my teaching goals?

CAT used: Goal Ranking and Matching (CAT 35, Chap. 8)

Exhibit 5.7. Goal Ranking and Matching Exercise.

What do you hope to get out of this course? Will it meet your needs and expectations? This exercise is designed to help you identify your learning goals and share them with the instructor. After you have completed it, you will learn what the instructor's goals are and see how well her teaching goals match your learning goals.

1. Under the left-hand column below, please list four or five learning goals you hope to achieve by taking this course.

2. Then, using the right-hand column, indicate each goal's relative importance to you. Make the most important goal 1, the next most important 2, and so on.

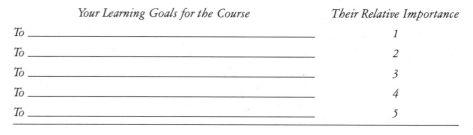

Your Learning Goals for the Course	*Their Relative Importance*
To _____	1
To _____	2
To _____	3
To _____	4
To _____	5

Background. For several years, a dance instructor had noticed that attendance in her large aerobics classes always dropped off sharply after the first few weeks of the semester. Although colleagues assured her that such attrition was, though unfortunate, to be expected, she remained dissatisfied with the retention rate. Hoping to increase student interest and motivation, she had experimented over the years with various teaching techniques and approaches, but none of them seemed to make an appreciable difference.

She remained convinced, however, that many students dropped her course because their initial high levels of interest and motivation were being negatively affected by something going on in the class. The instructor had a hunch that students were dropping because their expectations were not being met. In other words, she suspected that what she thought students should learn from the class did not correspond well to what the students expected. She realized that only the students could tell her what their goals were but that many of them probably were not explicitly aware of their own expectations. Therefore, her students would need to self-assess their goals before she could assess them. After working through the Goal Ranking and Matching exercise in a Classroom Research training workshop on her campus, she decided to adapt this CAT to find out how well her students' learning goals for the aerobics class matched her teaching goals.

Assessment Technique. In the second week of the semester, she asked students in the aerobics class to list their five most important goals in taking the course—what they hoped to learn, in other words—and how they hoped to benefit (see Exhibit 5.7). She then asked them to rank those five goals in the order of their relative importance. The instructor handed out large, lined index cards to use in the exercise. While the students wrote down and ranked their learning goals, she did the same for her teaching goals. She then collected the index cards, promised to talk with students about them at the next class meeting, and took the cards home to analyze.

She expected the students to rank their goals as follows (although these goals were not her actual teaching goals):

1. To improve cardiovascular fitness

2. To improve muscle tone; to shape up

3. To lose weight

4. To become a better, more graceful dancer

5. To have fun; to enjoy myself

The instructor's most important teaching and learning goals for the course were these:

1. To convince students of the importance of cardiovascular fitness and the value of regular aerobic exercise

2. To help students improve their cardiovascular fitness levels enough, in the short term, to make a noticeable difference in their daily lives

3. To help students develop a regular, sustainable aerobic exercise program to maintain lifelong cardiovascular fitness

Results. Much to her surprise, most of her students were not taking aerobics primarily to become more fit, get in shape, or lose weight, although many did mention these goals. The two most often mentioned, most important goals were (1) to improve self-image/self-confidence and (2) to reduce stress/relax. The content and ranking of students' goals surprised her for two reasons. First, she assumed that students had read and understood the course title and description, both of which stressed the development of cardiovascular fitness and healthy exercise habits. Second, although she had never equated aerobics directly with improving self-confidence or self-image, many of her students obviously did.

Being a professional dancer in excellent physical condition, the instructor personally found aerobics somewhat less than challenging. She worried that students were dropping the class because it was too easy or because they were not getting a rigorous enough workout. As a consequence, over the years, she had worked to make the class more physically challenging and faster paced. Each week she introduced new steps and new routines, assuming that students were mainly interested in getting a tough cardiovascular workout.

After assessing her students' goals, the instructor realized she had been teaching the class in a way that many students, given their expressed goals, probably found both threatening and stressful. For students whose goal was to improve self-image and self-concept, the steadily increasing challenge and pacing of the class could easily lead to feelings of failure and lower self-esteem; for students whose goal was to lower stress, the class could easily raise stress levels. In other words, the assessment showed the instructor that her teaching goals and the students' learning goals were inadvertently coming into conflict, and that this mismatch was probably encouraging students to drop the class.

Response. As she had promised, the instructor shared the results of the goals assessment with her aerobics class. She then presented and explained her teaching goals and admitted her surprise at discovering the mismatch between her goals and theirs. She assured the class that while she still aimed to achieve her goals, she also wanted to help them achieve theirs. She asked for specific suggestions on ways in which the course could help them lower stress and improve self-concept.

The students made a number of suggestions, most of which she found reasonable and thoughtful. After considering them, she decided to incorporate two of the best student ideas. To help lower the stress level, she began teaching simple, less challenging routines first; then, for students who were interested in a more rigorous workout, she presented more advanced variations. By offering a "two-track" workout, she allowed students more choice. Several students had expressed interest in learning more about self-concept; so the instructor decided to incorporate readings and discussion on the relationship between body concept and self-concept into the course syllabus.

Follow-Up. On subsequent assessments, the students made it clear that they appreciated the instructor's concern, flexibility, and willingness to help them meet their goals. In responding to the students' goals and interests, the instructor discovered new levels of intellectual challenge for herself. As she prepared to teach about body concept and self-concept, she had to read and integrate materials she would not otherwise have encountered and began to see the course in a new light. Her students helped her recognize that the aerobics course could be more than just physically challenging.

In a meeting of her college's Classroom Research group, the instructor admitted that she had never before considered assigning academic readings in an elective, one-unit aerobics course. The students' interest in the readings and the level of participation in the subsequent discussion convinced her to incorporate more intellectual content in her syllabus. The Goal Ranking and Matching technique became a permanent part of her teaching repertoire, an assessment she used in the first week of all her courses. In her aerobics course that semester, attendance and retention improved and have remained consistently higher than in the past.

SPEECH COMMUNICATION: ASSESSING STUDENTS' AWARENESS OF THEIR ATTITUDES AND VALUES

Example 8: Assessing Students' Awareness of Ways of Knowing

Discipline:	Speech communication
Course:	Essentials of Interpersonal Communication
Teaching goals:	To help students develop an ability to work productively with others (TGI Goal 36)

Teacher's questions:	To what extent are students aware of their own preferred ways of learning and communicating? Do they recognize contexts in which their preferred ways of learning are more effective or less effective? How clearly do they understand that others with whom they communicate may not share their preferences?
CAT used:	Self-Assessment of Ways of Learning (CAT 36, Chap. 8)

Background. One of the most difficult things for this professor's undergraduate students to understand was that the ways that they communicated and learned best were not universally shared. He had long been acutely aware that some of his students seemed predisposed to an argumentative, almost adversarial style of communication, while others shrank in horror from conflict, adopting a much more empathetic approach.

Most students took his class in hopes that improving their interpersonal communication skills would help them succeed in their other courses, their jobs, and their personal lives. He had tried many times to make students aware of these different styles or approaches and the misunderstandings and hurt feelings that usually resulted when they collided. Although he had repeatedly tried to show them that any awareness of their own communication styles could help them achieve their personal and professional goals, his message clearly did not get across to most students. They could learn to identify various communication styles in others, but they rarely seemed able to monitor or adapt their own.

The student population of his course was usually about evenly divided between men and women, and about one-third were international students. He knew that some differences in communication style were related to, though probably not determined by, gender and culture; and he had followed with interest, although at somewhat of a distance, the development of theories and a research literature on communication between men and women and among different cultures. But since this was an undergraduate general education course, too much emphasis on the research literature seemed inappropriate.

It was only after hearing Blythe McVicker Clinchy (1990) speak, and going on to read *Women's Ways of Knowing: The Development of Self, Voice, and Mind* (Belenky, Clinchy, Goldberger, and Tarule, 1986), that the professor found a useful conceptual scheme to explain these differences. In a nutshell, he found that he could categorize most of his students and himself according to the framework presented in *Women's Ways of Knowing*, whether the students were women or men. Some students communicated as though they could really know something only if they got it from an expert source or authority ("received knowing"); others, only if it originated in or agreed with their own personal opinions and/or experiences ("subjective knowing"). A third group of students seemed to learn best by trying to understand and empathize with others ("connected procedural knowing"); a fourth group, by debating and arguing ("separate procedural knowing").

Assessment Technique. To see whether this framework made sense to his students and whether it could help them become more aware of their preferred or habitual communication styles, he decided to create an assessment focusing on these "ways of knowing."

About halfway through the course, after the students had some grounding in various communication styles, the instructor decided to try out his self-assessment technique. He scheduled the assessment for the session in which he lectured on unintentional conflicts in interpersonal communications. Stopping twenty minutes before the end of the two-hour class meeting, he handed out a two-page assessment (for a slightly modified version, see Exhibit 5.8) and went over the directions. He asked the students to read the statements on the first page carefully and then to provide the requested background information. He suggested that they answer questions 1 through 4 quickly—according to their "gut" feelings—and to spend most of their time answering question 5. He also asked them to try to come up with a brief example for each of the four approaches. At that point, the students had fifteen minutes to complete the self-assessment. Several finished early.

Results. The speech communication professor took the nearly forty self-assessments back to his office and began tallying up responses. He decided to categorize the responses by gender and nationality. He began by drawing up a simple tally sheet, a four-by-four matrix with very large cells (see Exhibit 5.9), and in the appropriate cells of the matrix he entered the answers each student gave for question 1. He used a copy of this matrix to tally the answers to each of the other questions.

After he had completed the tallying, the instructor looked carefully for any big differences between the responses of the men and women, or between the responses of U.S. and international students. He did find some notable differences between the men's and the women's responses on questions 1, 3, and 4. The only differences between U.S. and international students showed up in response to question 2.

In answer to question 1, which asked students which of the four statements reminded them most of themselves, more men saw themselves as "separate knowers" (A) and more women saw themselves as "connected knowers" (B). The instructor had expected that outcome, but he was surprised to see that the majority of his students, both male and female, saw themselves reflected most clearly as "subjective knowers" (C).

Question 2 concerned students' usual approaches in class. The most frequent response, across the board, was "separate knowing" (A), followed by "connected knowing" (B) and "received knowing" (D). "Subjective knowing" (C), which had been the most common answer to question 1, was now the least common answer to question 2. Once again, more women than men selected "connected knowing," but the difference was very slight. The majority of international students, but almost no U.S. students, chose "received knowing" (D) in answer to question 2.

In characterizing their most common ways of knowing and communicating in their personal and social lives, his students once again differed by gender. More than three-fourths of the women selected "connected know-

Note: The classroom assessment for ways of knowing is adapted from a workshop exercise presented by Blythe McVicker Clinchy at the 10th Lilly Conference on College Teaching, Miami University, Oxford, Ohio, November 16, 1990.

**Exhibit 5.8. A Self-Assessment Exercise:
Preferred Ways of Knowing/Communicating.**

[Page 1]

Directions: Read the four statements below carefully; then answer the self-assessment questions on the following page. Please don't write your name on the assessment. You may keep page 1, but be sure to turn in page 2 before you leave.

A. I never take anything for granted. When somebody states an opinion, I like to play the "devil's advocate" and take the opposite position. Even if I agree with the opinion, I try to find the flaws and weak points in my "opponent's" logic. I really enjoy a good argument and often learn a lot from responding to the tough criticisms of a "worthy opponent." Sometimes I even change my mind as the result of a hard-fought debate.

B. When I hear somebody state an opinion that is very different from mine, I try to look at it from that person's perspective, to get inside his or her head. I learn a lot from listening to people explain why they think the way they do. They usually have reasons. And sometimes they have better reasons than I do.

C. Most of the time, disagreements are just a matter of differences in personal opinions. Sure, it can be interesting to discuss issues with other people, and even to argue about them sometimes; but in the end, it comes down to their opinions against mine. My own experiences change my mind. Other people's opinions don't.

D. I don't really enjoy arguments or debates, and I'm not too interested in other people's opinions about important topics. Unless they're experts, why bother listening? For example, I'd rather listen to a professor lecture than have class discussions. Only people who really know what they're talking about are worth listening to. I respect and accept expert opinion on most things.

[Page 2]

Background information (Circle the responses that describe you.)

Male	Female
U.S. Student	International Student

Self-assessment questions (In 1–5, circle the appropriate letter.)

1. Which of the four statements above most clearly reminds you of yourself?

    A   B   C   D

2. Which of these four approaches do you actually use most when you are communicating in this class?

    A   B   C   D

3. Which of these four approaches do you actually use most in your social/personal life outside the classroom?

    A   B   C   D

4. When other people are communicating with you, which of these four approaches would you prefer them to use?

    A   B   C   D

5. Are there some interpersonal communication situations in which one approach is more appropriate than the others? (Briefly explain and give specific examples.)

---

ing" (B), and about 40 percent of the men made the same choice. The rest of the men's responses were almost evenly divided between "separate knowing" (A) and "subjective knowing" (C). No students selected "received knowing" as the habitual mode in their personal and social lives.

Exhibit 5.9. Sample Tally Sheet.

	A	B	C	D
Women				
Men				
U.S.				
International				
All				

In responding to question 4, the class exhibited its highest level of agreement. Over two-thirds of the students—strong majorities of men and women, U.S. and international students alike—preferred communicating with the empathetic, open-minded "connected knower." Even here, however, there were gender differences. Quite a few men, but almost no women, indicated a preference for the disputatious "separate knower."

The instructor found his students' answers to question 5—which asked for specific examples of interpersonal situations in which one of the four approaches would be more appropriate than the others—too diverse to categorize meaningfully. As a result, he simply chose a few of the best examples to use in class.

Response. One week later, the instructor presented his summary and analysis of the students' responses to questions 1 through 4 and asked them for their interpretations. Several students commented on the differences between men's and women's responses, and there was a lively discussion about possible reasons for these differences. The instructor cautioned against placing too much importance on one simple survey, but he admitted that the results were certainly provocative. He suggested that students who found the topic of gender differences in interpersonal communication fascinating might use their term paper assignments as an opportunity to learn more about it. And he made the same offer to those students interested in cultural differences, which seemed to have been expressed in responses to question 2.

The instructor focused the ensuing discussion on the broader distinctions students made between in-class and out-of-class approaches, and between what they preferred in conversation partners and what they thought they offered. Here again, the issue of gender differences came up. In general, both men and women agreed that they preferred talking with women about personal or sensitive subjects. A few women students complained that men either didn't know how to listen or didn't want to. One male student responded by saying that he had never even noticed his "argumentative" approach before, but that it probably contributed to misunderstandings with his girlfriend.

The instructor then raised the question of appropriateness and shared some of the best responses to question 5. These examples seemed to prompt the class, and many students offered other specific examples of situations in which one approach or another might work best. Interestingly, the class found very few situations in which "connected knowing" would be inappropriate or ineffective but relatively many in which "separate knowing" might not work.

Follow-Up. These "ways of knowing" came up throughout the rest of the term, and the students often referred to them in characterizing communication behaviors. Because students had internalized it, the instructor was able to use this framework as a point of reference and comparison in later lectures.

NURSING EDUCATION: ASSESSING STUDENTS' AWARENESS OF THEIR ATTITUDES AND VALUES

Example 9: Assessing Course-Related Self-Esteem and Self-Confidence

Discipline:	Nursing
Course:	Clinical Nursing Practicum
Teaching goal:	To help students improve self-esteem/self-confidence (TGI Goal 45)
Teacher's question:	How can I help students gain more control over their self-esteem and self-confidence, so that they can perform more successfully in clinical settings?
CAT used:	Course-Related Self-Confidence Surveys (CAT 32, Chap. 8)

Background. As she supervised her first-year nursing students in their hospital placements, this young nursing instructor noticed that many of them demonstrated the necessary skills and knowledge but lacked the self-confidence necessary to use them effectively. When these otherwise competent adults dealt with patients, they often became flustered and inarticulate, put themselves down, or even trembled noticeably.

In her previous career as a practicing registered nurse, the instructor had learned that patients appreciate and need nurses who are assured and confident—not just competent. In the hospital, there had been moments when she had to make judgments and act instantly to save lives. There was no place for uncertainty. She also needed a healthy self-esteem to deal successfully with doctors and other staff.

Convinced of the practical importance of self-confidence to success in nursing, the instructor decided to find out what she and her students could do to raise their self-confidence. After doing some library research, looking for a useful definition of the concept, she created a definition and developed a simple survey.

Assessment Technique. In the third week of the practicum, the nursing instructor handed out a short Self-Confidence Survey (Exhibit 5.10). She explained its purpose, talked about her definition of self-confidence, and responded to questions. She asked students to be as specific and detailed as possible in answering. Students were told not to write their names on the surveys and were given fifteen minutes of class time to fill them out.

Exhibit 5.10. Self-Confidence Survey.

Definition of Self-Confidence: For this survey, let's define self-confidence as your personal, subjective evaluation of your own ability or competence. You make this judgment by comparing your performance (as you see it) with the expectations you believe others have of you. In other words, your self-confidence depends on the distance you perceive between your "actual" ability to perform and the "ideal" performance you imagine.

Although all of us probably have a "global," general level of self-confidence, our feelings of self-worth and self-confidence can certainly vary with situations or settings. This survey focuses on your self-confidence in a particular situation, your clinical placement—not on your overall feelings. So, even though your levels of self-confidence in the placement and in the rest of your life are clearly related, focus your answers on the placement. Please be as specific and complete as possible.

1. Rate your self-confidence—how you feel about it in the practicum today—by circling the appropriate number below.

1	2	3	4	5
Extremely low	Low	Average for me	High	Extremely high

2. Briefly explain the factors that contributed most to the above rating.

3. Overall, for the semester so far, how would you rate your self-confidence?

1	2	3	4	5
Extremely low	Low	Average for me	High	Extremely high

4. If you were your own supervisor, what outwardly observable signs would tell you that your self-confidence was low?

5. What signs would tell you that your self-confidence was high?

6. Complete the following sentence:

   An instructor could raise (or has raised) my self-confidence by . . .

7. How, specifically, do you raise your own self-confidence? (What works?)

Results. In answer to the first question, about one-third of the students rated their self-confidence that day as "extremely low" or "low," half of the class rated it as "average," and the remaining fraction as "high." No one rated his or her self-confidence as "extremely high." Responses to question 3 allowed the instructor to compare ratings for that particular day with overall ratings for the semester. The semester ratings were somewhat higher. Half of those students who had rated themselves in the two lowest categories gave "average" as their response to the semester.

In looking over the responses to question 2, the instructor separated the forms into three piles: those whose ratings on question 1 were below average, the average ratings, and the above-average ratings. This simple categorizing highlighted an interesting difference among the responses. Those students who rated their self-confidence that day as "average" attributed it to very general conditions or feelings, most of them not directly connected to the course. For example, the "average" respondents mentioned factors such as supportive family relationships, balanced life-style, progress toward personal goals, and the like. Those who rated their immediate self-confidence as lower or higher than average tended to mention more specific, course-related factors, such as specific positive or negative feedback from the instructor, success or failure on a particular task, and good or poor preparation for that day's activities.

The students gave concrete and informative answers to questions 4 and 5, pointing out signals of high or low self-confidence. They mentioned willingness to participate, eye contact, posture, verbal fluency, facial expressions, hand movements, expressions of humor, and even the kinds of food they ate at breaks as indicators. While the content of their lists of signals did not surprise the instructor, she was pleased to see that the students were aware of their own behavior and understood what was revealed about their self-confidence.

Their sentence completions were also specific and helpful. Students wrote that instructors could raise or had raised their self-confidence by providing honest, balanced, regular feedback; giving them lots of praise and positive encouragement; treating them fairly and with respect; showing confidence in them and supporting them in front of patients; remaining calm in the placement site; trusting them enough to allow some risk-taking; and showing interest in them as individuals. Several of the students made it clear that they were writing about positive things the instructor herself had done in the practicum.

In responding to the last question, however, most of the students mentioned general approaches to improving self-confidence. For example, students reported that the following activities helped them improve their own self-confidence: focusing on the positive, making time for oneself, taking time to exercise, learning when to say "no," and associating with supportive people. The instructor recognized the value of these approaches, but she did not see their direct relevance to her course.

The nursing instructor interpreted the responses to the Self-Confidence Survey to mean that what happened in class could affect students' self-esteem at the margins, raising it or lowering it somewhat. The results also suggested that students differed in the degree to which the course influenced their feelings of self-confidence.

Their very descriptive lists of the signals of low and high self-confidence and their clear, specific examples of how instructors could help raise their self-confidence gave the instructor a foundation of awareness to build on. The students understood the phenomenon and many of the factors contributing to it. What they lacked were specific techniques for raising their own self-esteem in the context of their placements.

Response. She summarized the results, typed them up, and handed out a two-page summary and tabulation of the comments at the next class meeting. After giving them a few minutes to read the summary, she asked students for any other specific techniques she could use to raise their self-confidence. From the original suggestions and several more collected then, she later created a checklist of techniques to use as a reminder during clinical supervision. After pointing out the generic quality of their own confidence-raising strategies, she asked the class to come up with a pooled list of specific techniques they could use to help themselves in the placement. While the students had a hard time thinking of specifics at first, they soon realized that there were many small things they could do to increase self-confidence in the hospital. She made the resulting ideas into a second checklist, this one for students to use in monitoring their own behavior.

Both the instructor and the students used the checklists and benefited from them. From time to time, students would suggest additional techniques to add to her list or theirs. She noted that students were very willing to try each other's techniques and that they more frequently acted to support each other in the placement, modeling their behavior on hers.

By the end of the semester, the instructor felt that her efforts to improve student self-confidence had paid off. She, and several of her colleagues, noticed her students' unusually high level of competence and confidence. To test her perceptions, she administered a shorter version of the Self-Confidence Survey in the last week of class as a kind of posttest. She repeated questions 1, 2, and 3 and replaced the rest with two new sentence completions: "The instructor has increased my self-confidence by..." and "The instructor has decreased my self-confidence by..."

The results of the follow-up survey were overwhelmingly positive. Eighty percent of the students rated their self-confidence that day as "high" or "extremely high." The answers to the sentence completions offered more evidence for the success of her Classroom Assessment and its effects. All the students had detailed and highly positive examples of how the instructor had helped raise their self-confidence. Only a handful gave examples of ways in which she had lowered theirs, and most of those examples came from the beginning of the semester, before the Classroom Assessment Project. A number of the students added comments praising her for Classroom Assessment and for devoting time and energy to improving their self-confidence as nurses.

The students mentioned her innovations to their other instructors, who began to ask what she was doing that was working so well. Her success led the department as a whole to begin experimenting with Classroom Assessment as a tool for instructional improvement.

STATISTICS: ASSESSING COURSE-RELATED LEARNING AND STUDY SKILLS, STRATEGIES, AND BEHAVIORS

Example 10: Assessing Students' Use of Study Time

Discipline:	Statistics
Course:	Introduction to Statistics
Teaching goal:	To help students improve their ability to organize and use time effectively (TGI Goal 41)
Teacher's questions:	How much time do my students devote to studying for this course? How much of that study time is really productive? How can I help students use their study time more effectively?
CAT used:	Productive Study-Time Logs (CAT 37, Chap. 8)

Background. In this professor's institution, statistics is a required course for most majors. The introductory statistics course in which he carried out this Classroom Assessment Project was specifically designed and taught to meet the needs of students majoring in the social sciences or business. In other words, the course did not presuppose a high level of preparation in mathematics.

As a statistician himself, the instructor had at first feared he would be pressured into teaching a watered-down, undemanding course. To his surprise, he found that his freshman and sophomore students were generally very bright and willing, though woefully underprepared in mathematics. After a few years of teaching it, the instructor had become convinced that this statistics course was more demanding for this particular group of students than the introductory statistics courses he taught for mathematics and physical science majors.

All students in the introductory courses had to learn basic concepts of statistical thinking and basic skills of statistical analysis. For the social science and business students, however, there were added burdens. They had to learn or relearn enough algebra to carry out basic manipulations; and they had to learn what amounted to a new "language," complete with unfamiliar symbols and syntax. These students not only were learning new content and skills but also were developing a new way of thinking and communicating. These multiple challenges were daunting for most students and for the professor as well.

Nevertheless, over time, the instructor developed an effective approach to teaching the course. He stressed "real-life" applications, provided numerous opportunities for practice and feedback, and arranged for extra support through tutorials and section meetings led by graduate students. His social science and business students succeeded in large numbers, and many were inspired to take further courses in statistics.

Like most excellent, committed teachers, however, he continued to look for ways to improve the course, to help the students learn more and better. But after more than a decade of experimenting with and changing the course organization, materials, and his teaching, he felt it was time to focus directly on what the students could do to improve their learning.

His students — no matter how successful or satisfied they were overall — always complained that statistics demanded too much study time and crowded out their other courses. Like most teachers, he had suggested various techniques that students might use to study more efficiently, but to little apparent avail. To focus on learner behavior, he decided to use a Classroom Assessment Technique to find out how much time students were really spending on his course and how efficiently they were using that time. He hoped to find ways to reduce the amount of time required to succeed in the course without reducing the number or scope of the assignments.

Assessment Technique. To find out how much time students were spending preparing for this class and how well they were spending that time, the statistics instructor decided to use a simple time-logging device in which students rated the productivity of their study time. He asked the students whether they would participate voluntarily in this survey and explained that the survey would serve a double purpose. First, and most important, the students and the instructor would learn how the students were spending their study time, so that they and the instructor could look for ways to "work smarter, not harder." Second, the instructor could use the information obtained from the survey to illustrate a number of statistical concepts and procedures. Students who agreed to participate would earn extra credit equal to one homework assignment, or about 5 percent of the class grade, if they completed the assessment fully and well. There would be no credit for incomplete logs; for days when they did not study statistics, they should log zero hours. He took pains to point out the importance of entering honest, accurate information on the log. He urged students to report how much they really were studying, not to write in the amount they thought he expected.

Before he could implement the Classroom Assessment, the instructor had to resolve a dilemma: he would have to assure students of anonymity if he expected them to give an honest report of such grade-sensitive data; at the same time, he could not give students credit for doing the assignment unless he knew who had turned it in. He decided to ask the students to observe an honor code. On the day the assessment was due, they were asked to sign a brief form attesting that they had or had not turned in a complete log. In his view, the value of demonstrating trust in students was greater than the risk that one or two of them might take advantage of his proposal.

After answering a few questions, he passed out copies of the Productive Study-Time Log (PSTL) to the class and explained how it worked. As Exhibit 5.11 shows, the form required students first to enter the amount of time they studied statistics each day in half-hour blocks, and then to rate the productivity of each half hour logged as either (1) nonproductive, (2) low in productivity, (3) of average productivity or (4) high in productivity. To see whether it made any difference where students studied, the instructor asked for that information as well. At the bottom of each day's log, students were directed to enter the total hours studied and the subtotals for each of the four levels of productivity. The last section of the PSTL consisted of a few follow-up questions about study behavior.

The professor asked for a show of hands from those students who were interested in the extra-credit assessment. Easily 90 percent of the students raised their hands. That was on a Monday, and he directed the students to start logging that day and to continue through the following Sunday. They were to hand in their completed logs on the following Monday, one week after they had begun the process. The logs handed in were to be a complete record of seven days of studying for statistics.

Results. As noted, the Productive Study-Time Log forms were handed out on a Monday. At the next class meeting, on Wednesday, a number of students had questions about the log. Most wondered whether they were filling it out correctly, so the instructor took a few minutes to respond.

On the following Monday, almost 120 of the 140 students registered for his class turned in their PSTL forms. The instructor thanked the students and told them that his graduate assistants would tabulate and analyze the data as quickly as possible. He promised to report back to the students as soon as he could interpret the results.

Exhibit 5.11. Productive Study-Time Log—Day 1 of 7.

Directions: (1) Enter any block of thirty minutes or more you spent studying statistics today on the form below. If you started at 2 P.M. and ended at 2:40, use the lines next to 2:00 only. (2) Make a note of where you were studying as well. (3) Make sure to rate the productivity of each half-hour segment in the appropriate column, using the following scale:

1 = Nonproductive	Learning nothing or extremely little
2 = Low productivity	Learning something but not much
3 = Average productivity	Learning a fair amount
4 = High productivity	Learning a great deal

Productivity Ratings	Time	Place	Productivity Ratings	Time	Place
_____	8:00 A.M.	_____	_____	4:00 P.M.	_____
_____	8:30	_____	_____	4:30	_____
_____	9:00	_____	_____	5:00	_____
_____	9:30	_____	_____	5:30	_____
_____	10:00	_____	_____	6:00	_____
_____	10:30	_____	_____	6:30	_____
_____	11:00	_____	_____	7:00	_____
_____	11:30	_____	_____	7:30	_____
_____	12:00 P.M.	_____	_____	8:00	_____
_____	12:30	_____	_____	8:30	_____
_____	1:00	_____	_____	9:00	_____
_____	1:30	_____	_____	9:30	_____
_____	2:00	_____	_____	10:00	_____
_____	2:30	_____	_____	10:30	_____
_____	3:00	_____	_____	11:00	_____
_____	3:30	_____	_____	11:30	_____

Subtotal A: Hours of statistics study rated at Level 1 = _____
Subtotal B: Hours of statistics study rated at Level 2 = _____
Subtotal C: Hours of statistics study rated at Level 3 = _____
Subtotal D: Hours of statistics study rated at Level 4 = _____
Total hours spent studying statistics today = _____

Productive Study-Time Log: Follow-Up Questions

1. Look back over the seven days you have logged and recheck your daily subtotals and totals. Once they are correct, add the figures up for all seven days and enter the figures below.

Subtotals and Total Study Hours for the Seven-Day Period

Subtotal A: Hours of statistics study rated at Level 1 = _____
Subtotal B: Hours of statistics study rated at Level 2 = _____
Subtotal C: Hours of statistics study rated at Level 3 = _____
Subtotal D: Hours of statistics study rated at Level 4 = _____
Total hours spent studying statistics this week = _____

Please give concise, specific answers to the following questions:

2. What did you discover about the amount of time you studied that you find surprising or interesting?

3. What did you discover about the productivity of your studying that you find surprising or interesting?

4. What did you discover about the location(s) of your studying that you find surprising or interesting?

5. Overall, what is the most important thing you learned from this assessment?

6. Given what you have learned from the week you just logged, is there anything you are determined to do differently as you study statistics next week?

When it became clear that the graduate assistants would need more than a week to analyze the mountain of data the students had generated, longer than the instructor had originally predicted, he asked them to concentrate first on the simple subtotals and totals of hours spent studying. The comments on the follow-up page were much more difficult to interpret and categorize than the numerical data, of course, and the professor had to work with his assistants to come up with an adequate coding scheme.

The basic numbers were ready for Friday's class, two meetings after the PSTLs had been handed in. The instructor had prepared a simple one-page handout summarizing their responses. The handout served two purposes. It presented the basic results and provided in-class practice in simple descriptive statistical procedures. From that information, the students were asked to quickly calculate the class mean, median, and mode for hours studied, and to create a frequency distribution. Their answers became the basis for a class discussion.

The class mean was more than 11 hours for the week, with the range running from 2.5 hours to 27 hours reported. Overall, students logged nearly three-quarters of their weekly study hours on Saturday and Sunday. Only about 18 percent of the total hours logged were rated as highly productive; more than 50 percent were rated as low or nonproductive. In the ensuing discussion, several students admitted that they had not realized the amount of time they studied for statistics. Some were surprised to discover how many hours they themselves studied; others, how few. Still others were surprised to discover how many hours their peers studied. Many were dismayed by their own generally low productivity.

When the instructor asked them what they thought contributed to that low productivity, a number of students had ready answers. In reviewing their logs, they could see clearly that they got less done at certain times of the day than at others, or when they studied in certain locations rather than others. There was no consensus on the best times or places to study, but most students agreed that they studied best alone or with other students from the statistics class, and worst with friends who were not in the class.

Not wanting to spend too much class time on the discussion, the instructor urged the students to focus on the study time that was effective and to try to understand what made it so. He also suggested that nine to twelve hours a week should be plenty for most students, and invited those who were spending more than twelve hours to meet with him as a group. Several of those students did come, and the instructor made it a point to praise them for their hard work and dedication. He then talked with them about how they were studying and shared ideas on how they might get more done in less time.

Follow-Up. As soon as the graduate assistants completed their analysis and categorization of the comments, the instructor created and handed out a second summary sheet. Its content basically supported the comments that the students had made in class the previous week, but it illustrated a wider range of observations. Then the PSTL forms were handed back.

By the time the comments were analyzed, however, the students had taken their first important test, and the instructor correlated the hours reported on the PSTL with their test grades, which they had entered on the PSTL before handing it in a second time. By doing several simple analyses of these data in class, he was able to demonstrate that the expected positive relationship between total hours studied and grades worked only to a point. Beyond thirteen hours, on average, more study time did not seem to improve grades. Beyond seventeen hours, average grades began to decrease with additional study time. In other words, there was, on average, a curvilinear relationship between total study time and test scores. These trends provided the basis for a lively discussion of causation and correlation.

At this point, the instructor demonstrated the value of the productivity ratings by showing students that more time, if it was rated "average" or "high productivity," did correlate positively and continuously with higher scores. With productive study time, more did clearly appear to be better. Later in the semester, when the class studied correlation and regression, the instructor used these data sets in homework problems.

ACCOUNTING: ASSESSING LEARNER REACTIONS TO TEACHERS AND TEACHING

Example 11: Assessing Learner Reactions to New Approaches to Teaching and Learning

Discipline:	Accounting
Course:	Intermediate Financial Accounting
Teaching goal:	To help students develop appropriate learning skills, strategies, and habits (TGI Goal 16)
Teacher's question:	How and how well are students using a learning approach that is new to them—cooperative learning—to master the concepts and principles of accounting?
CAT used:	Classroom Assessment Quality Circles (CAT 45, Chap. 9)

Background. This accounting professor, interested in experimenting with new teaching and learning approaches, wanted to find simple, effective ways to assess student reactions to his instructional innovations. If his new teaching approaches did not improve student learning, he needed to find out immediately, since timely feedback would allow him to make adjustments to ensure that students learned the material needed to prepare for subsequent accounting courses. At the same time, feedback on student reactions to his experiments would help ensure his own professional success. Since end-of-semester student ratings of faculty play a major role in promotion and tenure decisions on his campus, he was understandably interested in finding out early whether students reacted strongly, negatively or positively, to the changes he had made. Regular feedback on student learning and reactions would also be useful in documenting his efforts to improve instruction. He hoped to incorporate this information in his annual self-evaluation, another element in the university's tenure and promotion process.

The course he focused on, Intermediate Financial Accounting, was a large upper-division class required of both accounting and finance majors. The more than one hundred students enrolled met weekly as a whole group for lectures, as well as in sections of thirty-six students each. Given the size of the class, getting useful feedback was a particular challenge.

Assessment Technique. The accounting instructor decided to use the Classroom Assessment Quality Circle, a Classroom Assessment Technique adapted from business and industry, as a means of getting information from students on their learning and their reactions. He explained the process to the class, and early in the semester each section of thirty-six students elected two representatives to the Quality Circle. The instructor encouraged all students to take their suggestions, complaints, or compliments to their representatives. One important ground rule that everyone agreed to was that representatives would never reveal the names of students who offered suggestions or criticisms and that the instructor would never ask. The instructor urged those who were particularly concerned about anonymity to feel free to give their section representatives written, unsigned feedback.

The Classroom Assessment Quality Circle representatives met frequently and regularly with the professor outside of class. To communicate the importance of the Quality Circle to its members, the professor arranged to hold their meetings in the dean's conference room, which was set up each time as if a corporate board meeting were taking place. The meetings were run in an informal, professional manner and gave these business school students an opportunity to practice important skills. In recognition of the extra time and effort required, the student representatives were awarded a small amount of extra credit for their participation.

The Quality Circle members served as information gatherers and as liaisons. As noted above, they were asked to bring to the meetings any and all feedback offered by their section mates. At the same time, the instructor often directed them to ask their peers for feedback on specific questions or issues during the section meetings. In this way, both the students and the instructor were able to express their concerns. As time passed, the members of the Quality Circle began to suggest questions that they felt should be posed to the class. The instructor usually discussed the feedback with the members of the circle and often asked them for their analysis and suggestions for response.

Illustration. While the accounting professor used the Classroom Assessment Quality Circle throughout the semester, the assessment technique proved of particular value when he introduced a new instructional approach, cooperative learning, in the course. To implement cooperative learning, he organized the students into small, structured working groups. These groups were

Note: The accounting example is based primarily on "Classroom Research in Accounting: Assessing and Accounting for Learning," by Philip G. Cottell, Jr., a chapter in *Classroom Research: Early Lessons from Success* (Angelo, 1991).

given the task of reviewing the homework problems. The students in each small group had to agree on the correct answers to the homework problems and actually "sign off" before their papers could be turned in. In effect, they had to convince one another of the "rightness" of their answers, teaching each other the relevant accounting principles in the process.

This structured group work replaced the instructor's traditional practice of reviewing the problems at the chalkboard, as the entire class watched and asked questions or commented. Instead of watching and listening to the instructor work through the problems, each student would now be responsible for working through one or more problems in the group and explaining it to the others. It was his hope that assigning the homework review to the cooperative-learning groups would lead to more active student involvement and result in better learning.

The instructor introduced cooperative learning in the middle of the semester, at a point when the Quality Circle was already well established. He made it a point to tell both the class and the members of the circle that he needed and wanted their feedback on this new instructional approach.

Results. Early on, the Classroom Assessment Quality Circle let him know that the new cooperative-learning process contained "bugs" that threatened student learning and satisfaction. Specifically, although most students in the class valued this new method of reviewing homework problems, many were concerned that the solutions they reached by group consensus might not be correct. Most students did not feel comfortable waiting a week or more until they received their papers back to find out whether their group answers were right. In other words, students were satisfied with the process but concerned about the product. From reading the group solutions, the instructor knew that their quality was higher than that of most individual answers, but the students were not yet convinced. So, to respond to the concerns raised by the Quality Circle, he began providing the correct answers after homework was handed in, and he put a solution manual on reserve in the library.

The class appeared satisfied with the instructor's response to their concerns, and he assumed that the problem had been solved. He soon learned from the Quality Circle members, however, that some students were photocopying problem solutions from the manual and bringing them to their cooperative-learning groups. Many students were upset by this behavior, which threatened to short-circuit the value of the homework review sessions and kill the spirit of cooperative learning. The students who did not copy solutions accused those who did of cheating. The instructor asked the members of the Quality Circle for their suggestions, and they voted that this unfair practice be banned. He was happy to concur with their vote, of course. The representatives then announced their decision to the sections, and subsequently reported that no more photocopies of solutions were brought to group meetings. Although some students undoubtedly still consulted the solution manual, they had to explain the "borrowed" solutions to the other members of the group, rather than just showing their peers a photocopy; therefore, they had to understand the manual's solutions, an outcome that required at least some learning.

Response. The Quality Circle continued to play an important role in the course throughout the semester, helping the instructor ensure both that students were learning successfully and that they were satisfied with his teaching. He reported that using the Classroom Assessment Quality Circle—in conjunction with a few other simple Classroom Assessment Techniques, such as the Minute Paper (CAT 6, Chap. 7)—helped him improve learning quality by focusing students' attention on their own learning processes and by encouraging active self-monitoring.

At the same time, this approach benefited the accounting professor personally and professionally in four ways. First, he received the highest student ratings of his career during the first semester he used Classroom Assessment. Second, in the annual performance review, the department head formally recognized the professor's initiative and his success. Third, as evidenced by students' written comments on formal evaluations and by spoken, informal feedback, he benefited from overwhelmingly positive student responses and reactions to his attempts to help students improve their learning. Fourth, his involvement in Classroom Research and cooperative learning provided intrinsic rewards, energizing his teaching and encouraging him to continue to experiment.

DEVELOPMENTAL EDUCATION: ASSESSING LEARNER REACTIONS TO CLASS ACTIVITIES, ASSIGNMENTS, AND MATERIALS

Example 12: Assessing Students' Reactions to Small-Group Work

Discipline:	Developmental education
Course:	Writing Skills for College Success
Teaching goal:	To help students develop an ability to work productively with others (TGI Goal 36)
Teacher's questions:	What kinds of help are students giving and getting from small-group work sessions in which they critique each other's first drafts? How can the group sessions become more productive vehicles for helping students learn to write well?
CAT used:	Group-Work Evaluations (CAT 47, Chap. 9)

Background. Although this instructor was convinced of the value of structured small-group work to promote active learning, she found herself dissatisfied with the quality of interaction during group work in her developmental education writing course. Her course was designed to help underprepared students succeed in "mainstream" college courses—specifically, in the required freshman composition course.

Beginning writers usually find it difficult to gauge accurately how much they need to tell the reader and how much they can assume the reader will know. As a result, novice writers often fail to make explicit on the page what is implicitly clear to them. To help these inexperienced student writers begin to see their writing from the reader's point of view, the instructor often divided the class into groups of four or five and asked them to read and critique each other's drafts.

Despite her best attempts to organize and direct the group-critiquing sessions, her students were not giving or getting much help. Even though she had given the students a format to follow and questions to answer about each other's papers, their comments were vague and their critiques pro forma. She could see that the students were beginning to dread these small-group sessions. In reading their subsequent drafts, she found very little improvement that could be linked to the group work. She was determined to find out why the small-group critique sessions were not working, so that she could either improve them or give up group work entirely.

Assessment Technique. The instructor decided to assess her students' awareness of how their own and their peers' behavior affected their learning in small-group work. Specifically, she wanted to find out whether students thought their writing was benefiting from the group critiques—and, if so, in what way. She came up with two questions and created the simple assessment form illustrated below (Exhibit 5.12). At the end of the subsequent half-hour critique session, the instructor handed out copies of the form to all students and gave them five minutes to answer. Students were asked not to put their names on the forms but to indicate their group number.

Results. As she read through the students' responses after class, she was struck by two things. First, although she had made a point of asking students to be specific in their responses, and had included in that request directions for the Group-Work Evaluation Form, many of the responses were general and vague. For example, students wrote, "I told X that I didn't understand his essay" or "The group didn't like my essay topic." In addition, those responses that were specific focused almost entirely on what she viewed as trivial spelling, punctuation, and grammar mistakes—even though she had repeatedly told the students not to worry about those kinds of "surface" mistakes in critiquing and revising first drafts. Over and over again, she had directed the students to read first drafts for meaning and to worry about the nonessentials only in final rewrites. Since most of the text in a first draft will be changed or thrown out during the revision process, she reasoned, why invest time and energy polishing prose before you are sure that it says what you want it to? Clearly, that message had not gotten through, despite many repetitions.

Exhibit 5.12. Group-Work Evaluation Form.

Directions: As soon as you have finished your group-work assignment, please take five minutes to answer the two questions below. Give as many specific examples as you can and answer in full sentences.

1. What specific comments, criticisms, and/or suggestions did other members of your group offer to you that are likely to help you improve your draft essay?

2. What specific comments, criticisms, and/or suggestions did you offer to other members of your group that are likely to help them improve their draft essays?

The second thing about the responses that caught her attention was their unequal distribution. Most, though not all, of the students could remember some example of a comment, criticism, or suggestion they had received that might be helpful. Almost none of them, however, could think of anything useful they might have said. The writing instructor had actually expected the reverse: that her students would recall what they had contributed to the group, but not what the group had contributed to them.

Since the evaluation responses were numbered by group, she could also see that the better answers were not randomly distributed but, instead, tended to cluster in three of the seven groups. When she checked her group assignment sheet, she realized that those three groups contained most of the women in her class. What were the women doing differently in their groups, she wondered, that was leading to more effective learning?

Response. At the midpoint of the next class meeting, the instructor summarized the results outlined above. She then asked the class to help her figure out what those results meant and what to do next. Specifically, she asked the students why so many of them were focusing on spelling, punctuation, and grammar instead of on meaning. The students gave a variety of informative answers. As the students spoke, the instructor listened carefully and took notes. Several said that they couldn't even tell what a piece of writing meant if it was full of "mistakes," so it needed to be cleaned up before they could really understand it. Other students admitted that they were simply following the example set by previous writing teachers, who had mainly pointed out their mechanical errors. A number of students agreed with the classmate who said that he didn't feel capable of criticizing his classmates' draft essays and was uncomfortable when he tried to do so. A young woman added that she didn't want to criticize her friends and they didn't want to criticize her. The students made it very clear that they expected the teacher to do the criticizing and correcting.

She reminded the students that, in their responses on the evaluation form, many of them mentioned helpful comments they had received, but few of them remembered comments they had offered. She asked the students why they thought their responses were so lopsided. One after another, they gave variations on the same two responses; and, seen in a certain light, the responses were reasonable. At that particular moment, however, they did not sound reasonable to the instructor. Resisting her strong impulse to take issue with the students, she forced herself to listen carefully and take notes, speaking only to move the discussion along or clarify their statements.

First, the students reminded her that she had instructed them to get comments from their groups so that they could improve their own drafts; she had never emphasized their responsibility to give helpful comments. If helping their classmates was so important, why hadn't she told them to do it? Second, the students pointed out that, although they knew what had or had not been helpful to them as individuals, they had no idea what any other person in their group considered helpful; so how could they tell whether their comments were helpful to others? By this time, to the instructor's relief, the class period was ending. She promised the students that she would respond to their comments at the next class meeting, reminded them of their homework assignment, and sent them off.

Follow-Up. The writing teacher was more than surprised; she was stunned by her students' comments during the class. Her initial reaction was disbelief. How could the students suggest with straight faces that it was her responsibility to require them to be helpful and to teach them how to be helpful? Wasn't it obvious that, in group work, students were supposed to try to be helpful and were supposed to find out from their peers what kind of help they needed and wanted? After recounting the experience, she confided to a colleague that she thought the students were simply making excuses, trying to escape responsibility.

But her colleague was not persuaded. He asked her where the students would have learned how to function effectively in groups. After discussing their own experiences, they agreed that productive cooperation was not usually taught in school or on the job. They also agreed, laughing, that—if the productivity of committee meetings were any indicator—there wasn't much evidence that most of their faculty colleagues had developed effective group-work skills. Since she did not assume that students came to college with adequately developed writing skills, her colleague pointed out, why should she assume that their group-work skills were any better?

The more the instructor thought about it, the more she realized that her students probably had been honest with her. She recognized that if she was going to use group work in the classroom, she would have to be willing to train her students to do it well. And if she was going to ask them to critique each other's papers, she clearly had to teach them how to do so. It would mean taking time away from other elements of the course, but she felt that learning to cooperate effectively was such a valuable skill that the tradeoffs would be worth it.

At the next class meeting, she thanked the students for their feedback and told them that she had decided to be more directive and explicit in her group-work assignments. She explained why she considered cooperation a necessary skill for college and work success and gave some examples to illustrate its value. Since several students had indicated their reluctance to be "critical," she pointed out the difference between "critiquing" a first draft and "criticizing" someone's writing. Using the students' earlier responses as a starting point, she worked with the class to identify the qualities that made critiques either helpful or harmful.

The class agreed that the most helpful critiques were specific, pointed out strengths and weaknesses, provided explanations for positive and negative judgments, and offered options for improvement whenever possible. In contrast, harmful or useless critiques were very general, focused exclusively on strengths or exclusively on weaknesses, provided no reasons for the judgments made, and offered no suggestions for improvement or insisted that there was only one way to improve.

The writing instructor used the criteria for helpful critiques in planning the next group-work session. She also reviewed the original group-work evaluations, using the results to help her reconstitute the groups to get a better mix of strong and weak contributors. Instead of asking students to read each other's drafts in class, she gave each student copies of two drafts from his or her new group to read as homework. Along with the drafts, students got two copies of a critiquing form. The form asked them to point out some positive element in the draft, a strength, and explain why they thought it was good; to do the same for a weakness; and to offer two or three suggestions for improving the weakness. Students were told that their group work would be based on these forms and that the instructor would collect them after the critiquing session.

As she had hoped, the next critiquing session was much more lively and seemed to be more productive. At the end of the group work, after she had collected the critiquing forms, the instructor handed out copies of the same Group-Work Evaluation Form she had used several sessions earlier. The overall level of feedback on the session was much higher. There was more writing, responses were more specific, the tone was more positive, and most students were able to answer both questions—commenting on what they had contributed as well as on what they received. Moreover, the quality of the revised essays that they handed in subsequently was markedly higher.

The writing instructor was, understandably, very pleased with the improvement, and she told the class so. Most agreed with her that the group work had been more useful and enjoyable. When she asked them what accounted for the improvement in the critiquing session, however, she once again got an answer that she would not have predicted. The teacher expected students to talk about the direct instruction she had given them, the list of characteristics of helpful and harmful critiques, or the critiquing form. Students did mention these instructional changes—but not immediately. The first student to respond said he had made sure to give helpful comments because he knew he was going to be asked about them as soon as the group work ended. Several other students agreed. They said they knew in advance that she was going to hand out the Group-Work Evaluation Forms again, and they wanted to be able to give better answers the second time around.

While the students probably could not have improved their group performance without more guidance and instruction and additional practice, it was the Classroom Assessment and the teacher's response to it that focused their attention on the importance of improving their performance. And some students were motivated to improve simply because they anticipated the assessment, even though they knew it would be ungraded.

Classroom Assessment Techniques

Choosing the Right Technique

6

Our aim in presenting the fifty different Classroom Assessment Techniques described in Chapters Seven, Eight, and Nine is to provide college teachers—from various disciplinary specialties and backgrounds—with a compendium of good ideas developed by their colleagues for assessing and improving student learning. These chapters are, in many ways, the heart of this handbook. On one level, they resemble a tool chest containing fifty different "feedback devices," from which teachers can select the right assessment tool to fit the particular assessment job at hand; on another level, these chapters can be regarded as a collection of favorite recipes, or a "how-to" book, a vehicle for sharing tried-and-true approaches among practitioners. We urge readers to view and use these CATs as starting points, ideas to be adapted and improved upon. And we hope these fifty will serve as models and inspiration for many more new CATs yet to be invented.

HOW TO FIND THE CLASSROOM ASSESSMENT TECHNIQUE YOU NEED

Part Two is the largest part of the handbook, and the one least likely to be read straight through. Instead, we expect that many readers will make use of the three indexes in this chapter to find specific Classroom Assessment Techniques. By using the alphabetical index of CAT names (Table 6.1), faculty can quickly locate techniques that they may have read about earlier in the handbook, or elsewhere, or heard colleagues mention. By referring to the index of examples by disciplines (Table 6.2), teachers can look at CATs that other faculty in their fields have already used. Finally, instructors can find assessment techniques related to their Teaching Goals Inventory responses in the index of CATs by related TGI clusters (Table 6.3).

For ease of use, the indexes are placed at the end of this chapter, immediately preceding the Classroom Assessment Techniques in the following three chapters. These three indexes, along with the topical index that the Table of Contents offers, provide readers with several ways to locate appropriate and useful Classroom Assessment Techniques. In addition, we hope that the organization of the following three chapters will encourage faculty to browse through the chapters for promising techniques. Chapter Seven includes twenty-seven Classroom Assessment Techniques for assessing course-related knowledge and skills. Chapter Eight contains thirteen CATs for assessing students' course-related attitudes and values, self-awareness, and learning strategies. Finally, the ten techniques in Chapter Nine are designed to assess student reactions to instruction.

The first and largest set of techniques are those for assessing academic skills and knowledge. Helping students learn the subject matter of their courses is the most common goal of college teachers, and virtually all teachers try to measure what students are learning about the content being taught. But most college teachers aspire to more than simply teaching students information about subject matter. They hope to use subject matter to teach students to think — that is, to develop higher-level cognitive skills: to solve problems, analyze arguments, synthesize information from different sources, and apply what they are learning to new and unfamiliar contexts.

From the 1950s through the 1970s, major advances were made in the description and measurement of "higher" cognitive outcomes, as Benjamin Bloom and other measurement specialists developed taxonomies of educational objectives (Bloom and others, 1956) and guidelines for formative and summative evaluation (Bloom, Hastings, and Madaus, 1971). During the 1980s and the early 1990s, educators and cognitive scientists joined in attempts to promote the development of "creative" and "critical" thinking skills through direct instruction. In choosing and organizing the techniques presented in Chapter Seven, we have drawn on these streams of research and pedagogical practice. We have given particular attention to the various ways in which researchers and theorists conceptualize intellectual development.

Chapter Eight presents techniques for assessing learners' course-related interests, opinions, attitudes, and values, and their views of themselves as learners. These "affective" dimensions of learning critically affect student motivation and success in the "cognitive" dimensions presented in Chapter Seven. Chapter Eight also focuses on skills that cognitive psychologists call "metacognitive," to convey the importance of students' attention to and awareness of their own learning processes. Research shows that successful students engage in metacognition to plan their learning, monitor it "in process," and continually assess their own skills as learners. Less successful students, in contrast, are more likely to view learning as memorizing a set of facts and answers that are "out there," apart from themselves, and are less likely to assume that they can control their own learning.

Chapter Nine contains assessment techniques for collecting information on teaching performance and instruction. In this chapter, we ask not so much what students are learning, or how they are learning it, as how they perceive and react to the classroom experience. Recent research on the evaluation of teaching and learning suggests that students are valid and reliable sources of information about the effects of teaching or its impact on their learning (Cross, 1988). Many instructors, especially beginning teachers, will find the direct, timely, and safe access to student responses provided by these CATs the most helpful feedback of all.

Chapter Nine is also based on the extensive and still-developing literature on students' reactions to their classroom experiences. Among the most informative studies are those by Centra (1977a, 1977b), Feldman (1977), Gleason (1986), Kulik and McKeachie (1975), and Seldin (1984). To date, student evaluations have been used primarily to help administrators make decisions about promotions and tenure. However, the assessment techniques presented in Chapter Nine are *not* for that purpose. Rather, they are designed to help teachers and students make decisions about which methods and materials are most helpful in promoting learning in the classroom.

Chapters Seven, Eight, and Nine represent broad-stroke topic-centered classifications of the CATs. The groupings of CATs in each of these chapters represent functional clusterings of the assessment techniques. Within each of these ten CAT groups, we have presented quicker and easier techniques first, more difficult and demanding ones last.

FORMAT USED TO PRESENT CLASSROOM ASSESSMENT TECHNIQUES

Each Classroom Assessment Technique format contains at least thirteen of the following elements; many of them contain all fourteen.

1. The CAT's number and name. Some techniques have alternate names; when possible, we have indicated the other names known to us.

2. Estimation of the levels of time and energy the technique requires. Each CAT is rated as "low," "medium," or "high" on the following three dimensions: the levels of time and energy required for (1) faculty to prepare to use the CAT, (2) students to respond to the assessment, and (3) faculty to analyze the data collected. In the first handbook, we used a single, five-point ease-of-use scale. One problem with such a scale is that easy-to-prepare devices often yield data that are complex to analyze and interpret. Other CATs may take considerable time to prepare but provide data that can be easily tallied. This tradeoff between front-end and back-end time investments is a familiar one to most classroom teachers. An essay exam, for example, usually requires quite a bit of time to read and interpret—a heavy back-end time investment—but rather less time to develop. An effective multiple-choice test is just the opposite. It requires a great deal of time to plan and produce—a heavy front-end commitment—but little time to score. We opted to separate estimates of front-end and back-end time commitments to inform faculty choices and aid planning. For similar reasons, we included an estimate of the time and energy required for students to respond. All these estimates are meant only as rough guidelines, since the many decisions faculty make in adapting and applying a given CAT strongly affect the overall time and energy it requires.

3. Description of the technique.

4. Purpose of the technique.

5. A list of related teaching goals, taken from the Teaching Goals Inventory. These lists suggest several goals that can be assessed, directly or indirectly, with that assessment technique. To encourage experimentation, we have made these lists inclusive rather than exclusive.

6. A few suggestions for use, usually concerning where and when a given technique is most likely to work well.

7. Examples taken from a wide and representative range of disciplines. We hope that readers whose disciplines or specialties are not represented will benefit from examples in related fields. The examples selected are mainly from general, lower-level courses in each field, rather than from specialized upper-division or graduate courses. To help faculty get off to a successful start, we have provided more examples, in general, for the simplest and most widely used CATs.

8. Simple directions for carrying out the CAT, the "Step-by-Step Procedure."

9. "Turning the Data You Collect into Useful Information" — suggestions for analyzing the feedback collected.

10. "Ideas for Adapting and Extending This CAT" — intended to stimulate thinking about next steps.

11. Benefits associated with the assessment technique ("pros").

12. Costs associated with the assessment technique ("cons").

13. Some cautions to keep in mind when using the technique ("caveats").

14. A listing of relevant references and resources (provided when possible).

A few final points are worth restating. First, these fifty techniques are meant to supplement and complement, not to replace, the testing and evaluation that teachers already do. Second, by virtue of their dual nature, these Classroom Assessment Techniques can and should be used to assess and, at the same time, to reteach and reinforce the knowledge and skills being assessed. Since there are enormous variations in teaching goals, we expect that some teachers will find certain of the techniques useful and helpful, whereas others will reject those same techniques as inappropriate and irrelevant. Our hope is that each teacher will find one or more assessment techniques that can be used as presented or, better yet, that can be adapted to fit the precise requirements of that teacher's course and students.

Table 6.1. CATs Indexed Alphabetically.

Classroom Assessment Technique	CAT Number	Chapter Number
Analytic Memos	12	7
Annotated Portfolios	18	7
Applications Cards	24	7
Approximate Analogies	15	7
Assignment Assessments	49	9
Audio- and Videotaped Protocols	22	7
Background Knowledge Probe	1	7
Categorizing Grid	8	7
Chain Notes	41	9
Classroom Assessment Quality Circles	45	9
Classroom Opinion Polls	28	8
Concept Maps	16	7
Content, Form, and Function Outlines	11	7
Course-Related Self-Confidence Surveys	32	8
Defining Features Matrix	9	7
Diagnostic Learning Logs	40	8
Directed Paraphrasing	23	7
Documented Problem Solutions	21	7
Double-Entry Journals	29	8
Electronic Mail Feedback	42	9
Empty Outlines	4	7
Everyday Ethical Dilemmas	31	8
Exam Evaluations	50	9
Focused Autobiographical Sketches	33	8
Focused Listing	2	7
Goal Ranking and Matching	35	8
Group Instructional Feedback Technique	44	9
Group-Work Evaluations	47	9
Human Tableau or Class Modeling	26	7
Interest/Knowledge/Skills Checklists	34	8
Invented Dialogues	17	7
Memory Matrix	5	7
Minute Paper	6	7
Misconception/Preconception Check	3	7
Muddiest Point	7	7
One-Sentence Summary	13	7
Paper or Project Prospectus	27	7
Pro and Con Grid	10	7
Problem Recognition Tasks	19	7
Process Analysis	39	8
Productive Study-Time Logs	37	8
Profiles of Admirable Individuals	30	8
Punctuated Lectures	38	8
Reading Rating Sheets	48	9
RSQC2 (Recall, Summarize, Question, Comment, and Connect)	46	9
Self-Assessment of Ways of Learning	36	8
Student-Generated Test Questions	25	7
Teacher-Designed Feedback Forms	43	9
What's the Principle?	20	7
Word Journal	14	7

Table 6.2. CATs Indexed by Disciplines in the Brief Examples.

Discipline	Technique	CAT Number	Chapter Number
Accounting	Classroom Assessment Quality Circles	45	5
	What's the Principle?	20	7
Advertising/Graphic Arts	Content, Form, and Function Outlines	11	7
African-American Studies	Goal Ranking and Matching	35	8
Anthropology	Assignment Assessments	49	9
	Background Knowledge Probe	1	5
	Classroom Opinion Polls	28	8
	One-Sentence Summary	13	4
	Pro and Con Grid	10	7
Art/Humanities	Focused Listing	2	7
	Memory Matrix	5	7
Asian-American Studies	Double-Entry Journals	29	8
Astronomy	Categorizing Grid	8	5
	Misconception/Preconception Check	3	7
Biology	Categorizing Grid	8	7
	Defining Features Matrix	9	7
	Human Tableau or Class Modeling	26	7
	Misconception/Preconception Check	3	7
	One-Sentence Summary	13	7
	Pro and Con Grid	10	7
Business/Management	Applications Cards	24	7
	Categorizing Grid	8	7
	Directed Paraphrasing	23	7
	Empty Outlines	4	7
	Pro and Con Grid	10	7
	Problem Recognition Tasks	19	7
	Profiles of Admirable Individuals	30	8
	What's the Principle?	20	7
	Word Journal	14	7
Calculus	One-Sentence Summary	13	4
Chemistry	Exam Evaluations	50	9
	Group Instructional Feedback Technique	44	9
	Muddiest Point	7	7
Child Development	Empty Outlines	4	7
Clinical Nursing Practicum	One-Sentence Summary	13	4
Computer Science	Audio- and Videotaped Protocols	22	7
	Directed Paraphrasing	23	7
	Electronic Mail Feedback	42	9
Cosmetology/Vocational Education	Categorizing Grid	8	7
Counseling Education	Problem Recognition Tasks	19	7
Criminal Justice	Analytic Memos	12	7
	Classroom Opinion Polls	28	8
	Directed Paraphrasing	23	7
	Everyday Ethical Dilemmas	31	5
Drama, Theater Arts	Double-Entry Journals	29	8
	Self-Assessment of Ways of Learning	36	8
Economics	Applications Cards	24	7
	Concept Maps	16	7

Table 6.2. CATs Indexed by Disciplines in the Brief Examples.

Discipline	Technique	CAT Number	Chapter Number
Education	Annotated Portfolios	18	7
	Audio- and Videotaped Protocols	22	7
	Course-Related Self-Confidence Surveys	32	8
	Directed Paraphrasing	23	7
	Group-Work Evaluations	47	5
	Interest/Knowledge/Skills Checklists	34	8
	Punctuated Lectures	38	8
	What's the Principle?	20	7
Engineering	Approximate Analogies	15	7
	Background Knowledge Probe	1	7
	Pro and Con Grid	10	7
	Student-Generated Test Questions	25	7
English/Writing	Approximate Analogies	15	7
	Chain Notes	41	9
	Goal Ranking and Matching	35	8
	Group-Work Evaluations	47	9
	Pro and Con Grid	10	7
	Process Analysis	39	8
English as a Second Language	Muddiest Point	7	7
	Reading Rating Sheets	48	9
Environmental Studies	Analytic Memos	12	7
	Classroom Opinion Polls	28	8
Finance/Management	Focused Listing	2	7
Fine Arts	Annotated Portfolios	18	7
	Human Tableau or Class Modeling	26	7
	Invented Dialogues	17	7
Foreign Languages	Approximate Analogies	15	7
	Memory Matrix	5	7
	RSQC2	46	9
History	Classroom Assessment Quality Circles	45	9
	Classroom Opinion Polls	28	8
	Exam Evaluations	50	9
	Minute Paper	6	7
	Misconception/Preconception Check	3	7
	Profiles of Admirable Individuals	30	8
History of Science	Concept Maps	16	7
Journalism	Minute Paper	6	7
Linguistics	Content, Form, and Function Outlines	11	7
	Defining Features Matrix	9	7
	Documented Problem Solutions	21	7
Literature	Approximate Analogies	15	7
	Background Knowledge Probe	1	7
	Word Journal	14	7
Management	Everyday Ethical Dilemmas	31	8
Mathematics	Audio- and Videotaped Protocols	22	7
	Course-Related Self-Confidence Surveys	32	8
	Documented Problem Solutions	21	5, 7
	RSQC2	46	9
Medicine	One-Sentence Summary	13	7
Music	Focused Listing	2	4
	Process Analysis	39	8
Nursing	Course-Related Self-Confidence Surveys	32	5
	Directed Paraphrasing	23	7
	Empty Outlines	4	7
	Human Tableau or Class Modeling	26	7
	Memory Matrix	5	7
	One-Sentence Summary	13	4, 7

Table 6.2. CATs Indexed by Disciplines in the Brief Examples.

Discipline	Technique	CAT Number	Chapter Number
Philosophy	Invented Dialogues	17	7
	Pro and Con Grid	10	7
	Reading Rating Sheets	48	9
	Student-Generated Test Questions	25	7
	Word Journal	14	7
Physical Education	Course-Related Self-Confidence Surveys	32	8
	Goal Ranking and Matching	35	5
Physics	Applications Cards	24	7
	Approximate Analogies	15	7
	Focused Listing	2	7
Political Science	Applications Cards	24	7
	Content, Form, and Function Outlines	11	7
	Defining Features Matrix	9	7
	Focused Listing	2	7
	Muddiest Point	7	7
	One-Sentence Summary	13	5
	Pro and Con Grid	10	7
Psychology	Applications Cards	24	5, 7
	Chain Notes	41	9
	Defining Features Matrix	9	7
	Interest/Knowledge/Skills Checklists	34	8
	Problem Recognition Tasks	19	7
	What's the Principle	20	7
Public Administration	Approximate Analogies	15	7
	Focused Autobiographical Sketches	33	8
Social Work	Group-Work Evaluations	47	9
Sociology	Approximate Analogies	15	7
	Classroom Opinion Polls	28	8
Speech Communication	Assignment Assessments	49	9
	Focused Autobiographical Sketches	33	8
	Self-Assessment of Ways of Learning	36	5, 8
Statistics	Applications Cards	24	7
	Minute Paper	6	7
	Problem Recognition Tasks	19	7
	Productive Study-Time Logs	37	5
Study Skills/Personal Development	Everyday Ethical Dilemmas	31	8
Theology	Pro and Con Grid	10	7
Vocational and Technical Education	Annotated Portfolios	18	7
	Audio- and Viodetaped Protocols	22	7
	Electronic Mail Feedback	42	9
	Goal Ranking and Matching	35	8
	One-Sentence Summary	13	7
Women's Studies	Concept Maps	16	7
	Profiles of Admirable Individuals	30	8
Zoology	Categorizing Grid	8	7

Table 6.3. CATs Indexed by Related TGI Clusters.

TGI Cluster		CAT Number	Chapter Number
Cluster I	*Higher-Order Thinking Skills*		
	Analytic Memos	12	7
	Annotated Portfolios	18	7
	Applications Cards	24	7
	Approximate Analogies	15	7
	Audio- and Videotaped Protocols	22	7
	Categorizing Grid	8	7
	Concept Maps	16	7
	Content, Form, and Function Outlines	11	7
	Defining Features Matrix	9	7
	Diagnostic Learning Logs	40	8
	Documented Problem Solutions	21	7
	Human Tableau or Class Modeling	26	7
	Invented Dialogues	17	7
	One-Sentence Summary	13	7
	Paper or Project Prospectus	27	7
	Pro and Con Grid	10	7
	Problem Recognition Tasks	19	7
	Process Analysis	39	8
	RSQC2	46	9
	Teacher-Designed Feedback Forms	43	9
	What's the Principle?	20	7
	Word Journal	14	7
Cluster II	*Basic Academic Success Skills*		
	Approximate Analogies	15	7
	Assignment Assessments	49	9
	Audio- and Videotaped Protocols	22	7
	Background Knowledge Probe	1	7
	Chain Notes	41	9
	Concept Maps	16	7
	Content, Form, and Function Outlines	11	7
	Defining Features Matrix	9	7
	Directed Paraphrasing	23	7
	Documented Problem Solutions	21	7
	Empty Outlines	4	7
	Exam Evaluations	50	9
	Focused Listing	2	7
	Memory Matrix	5	7
	Minute Paper	6	7
	Muddiest Point	7	7
	One-Sentence Summary	13	7
	Paper or Project Prospectus	27	7
	Problem Recognition Tasks	19	7
	Process Analysis	39	8
	Punctuated Lectures	38	8
	Reading Rating Sheets	48	9
	RSQC2	46	9
	Word Journal	14	7
Cluster III	*Discipline-Specific Knowledge and Skills*		
	Annotated Portfolios	18	7
	Applications Cards	24	7
	Audio- and Videotaped Protocols	22	7
	Background Knowledge Probe	1	7
	Categorizing Grid	8	7
	Concept Maps	16	7
	Invented Dialogues	17	7
	Documented Problem Solutions	21	7
	Electronic Mail Feedback	42	9

Table 6.3. CATs Indexed by Related TGI Clusters.

TGI Cluster		CAT Number	Chapter Number
	Empty Outlines	4	7
	Focused Listing	2	7
	Group Instructional Feedback Technique	44	9
	Memory Matrix	5	7
	Minute Paper	6	7
	Misconception/Preconception Check	3	7
	Muddiest Point	7	7
	Problem Recognition Tasks	19	7
	Student-Generated Test Questions	25	7
	Teacher-Designed Feedback Forms	43	9
Cluster IV	*Liberal Arts and Academic Values*		
	Approximate Analogies	15	7
	Chain Notes	41	9
	Double-Entry Journals	29	8
	Everyday Ethical Dilemmas	31	8
	Group Instructional Feedback Technique	44	9
	Human Tableau or Class Modeling	26	7
	Invented Dialogues	17	7
	Misconception/Preconception Check	3	7
	Pro and Con Grid	10	7
	Profiles of Admirable Individuals	30	8
	Student-Generated Test Questions	25	7
	What's the Principle?	20	7
Cluster V	*Work and Career Preparation*		
	Analytic Memos	12	7
	Annotated Portfolios	18	7
	Course-Related Self-Confidence Surveys	32	8
	Diagnostic Learning Logs	40	8
	Directed Paraphrasing	23	7
	Electronic Mail Feedback	42	9
	Focused Autobiographical Sketches	33	8
	Goal Ranking and Matching	35	8
	Group-Work Evaluations	47	9
	Interest/Knowledge/Skills Checklists	34	8
	One-Sentence Summary	13	7
	Productive Study-Time Logs	37	8
Cluster VI	*Personal Development*		
	Assignment Assessments	49	9
	Chain Notes	41	9
	Classroom Opinion Polls	28	8
	Classroom Assessment Quality Circles	45	9
	Course-Related Self-Confidence Surveys	32	8
	Double-Entry Journals	29	8
	Everyday Ethical Dilemmas	31	8
	Exam Evaluations	50	9
	Focused Autobiographical Sketches	33	8
	Goal Ranking and Matching	35	8
	Group Instructional Feedback Technique	44	9
	Group-Work Evaluations	47	9
	Interest/Knowledge/Skills Checklists	34	8
	Pro and Con Grid	10	7
	Productive Study-Time Logs	37	8
	Profiles of Admirable Individuals	30	8
	Punctuated Lectures	38	8
	Reading Rating Sheets	48	9
	RSQC2	46	9
	Self-Assessment of Ways of Learning	36	8
	Teacher-Designed Feedback Forms	43	9

Techniques for Assessing Course-Related Knowledge and Skills

The goals of college teachers differ, depending on their disciplines, the specific content of their courses, their students, and their own personal philosophies about the purposes of higher education. All faculty, however, are interested in promoting the cognitive growth and academic skills of their students. In the drive toward academic excellence, the assessment of cognitive skills and mastery of subject matter has been given major attention, especially in institutional and statewide assessment plans. The assessment movement has had an important impact on the design and content of standardized tests and, to a lesser degree, on curricula and graduation requirements. Its impact on the measurement of student learning in the classroom is less clear. Although classroom teachers have been testing students on their mastery of subject matter for centuries, there is a growing conviction that, as classroom assessment resources, tests are limited in scope and in usefulness. One problem is that traditional classroom tests are frequently used as summative evaluations—as "final" exams or other measures to grade students. They are not often used to provide feedback to both students and teachers on whether learning goals are being met.

Tests are, however, an effective way to define the goals of the course. Research suggests that students concentrate on learning whatever they think will be on the test. As McKeachie and his colleagues observe, "Whatever teachers' goals and no matter how clearly they present them, students' goals are strongly influenced by tests or the other activities that determine grades" (McKeachie, Pintrich, Lin, and Smith, 1986, p. 76). No matter how clear the teacher is about the "big picture," students are unlikely to share and appreciate the view unless tests and other assessment measures point them toward it. Formative, mid-course feedback at the classroom level, especially if it is repeated at regular intervals, helps students and teachers clarify their goals and assess progress toward them while there is still time to make changes based on that feedback.

A second problem in current classroom assessment is that the tests devised frequently measure low-level abilities to remember and reproduce what is presented by others. Yet the emphasis in the 1980s reform movement is on the development of critical thinking, problem solving, and independent thought—the capacity to analyze the ideas of others and generate ideas of one's own. This higher-order capacity is much more difficult to measure.

Assessing accomplishment in the cognitive domain has occupied educational psychologists for most of this century. "As yet, however, there is no comprehensive and universally accepted theory capturing complex human intellectual functions in a single conceptual framework" (Segal, Chipman, and Glaser, 1985, p. 7). Research on the assessment of academic skills and intellectual development is in a period of especially rapid change right now, and a number of potentially useful theories and taxonomies exist side by side.

The most influential mapping of the cognitive terrain for educational purposes is still the extensive classification system devised by Benjamin Bloom and his colleagues (Bloom and others, 1956; Bloom, Hastings, and Madaus, 1971). The assumption underlying what has become known as the "Bloom taxonomy" is that cognitive abilities can be measured along a continuum from simple to complex. A brief description of that taxonomy (as presented by Bloom, Hastings, and Madaus, 1971, pp. 271–273) follows.

1.0 Knowledge	Recalling specific facts or general concepts.
2.0 Comprehension	Demonstrating the lowest level of understanding. The individual can make use of what is being communicated without necessarily relating it to other material or seeing its fullest implication.
3.0 Application	Using abstractions in concrete situations. The abstractions may be principles, ideas, and theories that must be remembered and applied.
4.0 Analysis	Breaking down a communication into its constituent elements. The relationships between ideas are made explicit, and the organization of the communication is understood.
5.0 Synthesis	Putting together elements to form a whole—arranging elements to constitute a structure not clearly there before.
6.0 Evaluation	Making judgments about the value of materials and methods for given purposes. The individual can make appraisals that satisfy criteria determined by the instructor or by others.

Yet another view of the structure of cognition is presented by McKeachie and his colleagues (1986) at the National Center for Research to Improve Postsecondary Teaching and Learning (NCRIPTAL) at the University of Michigan. They conducted a comprehensive review of the literature on teaching and learning in higher education and decided to organize their discussion of student cognition under the rubrics of knowledge structure, learning strategies, and thinking and problem solving. Although these categories sound familiar, the emphasis of the NCRIPTAL group is less on measuring student outcomes than on understanding cognitive processes. For this reason, their definitions and their measures are more complex than those of the Bloom taxonomy.

Under knowledge structure, the NCRIPTAL group (pp. 16–35) advocates study of both the structure of the subject matter and students' internal representations of that structure. Students' learning in this area can be measured both indirectly (by word association, card sorting, ordered-tree techniques, and interviews) and directly (by concept mapping, networking, concept structuring, and similar techniques). Their second category of student cognition, learning strategies, deals with how students acquire and modify their knowledge base. McKeachie and his colleagues group these skills into three broad categories: cognitive, metacognitive, and resource management. "The cognitive category includes strategies related to the students' learning or encoding of material as well as strategies to facilitate retrieval of information. The metacognitive strategies involve strategies related to planning, regulating, monitoring, and modifying cognitive processes. The resource management strategies concern the students' strategies to control the resources (i.e., time, effort, outside support) that influence the quality and quantity of their involvement in the task" (p. 25). The third category, thinking and problem solving, includes critical thinking, problem solving, and reasoning—in general, the use of learning in new situations to solve problems or make decisions. There has been a great deal of research on problem solving and critical thinking in recent years, and a number of instruments exist for the measurement of these skills (see pp. 37–42).

McKeachie and his colleagues point out the recent advances made in the field of cognitive psychology—notably, the assimilative approach, which holds that meaningful learning occurs only when new inputs are linked with already existing schemata. In this view, learning is a creative, active process, and learners create new knowledge out of what's already in their heads. According to Ausubel (1968), an early advocate of this school of cognition, "If I had to reduce all of educational psychology to just one principle, I would say this: 'The most important single factor influencing learning is what the learner already knows. Ascertain this fact and teach him accordingly'" (prefatory note). In this view of learning, assessment depends not on tests— in the usual sense of questions asked and problems to be solved—but on the match between the conceptual map of the discipline or subject being taught and the internal cognitive map that illustrates what the learner knows.

It is not our intention to make classroom teachers into cognitive psychologists. However, since college teachers have a responsibility and a desire to promote their students' intellectual development, some acquaintance with current trends in cognitive psychology is clearly desirable. Moreover, since classroom teachers understand the structure of knowledge in their disciplines and have opportunities to observe learning in progress every day, they can contribute greatly to the improvement of their own teaching, and to our understanding of student learning, by becoming astute observers and skilled assessors of learning in process.

Our selection of feedback measures for assessing academic skills and intellectual development required a framework that could accommodate outcomes specified by these various theories and research currents but that was primarily teacher-oriented. To that end, the assessment techniques presented in this chapter provide information on skills and competencies identified in the latest developments in cognitive assessment, but the techniques are grouped in sets that are familiar and useful to the average classroom teacher.

Assessing Prior Knowledge, Recall, and Understanding

---

1. Background Knowledge Probe

2. Focused Listing

3. Misconception/Preconception Check

4. Empty Outlines

5. Memory Matrix

6. Minute Paper

7. Muddiest Point

The seven Classroom Assessment Techniques presented in this section assess students' learning of facts and principles, often called declarative learning; that is, they assess how well students are learning the content of the particular subject they are studying. The kind of learning task or stage of learning these techniques assess is what Norman (1980, p. 46) calls accretion, the "accumulation of knowledge into already established structures." Although such learning is not sufficient in higher education, it is certainly necessary. In most college classrooms, teachers and students focus a great proportion of their time and efforts on declarative learning. By investing a few minutes of class time to use one of these seven techniques, faculty can better gauge how well the content is being learned.

Two techniques, Background Knowledge Probes and Misconception/ Preconception Checks, allow faculty to assess students' prior knowledge and understanding, so they can teach accordingly. Focused Listing, the Empty Outline, and the Memory Matrix assess recall of "new" information presented in class or through homework assignments. These CATs focus on students' ability to remember the "new" declarative knowledge they are being exposed to, providing feedback on how well they are "accreting" or accumulating that content. To a limited extent, the Empty Outline and the

Memory Matrix also assess how and how well students are organizing the new content they are learning. The Minute Paper and the Muddiest Point, though extremely simple, focus on understanding, a somewhat deeper level of learning than simple recall. By asking students to judge what was clear and what was not, or what was most important and what they still have questions about, these CATs require learners to engage in simple acts of metacognition, to reflect on and assess their own understanding of the content they are learning.

Taken together, these seven CATs are among the most generic and most widely applicable tools in this handbook. They are also among the quickest and simplest CATs to use. For these reasons, they can be, and have been, successfully adapted to assess subject matter learning in almost every discipline.

CLASSROOM
ASSESSMENT
TECHNIQUE

1

Background Knowledge Probe

Estimated Levels of Time and Energy Required for:

Faculty to prepare to use this CAT	**MEDIUM**
Students to respond to the assessment	**LOW**
Faculty to analyze the data collected	**MEDIUM**

DESCRIPTION At the first class meeting, many college teachers ask students for general information on their level of preparation, often requesting that students list courses they have already taken in the relevant field. This CAT is designed to collect much more specific, and more useful, feedback on students' prior learning. Background Knowledge Probes are short, simple questionnaires prepared by instructors for use at the beginning of a course, at the start of a new unit or lesson, or prior to introducing an important new topic. A given Background Knowledge Probe may require students to write short answers, to circle the correct responses to multiple-choice questions, or both.

PURPOSE Background Knowledge Probes are meant to help teachers determine the most effective starting point for a given lesson and the most appropriate level at which to begin instruction. By sampling the students' background knowledge before formal instruction on that topic begins, these probes also provide feedback on the range of preparation among students in a particular class.

For students, the Background Knowledge Probe focuses attention on the most important material to be studied, providing both a preview of what is to come and a review of what they already know about that topic. Background Knowledge Probes can also be used as pre- and post-assessments: before instruction, to find out the students' "baseline" knowledge level; and immediately after, to get a rough sense of how much and how well they have learned the material. This CAT elicits more detailed information about what students know than Focused Listing (CAT 2) can.

RELATED TEACHING GOALS Improve memory skills (TGI Goal 11)
Develop appropriate study skills, strategies, and habits (TGI Goal 16)
Learn terms and facts of this subject (TGI Goal 18)
Learn concepts and theories in this subject (TGI Goal 19)
Develop an informed historical perspective (TGI Goal 32)

SUGGESTIONS FOR USE   You can use this technique as early as the first class meeting; it works well in classes of any size. Focus the questions in your probe on specific information or concepts that students will need to know to succeed in subsequent assignments, rather than on their personal histories or general knowledge. Make sure to ask at least one question that you are certain most students will be able to answer correctly, and at least one other that you judge to be more difficult. At the next class meeting, individual students can find out how the class as a whole did, and can gauge their level of preparation in relation to that of the group. To assess changes in students' knowledge and concision in responding, you can use the same or similar questions at the midpoint and at the end of the lesson, unit, or term. The probe can also be used to introduce important concepts that will subsequently be developed through a number of lessons, or throughout the entire course.

EXAMPLES

From a Survey of English Literature (English/Literature)

On the first day of class, to get an idea of how much exposure her students had had to Shakespeare's plays, this professor prepared a Background Knowledge Probe. The form asked students in her lower-level English literature course to list the plays that they were familiar with. For each work listed, they were to check off whether they had read it, seen it performed in a theater, or seen it in the movies or on television.

Most of the lists she got back were predictably short; and *Romeo and Juliet, Hamlet,* and *Macbeth* were the titles most frequently named. A handful of students turned in quite long lists, however, while a few turned in blank forms. Several other students included works on their lists that were not by Shakespeare. More students had seen Shakespeare's works on television or in the movies than had read them, and only a quarter had seen a live performance. As a result, most of the students were familiar with abridged and sometimes drastically altered versions of the original plays.

At the next class meeting, the English literature professor shared a summary of this information with the class, letting some of them know that they would be encountering a play for the second time and explaining that she had substituted *King Lear* for *Macbeth* because many already had seen or read the latter. She complimented the students who had already read and/or seen a work of Shakespeare and asked them to assist those in class to whom it would be totally new. She also alerted the class to major differences between the texts they would read and some of the filmed versions they had seen. She then passed out a handout summarizing the feedback gathered and giving the names of the authors of the works listed that were not by Shakespeare.

From Fundamentals of Electric Circuits (Electrical Engineering)

Before their first lecture-demonstration-lab session, this electrical engineering instructor wanted to determine what his students might already have learned—whether through course work or on-the-job experience—about measuring current, voltage, and resistance. To find out, he prepared a Background Knowledge Probe that contained five illustrations representing the displays of the following instruments: voltmeter, ammeter, ohmmeter, deflection multimeter, and digital multimeter. Each illustration clearly indicated a different reading or readings through the pointer positions and switch settings, or digital readouts shown. Near the end of the first class session, he presented students with these illustrations, reproduced on two pages, and asked them to determine, and write out, the readings for the five instruments shown.

The responses to his probe indicated that most students were more familiar with digital instrument displays and that most of them had some idea what the readings on at least one of the instruments meant. But he also saw that most students did not use standard electrical engineering notation and vocabulary in their responses and that there was quite a range of prior knowledge. A few students had no idea how to respond; a few others got everything correct.

To capitalize on the diversity in preparation, he decided to start the next class with a small-group warm-up exercise. He randomly assigned students to groups of four and then handed out clean copies of the same Background Knowledge Probe. He gave the groups fifteen minutes to come up with correct readings for all five instruments. They were told that each person in each group was expected to learn the correct answers. This, of course, meant that the more experienced students had to explain and teach their responses to the novices.

After the instructor had asked questions of each group, he commented on the diversity of the earlier, individual responses to the probe. To respond to this diversity, he told the class, he had to include material that would be totally new to some of them but would be review to others. He asked the more advanced students to consolidate their knowledge by helping their less experienced classmates. And he asked the beginners to recognize their responsibility to invest relatively more time and effort.

STEP-BY-STEP PROCEDURE

1. Before introducing an important new concept, subject, or topic in the course syllabus, consider what the students may already know about it. Recognizing that their knowledge may be partial, fragmentary, simplistic, or even incorrect, try to find at least one point that most students are likely to know, and use that point to lead into other, less familiar points.

2. Prepare two or three open-ended questions, a handful of short-answer questions, or ten to twenty multiple-choice questions that will probe the students' existing knowledge of that concept, subject, or topic. These questions need to be carefully phrased, since a vocabulary that may not be familiar to the students can obscure your assessment of how well they know the facts or concepts.

3. Write your open-ended questions on the chalkboard, or hand out short questionnaires. Direct students to answer open-ended questions succinctly, in two or three sentences if possible. Make a point of announcing that these Background Knowledge Probes are not tests or quizzes

and will not be graded. Encourage students to give thoughtful answers that will help you make effective instructional decisions.

4. At the next class meeting, or as soon as possible, let students know the results, and tell them how that information will affect what you do as the teacher and how it should affect what they do as learners.

TURNING THE DATA YOU COLLECT INTO USEFUL INFORMATION

After you have collected the responses, try dividing them into three or four piles, according to degree of preparation for the upcoming learning tasks. You can, for example, quickly rate both written answers and multiple-choice responses, classifying them into the following four categories: [– 1] = erroneous background knowledge; [0] = no relevant background knowledge; [+ 1] = some relevant background knowledge; [+ 2] = significant background knowledge. By summing the individual numerical ratings for each question, you can find out whether the class as a whole has more knowledge about some topics than about others. For an even faster analysis, you can simply sort responses into "prepared" and "not prepared" piles.

IDEAS FOR ADAPTING AND EXTENDING THIS CAT

After students have responded individually to the probes, ask them to work in pairs or small groups to come up with mutually acceptable, correct answers.

Divide the class into small groups of students and ask them to rate and sort responses from other groups.

If you have a small number of students in an upper-level course, consider having the students interview each other, taking notes on the responses to probe questions.

Use Background Knowledge Probes as a higher-level follow-up or alternative to Focused Listing (CAT 2).

PROS

Background Knowledge Probes can provide useful data not only about students' knowledge of the topic but also about their skills in communicating what they know.

They provide baseline data that teachers can use to make critical instructional decisions before instruction begins.

By building on specific background knowledge that students do have, the instructor can give students a familiar starting point, a "hook to hang new information on."

Like Focused Listing, this technique can "prime the pump" of recall, encouraging students to connect the lesson or course topic to their own past experiences and prior knowledge and prodding students to begin constructing their own "bridges" between old and new knowledge.

CONS   If student responses are at odds with the teacher's expectations, the feedback can sometimes be overwhelming and even demoralizing to the instructor.

In a similar fashion, trying to respond to the probe can be a difficult and frustrating experience for students who are underprepared.

In the process of reading and classifying responses, a teacher may form hard-to-change first impressions, which can affect his or her expectations of the students for the remainder of the term.

CAVEATS   Feedback from this technique can throw even the best-planned lesson or syllabus into serious question by demonstrating the need for quick and sometimes major revisions in instructional plans. Therefore, Background Knowledge Probes should be used only if you have the time, energy, and willingness to analyze and respond to the information they generate.

Do not generalize too much from the responses to a single administration of this CAT.

Although you will naturally be concerned with the underprepared students that a Background Knowledge Probe is likely to identify, you will also need to plan a response for those students who are adequately to extremely well prepared.

REFERENCES AND RESOURCES   A description of this technique, along with many other useful ideas on teaching and learning, can be found in an in-house publication of Roxbury Community College (1986, especially pp. 8 and 9). For an example of the Background Knowledge Probe used in a political science course, see *Early Lessons* (Angelo, 1991, pp. 20–21).

Focused Listing

Estimated Levels of Time and Energy Required for:

Faculty to prepare to use this CAT	**LOW**
Students to respond to the assessment	**LOW**
Faculty to analyze the data collected	**LOW**

DESCRIPTION

As the name implies, this Classroom Assessment Technique focuses students' attention on a single important term, name, or concept from a particular lesson or class session and directs them to list several ideas that are closely related to that "focus point."

PURPOSE

Focused Listing is a tool for quickly determining what learners recall as the most important points related to a particular topic. It can help faculty assess how well students can describe or define a central point in a lesson, and it can begin to illuminate the web of concepts students connect with that point. Practicing this technique can help students learn to focus attention and improve recall.

RELATED TEACHING GOALS

Improve skill at paying attention (TGI Goal 9)
Develop ability to concentrate (TGI Goal 10)
Improve memory skills (TGI Goal 11)
Improve listening skills (TGI Goal 12)
Develop appropriate study skills, strategies, and habits (TGI Goal 16)
Learn terms and facts of this subject (TGI Goal 18)
Learn concepts and theories in this subject (TGI Goal 19)

SUGGESTIONS FOR USE

Focused Listing can be used before, during, or after the relevant lesson. As a result, teachers can use this technique to gauge the best starting point, make midpoint corrections, and measure the class's progress in learning one specific element of the course content. Because of its simplicity, Focused Listing works well in classes of all sizes. It can be used relatively frequently in courses where a large amount of new information is regularly introduced. Perhaps for this reason, Focused Listing has been particularly popular with instructors in undergraduate survey courses and those who teach courses in vocational and preprofessional education.

EXAMPLES

From Introductory Physics for Nonscience Majors (Physics)

Over the years, this physics professor has found that, for many first-year students, the specialized vocabulary of her field is almost as great a barrier to learning as the level of mathematical sophistication that most such courses assume. For that reason, she and her colleagues developed a challenging introductory physics course that focuses on conceptual understanding and teaches students the necessary terminology and mathematics as they go.

She often uses Focused Listing to assess her students' knowledge of critical physical science terminology and to raise their awareness of the important information and concepts represented by those terms. On the first day of class, for example, she hands out half-sheets of scrap paper and asks students to write a list of five or so words or phrases that define *work* in physics. After about two minutes, she collects their responses.

Once she has read them through quickly, the physics professor sorts the responses into three piles: those that do at least a fairly good job of defining *work* in physics; those that confuse work in physics with work in everyday life; and all the rest. As she prepares for the second class meeting, the professor works the results of the Focused Listing and several quotes from student responses into her lecture notes. In the next class, using concepts and words that the students provided in their Focused Listings, she explains and differentiates the two distinct but easily confusable meanings of work: the everyday and the scientific. Throughout the semester, she uses Focused Listing to assess and help students learn other key concepts, such as mass, velocity, energy, impulse, and momentum.

From Investments (Finance/Management)

After an initial lecture on stocks in this core management course, the finance professor asked his fifty students to list and quickly define five to seven fundamental concepts related to stocks. Since they were writing brief definitions in addition to listing concepts they recalled, he allowed the class ten minutes for this assessment. Reading quickly through student responses afterward, he found that more than half of the class had listed and adequately defined at least three of the six concepts on his Focused List; some of the students had included other important and valid concepts that were not on his list (seven such concepts were included).

At the following class meeting, the finance professor gave out a printed list of some of the best definitions and reviewed the three fundamental concepts from his list that had not been included by most students. This experience led him to begin each class session by writing on the chalkboard a list of several key concepts and terms that students should focus on throughout the lecture.

From an Introduction to Non-Western Art and Music (Art/Humanities)

With no introduction except directions to listen and watch attentively, the instructor in this general education survey course showed a twenty-minute slide and audiotape presentation on classical Persian art and music. After turning the lights back up, she asked the students to make a Focused Listing of terms they would use to describe classical Persian culture, based on what they had seen and heard. She allowed students a couple of minutes to make individual lists. Then, rather than collecting the Focused Lists and analyzing them out of class, the instructor asked students to share what they had written.

By eliciting responses from around the room, she made a composite list of a dozen terms on the chalkboard and used that list as a starting point for her lecture on the topic. Now that she knew the students' vocabulary of concepts, she could help them connect her new, very specific set of terms and concepts to their general impressions and previous knowledge. She also used the class's Focused List to demonstrate to the students that although most of them had never encountered Persian culture before, they could begin to appreciate it with the cultural vocabularies they already possessed.

From United States Government and Politics (Political Science)

(This last example is a somewhat more complicated one, in which Focused Listing was used as a pre- and post-assessment of students' learning in the course of a single class session.)

At the beginning of the ninety-minute session, before leading a lecture/discussion on basic concepts of United States government, this political science professor handed out 3-by-5-inch index cards to his thirty first-year students, telling them to label one side of the card "Before." He then gave them two minutes to make a Focused List of a half-dozen words and short phrases they would use to define or describe Federalism. When two minutes had passed, the professor asked them to turn over the index cards, but to keep them handy.

At the conclusion of the lecture/discussion on Federalism, but about ten minutes before the end of class, the instructor asked students to write another half-dozen or so terms defining or describing Federalism on the blank side of their index cards, and to label the second list "After." He then directed them to circle the three most important terms and hand in the index cards.

Even a quick scan of the cards highlighted the students' inclusion of more specific and more appropriate terms in their "After" lists. This was, of course, the kind of learning the professor was hoping his lesson would provoke. As he compiled a list of the terms that students had circled as the three most important, however, he noticed a great deal of variation. In fact, his thirty students had come up with twenty-three different terms as "most important." The five fundamental terms that the instructor had emphasized in his lecture were there on the composite list, but not on every individual list. He saw that many of the class's eighteen remaining terms could be subordinated to his five big ideas but that some clearly did not relate to Federalism.

The political science instructor decided to use the students' list as a starting point for the next class session. He created three overhead transparencies. The first overhead contained the twenty-three terms from the composite list; the second consisted of the same items organized into six subgroups, headed by his five topics and one other; and the third transparency was his own Concept Map (see CAT 16) showing the relationships between Federalism and those items from the class list that he could connect. In the next class, those three transparencies served as launching points for a lively twenty-minute discussion focusing on why and how particular concepts from their lists did or did not relate to Federalism.

STEP-BY-STEP PROCEDURE

1. Select an important topic or concept that the class has just studied or is about to study and describe it in a word or brief phrase.

2. Write that word or phrase at the top of a sheet of paper as the heading for a Focused List of related terms important to understanding that topic.

3. Set a time limit or a limit on the number of items you will write, or set both time and item-number limits. Two or three minutes and five to ten items are usually sufficient.

4. Adhering to your own limits, make a list of important words and phrases you can recall that are related to and subsumed by your heading.

5. Look over your list quickly, adding any important items you may have left out.

6. If you are still convinced that the topic is important and well defined — worth class time to assess and respond to — give your students the same focus topic, tell them the time and/or length limits, and ask them to make Focused Lists. (You will probably need to allow students somewhat more time than you gave yourself to carry out this task.)

TURNING THE DATA YOU COLLECT INTO USEFUL INFORMATION

In analyzing responses to the Focused Listing, as with any other CAT, organize the data to highlight the information, categories, or relationships you want students to pay attention to and learn from. You may find it useful to compare the number of items (quantity) and the identity of those items (quality) on the students' lists with the content of your own lists. While your own Focused List should serve as the "master list" — the criterion against which to compare the students' lists — you might want to read at least a sample of the students' lists to see whether they have come up with any acceptable items that you missed.

The simplest way to categorize students' responses is to sort them into groupings of "related" and "unrelated" or "appropriate" and "inappropriate" items. A second level of analysis is to categorize responses according to the type or degree of relationship they have to the focus topic. For instance, you might sort students' responses into groups of definitions, examples, descriptions, and illustrations; or into those that have primary, secondary, and tertiary relationships to the focus term.

IDEAS FOR ADAPTING AND EXTENDING THIS CAT

Provide students with the focus topic along with their homework assignment and ask them to complete the Focused List before class.

Allow students to work in small groups to develop collective Focused Lists.

Make your Focused List available to the students for comparison and, if possible, for questions and discussion in class.

Make — or have students working in small groups make — a follow-up list that combines the best of the students' lists with your own. This activity provides students with an opportunity to think about what is most important to learn, know, and remember about that topic.

Encourage students to keep a notebook or journal of their Focused Lists and to use the technique whenever they find it useful.

Ask students to write definitions for each of the key terms on their Focused Lists.

Have students turn their lists into expository prose, clearly explaining the relationships between the focus point and the items and/or the relationships among the items.

Use Focused Listing again at intervals after the first administration. It then becomes a technique not only for assessing longer-term recall but also for reinforcing and deepening learning and encouraging restructuring.

Build on this CAT by assessing students' knowledge of the same focus point with Concept Maps (CAT 16), the One-Sentence Summary (CAT 13), Directed Paraphrasing (CAT 23), or the Memory Matrix (CAT 5).

To assess students' understanding of two related concepts, try the Defining Features Matrix (CAT 9).

PROS

Focused Listing is an extremely simple, quick, and flexible way to collect information on student knowledge about a particular topic.

It gives the teacher a clear idea of which specific terms and concepts the students recall and which they don't, allowing for more focused and effective review.

When the amount of time allotted for list making is very limited, the resulting responses often indicate what the most salient information is from the learner's point of view, rather than what the students think the teacher wants to hear.

If Focused Listing is used before instruction, it can "prime the pump," stimulating students to recall anything they may know about a topic before reading or hearing about it. They will therefore be more likely to connect and remember the new information they encounter.

CONS

In its basic form, Focused Listing requires only recall, and so makes no demands, or very limited ones, on higher-level cognitive skills.

Some students may be able to produce a list of relevant terms without necessarily understanding their meanings or interrelationships.

This technique focuses on one idea at a time, but many of the most difficult learning problems have to do with students' difficulty in understanding the relationships between and among ideas.

CAVEATS   Always work through this technique yourself before using it in class. Make sure you have your own Focused List ready.

Focus on a term or concept so important that you want students to remember it three years after the class is over.

Choose a focus topic that is neither too broad nor too narrow. A topic that is too broad will lead to hopelessly divergent lists, while too narrow a focus can lead to extremely limited and trival lists.

Make sure that both the task and the limits are clear and that students know if you expect them to apply any particular criteria in generating their lists, such as listing only defining words, synonyms, or examples.

REFERENCES AND RESOURCES   See Obler, Arnold, Sigala, and Umbdenstock (1991, pp. 111–112) for an example of Focused Listing used in a U.S. history class.

CLASSROOM
ASSESSMENT
TECHNIQUE

3

Misconception / Preconception Check

Estimated Levels of Time and Energy Required for:

Faculty to prepare to use this CAT	**MEDIUM**
Students to respond to the assessment	**LOW**
Faculty to analyze the data collected	**MEDIUM**

DESCRIPTION   Focused Listing and Background Knowledge Probes are simple techniques for gathering information on what students already know in order to determine effective starting points for instruction. The Misconception/Preconception Check also assesses students' prior knowledge, but with a twist. Its focus is on uncovering prior knowledge or beliefs that may hinder or block further learning.

PURPOSE   The greatest obstacle to new learning often is not the student's lack of prior knowledge but, rather, the existence of prior knowledge. Most college teachers know from experience that it's much harder for students to unlearn incorrect or incomplete knowledge than to master new knowledge in an unfamiliar field. Consequently, teachers can benefit from discovering early in the term which common misconceptions and preconceptions students have that are likely to interfere with their learning in a given course. This CAT is designed to uncover specific instances of incorrect or incomplete knowledge, attitudes, or values that represent likely barriers to new learning. Because assessment activities such as this CAT identify misconceptions and preconceptions early on and help students explicitly recognize and understand them, students stand a much greater chance of learning new material correctly and integrating it into their "revised" and often "transformed" knowledge structures.

RELATED TEACHING GOALS   Develop ability to distinguish between fact and opinion (TGI Goal 8)
Learn terms and facts of this subject (TGI Goal 18)
Learn concepts and theories in this subject (TGI Goal 19)
Develop an openness to new ideas (TGI Goal 27)
Cultivate an active commitment to honesty (TGI Goal 50)

SUGGESTIONS FOR USE   Although there are common misperceptions or preconceptions about every field, they seem to be most pernicious and common in those areas of the curriculum that have the greatest overlap with life outside the university

132   CLASSROOM ASSESSMENT TECHNIQUES

classroom. For instance, virtually all incoming first-year college students have knowledge, beliefs, and attitudes about the phenomena they will study in political science, economics, anthropology, sociology, history, and psychology courses. While these same students are likely to have fewer strongly held preconceptions and misconceptions about mathematics, the natural sciences, and related fields, some of the wrongheaded, implicit "common-sense" notions that they cling to can still effectively derail learning.

Thus, this CAT can be particularly useful in social and behavioral science courses, especially those dealing with controversial or sensitive issues. In the natural sciences and mathematics, the Misconception/Preconception Check can help faculty uncover naive and sometimes magical beliefs that can act like filters: allowing disconnected facts and principles through but blocking out a deeper understanding of method or worldview. Although two of the three examples below concern beginning-of-term applications, this technique can be used at any point in a course when students encounter new information or interpretations that they may find counterintuitive or disturbing.

EXAMPLES

From the Americas Before Columbus (History)

> On the first day of class, after initial introductions, the instructor in this upper-division course on pre-Columbian history administered a Misconception/Preconception Check. She explained to the twenty-five or so students that she was gathering information on what the class as a whole already knew about the Americas and Native Americans before 1492, so that she could better tailor her teaching to fit them. She then passed out sheets of lined paper and asked the students to write their best answers to three questions, but not their names. She told them they would have five minutes to write. The three questions she wrote on the chalkboard were:
>
> 1. About how many people lived in North America in 1491?
>
> 2. About how long had they been on this continent by 1491?
>
> 3. What significant achievements had they made in that time?
>
> After five minutes, she collected the papers, shuffled them, and handed them back, asking anyone who got his or her own paper back to trade with someone else. Once everyone had someone else's paper, she asked the students to share those responses. First, she elicited the lowest and highest numerical answers for questions 1 and 2, establishing the ranges. The ranges were quite spectacular, and there wasn't much agreement between the poles. For question 3, she simply listed answers on the board until they began to repeat. The list was not particularly long.
>
> Having finished the list, the history professor stood quietly. Finally, one of the students asked her what the right answers were. She allowed that his was an important question, but one that would have to wait until they had explored an even more critical question. She collected their responses again, so that she could read them at home, and then wrote her fourth question on the board: "Where did you get those first three

answers?" The students spent the rest of that session trying to answer question 4. Most of them soon realized that their impressions of pre-Columbian America were based on shaky ground. Then the professor gave them their first library research assignment. They were to work in pairs to double-check the accuracy of their first three answers and, in the process, to find the "right" answers. The students found, of course, that there are no generally accepted right answers but that some answers are more plausible and better supported than others.

From Human Sexuality (Health Science/Biology)

Several weeks into the semester, before students in his large general education course began the unit on sexually transmitted diseases and AIDS, this biology professor constructed a Misconception/Preconception Check focusing on these related topics. He developed a simple questionnaire containing ten prompts designed to uncover commonly held, incorrect ideas and beliefs about how diseases such as gonorrhea, syphilis, hepatitis, and AIDS are transmitted; how prevalent these diseases are among college students; and how individuals can avoid exposure entirely or greatly reduce the risks of infection. Each prompt was a statement, such as "Most of those now infected with the AIDS virus became infected through homosexual activities or intravenous drug use." In response to each statement, the student was to circle one of the answers below.

I'm absolutely certain this is true	I'm pretty sure it is true	I have no idea whether it's true or false	I'm pretty sure it is false	I'm absolutely certain it is false

He asked students to circle the one most appropriate answer for each question, but not to put their names on the questionnaires. After class, he quickly tallied the responses and found that a majority of his students were either operating under dangerously incorrect notions or simply unsure about nine out of the ten issues. The Misconception/Preconception Check also revealed that his students felt more certain about some wrong answers than others. Knowing what the common misconceptions were, and just how common they were in that class, the biology professor could tailor his teaching plan to respond to the particular needs of that group. And knowing that some incorrect notions were more deeply ingrained than others, he could prepare more effectively to meet different degrees of resistance.

At the beginning of the first class meeting on this topic, he displayed a series of ten overhead transparencies, each illustrating the range of responses to each statement. In the lecture and discussion that followed, he explained why the incorrect answers were incorrect and what implications the general "true" information he presented might have for specific individuals. He also talked with students about the evolution of knowledge about these diseases over time, and ways in which the media sometimes encourage or reinforce misconceptions.

From Introduction to the Structure of the Universe (Astronomy)

Ten minutes before the end of the first meeting of a large undergraduate science course, the professor handed out half-sheets of paper and asked students to write their best answers to the following question: "What makes the seasons change on Earth?" She told them that any sincere answer was acceptable except "I don't know." She explained why she was asking them this question and what she would do with their responses. She also directed the students not to write their names on the papers and assured them that, on the first day of class, she certainly could not yet identify them by their handwriting.

The professor stood by the exit as class ended, holding a small cardboard box for students to drop their answers in, thereby encouraging a high response rate. Later that day, she looked through the student responses very quickly, dividing them into the following four piles, based on the type of explanations given: the "correct" pile, the "distance" pile, the "weather" pile, and the "others" pile. The pile of correct answers was fairly small, representing less than one-tenth of the class. The pile of answers that explained seasons as the result of distance from the sun was the largest, with over 50 percent of the responses. Those who thought that weather somehow caused seasonal change represented almost 20 percent, and the rest came up with a bewildering variety of other explanations, including references to the moon's gravitational pull!

Before the next class, she picked out the clearest, most articulate example from each of the four piles and transcribed those four answers onto a one-page handout, which she then distributed to the students at the beginning of the next class. After they had read all four explanations, she asked them simply to circle the one correct answer and to turn in the handouts. While she went on with her lecture, her teaching assistant quickly tallied the responses. The assistant then wrote the percentages of the various answers from the first assessment and those from the second assessment side by side on the board. The second time around, the proportion of correct responses was much higher, nearly 40 percent. This is a common effect, occurring because students can more often recognize the correct answer when it is presented to them than they can independently produce that same answer.

At that point, the professor stopped her lecture and invited several students to explain their choices to the class. Proponents of each of the four major positions explained their models of seasonal change. That weekend, each student's assignment was to find out which of the answers really was correct and to explain, in less than a page, how he or she could be certain that it was indeed the correct explanation. Students then provided the explanations during the next class, with the professor offering minor corrections and qualifications. The class then discussed the adequacy of the arguments and evidence for each position. The instructor concluded the lesson on seasons by explaining why several other models, though incorrect, were reasonable. She also reminded the class that it had taken humans, as a species, quite a long time to figure out what caused the seasons.

STEP-BY-STEP PROCEDURE

1. Start by identifying some of the most troublesome common misconceptions or preconceptions students bring to your course. Brainstorming this question with colleagues in your department or field can be a very effective way to generate such a list.

2. Select a handful of these troublesome ideas and beliefs—ones that are likely to interfere most with learning in your course—and focus your Misconception/Preconception Check on them.

3. Create a simple questionnaire to elicit information about students' ideas and beliefs in these areas. You may want to use a multiple-choice format or a short-answer format. Short-answer questions can uncover more useful information, but they compromise anonymity. Multiple-choice questionnaires are therefore safer, and the responses are easier to analyze. If you need to know how strongly held the beliefs or ideas are, consider providing Likert-scale responses such as those used by the biology instructor in the example above.

4. Have another faculty member read your questions to make sure they do not seem patronizing, threatening, or obvious.

5. Before giving the questionnaire to your students, think through how you will respond to several likely outcomes. Strike any questions or topics you do not feel prepared to deal with.

6. Explain your reasons for using this CAT to the students, make sure the anonymity of their responses is ensured, and announce when and how you plan to respond to their feedback.

TURNING THE DATA YOU COLLECT INTO USEFUL INFORMATION

Depending on the way the questionnaire is designed, analyzing the feedback from this CAT can answer one or more of the following three questions: What specific misperceptions or preconceptions do my students have about the course material that might interfere with their learning? How many of the students have them? How deeply embedded are these "problematic" ideas or beliefs?

To answer the first two questions, you can quickly organize the responses into rough categories by type of misconception or preconception, and then tally them, as in the example above from the physics course. You can best answer the third question if you have constructed the Misconception/Preconception Check to provide information on the students' degree of certainty or strength of beliefs, as in the example from the Human Sexuality course. As you read through and tally responses to this type of question, look for patterns within and across items. For example, watch for questions or topics on which the students' responses are clearly divided. Looking across items, group the topics into four categories: those that elicit strong reactions at both the "correct" and the "incorrect" ends of the scale, those that elicit mostly incorrect or mostly correct responses, and those that most students are unsure of or that elicit thoroughly mixed results.

IDEAS FOR ADAPTING AND EXTENDING THIS CAT

To encourage candid responses to sensitive topics, begin by asking students to identify common misconceptions and preconceptions that they think other people have about the topic or field.

Have students work in teams to come up with "reasonable" explanations or justifications for the misconceptions uncovered through this assessment.

Readminister the same questionnaire later in the term—after your instructional response—to see what, if anything, has changed and how.

PROS

The Misconception/Preconception Check gives teachers a quick way to uncover likely barriers to learning and thus to prepare to meet and overcome them.

Since this CAT is carried out anonymously, individual students are likely to reveal their own ideas and beliefs, rather than providing "safe" answers.

Many students are both surprised and relieved to learn that they are not alone in being mistaken or unclear about a given topic. The feedback session can provide that reassurance.

When students do explicitly recognize and question their own knowledge, beliefs, and attitudes, they gain a measure of control over their own thinking. This technique can help students take one small step in the direction of self-knowledge and self-awareness.

CONS

The first and most obvious disadvantage of using this technique is that virtually no one enjoys having his or her certainties questioned. As noted above, unlearning—though often necessary—can be very difficult and even painful.

A related problem is time. Changes in fundamental ideas, beliefs, and attitudes take time and rarely occur in a linear fashion. For many students, the developmental changes involved in moving from a "magical," prescientific view of the universe to an empirical approach will take much more than a semester to solidify.

CAVEATS

One person's unquestioned fact is often another's questionable theory—or pernicious falsehood. Tread lightly when dealing with potentially sensitive issues if you want students to open up enough to risk having their assumptions challenged. In general, do not use this technique to focus on issues that students may find personally threatening until a climate of trust and civility has been established in the class.

REFERENCES AND RESOURCES

For an example of this CAT applied to a chemistry course, see *Early Lessons* (Angelo, 1991, pp. 21–22).

A Private Universe is a fascinating videotape that explores high school and college students' (mis)understandings of the causes of seasons and the difficulty one student faces in unlearning her incorrect, though highly original, explanation. This videotape illustrates the importance and difficulty of uncovering powerful misperceptions and helping students unlearn them. (Videotape distributed by Pyramid Film and Video, Box 1048, Santa Monica, Calif. 90406.)

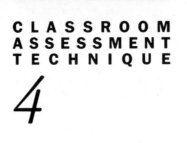

CLASSROOM
ASSESSMENT
TECHNIQUE

4

Empty Outlines

Estimated Levels of Time and Energy Required for:

Faculty to prepare to use this CAT	**MEDIUM**
Students to respond to the assessment	**LOW**
Faculty to analyze the data collected	**MEDIUM**

DESCRIPTION The name of this technique is self-explanatory. The instructor provides students with an empty or partially completed outline of an in-class presentation or homework assignment and gives them a limited amount of time to fill in the blank spaces. To help students better organize and learn course content, many instructors already provide outlines of their lectures at the beginning or end of class sessions. In our experience, however, fewer teachers use the outline format to assess students' learning of that same content.

PURPOSE The Empty Outline technique helps faculty find out how well students have "caught" the important points of a lecture, reading, or audiovisual presentation. It also helps learners recall and organize the main points of a lesson within an appropriate knowledge structure, making retention more likely and aiding understanding.

RELATED TEACHING GOALS Improve skill at paying attention (TGI Goal 9)
Develop ability to concentrate (TGI Goal 10)
Improve listening skills (TGI Goal 12)
Develop appropriate study skills, strategies, and habits (TGI Goal 16)
Learn terms and facts of this subject (TGI Goal 18)

SUGGESTIONS FOR USE This technique works best in courses where a large amount of content—facts and principles—is presented regularly in a highly structured manner. For example, Empty Outlines have been used with success in introductory courses in physical and life sciences, nursing, law, art history, and music history. The technique can be used at the conclusion of a class session or at the beginning of the next one. Because it generates quite a bit of feedback, the instructor usually can read every response only in small classes. In large courses, the instructor can collect only group responses, or read and respond to only a sample of student outlines.

From Pathophysiology (Nursing)

Experience and examination results had convinced this nursing professor that her students had difficulty recognizing, organizing, and recalling the most important points in her lectures. To gain specific insights into how students were managing the heavy information load of her lectures, she handed out copies of an Empty Outline form ten minutes before the end of class. The outline contained four main headings, representing the four main topics she had just lectured on. Each main heading was followed by empty lines for three to five subheadings. She directed the students to fill in the subheadings quickly, making use of their class notes. At the end of the session, she collected the forms.

The Empty Outline form was based on her lecture outline, of course; so she could easily compare the students' subheadings with her own. A quick reading showed her that most of the students placed their responses under the correct headings. However, they often made their subheadings too specific, or they mixed items of different levels of specificity. The responses demonstrated that students were missing at least some important subtopics because they were distracted by facts.

Armed with examples from the Empty Outlines, the instructor was better able to illustrate the level on which she wanted students to focus their attention during the lectures. By the third application of this CAT, most students had located that level and were therefore more successful at "seeing the forest for the trees."

From Child Language Acquisition (Child Development)

Before he showed a videotape of an educational television program on the stages of language acquisition from birth to five years, the instructor watched the video himself and sketched a simple outline of its topics and major points. The major topics in his outline were the developmental stages of language acquisition; the subheadings were the developmental milestones that characterize each stage. To create an Empty Outline assessment form, he simply deleted the content of his subheadings, leaving the main headings intact.

After the class had viewed the hour-long videotape, the instructor passed out the one-page Empty Outline forms and asked students to work in pairs to fill them in. He allowed five minutes for the work and then collected the completed forms. A quick analysis of the results showed him that his students most clearly recalled the milestones from the first and last stages presented in the video. Their responses to the intermediate stages were much sketchier. This information gave the teacher clear directions on where to begin the follow-up discussion and what to focus on. It also convinced him of the need to stop in the middle of the videotape to allow students time to take notes and review what they had seen and heard to that point.

From International Marketing (Business/Management)

In this upper-division course, taught primarily through the case method, the instructor wanted to determine whether her students were noting the major points brought out during case discussions. She drew up her outline before the discussion and then revised it as the case discussion took place. Ten minutes before the end of the two-hour class meeting, the marketing professor sketched a simple Empty Outline on the board. It consisted of four Roman numerals, each followed by three capital letters. She directed the students to copy the outline on a blank sheet of paper, to fill in the main points illustrated by the case discussion, and to follow each with at least three supporting comments made by class members.

While she had expected some range of responses, the width of that range surprised her. There was general agreement on only two major points, and very little consistency in the supporting comments cited. Many students had difficulty coming up with supporting comments. Her outline and the students' were often far apart, and not in ways that simply reflected reasonable differences in focus or interests.

The marketing professor summarized these differences broadly and reported back to the students, letting them know what she saw as the main points and strong supporting comments, and why. She invited discussion of her outline content—and got it. Several students were able to explain their responses persuasively.

At the suggestion of members of the class, she repeated the Empty Outlines exercise halfway through the next case discussion, and made time for small-group discussion of responses and revision of responses before they were handed in. Over several class sessions, the use of this technique led to much greater consensus on the important points and much more careful listening and questioning during the case discussions.

STEP-BY-STEP PROCEDURE

1. Create an outline of the lecture, presentation, discussion, or reading you want to focus on.

2. Make conscious decisions about the level on which you will focus the Empty Outline and, thus, the students' attention. Do you want students to supply the main topics, the main subtopics, or the supporting details? These decisions will determine what information you supply in the form and what you leave out.

3. When students are to complete the form from memory—that is, without any notes or other information—limit the number of items the Empty Outline elicits to fewer than ten.

4. If your Empty Outline focuses on a live presentation or a discussion, make sure that your own notes reflect any important changes that may have occurred between what was scripted and what actually happened.

5. Let students know how much time they will have to complete the outlines and the kinds of responses you prefer—words, short phrases, or brief sentences.

6. Be sure to announce the purpose of the assessment and the time when the students will receive feedback on their responses.

TURNING THE DATA YOU COLLECT INTO USEFUL INFORMATION

As with the responses from many other CATs, you can take your analysis in two useful directions. You may wish simply to compare the actual responses to those you expected, counting the number of students who agreed or disagreed with your responses for each item. As an alternative, or as a second step, you can look at the range of responses among students, focusing more on the patterns that emerge than on how well they match your expectations.

IDEAS FOR ADAPTING AND EXTENDING THIS CAT

If students have a great deal of difficulty completing the Empty Outline, try providing the class with a jumbled list of headings and subheadings and letting them structure the outline by using that content. Provide main headings but not subheadings; at other times, list the subheadings or details and ask students to fill in the main points. For more advanced learners, provide nothing more than guidelines. Simply ask them to create outlines of the focus lesson and indicate how much detail you expect.

Use the technique to assess student expectations of the lesson by having them fill in the Empty Outline before the presentation or reading. Allow students a few minutes to work in pairs or small groups to fill in the outlines. Use Focused Listing (CAT 2) as a warm-up or step-up to Empty Outlines. Consider using Concept Maps (CAT 16) as an alternate or next step.

PROS

Repeated use of this CAT can promote more careful listening and note-taking.

Feedback on responses gives important direction and useful models to less experienced students.

Empty Outlines can help students better organize and more effectively reorganize their memories of the material they are learning.

The Empty Outline can be used to demonstrate the basic organizing schemes of the discipline and to give students practice in using these schemes.

CONS

Once you have decided to use the Empty Outline at the end of a session, you may feel more constrained to follow your own outline than you otherwise would.

Not all information is best organized or best remembered in the hierarchical, linear fashion commonly associated with outlines.

Unless students are creating their own outlines from "scratch," little if any higher-order thinking is required.

CAVEATS

Because learners start at different points and process information differently, there will always be some variation in the way students complete the Empty Outlines.

Don't try to assess too much at any one time. If there are twenty main points in your lecture or in the chapter you are focusing on, for example, use the Empty Outline to assess understanding of only one-third or half of that material.

Memory Matrix

Estimated Levels of Time and Energy Required for:

Faculty to prepare to use this CAT — **MEDIUM**
Students to respond to the assessment — **LOW**
Faculty to analyze the data collected — **MEDIUM**

DESCRIPTION The Memory Matrix is simply a two-dimensional diagram, a rectangle divided into rows and columns used to organize information and illustrate relationships. In a Memory Matrix, the row and column headings are given, but the cells, the boxes within, are left empty. When students fill in the blank cells of the Memory Matrix, they provide feedback that can be quickly scanned and easily analyzed.

PURPOSE The Memory Matrix assesses students' recall of important course content and their skill at quickly organizing that information into categories provided by the instructor. By using this technique, teachers can quickly see not only whether their students have memorized the basic information but also how well they have organized that information in their memories.

RELATED TEACHING GOALS Improve memory skills (TGI Goal 11)
Improve reading skills (TGI 14)
Develop appropriate study skills, strategies, and habits (TGI Goal 16)
Learn terms and facts of this subject (TGI Goal 18)
Learn concepts and theories in this subject (TGI Goal 19)

SUGGESTIONS FOR USE The Memory Matrix is useful for assessing student recall and basic comprehension of facts and principles in courses with a high informational content. It works particularly well, for example, in introductory courses in the natural sciences, foreign languages, music theory, history, and law. This assessment technique is often used after lectures, reading assignments, films, or videotapes that present a substantial amount of clearly categorizable information. Like the other CATs in this section, however, the Memory Matrix also can be used as a preinstructional assessment.

EXAMPLES

From Elementary Spanish I (Foreign Languages)

Several classes after teaching the introductory lessons on verb endings, this Romance languages instructor wondered how well students in her first-semester Spanish class had internalized the organizing logic of "families" of verbs. Specifically, she wanted to find out whether they could quickly and easily categorize common verbs they had recently learned. She handed out the matrix shown as Exhibit 7.1 and gave students ten minutes to fill the blank cells with as many different "base form" verbs as they could recall.

Exhibit 7.1. A Sample Memory Matrix for Spanish Verb Endings.

	-ar	*-er*	*-ir*
Irregular			
Regular			

By quickly looking over the students' completed matrices, the Spanish teacher identified two problem areas. First, students almost never misclassified irregular verbs as regular, but they did mistakenly categorize regular verbs as irregular ones fairly frequently. Second, students confused the *-er* and *-ir* verbs—something she often noted during conversational practice. This feedback gave the instructor a clearer picture of what to review in the next class meeting. It also helped students decide how to focus their study time before the first test.

From a Survey of Nineteenth- and Twentieth-Century Western Art (Art/Humanities)

This art history professor used a Memory Matrix to find out how well her students were connecting major artists, the countries they were associated with, and the important trends they exemplified, as well as to provide the class with a foreshadowing of the midterm examination. She allowed students in her large survey course ten minutes to fill in the matrix shown as Exhibit 7.2 by placing the names of major artists they had studied in the appropriate cells.

Exhibit 7.2. A Memory Matrix for Major Artists and Styles.

	France	*United States*	*Britain*
Neoclassicism			
Impressionism			
Postimpressionism			
Expressionism			

The instructor then divided the students into groups of five and directed each group to work together for ten minutes and come up with the most complete, correct matrices possible. Each of the seven groups was given a larger, blank copy of the matrix to write the group response on. At the end of ten minutes, the groups were still so enthusiastically engaged that she decided to give them five more minutes to work. Finally, after fifteen minutes of group work, she convinced the students to hand in their individual and group matrices.

Just by flipping through the responses, she could see that the group memory was much better than almost any individual student's recall. She also noted that categorizing artists by nationality was easy for most students. But even the groups had some trouble distinguishing Impressionists from Postimpressionists or Postimpressionists from Expressionists. That feedback gave her the starting point for a lecture/discussion on how and why art historians categorize artists in this fashion, and how and why they sometimes disagree on who belongs where.

From Anatomy and Physiology I (Nursing/Biology)

One of this biology instructor's primary teaching goals was to help students make the connections between structures, processes, and functions. To assess how well his first-year nursing students understood these connections in relation to the digestive system, he drew the Memory Matrix shown as Exhibit 7.3. He decided to use the assessment after the students had read a chapter on that system but before he had lectured on it.

Exhibit 7.3. A Memory Matrix for Biology: The Digestive System.

	Structure	*Functions*	*Enzymes*
Mouth			
Esophagus			
Stomach			
Small intestine			
Large intestine			
Pancreas			
Liver			
Gall bladder			

Since this particular biology instructor was a firm believer in the value of cooperative learning, he organized the forty or so nursing students into eight more or less equal groups. Then he gave a piece of newsprint to each group, projected the Memory Matrix on a screen, and asked one person from each group to draw the diagram on the newsprint. After the empty matrices were sketched out, he allowed the groups fifteen minutes to fill in the missing information. A remarkable flurry of activity followed as the groups scrambled to complete their matrices.

When the time was up, the instructor collected the eight sheets. During the next twenty minutes, while the students watched an instructional videotape on enzyme functioning in the digestive system, he quickly scanned their group matrices for misplaced and missing information. The professor made quick notes on his own master version of the matrix, tallying up the number of groups that included critical information and jotting down errors. As he had expected, remembering all the enzymes and associating them with the correct structures were the most difficult tasks.

By the time the videotape ended, the instructor was ready to lead a short, very focused discussion on the digestive system. He first pointed out some of the more common errors that the groups had made; then, using his "model" transparency of the matrix, he reinforced those points that most groups had gotten right. After the students had asked clarifying questions, he handed out individual copies of the same Memory Matrix, giving the students the last five minutes of class to fill them in. Their responses, which he looked over after class, indicated that all but a handful of students had successfully integrated the information.

STEP-BY-STEP PROCEDURE

1. Draw a simple Memory Matrix in which row and column headings represent useful categorizing variables for important information covered in the lesson.

2. Fill in the blank cells yourself with the appropriate facts. Use the same vocabulary as that used in the relevant lectures, discussions, readings, or other instructional material.

3. Check to see that there is a good "fit" between row and column headings and the facts in the cells. Revise the Memory Matrix if necessary.

4. When you are satisfied with your matrix, draw a new one with only the row and column headings and spacious but empty cells. To encourage high achievers, provide enough space in the cells for a larger number of items than you expect students to come up with. Duplicate this matrix on scrap paper and hand out copies, or draw it on an overhead transparency or the chalkboard and have students copy it.

5. Direct students to provide the information needed to fill in the cells. Ask them to write only words or brief phrases. Set a realistic lower limit for the number of items you expect them to insert in each cell. Asking students to provide at least three items, for example, can keep them from stalling and blocking in search of the one best answer.

6. Collect the matrices and assess the correctness and completeness of the information given.

TURNING THE DATA YOU COLLECT INTO USEFUL INFORMATION

One way to analyze the data in the cells of the matrices is first to tally the number of instances (frequencies) of correct items in each cell and then to look for noticeable differences, both in total and in average numbers of correct responses, between and among the cells. This analysis will quickly show you what the students know well. A second useful approach is to focus on the incorrect or marginal items, once again by tallying them and looking for patterns. After you have tallied responses either way, you can look for patterns in the kinds of errors made. If there are clear imbalances in numbers of correct items in cells, they may indicate a failure to recall or correctly categorize specific types of information; or they may simply indicate that less teaching or study time was devoted to certain categories of information than to others.

IDEAS FOR ADAPTING
AND EXTENDING
THIS CAT
Use the Memory Matrix as a whole-class assessment by drawing the diagram on the chalkboard, eliciting the missing information from the class, and filling it in as you go. Ask a student or students to take notes, or write the elicited information on the chalkboard or on an overhead projector transparency.

Allow students to work in pairs or small groups to fill in the matrix, providing a bit more time for the task than you would for individuals.

Provide students with a Memory Matrix that is missing elements other than the contents of the cells. Leave out one column heading, for example. Then fill in one cell to serve as a clue to the identity of the missing column heading.

Break the class into small groups, giving each group a list of facts or terms that can be categorized into a Memory Matrix. The groups' task will be to decide how many and which categories to use as the row and column headings for their matrices. Responses from the various groups can then be compared and discussed.

PROS
The Memory Matrix allows you to assess not only how many facts the students can recall about a lesson but whether they can correctly categorize those facts and understand relationships among them.

It produces a bare minimum of written information displayed in a simple graphic framework, so the information can be read and assessed quickly.

Because of its graphic qualities, students who are strong visual learners may find this technique particularly helpful.

The Memory Matrix helps students manage, organize, and learn large amounts of information, making retrieval from memory easier and more efficient.

CONS
By providing row and column headings, the matrix precludes the students from using their own categorizing schemes. Therefore, the teacher may not find out whether some students have alternate ways of organizing and storing the information covered in the course.

Because the matrix provides very basic categories and information, the teacher may not be able to determine whether the students' answers represent what they have learned in the course or what they knew before they took the course.

The matrix format can make complex, dynamic systems appear static and lifeless.

If your students have had little experience with this format, start out with simple matrices, preferably no larger than two by two (rows by columns), or three by three. Limiting the number of categories initially will help students master the technique more quickly.

Not all data can be neatly arranged in matrix cells; hence the distinction between categorical and sequential data so familiar to statisticians. If categories do overlap or blend, make sure those blurred lines get illuminated and clarified in subsequent feedback sessions. When distinctions are of degree rather than kind, the Defining Features Matrix (CAT 9) may be a more appropriate and useful assessment tool.

While it is a useful way to assess and organize information of many kinds, the Memory Matrix needs to be acknowledged as a convenient simplification of a more complex reality.

REFERENCES AND RESOURCES See Walker (1991, pp. 70–71) for an example of the Memory Matrix used in a large undergraduate psychology class.

CLASSROOM ASSESSMENT TECHNIQUE

6

Minute Paper

Estimated Levels of Time and Energy Required for:

Faculty to prepare to use this CAT	**LOW**
Students to respond to the assessment	**LOW**
Faculty to analyze the data collected	**LOW**

DESCRIPTION   To the best of our knowledge, no other Classroom Assessment Technique has been used more often or by more college teachers than the Minute Paper. This versatile technique—also known as the One-Minute Paper and the Half-Sheet Response—provides a quick and extremely simple way to collect written feedback on student learning. To use the Minute Paper, an instructor stops class two or three minutes early and asks students to respond briefly to some variation on the following two questions: "What was the most important thing you learned during this class?" and "What important question remains unanswered?" Students then write their responses on index cards or half-sheets of scrap paper—hence the "Half-Sheet Response"—and hand them in.

PURPOSE   The great advantage of Minute Papers is that they provide manageable amounts of timely and useful feedback for a minimal investment of time and energy. By asking students what they see as the most significant things they are learning, and what their major questions are, faculty can quickly check how well those students are learning what they are teaching. That feedback can help teachers decide whether any mid-course corrections or changes are needed and, if so, what kinds of instructional adjustments to make. Getting the instructor's feedback on their Minute Papers helps students learn how experts in a given discipline distinguish the major points from the details. The Minute Paper also ensures that students' questions will be raised, and in many cases answered, in time to facilitate further learning.

Despite its simplicity, the Minute Paper assesses more than mere recall. To select the most important or significant information, learners must first evaluate what they recall. Then, to come up with a question, students must self-assess—asking themselves how well they understand what they have just heard or studied.

RELATED TEACHING GOALS

Develop ability to synthesize and integrate information and ideas (TGI Goal 5)

Develop ability to think holistically: to see the whole as well as the parts (TGI Goal 6)

Improve skill at paying attention (TGI Goal 9)

Develop ability to concentrate (TGI Goal 10)

Improve listening skills (TGI Goal 12)

Develop appropriate study skills, strategies, and habits (TGI Goal 16)

Learn terms and facts of this subject (TGI Goal 18)

Learn concepts and theories in this subject (TGI Goal 19)

SUGGESTIONS FOR USE

Minute Papers are probably most useful in lecture or lecture/discussion courses, although the technique can be easily adapted to other settings. For example, the Minute Paper can also be used to assess what students have learned from a lab session, study-group meeting, field trip, homework assignment, videotape, or exam. Minute Papers work well at the end or the beginning of class sessions, serving either as warm-up or wrap-up activities. Like other simple techniques in this section, Minute Papers can be used frequently in courses that regularly present students with a great deal of new information. Because it is quick to administer and easy to analyze, the Minute Paper is well suited for use in large classes.

EXAMPLES

From European History: Renaissance to Modern Times (History)

At the end of an exquisitely prepared, well-illustrated lecture on the Renaissance entitled "Why Italy?" the veteran history professor decided to use a new feedback technique she had heard about from a younger colleague. She passed out small, blank index cards and then raised the projection screen to reveal two questions, which she had written on the chalkboard before class. She told the students that she wanted thoughtful, brief, and legible answers, but no names. Then she read the two questions aloud: "What is the single most significant reason Italy became a—if not the—center of the Renaissance?" "What one question puzzles you most about Italy's role in the Renaissance?"

After five minutes, the history professor collected the index cards, told the students that she would respond to them at the next meeting, and dismissed the class. Reading through the forty-plus cards in her office, she was pleased that many of the students offered reasons she had underlined in her lecture. For this professor, acceptable reasons for Italy's central role in the Renaissance included its geographical proximity to Asia and Africa, its political organization into city-states, its historical links to Greece and Rome, and its highly developed mercantile economies.

She was irritated, on the other hand, because some students insisted on confusing cause and effect, reasoning that Italy became a Renaissance center because it had so many great artists and learned men. A few students even seemed to think that the Renaissance was created by Marco Polo, Leonardo da Vinci, Michelangelo, or the Medicis—a "Great Man" view of history that annoyed her even more!

How on earth, she wondered, could these students have missed the main points of her excellent, crystal-clear lecture?

She was so delighted with their questions, however, that she soon got over her irritation and began to reshape her outline for the next class meeting. On the whole, they were much more thoughtful questions than students asked in class. She prepared an overhead transparency that categorized the students' responses as Major Causes, Minor Causes, Effects, Actors, or To Be Discussed, this last category for answers she could not fit in the other categories. She then listed five questions that had been asked by more than two students and tried to answer them by referring to information the class had provided. Although her response to the Minute Papers and the ensuing discussion devoured one-third of the following class, she considered it time well spent. The class's excellent performance on the midterm essay question dealing with causes of the Renaissance was further evidence that her personalized Minute Paper had improved their learning.

From Introductory Statistics (Statistics)

Intrigued by a demonstration of the Minute Paper during a faculty development workshop at his college, this young mathematics instructor decided to adapt the technique for use in his intensive Introductory Statistics course. Although he liked the format, he felt that asking for only one significant point was too limiting, and decided to ask students to come up with several. Consequently, a few minutes before the end of each lecture, he asked students to list the five most important points from that session, along with one or two important questions they had. He then collected the responses and quickly read them after class, making a list of the "important points" and questions and tallying how often each item was repeated.

At first, the variety of points that students listed as important astounded the statistics instructor. He found that, as a group, his thirty-five students came up with as many as twenty different important points from the same lecture. Many of the points they listed were ones he considered details; others were distortions of things he had said; still others were points he was sure he had never mentioned at all! The bewildering variety of responses on Minute Papers from the first few class meetings convinced him of the need to teach students how to tell the "wheat from the chaff."

He began by listing the ten or twelve most common responses on the board before class. He then took the first five to ten minutes of class to explain the relative importance of these points and their relationships to one another. He also let students know which points were definitely not related. In the course of these "feedback sessions," he could often weave in responses to two or three commonly asked questions as well. The Minute Paper responses convinced him that his students needed a more explicit road map than he had been providing. Therefore, in addition to the list of responses to the preceding lecture, he wrote his own list of most important points for that day. With both lists on the board, he could make connections between one class and the next graphically clear.

After a month of following the Minute Paper at the end of one class with a feedback session at the beginning of the next, the average total number of different "important points" had dropped from nearly twenty to eight or nine. That was a level of variation he could live with. Repeated use of the Minute Paper helped his students learn to listen more carefully and focus more effectively during lectures. The CAT helped the instructor realize the importance of being explicit in teaching statistics to students with very little or no previous knowledge of the subject.

From Writing for Magazines and Newspapers (Journalism)

As she neared the end of the hour, the journalism instructor suddenly realized that she had spent far too much time on one topic, slighting two other important themes she had planned to develop in her lecture on the life cycle of magazines. She felt guilty of self-indulgence, since the topic she had lingered on—the death of general-interest magazines—was one she found particularly fascinating. It was clear to her that she had been carried away in her enthusiasm and had pounded the same points home too many times.

Although she was certain that she could predict their responses, the journalism instructor went ahead with the Minute Paper anyway. She had established the use of CATs as part of the classroom routine from the first day of class and did not want to break the pattern. So she handed out squares of scrap paper and asked students to write down the three most important things they had learned from her lecture, and one important question they would like to pursue further.

To her astonishment, very few of the Minute Papers even mentioned the topic to which she had devoted most of the lecture: the demise of weekly magazines such as the *Saturday Evening Post* and *Life*. Instead, most of the students had focused on the rise of the more specialized, current magazines they were familiar with and on her few comments about getting published. In essence, her students had paid scant attention to information the instructor worried she had overstressed. When she asked why a major portion of the lecture was poorly represented in their Minute Papers, the students explained that they considered it background information—interesting but not very relevant history. To them, the most important information was that which they thought might help them succeed as professional writers. This response made the journalism teacher realize that she should continually point out the connections between the content of her course and the "real world" of journalism and the job market.

STEP-BY-STEP PROCEDURE

1. Decide first what you want to focus on and, as a consequence, when to administer the Minute Paper. If you want to focus on students' understanding of a lecture, the last few minutes of class may be the best time. If your focus is on a prior homework assignment, however, the first few minutes may be more appropriate.

2. Using the two basic questions from the "Description" above as starting points, write Minute Paper prompts that fit your course and students. Try out your Minute Paper on a colleague or teaching assistant before using it in class.

3. Plan to set aside five to ten minutes of your next class to use the technique, as well as time later to discuss the results.

4. Before class, write one or, at the most, two Minute Paper questions on the chalkboard or prepare an overhead transparency.

5. At a convenient time, hand out index cards or half-sheets of scrap paper.

6. Unless there is a very good reason to know who wrote what, direct students to leave their names off the papers or cards.

7. Let the students know how much time they will have (two to five minutes per question is usually enough), what kinds of answers you want (words, phrases, or short sentences), and when they can expect your feedback.

TURNING THE DATA YOU COLLECT INTO USEFUL INFORMATION

Simply tabulating the responses and making note of any useful comments is often all the analysis needed. Consider saving Minute Papers from early in the term to compare with responses at midterm and later. Comparing responses over time can allow you to see changes and development in the clarity of student writing and thoughtfulness of answers.

IDEAS FOR ADAPTING AND EXTENDING THIS CAT

Use only half of the Minute Paper. That is, ask students either for the most important point(s) or for their question(s). These "Half-Minute Papers" are the most common adaptations because they make the assessment process even simpler and quicker. The Muddiest Point (CAT 7) is a particularly creative example of such an adaptation.

Change the wording to make the prompt more appropriate and specific. For example, instead of asking students to identify the most significant point, ask them for one of the following: the most illuminating example, the most powerful image, the most convincing argument or counterargument, the most surprising information, the most memorable character, or the most disturbing idea.

Allow students a few extra minutes to compare and discuss their Minute Paper responses with their classmates in pairs or small groups.

Assign students to small groups. Give each group, in turn, the opportunity to suggest questions for the Minute Papers and let the members of the group analyze and present the results to the whole class.

PROS

Minute Papers provide immediate mid-course feedback to teachers and allow quick response to students.

This advantage is especially important in college classrooms, where many issues and questions have limited life spans and time is always in short supply.

The responses—even from a very large class—can be read, tabulated, and analyzed quickly and with limited effort.

Faculty using the Minute Paper demonstrate respect for and interest in student feedback, thereby encouraging active listening and engagement, which are often lacking in large classes.

Feedback on the Minute Paper allows individual students to compare their responses with those of the class as a whole.

CONS

If Minute Papers are overused or poorly used, students will begin to view the technique as a gimmick or a pro forma exercise in polling.

It is more difficult than it may seem to prepare questions that can be immediately and clearly comprehended and quickly answered.

CAVEATS

Not all learning experiences can be meaningfully assessed by an instrument that asks learners to note significant points or remaining questions. In other words, this technique is flexible but not universally applicable.

When students seem to confuse trivial details with significant themes, or pose questions that you have already answered several times, remind yourself that they see the material through different eyes, hear it with different ears, and make sense of it differently than you do. Hold off responding until the irritation has faded. Accepting their starting points is often a necessary step in getting them to the desired learning goal.

Responding to Minute Papers often takes longer than planned, because questions lead to further questions. Build in some flexibility but set clear limits for the time you will spend on feedback.

To temper expectations and prevent individual disappointment, let the class know in advance that you may not be able to comment on every important point and question submitted. It is often wise to promise less feedback than you think you can deliver. Let students know in advance, for example, that you will respond to the three most commonly raised points and questions from their Minute Papers, even though you hope to do more.

REFERENCES AND RESOURCES

Wilson (1986) describes the Minute Paper in an article on using feedback from students and consultants to improve college teaching. The term *half-sheet response* comes from an article on a similar technique by Weaver and Cotrell (1985). Of course, versions of the Minute Paper, and many other CATs, probably have been invented and reinvented time and again by instructors in various colleges at different times.

Muddiest Point

Estimated Levels of Time and Energy Required for:

Faculty to prepare to use this CAT	**LOW**
Students to respond to the assessment	**LOW**
Faculty to analyze the data collected	**LOW**

DESCRIPTION

The Muddiest Point is just about the simplest Classroom Assessment Technique imaginable. It is also remarkably efficient, since it provides a high information return for a very low investment of time and energy. The technique consists of asking students to jot down a quick response to one question: "What was the muddiest point in _____?" The focus of the Muddiest Point assessment might be a lecture, a discussion, a homework assignment, a play, or a film.

PURPOSE

As its name suggests, the Muddiest Point technique provides information on what students find least clear or most confusing about a particular lesson or topic. Faculty use that feedback to discover which points are most difficult for students to learn and to guide their teaching decisions about which topics to emphasize and how much time to spend on each. In response to this CAT, learners must quickly identify what they do not understand and articulate those muddy points. Consequently, even though the technique is extremely simple to administer, responding to it requires some higher-order thinking.

RELATED TEACHING GOALS

Improve skill at paying attention (TGI Goal 9)
Develop ability to concentrate (TGI Goal 10)
Improve listening skills (TGI Goal 12)
Develop appropriate study skills, strategies, and habits (TGI Goal 16)
Learn terms and facts of this subject (TGI Goal 18)
Learn concepts and theories in this subject (TGI Goal 19)

SUGGESTIONS FOR USE

While this technique can be used in virtually any setting, it is particularly well suited to large, lower-division classes. Since students' responses to the Muddiest Point question usually consist of a few words or phrases, a teacher can read and sort a great many in a few minutes. The Muddiest Point question should be posed at the end of a lecture, at the close of a discussion or presentation, or immediately after a reading assignment. This CAT can be used quite frequently in classes where a large amount of new information is presented each session—such as mathematics, statistics, economics, health sciences, and the natural sciences—probably because there is a steady stream of possible "muddy points." On the other hand, the Muddiest Point is best used sparingly in courses where the emphasis is on integrating, synthesizing, and evaluating information.

EXAMPLES

From the Decline and Fall of the Soviet Union (International Relations/ Political Science)

This professor used the Muddiest Point in his senior-level honors course to assess students' understanding of a prerecorded videotape. The videotape was a recording of an hour-long speech on the reasons for the collapse of the Soviet Union. The speech had been delivered by one of the professor's eminent colleagues to foreign policy consultants and journalists in Washington, D.C. At the conclusion of the tape, the international relations professor asked his eighteen students to write the "muddiest point" they found in the videotape.

As the professor read through the responses, he noted that almost half of his students mentioned the same "muddy point": the videotaped speaker's thesis that "imported inflation" seriously undercut the Soviet economy in the 1980s. Since the instructor regarded that thesis as the most important and original element of his colleague's analysis, he was pleased to discover the students' confusion right away. To clear it up, he prepared a detailed explanation of that critical point, which he presented during the next class meeting.

From Fundamentals of English (English as a Second Language)

After two lectures and related homework assignments on English pronoun usage, the new ESL instructor decided to try the Muddiest Point technique. So, just before class ended, she asked students to write down the "muddiest point" in their minds about pronoun usage. When several students quickly raised their hands to ask what she meant by a "muddy point," she realized that even widely used colloquialisms can stymie nonnative English speakers. As soon as she explained that "muddy" in this phrase meant unclear, confusing, or hard to understand, they were able to carry out the assessment.

Later, shuffling through the index cards containing their responses, the instructor was dismayed and disappointed by what she read. Although she had worked hard to explain the pronominal system on a conceptual level, stressing what pronouns do in English and why it is important to use them correctly, the muddy points that students mentioned were virtually all about very specific, and sometimes rather minor, rules of usage—such as the difference between "who" and "whom."

Feeling that her class had failed to see the forest for the trees, the ESL instructor asked one of her veteran colleagues for advice. Her colleague assured her that the students' responses were quite normal, given their low level of experience with and knowledge of English. The veteran teacher reminded the new faculty member to keep her audience in mind. Teaching the pronominal system conceptually makes sense if students are English-speaking linguistics majors or future English language teachers, but is less useful with beginning or intermediate language learners.

After that conversation, the new ESL teacher again looked at the muddy points. This time she realized that she had been teaching about pronouns as she had been taught in graduate linguistics courses, rather than thinking about what her ESL students needed to learn and how they could best learn it. That realization caused her to change her approach to the next few lessons. Specifically, she provided many more examples and much more practice, helping students move from the specifics to the more general concepts and back to specifics—and helping them see the connections.

From General Chemistry (Chemistry)

From the first week of class, students in this general education science course had been responding to the Muddiest Point. Now, several weeks into the course, the professor used this CAT to assess the students' understanding of a lecture on enthalpy and entropy. The most commonly mentioned muddy point concerned the difference between enthalpy of activation and entropy of activation. Other students mentioned the difference between enthalpy of formation and enthalpy of activation. These responses let the professor know that the students had not firmly grasped the differences between entropy and enthalpy and that many of them probably did not understand either principle in isolation. Looking back on her lecture, she realized it had probably contained too much detail and too little differentiation of concepts—resulting in highly "entropic" learning.

STEP-BY-STEP PROCEDURE

1. Determine what you want feedback on: the entire class session or one self-contained segment? A lecture, a discussion, a presentation?

2. If you are using the technique in class, reserve a few minutes at the end of the class session. Leave enough time to ask the question, to allow students to respond, and to collect their responses by the usual ending time.

3. Let students know beforehand how much time they will have to respond and what use you will make of their responses.

4. Pass out slips of paper or index cards for students to write on.

5. Collect the responses as or before students leave. Stationing yourself at the door and collecting "muddy points" as students file out is one way; leaving a "muddy points" collection box by the exit is another.

6. Respond to the students' feedback during the next class meeting or as soon as possible afterward.

TURNING THE DATA YOU COLLECT INTO USEFUL INFORMATION

As with everything else about this technique, data analysis can and should be kept very simple. Quickly read through at least half of the responses, looking for common types of muddy points. Then go back through all the responses and sort them into piles—several piles containing groups of related muddy points, and one "catch-all" pile made up of one-of-a-kind responses. You may want to count the responses in each group before you decide which to deal with. Or you may want to group together the muddy points that concern facts and principles, those that concern concepts, and those that concern skills.

IDEAS FOR ADAPTING AND EXTENDING THIS CAT

Ask students to identify the muddiest points in a homework assignment or an out-of-class reading and to turn in their responses at the next class meeting. For example, ask them to list the three muddiest points in a chapter or a case that they have been assigned to read.

Ask students to read each other's drafts of writing assignments and to point out the muddiest points in those drafts.

When students are familiar with the material and are relatively articulate, ask them to indicate the muddiest point and then to explain briefly what it was about that point that they found "muddy."

At each class meeting, ask a few different students to categorize and summarize the data and to present the results—and perhaps even their responses—at the beginning of the next class.

Use other CATs (such as Directed Paraphrasing, Memory Matrix, or Concept Maps) to check later on how much clearer the most critical muddy points have become since you responded to them.

Let students know that some of your exam questions will concern the muddy points that you have responded to in class.

PROS

The Muddiest Point is not only quick, simple, and easy to administer; it also requires very little preparation. This is one of the few CATs you can successfully use on the spur of the moment.

For students who are hesitant to ask questions in class, this technique is a safe alternative. For students who are lost, it can be a "lifeline."

This technique can give the instructor a "snapshot" diagnosis of what students are finding difficult to learn. As a result, the teacher can focus subsequent lessons and assignments much more accurately and effectively.

This technique enables teachers to see the material through their students' eyes and reminds them of the range of intellectual and perceptual diversity present in each classroom.

If students are regularly asked to identify the "muddiest point," they tend to pay more attention to how well they are understanding the relevant session or assignment because they expect to be asked about it. This expectancy can lead, on the simplest level, to more care in listening and studying. Because of the nature of the question, however, this technique also promotes introspection and self-assessment.

This is a simple technique that students can easily internalize, making self-assessment a regular part of their own classroom and study routines. Students can learn to habitually ask themsleves, "What was the muddiest point in _____?" whether or not other instructors ask them for such feedback.

CONS

As Mosteller (1989) points out, there are drawbacks to asking students to focus only on what they don't understand. Such an emphasis can undermine both the students' and the teacher's motivation and sense of self-efficacy. To restore some balance, teachers need to focus on what students do understand as well as on the muddy points.

It can be disconcerting to realize that even your best-prepared, most lucid lecture or lab will be misunderstood or poorly understood by some of your students.

Initially, a number of students may have difficulty explaining, or even naming, what it is that they don't understand. Becoming effective self-assessors takes time and practice, and you may not wish to develop that skill on class time.

As students become more adept at identifying and explaining the points they find "muddiest," they become more likely to raise difficult questions that you may be unable to answer on the spot.

CAVEATS

Don't become angry or disappointed when students identify something as a "muddy point" that you're positive you presented with absolute clarity. At least, don't respond to the class until you have dealt with those feelings. (Remember: don't ask if you don't really want to know.)

Don't spend so much class time responding to "muddy points" from past sessions that you risk losing the momentum of your course.

Don't give students the impression that all confusions and questions can be cleared up in a few minutes — or even a few days. Make it clear that some points are "muddier" than others and that a few are real landslides that will take a lot of digging out!

REFERENCES AND RESOURCES

In an informative and thoughtful journal article, Mosteller (1989) describes how he developed and used the Muddiest Point in his large undergraduate statistics course at Harvard. To request copies of the journal (*The Journal of the Harvard-Danforth Center*) or reprints of the Mosteller article, contact:

The Derek Bok Center for Teaching and Learning
318 Science Center
Harvard University
Cambridge, Mass. 02138

See also Cottell (1991, pp. 50–51) for a clear and humorous example of the Muddiest Point applied to accounting. In this example, the author refers to the CAT as an adaptation of the Minute Paper.

Assessing Skill
in Analysis and
Critical Thinking

Each of the five techniques in this section is designed to assess students' skills at analyzing, or "breaking down," information, questions, or problems in order to understand them more fully and solve them more effectively. These analytical and critical-thinking skills are examples of procedural learning, learning the "how" rather than the "what."

These techniques make progressively greater demands on students. The Categorizing Grid, for example, simply requires students to sort information into the appropriate conceptual categories—a very low level of analysis. The Defining Features Matrix raises the ante a bit, by asking students to notice and respond to discriminating features. Content, Form, and Function Outlines assess students' skill at analyzing a message by unwinding its interwoven strands to isolate the threads of "what, how, and why." The Pro and Con Grid elicits and assesses evaluation—an important component of cricital thinking—as students identify the advantages and disadvantages of a given plan or idea. The most ambitious technique in this group is the Analytic Memo, an assessment that stimulates students to read analytically, evaluate, and write concisely.

CLASSROOM ASSESSMENT TECHNIQUE

8

Categorizing Grid

Estimated Levels of Time and Energy Required for:

Faculty to prepare to use this CAT	**LOW**
Students to respond to the assessment	**LOW**
Faculty to analyze the data collected	**LOW**

DESCRIPTION The Categorizing Grid is the paper-and-pencil equivalent of sorting objects in a warehouse and putting like ones together in the right bins. Students are presented with a grid containing two or three important categories—superordinate concepts they have been studying—along with a scrambled list of subordinate terms, images, equations, or other items that belong in one or another of those categories. Learners are then given a very limited time to sort the subordinate terms into the correct categories on the grid.

PURPOSE The Categorizing Grid provides faculty with a snapshot of the students' "sorting rules." This feedback allows the teacher to determine quickly whether, how, and how well students understand "what goes with what." The Categorizing Grid prompts students to make explicit the implicit rules they are using to categorize information in their memories. As a consequence, it gives learners the opportunity to rethink and revise their categorizing rules. By making these implicit ways of organizing explicit, students and teachers can gain more control over what is remembered, how it is remembered, and how well it can be recalled when needed.

RELATED TEACHING GOALS Develop analytic skills (TGI Goal 2)
Develop ability to draw reasonable inferences from observations (TGI Goal 4)
Improve memory skills (TGI Goal 11)
Develop appropriate study skills, strategies, and habits (TGI Goal 16)
Learn terms and facts of this subject (TGI Goal 18)
Learn concepts and theories in this subject (TGI Goal 19)

SUGGESTIONS FOR USE Thanks to its simplicity, the Categorizing Grid can be adapted to courses in most disciplines and easily used in classes of all sizes. Given the skills it assesses, this CAT is probably most useful in introductory-level courses, where students are most likely to be learning the categorizing rules of the discipline.

EXAMPLES

From Colors: Theories, Systems, and Applications (Cosmetology)

> Students in this vocational education course had read about the "season" system of color matching and had seen a short videotape demonstrating how this system is used to help clients match the colors of clothes and makeup to their hair and skin colors. To assess the students' understanding of which colors go with which "seasons"—four categories of skin and hair coloration—this instructor used a Categorizing Grid. The grid simply consisted of a large rectangle divided into four smaller ones, labeled for the four seasons. Students were given a list of twenty-four color names and asked to write them in the appropriate boxes for the seasons they matched.
>
> To her dismay, many of the students did poorly on the assessment. After discussing the feedback with them, she began to suspect that many of them either did not know the color names well or could not associate them with the tones they represented. She knew that many of her students were strong visual learners but poor readers. To test her hypothesis, she constructed a second Categorizing Grid, this one a large poster with pictures of models representing the "season" types. She also made a poster with samples of the twenty-four colors next to their names. The feedback on this second assessment bore out her hypothesis: most of the students did very well in visually categorizing the colors with the "seasons." The instructor followed up by explicitly helping students connect the verbal and visual information in that and subsequent lessons.

From Comparative Animal Physiology (Zoology/Biology)

> At the end of two weeks of work on mammals, this zoology professor decided to assess his class's skill at categorizing mammals visually. He did the assessment in two stages, projecting numbered slides and directing students to write the numbers in the correct boxes on mimeographed grids. For the first assessment, he used a grid divided into boxes for the three mammalian subclasses: Prototheria, Metatheria, and Eutheria. He projected thirty slides of animals, with the examples more or less evenly divided among subclasses. He was pleased but not surprised to see that the class did quite well, with only a few confusions here and there. At the next class meeting, he asked students to categorize thirty-five slides of members of subclass Eutheria into seven of its major orders. Results on the second assessment were very uneven. About half the class did extremely well again; the other half, rather poorly. The professor went over the results of both assessments quickly and suggested the most critical areas for review, reminding students that the midterm would include questions requiring exactly this sort of categorizing.

From Introduction to Management Theory (Business/Management)

> To get an idea of how well her students were understanding the distinctions between the concepts of Theory X and Theory Y management (MacGregor, 1960, especially chaps. 3–4), this business professor decided to use the Categorizing Grid. She began by jotting down a list of

about a dozen terms and short phrases she associated with each concept. She made sure that each item clearly related to one theory or the other, and she discarded those that could be categorized in either camp. She then made an overhead transparency with the concepts, Theory X and Theory Y, in large letters at the top, followed by a list of the two dozen terms in more or less random order. In class, she gave the students five minutes to sort the terms into two lists under the two concepts and then collected their responses.

By quickly reading through the responses, the instructor realized that the students had focused almost entirely on the human-nature and motivational aspects of these two theories, neglecting the managerial and organizational consequences. In other words, students had little trouble categorizing the terms that related directly to Theory X or Theory Y in the abstract, but they did less well with those items related to applications. Since she especially wanted the students to remember possible applications, that information gave her a clear sense of what to stress in subsequent class meetings.

STEP-BY-STEP PROCEDURE

1. Select two or three related categories that are particularly useful for organizing the information presented in class. Make a list of several good examples of items in each category. Review your list to make sure that all items clearly belong only to one category and that all items are ones students can be expected to recognize from class or homework.

2. Make a grid by drawing a large rectangle and dividing it into as many rectangles of equal size as you have categories. You can either hand out copies of the Categorizing Grid or draw it and have students copy it themselves. With simple grids, the latter is more economical and probably no more time-consuming than passing out copies.

3. The items that students are to categorize can be listed, in scrambled order, next to the grid on the copies or on the chalkboard, or they can be projected from an overhead transparency. Alternately, you can use real objects or slides as the examples to be categorized.

TURNING THE DATA YOU COLLECT INTO USEFUL INFORMATION

In most cases, you can simply check the grids to see whether students have placed the right items in the correct boxes, making note of those items that are most often miscategorized or left out entirely. Look for patterns in the incorrect responses that can help you see which kinds of examples, and/or which categories, are most difficult for students to deal with.

IDEAS FOR ADAPTING AND EXTENDING THIS CAT

Ask students to explain briefly why the items they have placed in a given category belong together.

Provide students with the categories but have them come up with their own lists of category members.

To assess their knowledge of superordinate terms, provide students with grids containing a few examples of category members but no category names.

Move from broad, general categories to more specific subcategories as students demonstrate their mastery.

Use the Defining Features Matrix (CAT 9) as a follow-up to assess student understanding of the features that define category membership.

To assess the students' understanding and categorization of the "fence straddlers" or "in-between" cases that exist in many categorizing schemes, draw a Categorizing Grid with dotted lines or buffer zones between categories.

PROS

The Categorizing Grid is a quick, simple procedure that assesses students' basic analytic and organizing skills and also reinforces effective categorization and recall.

Practice in this simple CAT provides students with one more tool they can use in studying other subjects.

CONS

Unless there are challenging items or categories in the grid, or the instructor helps students see the logic behind the categorization scheme, this technique may simply assess rote memory.

CAVEATS

The categories that you put forth on the grid, although correct, may not be identical to those the student is using to organize the material. This CAT does not help you assess a student's memory organization schemes if they are very different from those common to the discipline.

Defining Features Matrix

Estimated Levels of Time and Energy Required for:

Faculty to prepare to use this CAT	**MEDIUM**
Students to respond to the assessment	**LOW**
Faculty to analyze the data collected	**LOW**

DESCRIPTION The Defining Features Matrix requires students to categorize concepts according to the presence (+) or absence (−) of important defining features, thereby providing data on their analytic reading and thinking skills.

PURPOSE The Defining Features Matrix is designed to assess students' skills at categorizing important information according to a given set of critical defining features. It allows faculty to see quickly how well students can distinguish between apparently similar concepts, and it helps learners identify and make explicit the critical distinctions between such concepts.

RELATED TEACHING GOALS
Develop analytic skills (TGI Goal 2)
Develop ability to draw reasonable inferences from observations (TGI Goal 4)
Improve memory skills (TGI Goal 11)
Improve listening skills (TGI Goal 12)
Improve reading skills (TGI Goal 14)
Develop appropriate study skills, strategies, and habits (TGI Goal 16)
Learn terms and facts of this subject (TGI Goal 18)
Learn concepts and theories in this subject (TGI Goal 19)

SUGGESTIONS FOR USE The Defining Features Matrix is best used in courses that require students to distinguish between closely related or seemingly similar items or concepts. Some disciplines in which this skill is particularly important are biology, geography, chemistry, astronomy, and medicine. Since it is in a matrix format, student responses to this CAT are very easy to score and evaluate. For this reason, the Defining Features Matrix can be administered quickly and easily, even in very large classes.

An Example from Classroom Research

The Defining Features Matrix shown as Exhibit 7.4 draws some distinctions between the generally accepted model of institutional assessment in higher education and our model of Classroom Assessment.

Exhibit 7.4. Defining Features of Institutional and Classroom Assessment.

Features	Institutional Assessment	Classroom Assessment
Teacher-designed and directed	–	+
Large sample sizes required	+	–
Sophisticated statistical data analysis required	+	–
Standardized and validated instruments preferred	+	–
Focused on classroom teaching and learning	–	+
Replicable and comparable	+	–
Useful to students and teachers	–	+
Useful to administrators	+	–
Aims to improve quality of higher education	+	+

From an Introduction to Psychology (Psychology)

After lectures and assigned readings on Freudian and behaviorist views of human psychology, this instructor constructed a Defining Features Matrix form to assess students' ability to distinguish between these two schools.

From Comparative Political Systems (Political Science)

This professor used a Defining Features Matrix to assess how well his students understood the detailed differences among the federal systems of the United States, Canada, and Germany, after they had read chapters on each of the three systems.

From History and Development of the Romance Languages (Linguistics)

To assess how clearly students understood the surface differences between modern Spanish and Portuguese, two closely related Romance languages, this linguistics professor created a Defining Features Matrix focused on the characteristic syntactic, morphological, and phonological contrasts.

From Human Evolution (Biology)

Students in this general education science course were assigned several magazine and journal articles on recent discoveries and theories about Neanderthals and their relation to *Homo sapiens*. To find out how closely students had read the material, and how well they understood the generally agreed-upon differences between modern humans and the Neanderthals, this biology professor created a Defining Features Matrix. The matrix contained features related not only to anatomy but also to likely cultural and social differences and similarities.

STEP-BY-STEP PROCEDURE

1. Focus the matrix on two or three important concepts that are similar enough to confuse your students.

2. Determine which features of these concepts are most critical for the students to recognize.

3. Make a list of defining features that each concept either clearly does or does not possess. After drawing up that list, you may want to add a limited number of shared features.

4. Sketch out a matrix with features listed down the left side and concepts across the top, or vice versa.

5. Check to see that each cell in the matrix can be reasonably responded to with a plus or a minus sign or a "yes" or "no." If you cannot give an either/or response to the cell, that feature probably should be removed from the matrix.

6. Draw up a finished matrix and give copies to your students or, if it is very simple, have them copy it off the chalkboard.

7. Clearly explain the purpose of the matrix and the directions for filling it in, as well as the time limit for doing so.

TURNING THE DATA YOU COLLECT INTO USEFUL INFORMATION

It is relatively easy to compare the students' matrices with your master copy. You can scan them one by one, indicating incorrect responses on each student's matrix with a slash or an X and, at the same time, keeping a running tally of incorrect responses on a larger copy of the matrix with empty cells. (By investing a little more preparation time, you can create an answer format that can be scanned electronically.) Or you can simply count all the plusses and minuses for each cell and tally them on an oversized copy. Look for those cells where several students made the wrong choice and see whether there are patterns in the errors. Are students paying more attention to certain features than to others? Are they failing to notice defining differences of specific kinds that would be obvious to an expert?

IDEAS FOR ADAPTING AND EXTENDING THIS CAT

Present students with a sample Defining Features Matrix on a familiar, course-related topic. Then ask them to create their own matrices to define concepts or items related to a different important topic covered in the course.

Work up to matrices that allow for more than simple binary responses in the cells. For example, for certain topics, the features might be more appropriately categorized as "always present," "often present," "rarely present," and "never present."

Ask each student to write brief statements explaining what the configuration of data—that is, the pattern of responses—in his or her completed matrix means.

Ask each student to write brief statements explaining what the configuration of data—that is, the pattern of responses—in his or her completed matrix means.

PROS The Defining Features Matrix is a quick way to check students' skills at distinguishing between items or concepts that are easily confused and to pinpoint any areas of confusion. Once those confusing areas are isolated, students and teachers can more effectively clear them up.

It helps students and teachers break down (analyze) complex comparisons and contrasts into more manageable component parts.

It gives students practice in using a simple, powerful, and highly transferable approach to categorizing data.

CONS This technique requires careful and thoughtful preparation and therefore may be too time-consuming for some teachers. (In compensation, it is easy to score.)

Not all information can be easily or accurately expressed with only a plus or minus. Many important definitions depend on differences in level or degree, rather than on the absolute presence or absence of a feature.

Unless students understand that the purpose of the matrix is to help them see important patterns of defining features in the data, it can easily become a low-level assessment of their recall of isolated facts.

CAVEATS Try to keep the features in the matrix parallel in kind or in level of importance.

To avoid overload, don't include more than two or three concepts or seven to ten defining features in the matrix, at least in the first few applications of this technique.

REFERENCES AND RESOURCES For a discussion of the use of the Defining Features Matrix and other organizational devices in integrated reading and writing lessons, see Cunningham and Cunningham (1987).

Pro and Con Grid

Estimated Levels of Time and Energy Required for:

Faculty to prepare to use this CAT	**LOW**
Students to respond to the assessment	**LOW**
Faculty to analyze the data collected	**LOW to MEDIUM**

DESCRIPTION

At one time or another, most people have jotted down quick lists of pros and cons to help them think more clearly about a pressing decision. The Pro and Con Grid turns that familiar decision-making exercise into a simple Classroom Assessment Technique with many possible applications.

PURPOSE

The Pro and Con Grid gives faculty a quick overview of a class's analysis of the pros and cons, costs and benefits, or advantages and disadvantages of an issue of mutual concern. Even a cursory reading of students' lists of pros and cons provides important information on the depth and breadth of their analyses and on their capacity for objectivity. This assessment forces students to go beyond their first reactions, to search for at least two sides to the issue in question, and to weigh the value of competing claims.

RELATED TEACHING GOALS

Develop analytic skills (TGI Goal 2)
Develop ability to draw reasonable inferences from observations (TGI Goal 4)
Learn to evaluate methods and materials in this subject (TGI Goal 24)
Develop an informed concern about contemporary social issues (TGI Goal 28)
Develop capacity to make informed ethical choices (TGI Goal 35)
Develop a commitment to one's own values (TGI Goal 46)
Develop capacity to think for oneself (TGI Goal 51)
Develop capacity to make wise decisions (TGI Goal 52)

SUGGESTIONS FOR USE

The Pro and Con Grid can be put to good use in any course where questions of value are an explicit part of the syllabus; specifically, this assessment works well in many humanities, social science, and public policy courses. It can also be used to assess students' awareness of potential costs and benefits or of alternate technical solutions to the same problem; used in these ways, this technique can be applied in many science and mathematics courses, as well as in preprofessional and vocational training.

The brief examples below are meant to give an idea of the range of issues that can be used as focal points for the Pro and Con Grid.

From Introduction to English Literature (English)

To first-year students reading Shakespeare's *Hamlet*: Imagine that you are Hamlet, the day after the encounter with your father's ghost. Make a list of pros and cons of murdering your stepfather, Claudius. (Three pros and three cons will be enough.)

From Ethics in Anthropological Fieldwork (Anthropology)

Several Native American tribes have demanded that universities and museums return tribal objects and human remains taken from their lands by anthropologists and archaeologists. Suppose you are the curator of Native American collections at the city's natural history museum. Come up with a balanced three-minute report for the museum's board of directors on the potential advantages and disadvantages of agreeing to return these objects and remains.

From Personal Financial Planning (Business/Management)

After reading a short case outlining the financial situation of a two-career couple, quickly list the potential costs and benefits to these two individuals of filing their federal income taxes jointly. (You should come up with at least three "costs" and at least three "benefits."

From U.S. Electoral Politics (Political Science)

In the wake of the last federal census, the state legislature has just issued a draft plan for redistricting. Study this plan carefully, as though you were the governor's special assistant for legislative relations. Then write a short list of political costs and benefits that the governor should consider before deciding whether to support this plan.

From Seminar in Bridge and Highway Design (Civil Engineering)

The seminar has just studied two proposed designs for a new suspension bridge. The second design proposes a structure that is significantly more massive and more rigid than the first. Briefly list three to five major advantages and disadvantages you see in the second design.

From Issues in Bioethics (Biology/Philosophy)

You have read several recent articles on the current debate about patenting human genetic material. From your viewpoint as consumers, what are the principal pros and cons of allowing the patenting of genes? Come up with about six of each.

From Contemporary Catholicism (Theology)

> For some time now, certain critics within and outside of the Roman Catholic Church have argued that priests should be allowed to marry and have children. In responding to this assessment exercise, consider the pros and cons of abolishing the requirement of celibacy from the perspective of the church as an organization. List about five important potential advantages and an equal number of disadvantages.

STEP-BY-STEP PROCEDURE

1. Focus on a decision, a judgment, a dilemma, or an issue that has teaching and learning implications in your discipline and for your students.

2. Write out a prompt that will elicit thoughtful pros and cons in relation to this issue or dilemma. You may wish to indicate a specific point of view that students should adopt in coming up with their lists. Doing so will make the pros and cons more comparable.

3. Let students know how many pros and cons you expect and how they are to be expressed. Are parallel lists of words and phrases adequate, or should the pros and cons be expressed in sentences?

TURNING THE DATA YOU COLLECT INTO USEFUL INFORMATION

Start by listing the points that students have put forth as pros and as cons and doing a simple frequency count. Which points are most often mentioned? Compare the students' grids with yours. Have they omitted some points that you expected them to mention? Have they included some points that you regard as extraneous? How balanced are the two "sides" of the grid? These are all possible matters to report on and to discuss when you give the class feedback.

IDEAS FOR ADAPTING AND EXTENDING THIS CAT

Assess students' ability to imagine and list pros and cons on the same issue from two different viewpoints—such as customer and salesperson, defense attorney and prosecutor, or parent and child.

Once students have completed the Pro and Con Grid and received feedback on their responses, ask them to back up their pros and cons with evidence and/or reasoned analysis.

Use the results of this assessment as the springboard for an organized class debate or for a pro and con essay assignment.

PROS

The Pro and Con Grid is a quick and easy way to assess whether and how well students can imagine more than one side to an issue. For some college students, this is a difficult but valuable step in their intellectual development.

The points that students raise can indicate which arguments, whether for or against, they find most persuasive or troubling. These can be the most promising arguments to focus on in subsequent class discussions.

CONS   Not all issues or questions have merely two sides, of course; so this technique risks oversimplifying complex matters.

Students who are not convinced of the value of this exercise may submit superficial or flippant responses.

On certain issues, especially those freighted with ethical or moral overtones, some students may reject the notion that there can be two sides.

CAVEATS   In asking students to generate lists of pros and cons related to important questions of ethics and values, you are bound to meet with some resistance and generate some controversy — if only for bringing up the questions. Be prepared to explain your educational rationale for carrying out this assessment. Make sure that you ensure anonymity and show respect for various viewpoints in responding.

**CLASSROOM
ASSESSMENT
TECHNIQUE**

11

Content, Form, and Function Outlines

Estimated Levels of Time and Energy Required for:

Faculty to prepare to use this CAT	**MEDIUM**
Students to respond to the assessment	**HIGH**
Faculty to analyze the data collected	**HIGH**

DESCRIPTION This Classroom Assessment Technique is also called "What, How, and Why Outlines." To respond to it, the student carefully analyzes the "what" (content), "how" (form), and "why" (function) of a particular message. That message may be a poem, a newspaper story, a critical essay, a billboard, a magazine advertisement, or a television commercial. The student writes brief notes answering the "what, how, and why" questions in an outline format that can be quickly read and assessed.

PURPOSE Content, Form, and Function Outlines are designed to elicit information on the students' skills at separating and analyzing the informational content, the form, and the communicative function of a piece of writing, a film or video, or any other form of communication. Put another way, this CAT can help faculty see how well students can analyze not only the message but also the way in which that message is presented and its purpose. In a society where individuals are bombarded daily by messages of all kinds through all media, students need to develop this valuable analytic skill.

RELATED TEACHING GOALS Develop analytic skills (TGI Goal 2)
Improve reading skills (TGI Goal 14)
Improve writing skills (TGI Goal 15)
Develop appropriate study skills, strategies, and habits (TGI Goal 16)
Learn to evaluate methods and materials in this subject (TGI Goal 24)
Develop capacity to make informed ethical choices (TGI Goal 35)
Develop capacity to think for one's self (TGI Goal 51)

SUGGESTIONS FOR USE The Content, Form, and Function Outline is useful in courses focusing on written form, such as composition, literature, technical writing, or creative writing. This CAT is also effective in courses focusing on communication that is not — or not exclusively — written, in fields such as advertising, marketing, fine arts, graphic design, communications, and radio and television.

EXAMPLES   In Exhibit 7.5, this technique is applied to the material directly above.

Exhibit 7.5. A Content, Form, and Function Outline.

Content (What?)	Form (How?)	Function (Why?)
"CAT Title"	Phrase	To capture the essence of the technique and readers' attention
"Estimated Levels of Time and Energy Required for . . ."	Grid	To give readers information on the overall difficulty of the technique
"Description"	Expository prose	To help readers decide whether to read further
"Purpose"	Expository prose	To explain what information this technique is designed to elicit
"Related Teaching Goals"	List	To specify the TGI goals for which this technique is most applicable
"Suggestions for Use"	Expository prose	To describe where and how the CAT is best used
"Examples"	Narrative prose	To provide readers with vignettes that illustrate how these techniques are used by instructors

From Advertising Design (Advertising/Graphic Arts)

To assess her students' skill at taking apart and learning from television commercials, this instructor first asked her Advertising Design students to watch a video clip of a well-known cigarette commercial and then to fill out a Content, Form, and Function Outline analyzing it. In reading their responses, she was surprised to find that more than half of her students had great difficulty breaking the commercial into its component segments. They saw the entire sixty seconds as one seamless whole. As a result, these students did a poor job of completing the assessment. She responded by leading the class through the assessment procedure step by step, inviting comments from those who had done well.

The advertising instructor then asked the students to study and outline an antismoking commercial that paralleled and parodied the cigarette commercial they had just finished analyzing in depth. This time, about two-thirds of the students in the class were able to complete the Content, Form, and Function Outline with varying degrees of success. She then broke the class of thirty into six small groups, showed the antismoking commercial again, and asked them to work through the assessment technique quickly and to produce group outlines. She assigned group work mainly to help the one-third who still were not able to analyze the commercials adequately.

After the groups had finished, she led an exercise comparing the two commercials in content, form, and purpose. The students soon recognized that the two advertisements were almost exactly the same in form, and very similar in content, but were diametrically opposed in purpose. Thanks to the close analyses they had performed, many of the students were able to discuss the similarities and differences in great detail.

From Language and Politics (Linguistics/Political Science)

One of the central goals of this team-taught course is to help students get beyond the rhetoric of campaign speeches and better understand the uses of political language. To help students do so, the two professors—one from linguistics and the other from political science—analyzed a speech given by a presidential candidate. They went through the speech paragraph by paragraph—emphasizing its content, form, and purpose—and outlined the analysis on the chalkboard. They then passed out a copy of another candidate's speech and asked the students to complete a Content, Form, and Function Outline at home, analyzing only the first ten paragraphs of the text.

In reading through the outlines, the instructors noted that most students did a very good job analyzing the content. Form was not much of an issue in the speech. Instead of analyzing the political purpose of the paragraphs, however, most of the students responded by agreeing or disagreeing with the content. This feedback convinced the instructors to spend time in class discussing the need to separate the analysis of the politician's message from the evaluation of that message.

STEP-BY-STEP PROCEDURE

1. Choose a short text, a passage, or a film clip that contains important content and is clearly structured in a form that is common to the genre—for example, a five-paragraph essay.

2. If the structural subsections of the message are not explicitly defined—by subheadings or numbers, for example—you may want to mark them clearly yourself, so that all the students will divide the text into the same subsections.

3. Find a parallel text that you can use as an example and write a Content, Form, and Function Outline for that text.

4. Hand out your outline to the students and take them through your analysis step by step, modeling the process you want them to use. Many students find it difficult to understand and then express the distinction between function and content at first; so give several clear examples. The handout detailing your analysis allows students to review the steps you have demonstrated.

5. You may wish to prepare an outline form for students to use. Such a form can help you read and compare responses more quickly.

6. After you are confident that the students understand the technique, present the message they are to analyze. Go through the directions

carefully and give them sufficient time to carry it out. Unless it is a very short text or message, the assessment should probably be completed outside of class.

TURNING THE DATA YOU COLLECT INTO USEFUL INFORMATION

There are three main types of related yet separable data to be analyzed in the students' responses: (1) the paraphrase of the content, (2) the identification or description of the form, and (3) the analysis of the segment's function within the larger text or message. A simple way to assess the class's understanding of these three elements is to keep a running tally of the problem spots in the text — those segments that students have trouble analyzing — and of the question or questions that seem most difficult to answer in relation to each problem spot.

IDEAS FOR ADAPTING AND EXTENDING THIS CAT

Use this technique with several different types of writing or media and ask students to compare the forms used and the effectiveness of the content and functions in those different examples.

Take an interesting text that you have analyzed and scramble the order of your outline by cutting and pasting. Photocopy the scrambled version and give it to the students. Assess their skills at putting the pieces into their original — or another plausible — order.

PROS

The Content, Form, and Function Outline can prompt students to analyze messages carefully for their intent as well as their content, thereby promoting critical thinking.

It stimulates thinking about patterns and common structures, helping students see why different genres may encode the same information in different forms.

It allows teachers to zero in on particular sticking points in text or communication analysis, rather than giving them a global assessment of students' skills. It shows teachers what their students can do well and what less well, allowing for more fine-tuned teaching.

CONS

This is a time-intensive technique. Some students may have trouble learning this type of analysis, and many will not succeed at it the first time. It generally takes more than one administration to work well.

Many texts and messages, particularly in the visual media, cannot easily be categorized in neat and simple ways.

Many texts and messages perform several functions in each component part, making analysis even more difficult for students.

CAVEATS

Choose a clear, simple, and easily analyzed text for the first administration—as well as for the examples used to demonstrate the technique.

Allow enough time to work through at least part of your examples, but don't feel constrained to do it all at once. This technique is often learned better if it is repeated over a period of days.

Recognize that students will come to different conclusions about a message—particularly about its function—and that their responses can be valid even if they do not match yours.

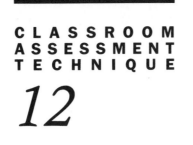

Analytic Memos

Estimated Levels of Time and Energy Required for:

Faculty to prepare to use this CAT	**HIGH**
Students to respond to the assessment	**HIGH**
Faculty to analyze the data collected	**HIGH**

DESCRIPTION

The Analytic Memo is basically a simulation exercise. It requires students to write a one- or two-page analysis of a specific problem or issue. The person for whom the memo is being written is usually identified as an employer, a client, or a stakeholder who needs the student's analysis to inform decision making.

PURPOSE

Analytic Memos assess students' ability to analyze assigned problems by using the discipline-specific approaches, methods, and techniques they are learning. This CAT also assesses students' skill at communicating their analyses in a clear and concise manner. This short, structured writing assignment provides high-quality feedback on students' analytic and writing skills as a by-product of an intellectually challenging and realistic skill-building exercise.

RELATED TEACHING GOALS

Develop analytic skills (TGI Goal 2)
Develop problem-solving skills (TGI Goal 3)
Improve writing skills (TGI Goal 15)
Develop management skills (TGI Goal 37)
Develop leadership skills (TGI Goal 38)
Develop ability to perform skillfully (TGI Goal 43)

SUGGESTIONS FOR USE

Analytic Memos are particularly useful in disciplines that clearly relate to public policy or management, such as political science, economics, criminal justice, social work, education, environmental studies, management, and public health. This CAT works best when used early in the term, as a means to help students prepare for later graded memo-writing assignments. Because preparing and assessing the Analytic Memos takes quite a bit of time and effort, this technique is best suited to seminars and small classes.

EXAMPLES

From a Seminar in Law Enforcement Leadership (Criminal Justice)

The dozen young men and women in this graduate seminar were all being groomed for future leadership roles in the police and sheriff's departments of a large metropolitan area. Their instructor wanted to help them learn to analyze problems and improve their writing skills. He used the Analytic Memo technique to get feedback on their progress toward both goals.

The officers participating in the seminar were given a short case involving a precinct commander faced with proposed budget cutbacks. They were to write analytic Memos to the commander, taking into consideration the stakeholders, the potential winners and losers, and the political resources available. A quick reading of their memos uncovered the officers' strengths and weaknesses. Nearly all had done a good job of identifying the stakeholders and figuring out who stood to lose or win. They were relatively poor at identifying political resources, particularly informal ones. The instructor also told the group that very little of the writing would stand up to scrutiny if the commander's superiors, or the newspapers, were to gain access to their memos. With that general feedback in mind, the students rewrote their memos, this time as a graded assignment. Though far from perfect, the memos were more informative and better written the second time around.

From Environmental Policy Analysis (Environmental Studies)

During the first month of this environmental studies course, the instructor decided to find out how well her students could analyze a typical environmental policy problem. Since a story about contaminated groundwater had recently appeared in the local newspapers, she directed her students to write an Analytic Memo about this topic. They were told to write as environmental policy analysts, to address their memos to the state's secretary of environmental affairs, and to point out the major policy implications of the groundwater crisis.

The students were given three days to prepare their memos. After collecting them, the teacher assessed and responded to each memo with a five-point checklist and short comments. From her quick assessment of the memos, the instructor realized that her students were generally successful at describing the problem and probable causes but demonstrated little ability to analyze its policy implications and the interests of various actors and agencies involved. In response, she planned several increasingly challenging assignments on applying political and policy analyses to environmental problems.

STEP-BY-STEP PROCEDURE

1. Determine which analytic methods or techniques you wish to assess.

2. Locate or invent an appropriate, well-focused, and typical problem or situation for the students to analyze. Get background information on the problem or invent some plausible information.

3. Specify who is writing the memo and for whom it is being written, as well as its subject and purpose.

178 CLASSROOM ASSESSMENT TECHNIQUES

4. Write your own Analytic Memo on the subject. Keep track of any difficulties you have in writing the memo and note how long it takes you from start to finish. Ask yourself whether it really required the type of analysis you were hoping to assess and whether you found it an informative and instructive exercise.

5. Decide whether you want students to work alone, in pairs, or in small groups.

6. Develop an explicit, half-page directions sheet for your students. Specify the students' role, the identity of the audience, the specific subject to be addressed, the basic analytic approach to be taken, the length limit (usually one or two pages), and the assignment deadline.

7. Explain to students how this assessment can help prepare them for subsequent course assignments and for their careers.

TURNING THE DATA YOU COLLECT INTO USEFUL INFORMATION

The basic challenge in analyzing Analytic Memos is to extract useful information while severely limiting the amount of time and energy you spend. Promise yourself to read each memo quickly, and only once, before assessing it. As an aid, devise a short checklist of three to five major points to look for in each memo read—and limit yourself to just those points. For example, you might want to evaluate your students' Analytic Memos for "content" (the breadth of the analysis and the quality of the information), "skill" (the skill with which the relevant tools or methods were employed in the analysis), and "writing" (clarity, conciseness, appropriateness of format, and overall writing quality). Make up a simple grid on which you can check off "Well done," "Acceptable," or "Needs work" for each of the major points you focus on as you read. If you must write comments, limit yourself to two or three very specific ones. After reading all the Analytic Memos quickly, or a sample of the memos in a large class, you can add up the number of "Needs work" check marks in each category and prepare your teaching response accordingly. For example, if you find that more memos need work on analytic "skill" than on writing "quality," you could focus your next lesson on the former.

IDEAS FOR ADAPTING AND EXTENDING THIS CAT

Before they rewrite their memos, have students read and evaluate each other's memos. Be sure to provide guidelines for this peer-evaluation task.

Use the Analytic Memo as the first draft of a graded memo-writing assignment.

Divide the class into "policy analysts" and "policy makers"; then have the policy makers respond, in memo format, to the policy analysts' memos.

PROS

Analytic Memos are valuable, realistic, and substantial learning exercises in themselves; they build and sharpen skills, in addition to providing feedback for assessment.

The memos provide rich data on the students' skills in applying analytic thinking and writing to a real or realistic problem related to the course.

Since memo writing is an important skill in many jobs, this exercise can also serve as an assessment of job-related skills.

CONS
Preparing an Analytic Memo is time-consuming.

The task of reading, assessing, and commenting on these one- to two-page memos requires more time and concentration than do most other CATs.

Students may resist investing their time and energy in an exercise that will not be graded.

CAVEATS
To get good feedback with this CAT, choose a problem that is both real enough and rich enough to generate thoughtful analysis.

The problem must also be one that is familiar to the students or one that they can quickly become familiar with.

You may need to offer students some course credit for successfully completing the Analytic Memos, even though they will not be graded, in order to motivate them to do a good job.

Assessing Skill in Synthesis and Creative Thinking

Creative thinking is a topic about which there is much discussion and speculation, but little agreement among teachers, researchers, and theorists. One simple definition of creative thinking is "the ability to interweave the familiar with the new in unexpected and stimulating ways." In the context of a college classroom, from the student's point of view, the familiar is what the student already knows, and the new is often the course content. Given this definition, students can demonstrate creative thinking in the ways they synthesize prior knowledge and course content. The six techniques in this section all stimulate students to create, and allow faculty to assess, original intellectual products that result from a synthesis of the course content and the students' intelligence, judgment, knowledge, and skills. Thus, all six CATs assess what Bloom would classify as "synthesis," which we regard as a type of creative thinking.

Four of the six techniques elicit written responses: the One-Sentence Summary, the Word Journal, Approximate Analogies, and Invented Dialogues. But the kinds of writing and synthesis they call for vary greatly. The other two CATs, Concept Maps and Annotated Portfolios, can involve a variety of media as well as writing. McKeachie and his colleagues (1986) note the importance of helping learners make their "knowledge structures" explicit, so that they and their teachers can better assess and understand them. Concept Maps provide a simple way to get at these conceptual structures. Annotated Portfolios invite the assessment of visual, musical, and other expressions of creativity and synthesis, since the portfolios can include photographs, drawings, slides, sound recordings, videotapes, or software.

One-Sentence Summary

Estimated Levels of Time and Energy Required for:

Faculty to prepare to use this CAT	**LOW**
Students to respond to the assessment	**MEDIUM**
Faculty to analyze the data collected	**MEDIUM**

DESCRIPTION   This simple technique challenges students to answer the questions "Who does what to whom, when, where, how, and why?" (represented by the letters WDWWWWHW) about a given topic, and then to synthesize those answers into a single informative, grammatical, and long summary sentence.

PURPOSE   The One-Sentence Summary enables teachers to find out how concisely, completely, and creatively students can summarize a large amount of information on a given topic. As the name indicates, this technique requires students to summarize the information within the grammatical constraints of a single sentence. This response format has advantages for the teacher and the students. It allows faculty to scan and compare responses quickly and easily. The One-Sentence Summary also gives students practice in using a technique for "chunking" information—condensing it into smaller, interrelated bits that are more easily processed and recalled.

RELATED TEACHING GOALS   Develop ability to synthesize and integrate information and ideas (TGI Goal 5)
Improve memory skills (TGI Goal 11)
Improve listening skills (TGI Goal 12)
Improve reading skills (TGI Goal 14)
Develop appropriate study skills, strategies, and habits (TGI Goal 16)
Prepare for transfer or graduate study (TGI Goal 22)
Develop management skills (TGI Goal 37)
Develop ability to perform skillfully (TGI Goal 43)

SUGGESTIONS FOR USE   This assessment technique can provide feedback on students' summaries of just about any information that can be represented in declarative form, from historical events, to the plots of stories and novels, to political processes, to chemical reactions and mechanical processes.

An Example from Classroom Research

In the following example, the task is to summarize the information provided throughout this handbook on Classroom Assessment in just one sentence. The matrix immediately below is a helpful intermediate step leading to the One-Sentence Summary.

Who?	teachers
Does what?	assess
To what or whom?	their students' learning
When?	regularly during the semester
Where?	in their own classrooms
How?	using Classroom Assessment Techniques and any other appropriate tools and methods of inquiry
Why?	so that they can understand and improve teaching effectiveness and the quality of student learning
In sentence form:	Teachers assess their students' learning regularly during the semester in their own classrooms, by using Classroom Assessment Techniques and any other appropriate tools and methods of inquiry, so that they can understand and improve teaching effectiveness and the quality of student learning.

From Immunology (Biology/Medicine)

Most of the students in this course, taught by a biology professor, plan to pursue graduate education in medical fields. Therefore, the instructor stresses the importance of understanding the heart of the concepts and recognizing their applications. After an initial lecture and reading assignment on AIDS, the professor gave students five minutes to write a One-Sentence Summary explaining how HIV infects and affects the immune system. She stipulated only that the HIV virus had to be the subject of the summary sentence. In other words, the answer to the "who" question in this case was HIV. At the end of five minutes, almost no one in the large class was finished; so she allowed five more minutes and then collected the responses.

In the quality and completeness, the range was rather wide. Students had the most difficulty answering the "how" and "why" prompts. To provide feedback, she selected three of the well-written summaries and read them to the class, pointing out that each writer had answered the questions in different ways. After taking a few questions on the issues raised by the summary, she reviewed the HIV infection process

184   CLASSROOM ASSESSMENT TECHNIQUES

again, this time in more detail and using much more specific terminology.

From Fundamentals of Nursing (Nursing)

The instructor in this required first-year course for nursing students used the One-Sentence Summary to assess her students' understanding of the five steps in the nursing process: assessing, diagnosing, planning, implementing, and evaluating. After they had been assigned a chapter on this topic as homework, she asked students to summarize each step in one sentence, beginning with "nurses" as the subject.

From Physics for Technicians (Physics/Vocational and Technical Education)

To make sure that his students really understood the process of generating electricity by converting fluid energy to mechanical energy, this instructor asked the part-time students in his evening class to write a One-Sentence Summary. They were asked to summarize the hydroelectric power generation process in one sentence. To help them get started, he provided a photocopied matrix with the questions "What? Does what? To what? When? Where? How? Why?" listed down the left side of the page. He suggested that they begin by answering the first "What?" with "water."

After reading their summaries, the instructor picked three of the clearest correct summaries and read them to the class. After he was sure that everyone understood the process, he gave his students a follow-up homework assignment. The task was to draw a schematic illustration of the hydroelectric power generation process, briefly explaining each step in writing. He provided the students with a few relevant facts about the system and asked them to calculate force and torque exerted on the turbine, and the maximum ideal power output as well.

STEP-BY-STEP PROCEDURE

1. Select an important topic or work that your students have recently studied in your course and that you expect them to learn to summarize.

2. Working as quickly as you can, answer the questions "Who Did/Does What to Whom, When, Where, How, and Why?" in relation to that topic. Note how long this first step takes you.

3. Next, turn your answers into a grammatical sentence that follows WDWWWWHW pattern. Note how long this second step takes.

4. Allow your students up to twice as much time as it took you to carry out the task and give them clear directions on the One-Sentence Summary technique before you announce the topic to be summarized.

TURNING THE DATA YOU COLLECT INTO USEFUL INFORMATION

Perhaps the easiest way to organize the data from these summaries is to draw slash marks between the focus elements of the sentence, separating the responses to the various questions ("Who?" "Did/Does What?" and so on) with penciled-in vertical lines. To make the analysis faster and easier, ask the students to insert the separating lines after they have completed their sentences. As you separate the components of the summary sentence, evaluate the quality of each by writing a zero, a check mark, or a plus above that element. Zero indicates an "inadequate" or "incorrect" element; the check means "adequate"; and the plus sign indicates "more than adequate." You can then make a simple matrix to represent the whole class's responses, with the questions as column headings and the three marks—zero, check, plus—as row headings. When you have totaled the responses, insert the totals in the cells of the matrix and look for patterns of strength and weakness in the responses. For example, the totals can tell you whether your students are better at answering "who" and "what" questions than "how" or "why" questions.

IDEAS FOR ADAPTING AND EXTENDING THIS CAT

After questions of content have been resolved, ask students to turn the one-sentence summaries into concise, informative, and elegant two- or three-sentence summaries. Have them share these revised, but still very brief, summaries with each other.

Give students a few minutes to work in pairs or small groups to critique and improve each other's summaries, either before handing them in or after getting them back.

Use this technique a number of times to summarize different chapters of the same book or facets of the same subject. Then ask students to summarize the entire book or subject in one paragraph by rewriting and linking their individual single-sentence summaries.

PROS

The One-Sentence Summary provides a quick and easy way to assess students' ability to summarize a topic succinctly and coherently.

This is a powerful technique for helping students grasp complex processes and explain them to others in nontechnical language.

Students must organize the information they are summarizing within a familiar, useful, and memorable framework—the sentence. Once summarized in this way, that information is easier to recall.

CONS

Some material cannot easily be summarized in this form because some or all of the focus questions would have multiple answers.

Some teachers and some students may feel that "squeezing" a lesson or reading into a one-sentence "straitjacket" oversimplifies the material.

CAVEATS

Don't ask the students to write a One-Sentence Summary of a topic unless you have first determined that you can coherently summarize the topic in one sentence.

Limit the topic so that the summary task will deal with a manageable part of it. For example, if there are several main characters and actions in a chapter to be summarized, limit the One-Sentence Summary assignment by specifying which character to use as the subject of the sentences.

Encourage students to make their sentences grammatical, factually accurate, complete, and original. But tell them not to be too disappointed if their One-Sentence Summaries are not particularly elegant—especially at first.

REFERENCES AND RESOURCES
We owe the inspiration for the One-Sentence Summary to Anne Berthoff. In her book on composing, *Forming/Thinking/Writing* (1982, pp. 70–79), she presents a technique for organizing the sometimes chaotic information generated by brainstorming; she labels this technique HDWDWW (How Does Who Do What and Why?). Following our own advice, we adapted her excellent prewriting technique for use as an assessment tool.

Word Journal

Estimated Levels of Time and Energy Required for:

Faculty to prepare to use this CAT	**LOW to MEDIUM**
Students to respond to the assessment	**MEDIUM to HIGH**
Faculty to analyze the data collected	**MEDIUM to HIGH**

DESCRIPTION

The Word Journal prompts a two-part response. First, the student summarizes a short text in a single word. Second, the student writes a paragraph or two explaining why he or she chose that particular word to summarize the text. The completed response to the Word Journal is an abstract or a synopsis of the focus text.

PURPOSE

The Word Journal can help faculty assess and improve several related skills. First, it focuses on students' ability to read carefully and deeply. Second, it assesses skill and creativity at summarizing what has been read. And third, it assesses the students' skill at explaining and defending, in just a few more words, their choice of single summary word. Practice with this CAT helps students develop the ability to write highly condensed abstracts and to "chunk" large amounts of information for more effective storage in long-term memory. These skills are useful in almost any field, particularly the professions.

RELATED TEACHING GOALS

Develop ability to synthesize and integrate information and ideas (TGI Goal 5)

Develop ability to think holistically: to see the whole as well as the parts (TGI Goal 6)

Improve memory skills (TGI Goal 11)

Improve listening skills (TGI Goal 12)

Improve reading skills (TGI Goal 14)

Develop appropriate study skills, strategies, and habits (TGI Goal 16)

Prepare for transfer or graduate study (TGI Goal 22)

Develop ability to perform skillfully (TGI Goal 43)

Develop capacity to think for oneself (TGI Goal 51)

SUGGESTIONS FOR USE

The Word Journal works wherever students are expected to read carefully and thoughtfully—to understand concepts, not simply to memorize information. It works especially well in courses that focus on primary texts rather than textbooks. This technique can easily be adapted for use in courses in literature, anthropology, sociology, criminal justice, history, management, and law. Because of the extreme condensation required to summarize a reading in one word, however, this CAT is best used to assess the reading of short texts, such as essays, poems, short stories, short articles, and cases.

EXAMPLES

From the Socratic Dialogues of Plato (Philosophy)

To help her students prepare for seminar discussions, and to assess their reading of the Socratic dialogues, this philosophy professor used the Word Journal regularly. All fifteen students in the seminar, as well as the professor, completed Word Journals on the first three dialogues read, the *Meno*, the *Crito*, and the *Phaedo*. The students' summary words became the starting points for the discussions. At first, the students' explanatory paragraphs were not well anchored in the dialogues themselves. Students used the paragraphs to express their beliefs and opinions about the dialogues but failed to support those beliefs and opinions with references to the dialogues. This was a central skill that the professor chose to promote and assess.

For the remainder of the semester, a different group of three students was responsible for completing and presenting Word Journals each week and for leading discussions based on their summaries. The instructor used the students' words as illustrations of different, valid ways to read the Socratic dialogues. At the same time, she helped the students learn to use their explanatory paragraphs to provide text-based justification and evidence for their readings, and to see that some justifications are better than others.

From Contemporary Eastern European Fiction (Slavic Languages and Literature)

The readings for this course, mostly short stories, are all English translations from the original Polish, Czech, Russian, German, and Hungarian texts. The instructor, a professor of Slavic languages and literature, conducts the course entirely in English. He used the Word Journal to encourage his students to read beyond the surface features of the stories. In reading their responses, the instructor quickly realized that most of his students were focusing only on the depressing or absurd aspects of the stories, failing to make connections to their own realities. This feedback convinced the Slavic professor to use his lectures to help students uncover the more universal themes in the stories and to take their possible personal relevance more seriously.

From Managing for Quality (Management/Business)

In this graduate course for M.B.A. students, class discussions were based on cases written about attempts to apply Edward Deming's "total quality management" approach to various corporate and industrial settings. The first case discussion of the semester went rather poorly, and the instructor suspected that the students had not read the case carefully. To assess their reading of the following case, she assigned the Word Journal. Adapting the CAT to her own purposes, she directed students to come up with one word to summarize the central problem or issue illustrated by the case, and then to explain and defend their choice of that word.

The management instructor began the next class session by asking students to volunteer their Word Journal words. She listed a number of those words on the board and then asked students to explain their particular characterizations of the case's central problem. Many of the words referred to surface problems in the case, but a few indicated that students were looking deeper. At the end of the class, she collected the Word Journals and read them quickly. She was surprised to see that several students who had writen insightful responses had not volunteered their words at any point in the discussion. To encourage wider participation, the instructor collected the next set of Word Journal responses at the beginning of class. While students were involved in a short group-work task, she scanned the Word Journal responses and selected a handful of words to put on the chalkboard for discussion. As she had suspected, most of the students who came forward to claim and explain the words she had selected were women.

STEP-BY-STEP PROCEDURE

1. Choose one of the short texts that your students will be assigned to read.

2. Decide what aspect of that text—main theme, central conflict or problem, core metaphor—you want students to focus on.

3. To determine whether the exercise is feasible and productive, try following your own directions.

4. If you find the Word Journal process thought-provoking, prepare to explain and administer the technique in your course.

5. Tell the students that the choice of a specific word is less important than the quality of the explanation for that choice. Give them some ideas about what their explanations should contain, and inform them that the words they choose must be connected to their interpretations of the text.

TURNING THE DATA YOU COLLECT INTO USEFUL INFORMATION

Before you collect responses to the Word Journal, take a few minutes to come up with your own list of reasonable "summary words" for the assigned text. Jot down some notes about the kinds of arguments and analyses you hope students will offer in defense of their word choices. As you read the journals, keep track of words that are used by more than one student, or related terms that crop up. Pay close attention to the justifications that students give for their word choices. When possible, categorize Word Journal responses not only by the summary words but also by the types of explanations offered. After analyzing the responses, select examples of three or four different approaches that you can share with the class.

If you believe that your students will find this technique too challenging at first, begin by providing them with a list of possible words to choose from. Their task will be to select a word from that list and then to justify that choice.

Work with students to develop criteria for judging their Word Journals. Have the class come up with a list of the qualities that characterize an excellent response.

Focus the Word Journals by directing students to summarize one aspect of the text—either the central problem or issue (as in the management example above) or the main conflict, theme, or unifying metaphor in a reading.

In fields where abstracts are commonly required, use the Word Journal to teach students the particular conventions for writing abstracts in your discipline.

Divide the class into pairs or small groups and ask students to read each other's Word Journals and analyze the strengths and weaknesses of each individual approach.

PROS

The Word Journal requires students to read deeply and to construct meaning from what they have read. It thereby promotes active learning through reading.

The act of choosing a single word to sum up a reading, and then explaining and advocating for that word, encourages students to make personal connections with the texts they are reading and to take responsibility for their ideas.

As with the One-Sentence Summary (CAT 13), this CAT helps students develop skills in summarizing, remembering, and communicating information—skills that they can use in academic and professional life.

CONS

The Word Journal takes time and energy to prepare, carry out, analyze, and discuss. It is worth using only if the development of these reading and summarizing skills is a central goal of the course.

Unless students have opportunities to discuss and compare their responses, they will benefit relatively little from the assessment.

Given the importance of discussion, it is very difficult to ensure the anonymity of student responses to the Word Journal.

CAVEATS

This is not an effective technique to use in cases where there is only one acceptable way to summarize a given text. The Word Journal works only when students have the freedom to explore and express their own interpretations.

Students who have never practiced this kind of reading and summarizing are likely to find this technique challenging, and even baffling, at first. Such students are likely to resist using the Word Journal.

REFERENCES AND RESOURCES See *Early Lessons* (Angelo, 1991, pp. 22–23) for an example of the Word Journal used in an English course.

Approximate Analogies

Estimated Levels of Time and Energy Required for:

Faculty to prepare to use this CAT	**LOW**
Students to respond to the assessment	**LOW**
Faculty to analyze the data collected	**MEDIUM**

DESCRIPTION   To respond to the Approximate Analogies assessment technique, students simply complete the second half of an analogy—A is to B as X is to Y—for which their instructor has supplied the first half (A is to B). Consequently, the student can respond to this CAT in as few as two words. For the purposes of Classroom Assessment, student responses need not always display the rigor required of analogies in formal logic or mathematics; therefore, we call these analogies "approximate."

PURPOSE   Responses to the Approximate Anologies technique allow teachers to find out whether their students understand the relationship between the two concepts or terms given as the first part of the analogy. Those responses also show faculty how effectively—and how creatively—students are able to connect the "new" relationship to one they are more familiar with. For learners, this technique provides guided practice in making connections, practice that helps them strengthen and extend their "knowledge networks."

RELATED TEACHING GOALS   Develop ability to synthesize and integrate information and ideas (TGI Goal 5)
Develop ability to think creatively (TGI Goal 7)
Improve memory skills (TGI Goal 11)
Learn concepts and theories in this subject (TGI Goal 19)
Develop an openness to new ideas (TGI Goal 27)
Develop capacity to think for oneself (TGI Goal 51)

SUGGESTIONS FOR USE   The Approximate Analogies technique can be adapted to any discipline, since virtually all disciplines require students to understand critical relationships. Its brevity and simplicity make it applicable to classes of any size.

EXAMPLES   The following examples—all simple Approximate Analogy prompts—are meant to suggest the wide range of possible applications of this technique.

From Freshman Composition (English)

> The theme is to an essay as
> _____ is to _____.

From Physics for Nonscience Majors (Physics)

> Mass is to volume as
> _____ is to _____.

From Fundamentals of Electrical Engineering (Engineering)

> Voltage is to wattage as
> _____ is to _____.

From Environmental Policy Issues (Public Administration)

> Depletion of the ozone layer is to the Environmental Protection Agency
> as _____ is to _____.

From Elementary Japanese (Japanese)

> Honorifics are to the Japanese language as
> _____ is to _____.

From Social Analysis (Sociology)

> Income is to social class as
> _____ is to _____.

From the Rise of the Novel (Comparative Literature)

> Dickens is to the nineteenth-century British novel as
> _____ is to _____.

STEP-BY-STEP PROCEDURE

1. Select a key relationship between two facts or concepts that is important for your students to understand well.

2. Create an Approximate Analogy, using the two related concepts or facts as the A and B elements in the "A is to B as X is to Y" format.

3. Quickly generate a number of appropriate completions—the "X is to Y" part—each of which results in an Approximate Analogy. Try to come up with relationships from everyday life.

4. If you are convinced that the original relationship is worth assessing, and that most of your students will be able to respond, prepare to use it as a prompt. Present one or two sample analogies to the students before asking them to complete an Approximate Analogy on their own.

5. When you are ready to carry out the assessment, simply write the prompt on the board, or display it on an overhead, and explain what students are to do. You may wish to hand out small index cards or slips of paper for the responses.

6. In most cases, students will need only a minute or two to complete the Approximate Analogy, after which you can collect the feedback.

TURNING THE DATA YOU COLLECT INTO USEFUL INFORMATION

The analysis of the responses can be almost as quick and simple as using this CAT. Read through the analogy completions very quickly, sorting them into piles of "good," "questionable," and "poor or wrong" responses. Read through the "questionable" pile again, to see whether any of the answers make more sense upon second reading. Re-sort as many of these as you can into one of the remaining two categories. Look for responses that not only make sense but also show creativity or humor. Choose three or four of the best completions to present to the class as good examples. Pick out a couple of marginal or poor examples as well. Be prepared to explain what makes the former good examples and the latter poor examples, in case you cannot elicit those explanations from the students.

IDEAS FOR ADAPTING AND EXTENDING THIS CAT

- To specify the response range more tightly, provide one part of the completion: "Dickens is to the nineteenth-century British novel as _____ is to the nineteenth-century French novel."

- Invite students to classify and explain the type of relationship that the analogy embodies. For example, is it a part-whole, cause-effect, or exemplar-to-class relationship — or some other type?

- Allow students to work in pairs or small groups to generate and critique Approximate Analogies. You might request that each group propose three to five responses and be ready to explain the differences and similarities among them.

- Suggest that students keep a log or journal of Approximate Analogies, practicing this learning strategy on their own whenever they encounter new relationships in the course material.

PROS

Thinking by analogy is a skill that plays an important part in transferring and applying knowledge, and in creative thinking. This CAT assesses and promotes that skill.

Approximate Analogies encourage students to connect new knowledge about relationships between concepts and terms in the discipline to prior knowledge — relationships they are already familiar with. These connections promote more powerful and lasting learning.

Many students find this technique challenging, intellectually stimulating, and fun.

CONS

Approximate Analogies can be difficult and frustrating for students who do not understand the relationship represented by the prompt or cannot think of any analogous relationship.

This technique may seem more difficult to apply in science, math, and technical courses. Paradoxically, these are precisely the fields in which many students most need help in making connections between their previous knowledge and the course material.

CAVEATS   Some students may not be familiar with the analogy format. These students may need several examples before they understand what they are being asked to do.

Some students' responses may be so personal or implicit that you may not be able to understand them at all—much less assess their usefulness.

All other things being equal, analogies of this sort tend to favor students with larger vocabularies and broader reading experience.

16

Concept Maps

Estimated Levels of Time and Energy Required for:

Faculty to prepare to use this CAT	**MEDIUM**
Students to respond to the assessment	**MEDIUM**
Faculty to analyze the data collected	**MEDIUM TO HIGH**

DESCRIPTION Concept Maps are drawings or diagrams showing the mental connections that students make between a major concept the instructor focuses on and other concepts they have learned. An analogy would be to ask students to draw a map of the area in a twenty-mile radius around Boston, putting in only the features they regard as most important. To prompt students to make Concept Maps, we might ask them to sketch the important features of the "geography" around major concepts such as democracy, racism, art, or free trade.

PURPOSE This technique provides an observable and assessable record of the students' conceptual schemata — the patterns of associations they make in relation to a given focal concept. Concept Maps allow the teacher to discover the web of relationships that learners bring to the task at hand — the students' starting points. This CAT also helps the teacher assess the degree of "fit" between the students' understanding of relevant conceptual relations and the teacher's Concept Map — which is often a "map" commonly used by members of that discipline. With such information in hand, the teacher can go on to assess changes and growth in the students' conceptual understandings that result from instruction.

By literally drawing the connections they make among concepts, students gain more control over their connection making. The Concept Map allows them to scrutinize their conceptual networks, compare their maps with those of peers and experts, and make explicit changes. As a consequence, this technique can be used to assess and develop valuable metacognitive skills.

RELATED TEACHING GOALS Develop ability to draw reasonable inferences from observations (TGI Goal 4)

Develop ability to synthesize and integrate information and ideas (TGI Goal 5)

Develop ability to think holistically: to see the whole as well as the parts (TGI Goal 6)

Develop appropriate study skills, strategies, and habits (TGI Goal 16)

Learn concepts and theories in this subject (TGI Goal 19)

Learn to understand perspectives and values of this subject (TGI Goal 21)

Develop an openness to new ideas (TGI Goal 27)

Develop capacity to think for oneself (TGI Goal 51)

SUGGESTIONS FOR USE   This technique is useful in any course that requires conceptual learning. In courses with a high theoretical content, Concept Maps provide insights into the connections students are making among theories and concepts. At the same time, Concept Maps can be used to assess the connections students make between theories or concepts and information. In courses where students must learn large numbers of facts and principles, Concept Maps can help faculty see how and how well students are organizing those details into correct and memorable conceptual networks.

Before beginning instruction on a given concept or theory, teachers can use Concept Maps to discover what preconceptions and prior knowledge structures students bring to the task. This information can help instructors make decisions about when and how to introduce a new topic — as well as discover misconceptions that may cause later difficulties. During and after a lesson, they can use Concept Maps to assess changes in the students' conceptual representations. An ideal use of this technique is to employ it before, during, and after lessons on critical concepts.

EXAMPLES

An Example from Classroom Research

The simple Concept Map in Figure 7.1 represents "Classroom Research" in relation to other types of assessment in higher education.

From Introduction to Feminist Thought (Women's Studies)

Ten minutes before the end of the first class meeting of this lower-division course, the instructor asked students to draw a Concept Map focused on the concept of "feminism." She directed students to write "feminism" in the center of a blank sheet of paper and, around that center, to add related words or concepts that came to mind. She told students not to write their names on the maps and to be honest. She asked a student to collect the Concept Maps as class ended.

As the women's studies professor had expected, many of the maps contained what she saw as negative associations. But many others contained a mixture of positive and negative concepts—often very stereotypical ones in either case. Some students included the names of public figures; others included personal references. To give students feedback, she made up three composite Concept Maps—based on their drawings—to discuss with the class. She also kept their maps and, throughout her subsequent lectures, referred to ideas and individuals they had mentioned. At midterm, she repeated the assessment exercise and got back much more detailed and coherent Concept

Figure 7.1. A Concept Map Relating Classroom Research to Other Types of Higher Education Assessment.

Type	**Systemwide Assessment**
Level	Community college, four-year, or university systems
Goal	To provide public accountability

Type	**Institutional Assessment**
Level	Individual college or university
Goals	To provide public accountability; to gain and maintain accreditation

Type	**Program Review and Assessment**
Level	School, program, or department
Goals	To gain and maintain accredication; to improve program quality and success

Type	**Classroom Research**
Level	Individual course
Goals	To understand and improve teaching and learning in that individual course

Type	**Classroom Assessment**
Level	Individual class meeting or assignment within the course
Goals	To understand and improve teaching and learning of a single lesson or unit

Maps, which demonstrated much change in knowledge but little appreciable change in attitudes.

From Charles Darwin: His World and Work (History of Science)

About halfway through this graduate seminar, the professor asked students to draw a Concept Map centered on Darwin's theory of natural selection. The map was to connect Darwin's theory with its predecessors, contemporaries, competitors, and descendants. He urged the graduate students to use their imaginations in representing the relationships but to stick to the facts in characterizing them. In response, seminar participants created everything from flowcharts to family trees to mock maps full of topographical features.

From International Trade (Economics)

During the first week of class, the instructor in this course asked students to draw a Concept Map to illustrate their understanding of "free trade." To illustrate what he meant by a Concept Map, he used the overhead projector to show the class an example he had drawn—a Concept Map of his understanding of the gross national product (GNP). To assess students' responses, he drew his own Concept Map on "free trade" and extracted a list of critical related concepts to look for in their maps.

STEP-BY-STEP PROCEDURE

1. Select the concept you wish to use as the stimulus or starting point for the Concept Map. It should be a concept that is both important to understanding the course and relatively rich in conceptual connections.

2. Brainstorm for a few minutes, writing down terms and short phrases closely related to the stimulus.

3. Draw a Concept Map based on your brainstorming, placing the stimulus in the center and drawing lines to other concepts. You might make your Concept Map roughly resemble a wheel with spokes, with the focus concept at the hub. Or it might be based on a model of the solar system, with the stimulus in the sun's position. A third option is to make the Concept Map resemble a geographical map.

4. After you have sketched in the primary associations, move on to add secondary and even tertiary levels of association, if appropriate.

5. Determine the ways in which the various concepts are related to each other and write those types of relations on the lines connecting the concepts.

6. Prepare a simple parallel example to use with the class.

7. Present the example to the students and work through it with them step by step, checking results at each step to make sure the process is clear.

In analyzing the students' Concept Maps, consider both the content (the concepts) and the types of relations identified among concepts. Your own Concept Map can serve as the master copy for comparison. Since the students probably will come up with elements and relationships that you had not identified, however, you might want to review the data with an eye toward unexpected, creative responses.

The data can be coded rather simply in a matrix that juxtaposes degree of relationship (primary-, secondary-, tertiary-level relationships, and so on) with type of relationship (set/subset, part/whole, parallel elements, cause/effect, defining quality, necessary condition, and so on). Once the data are coded, the numbers of responses in each cell can be counted and the balance among cells analyzed. Coding the data on 3-by-5-inch index cards or small slips of paper can make the data easier to manipulate and rearrange.

IDEAS FOR ADAPTING AND EXTENDING THIS CAT

Have students use large-format graph paper (for example, four squares per inch) for their Concept Maps. They can then determine and calculate specific distances between the focus concept and the various related concepts.

Assign a Concept Map as a small-group assessment project.

Ask students to write explanatory essays based on their maps.

PROS

Concept Maps reflect current research in cognitive psychology by directing teacher and student attention to the "mental maps" used to organize what we learn.

This CAT is a very "low-tech" way to get a graphic view of students' conceptual associations.

Because it calls for a graphic response, this technique favors students with strong visual learning skills. These same students are often at a disadvantage in verbal assessments.

It prompts students to consider how their own ideas and concepts are related, as well as to realize that those associations are changeable.

Concept Maps can serve students as prewriting and note-taking devices, in addition to being powerful self-assessment techniques.

CONS

Comparisons among student responses can be difficult to make unless the teacher restricts responses to choices from a closed list of terms. Such restriction, however, will diminish student creativity and the variability of responses.

Students with well-honed verbal skills but less developed graphic skills may find this assessment frustrating and question its value.

CAVEATS While students are likely to have some trouble identifying levels of association, they may have even more difficulty identifying the types of relationships among concepts. By going over a parallel example in class, you can clarify exactly what is expected of the students.

REFERENCES AND RESOURCES Louis Henry (1986) presents a similar technique, which he calls "clustering," as an effective means of writing and learning about economics. In their provocative book *Learning How to Learn*, Novak and Gowin (1984) describe and discuss concept mapping and other strategies for helping students learn.

CLASSROOM
ASSESSMENT
TECHNIQUE

17

Invented Dialogues

Estimated Levels of Time and Energy Required for:

Faculty to prepare to use this CAT	**MEDIUM TO HIGH**
Students to respond to the assessment	**HIGH**
Faculty to analyze the data collected	**HIGH**

DESCRIPTION   By inventing dialogues, students synthesize their knowledge of issues, personalities, and historical periods into the form of a carefully structured, illustrative conversation. There are two levels of "invention" possible with this technique. On the first level, students can create Invented Dialogues by carefully selecting and weaving together actual quotes from primary sources. On a second, more challenging, level, they may invent reasonable quotes that fit the character of the speakers and the context.

PURPOSE   Invented Dialogues provide rich information on students' ability to capture the essence of other people's personalities and styles of expression — as well as on their understanding of theories, controversies, and the opinions of others. This technique provides a challenging way to assess — and to develop — students' skills at creatively synthesizing, adapting, and even extrapolating beyond the material they have studied.

RELATED TEACHING GOALS   Develop ability to draw reasonable inferences from observations (TGI Goal 4)

Develop ability to synthesize and integrate information and ideas (TGI Goal 5)

Develop ability to think creatively (TGI Goal 7)

Learn to understand perspectives and values of this subject (TGI Goal 21)

Learn techniques and methods used to gain new knowledge in this subject (TGI Goal 23)

Learn to evaluate methods and materials in this subject (TGI Goal 24)

Learn to appreciate important contributions to this subject (TGI Goal 25)

Develop an informed historical perspective (TGI Goal 32)

Invented Dialogues are particularly useful in humanities and social science courses, such as history, literature, political science, philosophy, sociology, and theology. To focus the dialogues, instructors suggest the topics, issues, and/or personalities to be dealt with.

Invented Dialogues can be invented in at least two different senses of the word. First, students can use these dialogues to speculate on conversations that might have taken place between contemporaries in a given situation within a given historical context. A student in a U.S. history class might invent a dialogue between an abolitionist and a slaveholder in the United States of 1855, for example. Or the students can juxtapose times and places, reinventing history to achieve an effect. A student in a course on political leadership might convene Alexander, Caesar, and Napoleon to discuss the difference between the leadership skills required to conquer an empire and those needed to maintain one.

EXAMPLES

An Example from Classroom Research

Setting: A faculty lounge in a medium-sized college.

Characters: Two college teachers. One is a Classroom Research booster (CRB); the other, a thoughtful skeptic (TS).

TS: Just why is it you think we all should put more time and energy into assessing our classes? Good teachers, and I happen to think I am one, are constantly assessing their students' learning. We've always done that.

CRB: I don't think we necessarily need to spend more time and effort assessing student learning. I do think, however, that we can learn about our students' learning more effectively by using explicit, focused, and systematic techniques. In other words, I'm advocating working smarter, not harder.

TS: But what about tests and quizzes? Aren't they explicit, focused, and systematic enough to assess students' learning?

CRB: Sure they are, when they're used well. There are still some important differences, though, between those evaluation techniques and Classroom Assessment Techniques.

TS: Such as the cute names you give to the techniques, you mean?

CRB: No, I think there's more to it than that. Tests and quizzes usually come at the end of lessons or terms, and focus on how much students have learned. Right?

TS: Yes. So what?

CRB: Well, Classroom Assessment Techniques are meant to be used during the lessons, while students are actively engaged in the learning process—not after it's over. Classroom assessment also focuses on how and how well students are learning, not just on what and how much.

TS: Aren't you just advocating testing better, earlier, and more often?

CRB: I suppose some tests and quizzes would work quite well as formative assessment tools. But there are a lot of other things I want to know about: things we don't usually test for and things I don't necessarily want to grade for.

TS: You mean you want to know whether your students like you or not?

CRB: Don't be snide. We all want to know that. But I'm thinking more about assessing some very traditional goals that I have for my teaching, like fostering a deeper appreciation for the subject and developing critical-thinking skills.

TS: Amen. In your words, "We all want to know that." Even I have secret "higher-order" goals, but I don't think those kinds of things are assessable. I really don't believe you can collect meaningful data on those sorts of things.

CRB: Well, maybe my project will change your mind. Let's talk about this again at the end of the semester, and I'll show you the results of my assessments of analytic reasoning in my classes.

TS: O.K. If you show them to me over lunch, I'll even bring an open mind with me.

CRB: Fair enough. If neither of us expects miracles, there's a chance we might both be pleasantly surprised.

From Greek Political Philosophy (Philosophy)

As a way to assess students' understanding of the fundamental differences between Socrates' and Aristotle's views of the individual's role in political life, this philosophy professor asked students to work in pairs to create a short Invented Dialogue. Each pair was to invent a dialogue by juxtaposing selected quotes on citizenship and political involvement from Aristotle's *Politics* and from any of the several Socratic dialogues they had studied. All excerpts were to be correctly cited, of course. The instructor read and responded to the Invented Dialogues and asked the authors of three of the best to read their dialogues aloud in class.

From Shakespeare on Film (Fine Arts)

To assess her class's appreciation for the critical, necessary differences between staging Shakespeare's plays in the theater and presenting them on film, this art instructor asked students to come up with a short dialogue in which William Shakespeare and Orson Welles compared notes on their quite different "stagings" of *Othello*. (The class had read *Othello*, seen a traditional theatrical staging of it, and seen the restored versions of Welles's film.) Students were free to draw on any relevant sources, as long as the sources were carefully and correctly acknowledged. But the instructor let students know that they would need to exercise some "poetic license," especially in creating the Bard of Avon's lines.

STEP-BY-STEP PROCEDURE

1. Select one or more controversial issues, theories, decisions, or personalities that are important topics in your course and lend themselves to the dialogue format.

2. Write a short dialogue — no more than ten to twenty exchanges long — on the focus you have selected, and use this dialogue as an example in your class. Note how long it takes you to invent your model dialogue.

3. If transcripts of relevant dialogues exist, collect a few and make them available as examples also. The "Melian dialogue" in Thucydides' *History of the Peloponnesian War*, The Lincoln-Douglass and Kennedy-Nixon debates, Socratic dialogues such as the *Symposium*, and contemporary philosophical dialogues, such as the Chomsky-Skinner debates, are all possible examples.

4. Make an instructive handout to help students get started. Suggest a few possible topics, give time and length guidelines, explain what you expect in the way of citations, and list your criteria for a successful dialogue. Let students know how much, if any, of the material they can invent from whole cloth — and how much they should cut and paste. Make it clear to students that the object is to create an original, lively, persuasive, natural-sounding, and self-contained dialogue.

5. Encourage students to assess their own dialogues by reading the draft versions out loud before putting them in final form.

TURNING THE DATA YOU COLLECT INTO USEFUL INFORMATION

In these Invented Dialogues, you should look for the same elements you mentioned in your assignment handouts. You can, for example, simply count the number of important points that the students adequately address in their dialogues and rate the quality of reasoning expressed in the exchanges. Note whether remarks really follow and respond to one another and whether the exchanges are balanced, on target, and in character. You can also assess them for literary qualities, particularly when the students invented the lines. Do they "breathe"? Are the lines speakable? Most important, remember to assess the Invented Dialogues for their originality, creativity, and success at synthesizing and integrating the material. You might want to create a checklist of points to look for as you read through the dialogues.

IDEAS FOR ADAPTING AND EXTENDING THIS CAT

Have students work in pairs, with each individual responsible for researching one side of the issue but with both responsible for weaving together the dialogue.

Ask students to act out a few of the dramatic and original dialogues and present them live or on videotape to you and the class.

Let students expand and polish their dialogues after you have assessed them, recycling them as the basis for a more extensive, graded assignment.

Direct students to translate the basic ideas and arguments in the dialogues into essays.

PROS Inventing dialogues forces students to internalize and "process" course materials in profound ways. This process draws on higher-order thinking skills, often more effectively than term papers or essays do.

This technique allows students a great deal of choice in selecting, combining, and generating ideas.

Invented Dialogues provide the teacher with information on both the students' understanding of course material and their creative skills.

Invented Dialogues can provide students with a way to "get there from here": a vehicle for internalizing and personalizing theories, controversies, and concepts that might otherwise seem quite distant, abstract, and "academic."

CONS Writing persuasive dialogues is hard and time-consuming work, both for students and teachers. Reading and commenting on them is similarly demanding.

Students who feel that they are not creative or not gifted at writing may resist the technique.

Many students will have had little or no previous experience at constructing balanced, persuasive discussions of ideas—and even less at writing dialogues—and so may need coaching and encouragement.

CAVEATS Begin with limited topics and modest guidelines. Any major issue or controversy could require dozens or hundreds of exchanges to explore.

Don't be dismayed if the students' first efforts are less than totally convincing. Remind yourself and your students that this is a challenging task.

If you impose or suggest too many guidelines, the technique will no longer allow creative thinking. Remember, the major point of this exercise is to generate an original, personal intellectual product.

Tell the students about your own experiences in writing the example dialogue—the process you went through, the problems you faced, and the surprises you encountered. Your comments will reassure apprehensive students and show them how to proceed.

REFERENCES AND RESOURCES Richard Davis (1981) presents convincing arguments for the use of student dialogues to promote learning. His article is well illustrated with excerpts from dialogues written by his history students in Australia. In an appendix to the article, he also includes a dialogue he invented to illustrate the usefulness of this technique. Davis's example inspired the dialogue on Classroom Assessment included above.

CLASSROOM ASSESSMENT TECHNIQUE

18

Annotated Portfolios

Estimated Levels of Time and Energy Required for:

Faculty to prepare to use this CAT	**MEDIUM**
Students to respond to the assessment	**HIGH**
Faculty to analyze the data collected	**HIGH**

DESCRIPTION   In the fine and applied arts, assessment of portfolios is a common and well-accepted practice. Painters, photographers, architects, and graphic artists — as well as orthodontists, plastic surgeons, and fashion models — submit select samples of their work to potential employers, admissions committees, galleries, and foundations. Fiction writers, poets, composers, and journalists also use portfolios of their work. In a somewhat different though related way, academic programs that grant credit to adult students for experiential learning often require portfolios of personal narratives, usually supplemented by supporting documentation. Annotated Portfolios used for Classroom Assessment contain a very limited number of examples of creative work, supplemented by the students' own commentary on the significance of those examples.

PURPOSE   Annotated Portfolios provide the teacher with a limited sample of students' creative work, along with the students' explanation of that work in relation to the course content or goals. In this way, the technique allows teachers to assess students' skill at making explicit connections between their creative work and the course content. In other words, it helps faculty see how well students can apply what they have learned and how well they can explain those applications. Annotated Portfolios prompt students to show and tell their instructors — and themselves — how their creative and self-evaluative skills are developing.

RELATED TEACHING
GOALS   Develop ability to apply principles and generalizations already learned to new problems and situations (TGI Goal 1)
Develop ability to think creatively (TGI Goal 7)
Develop skill in using materials, tools, and/or technology central to this subject (TGI Goal 20)
Prepare for transfer or graduate study (TGI Goal 22)

Develop a commitment to personal achievement (TGI Goal 42)
Develop ability to perform skillfully (TGI Goal 43)

SUGGESTIONS FOR USE   This technique has clear applications in courses in the visual arts and creative writing, as well as in music, dance, drama, and broadcasting. In some of these courses, samples of student "work" might be presented on video- or audiotape. Portfolios can also be used in vocational fields to document the work of students fixing automobiles, writing computer programs, and learning nursing skills. In recent years, there has been a surge of interest in using portfolios to document and evaluate teaching effectiveness. To that end, this CAT can be used to assess the learning of student teachers and graduate teaching assistants.

EXAMPLES

From Intermediate Drawing (Fine Arts)

All students in the three sections of this second-year drawing course were asked to submit an Annotated Portfolio containing two or three drawings in which they felt they had creatively resolved problems of line, form, shading, or perspective. Along with those two or three drawings, they submitted one or two pages of comments explaining how they had creatively dealt with these traditional drawing problems and explicitly relating their solutions to the course content.

The three art instructors who taught these sections devoted a Saturday to reading and analyzing the brief portfolios together. Each instructor first read through his or her own students' work and made notes on strengths and weaknesses. Then they traded sets and read each other's Annotated Portfolios, once again making notes. After they had each assessed all three sets of portfolios, the instructors compared notes. They discussed the strengths and weaknesses they had seen in the classes and brainstormed teaching strategies for responding to them. In return for their investment of a Saturday, the instructors gained three benefits: (1) a much clearer knowledge of their own students' skills and understanding, (2) a better sense of how well their students were learning in relation to those in the other two sections, and (3) a few new teaching ideas.

From Practicum in Teaching Elementary Mathematics (Education)

The professor leading this practicum, herself a longtime mathematics teacher, required her student teachers to make Annotated Portfolios of lessons and materials they had created. Specifically, each student teacher was to put together a folder containing original lesson plans and materials from three related lessons, along with an explanation of the pedagogical and mathematical principles applied in those plans and materials.

The instructor was impressed by the amount of work and level of creativity evident in many of the lesson plans, and she found that most of her student teachers were able to articulate the pedagogical principles underlying their lessons. There were two common areas of weakness in their portfolios, however. First, many of the lessons were at inappropriate levels of difficulty for the students they addressed; second, many of the students did a poor job of identifying or explaining the mathematical principles their lessons were meant to illustrate. Since most of the student teachers were not math majors, the professor was not surprised that this task was difficult for them, but the level of their responses did shock her. As a result, she decided to spend much more meeting time on reviewing the fundamental mathematical principles to be taught and learned in elementary school and on assessing readiness and skill—and less time discussing lesson design and teaching techniques.

From Automobile Engine Repair (Automotive Technology)

During the first month of class, the instructor in this vocational education course required students to keep a detailed journal of the problems they had diagnosed and repaired. He encouraged them to take instant photographs, make sketches, and draw diagrams to illustrate what they had done and what they had learned. At the end of that month, he directed the students to prepare Annotated Portfolios. Each student was to choose two different, challenging engine problems that he or she had creatively and successfully diagnosed and repaired and—in five pages or fewer—to explain and illustrate what he or she had done and why. He encouraged students to use sketches and photos if they had them.

The students turned in quite a range of work, from very creative and complete portfolios to minimal responses. Almost all the students, however, had difficulty explaining what was challenging about the problems they had chosen for the portfolios and why they had taken the steps they had. The instructor shared several good examples with the class and talked about the value of learning by reviewing their own work. He also talked with them about the importance of being able to explain their work to customers—and to repair-shop owners. Most of the students agreed that they needed more practice in explaining what they had done and why; so the instructor began holding regular role-playing sessions, during which the apprentice car mechanics took turns playing skeptical customers and demanding shop supervisors.

STEP-BY-STEP PROCEDURE

1. Choose one of the central topics, questions, or problems dealt with in your course and invite students to respond to it with two or three samples of their work that demonstrate some creativity.

2. Ask the students to explain briefly, in writing, how the pieces in their portfolios respond to the topic, question, or problem you posed. You may need to give the class several examples of the kinds of annotations you are looking for.

3. Have students turn in their work samples and annotations in a folder, a binder, or an envelope.

TURNING THE DATA YOU COLLECT INTO USEFUL INFORMATION

Annotated Portfolios can be analyzed from two different but complementary points of view. You may first wish to assess the students' creativity in resolving or dealing with the question, topic, or problem assigned. Next, you may consider the quality of synthesis demonstrated in the annotations. That is, read the annotations to assess how well students have incorporated course topics, themes, or problems into their own work. A simple ranking scale containing letters or numbers will probably be adequate to give you a picture of the range of skills within the class. Taking brief notes on each portfolio as you read and rank it will provide you with a richer and more useful record for later comparison.

IDEAS FOR ADAPTING AND EXTENDING THIS CAT

Use the Annotated Portfolio as a first draft in an ongoing assignment, allowing students to get early, ungraded feedback on portfolios that will eventually be graded.

To assess change and growth throughout the term, invite students to add selected works to their portfolios as the course progresses and to rethink and rewrite their annotations.

Ask students to choose the topic or question on which to focus their portfolios, rather than assigning it yourself. Require only that it be clearly related to the course content.

Arrange an exhibition or showing of Annotated Portfolios so that students can learn from each other's works and annotations.

PROS

The Annotated Portfolio allows students to express their conceptions of problems or topics in images rather than in prose alone.

It requires students not only to select work samples that are personally meaningful but also to interpret the meaning of those samples for others.

Because this CAT allows students to choose the work on which they will be assessed, the teacher gains insights into what they value and appreciate.

In some fields, this technique also helps students prepare to present their work to prospective employers.

CONS

Unless the technique is presented carefully and is well integrated into the course, students in some fields may not consider it appropriately serious or academic.

No matter how you structure your assignments, Annotated Portfolios will take a significant amount of time to assess.

Students may spend so much time selecting or creating the components that they slight the task of interpreting the contents of their portfolios.

CAVEATS

To make the portfolios more useful, more comparable, or both, you may need to impose guidelines for their contents or form. If there are to be guidelines or rules of any sort, make sure to state them clearly at the beginning of the assignment.

Unless the Annotated Portfolio is clearly linked to other, graded assignments, some students will refuse to expend the amount of time and effort it requires.

You may need to offer students course credit for this CAT.

Assessing Skill
in Problem Solving

19. Problem Recognition Tasks

20. What's the Principle?

21. Documented Problem Solutions

22. Audio- and Videotaped Protocols

Effective problem-solving skills imply the previous mastery of necessary skills and knowledge. But problem solving requires metacognition as well. Good problem solvers recognize the types of problems they are dealing with and determine the principles and techniques needed to solve them. Good problem solvers look beyond different surface features and perceive underlying similarities among problems. They know how they work through problems, and they can reflect on and alter their problem-solving routines when necessary.

The four assessment techniques in this group allow faculty to assess and promote problem-solving skills of various kinds. Problem Recognition Tasks assess students' skill at determining exactly what kinds of problems they are faced with, so that they can choose the appropriate solution routines. What's the Principle? picks up at the next step, assessing students' skill at determining the relevant principles to apply to specific problems. Documented Problem Solutions focus directly on metacognitive skills, requiring the learners to make explicit each step they took in a solving a problem. Finally, Audio- and Videotaped Protocols allow students to demonstrate a problem-solving protocol in "real time," and to capture their narrated solutions for later assessment and study. Taken together, these CATs provide four different assessment perspectives on the development of problem-solving skills. They also offer the students who engage in them valuable opportunities to practice and improve metacognitive skills.

19

Problem Recognition Tasks

Estimated Levels of Time and Energy Required for:

Faculty to prepare to use this CAT	**MEDIUM**
Students to respond to the assessment	**LOW**
Faculty to analyze the data collected	**LOW**

DESCRIPTION

Problem Recognition Tasks present students with a few examples of common problem types. The students' task is to recognize and identify the particular type of problem each example represents.

PURPOSE

In many fields, students learn a variety of problem-solving methods, but they often have difficulty determining which kinds of problems are best solved by which methods. Problem Recognition Tasks help faculty assess how well students can recognize various problem types, the first step in matching problem type to solution method. As students work through this CAT, they practice thinking generally about problems they often view as individual, isolated exemplars. This practice helps them develop a valuable diagnostic skill.

RELATED TEACHING GOALS

Develop ability to apply principles and generalizations already learned to new problems and situations (TGI Goal 1)

Develop problem-solving skills (TGI Goal 3)

Develop appropriate study skills, strategies, and habits (TGI Goal 16)

Improve mathematical skills (TGI Goal 17)

Prepare for transfer or graduate study (TGI Goal 22)

Learn techniques and methods used to gain new knowledge in this subject (TGI Goal 23)

Develop ability to perform skillfully (TGI Goal 43)

SUGGESTIONS FOR USE

Problem Recognition Tasks lend themselves naturally to quantitative and technical fields in which students learn a variety of specific problem-solving techniques or methods. Examples of such disciplines include mathematics, physics, statistics, and accounting. But this assessment can also be applied to fields in which students learn more general heuristics—broad problem-solving approaches—such as in critical thinking, composition, policy analysis, nursing, medicine, law, and counseling.

EXAMPLES

From Issues in Student Counseling (Psychology/Counseling Education)

To assess their ability to recognize and diagnose different types of common problems, the instructor in this course for high school counselors presented his graduate students with six half-page mini-cases, each describing an adolescent referred for counseling. The graduate students were given a half-hour to read the cases and to make an initial judgment about the main problem in each case. Was it substance abuse, family conflicts, academic stress, conflicts with peers, or depression? The students were also asked to write one or two sentences explaining the basis for their judgments.

The psychology professor, himself a counselor, found that many of the graduate students missed important clues and evidence in the mini-cases and that they often failed to support reasonable diagnoses with relevant evidence. Several students refused to make any judgments, arguing that there was too little evidence presented in the mini-cases. As he read through and summarized the responses to the Problem Recognition Task, the professor planned his strategy for the next class. This feedback showed him that many of the graduate students did not appreciate the absolute need to make quick and accurate initial diagnoses in the high-volume, understaffed school environment. He also saw that many had not yet developed the diagnostic skills needed to counsel confidently and well. To build skills and confidence, the professor began assigning mini-cases requiring quick diagnosis for in-class discussion weekly. To assess progress, he used the Problem Recognition Task again at three-week intervals.

From Intermediate Statistics for Management (Statistics/Business/Management)

To determine how well his students had learned to distinguish different types of statistical procedures, this business professor created a Problem Recognition Task to use during the first week of his second-year course. The one-page assessment consisted of five word problems adapted from the introductory course's final exam. The students were asked to indicate what kind of statistical procedure would best solve each problem. Specifically, the assessment asked whether the problems could be solved by chi-square testing, one-way ANOVA, two-way ANOVA, simple linear regression, or multiple regression. The instructor found that the students had most trouble recognizing ANOVA problems and adjusted his review preparation accordingly.

STEP-BY-STEP PROCEDURE

1. Choose examples of several different but related problem types that students find difficult to distinguish. Make sure that each example illustrates one and only one type of problem.

2. Decide whether you will provide information about the types of problems that students are to recognize, allowing them simply to match type with example, or whether you will ask students to name the problem types as well.

3. Try out your examples on a colleague or an advanced student to see whether he or she agrees with your choice of examples. This run-through also can help you assess the difficulty of the task and the time that it will take to complete.

4. Make up a short Problem Recognition Task form or overhead projector transparency containing a handful of example problems for students to recognize. Allow your students twice or three times the amount of time it took your colleague to respond.

TURNING THE DATA YOU COLLECT INTO USEFUL INFORMATION

In most cases, you can quickly scan the responses and tally the number of correct and incorrect answers for each problem.

IDEAS FOR ADAPTING AND EXTENDING THIS CAT

Allow small groups of students to work together to respond to the Problem Recognition Task. Group work is especially valuable for students who are just learning diagnosis or in classes where there are wide variations in skill levels.

Encourage students to come up with parallel examples of each problem type.

Ask students to explain, in detail, what distinguishes the different types of problems and what clues an expert would seek to distinguish them quickly.

If you are using complex problems that allow for more than one interpretation, ask students to justify their responses with reference to the evidence presented in the examples.

PROS

The Problem Recognition Task is a quick, simple way to assess students' diagnostic skills. It focuses student attention on correctly recognizing and diagnosing problems first, rather than immediately trying to solve them.

By helping students make connections between the specific and general levels of problem solving, this CAT shows them how to apply the problem-solving skills they are learning to new and unfamiliar situations.

CONS

Many real-life problems are multiple and therefore do not fit easily into one category.

The fact that students can correctly recognize a problem type does not necessarily mean that they know how to solve that problem.

CAVEATS   As noted above, many real-world problems are complex and multi-faceted, so the examples used in Problem Recognition Tasks may have to be simplified to highlight the distinctions between problem types. Be sure to explain the need for and the limitations of these "streamlined" example problems to students.

This is a skill that many students have not been explicitly taught. Therefore, you may have to demonstrate problem recognition and provide practice in this skill before you can assess students in any meaningful way.

What's the Principle?

Estimated Levels of Time and Energy Required for:

Faculty to prepare to use this CAT	**MEDIUM**
Students to respond to the assessment	**LOW**
Faculty to analyze the data collected	**LOW**

DESCRIPTION
After students figure out what type of problem they are dealing with, they often must then decide what principle or principles to apply in order to solve the problem. This CAT focuses on that second step in problem solving. It provides students with a few problems and asks them to state the principle that best applies to each problem.

PURPOSE
What's the Principle? assesses students' ability to associate specific problems with the general principles used to solve them — or the principles that, having been violated, created the problems. Responses to this technique tell faculty whether students understand how to apply basic principles of the discipline. What's the Principle? helps students recognize the general types of problems they can solve with particular principles, rather than merely learning how to solve individual problems.

RELATED TEACHING GOALS
Develop ability to apply principles and generalizations already learned to new problems and situations (TGI Goal 1)
Develop problem-solving skills (TGI Goal 3)
Develop appropriate study skills, strategies, and habits (TGI Goal 16)
Improve mathematical skills (TGI Goal 17)
Prepare for transfer or graduate study (TGI Goal 22)
Learn techniques and methods used to gain new knowledge in this subject (TGI Goal 23)
Learn to evaluate methods and materials in this subject (TGI Goal 24)
Develop a commitment to accurate work (TGI Goal 39)
Develop ability to perform skillfully (TGI Goal 43)

SUGGESTIONS FOR USE
What's the Principle? is an easy assessment to use in any course where students learn rules or principles of practice, however precise or imprecise those principles may be. Like Problem Recognition Tasks (CAT 19), this CAT

can be used in quantitative and scientific fields that make use of tightly defined algorithms, or in social sciences and applied disciplines that depend on more general "rules of good practice."

EXAMPLES

Principles of Financial Accounting (Accounting/Business/Management)

Although this accounting professor put great emphasis on the basic principles of financial accounting in his lectures, he suspected that many of his students were not making connections between the problems on their homework assignments and those principles. To find out, he created a simple What's the Principle? form, listing five major principles the class had heard and read about, and seven problems. The accounting principles were numbered I through V; so the students simply had to put the correct principle number in front of each problem.

The professor administered this CAT to his large class during the last ten minutes of the period, sure that he had given students more than enough time. To his surprise, about half of the students did not complete their assessments by the end of class, and many still had not finished when he collected the forms five minutes later. When he quickly tallied the results, he found widespread confusion and evidence of much guessing. He used this feedback to justify his decision to give the financial accounting class more assignments requiring them to connect principles and problems.

Teaching and Learning in Higher Education (Education/Psychology)

To find out how well and how quickly graduate students in this required course could connect general principles and specific practices, this higher education professor constructed a What's the Principle? assessment based on Gamson and Chickering's (1987) "Seven Principles for Good Practice in Undergraduate Education." Her assessment form contained the list of seven principles, reproduced below.

Good Practice in Undergraduate Education

1. Encourages contact between students and faculty

2. Develops reciprocity and cooperation among students

3. Encourages active learning

4. Gives prompt feedback on performance

5. Emphasizes time on task

6. Communicates high expectations

7. Respects diverse talents and ways of learning

Following these principles were ten brief descriptions of specific teaching behaviors. After she gave a brief lecture on the "Seven Principles," the professor handed out her assessment, allowing students the last ten minutes before the mid-class break to complete it. The graduate students were directed to write the number of the relevant principles in front of the examples, and then to add a "plus" sign if the example embodied the given principle or a "minus" sign if it contradicted the principle.

During the fifteen-minute break in her three-hour class, the professor quickly tallied the responses. The students did quite well, in general, but had some problems recognizing applications of "active learning" and "time on task." Informed by this assessment, she spent a few minutes after the break sharing the results and discussing these two less familiar principles.

STEP-BY-STEP PROCEDURE

1. Identify the basic principles that you expect students to learn in your course. Make sure to focus only on those that students have been taught.

2. Find or create sample problems or short examples that illustrate each of these principles. Each example should illustrate only one principle.

3. Create a What's the Principle? form that includes a listing of the relevant principles and specific examples or problems for students to match to those principles.

4. Try out your assessment on a graduate student or colleague to make certain it is not too difficult or too time-consuming to use in class.

5. After you have made any necessary revisions to the form, apply the assessment.

TURNING THE DATA YOU COLLECT INTO USEFUL INFORMATION

What's the Principle? forms should be very easy and quick to score. Simply tally the number of right and wrong answers, and note patterns in the specific wrong answers given. If you find lots of wrong answers and no sensible patterns, students are probably guessing.

IDEAS FOR ADAPTING AND EXTENDING THIS CAT

Provide students with only the principles, and ask them to come up with good and bad examples of applications.

Give students only the examples, and assess their ability to recall important principles, as well as to apply them.

Follow up by asking students to justify each of their choices of principles in a sentence or two.

PROS

What's the Principle? is an extremely simple, very quick way to get useful information on a complex skill: recognizing general principles embodied in or violated by specific examples.

It provides students with quick feedback on their level of skill at moving between the general and the specific, and it gives them practice in developing that skill.

Use of this CAT promotes the learning of transferable problem-solving skills that students may remember long after they have forgotten specific examples.

CONS

Unless students understand that the point is to develop skill at deciding which principles to apply in dealing with new and unfamiliar problems, they may see this assessment simply as a kind of lower-level item-matching task.

Skill in matching principles to problems does not translate directly into skill in solving those same problems.

CAVEATS

This assessment usually does not work well with raw beginners, because they have not seen enough examples and worked enough problems to generalize effectively. It also does not work well with advanced students, who are more interested in the "gray areas," where no general principles or several principles may apply.

As with problem recognition, connecting principles and problems is a skill that many students have not been explicitly taught. Therefore, you may have to teach it before you can assess it.

CLASSROOM ASSESSMENT TECHNIQUE

21

Documented Problem Solutions

Estimated Levels of Time and Energy Required for:

Faculty to prepare to use this CAT	LOW
Students to respond to the assessment	MEDIUM
Faculty to analyze the data collected	MEDIUM to HIGH

DESCRIPTION

To become truly proficient problem solvers, students need to learn to do more than just get correct answers to textbook problems. At some point, they need to become aware of how they solved those problems and how they can adapt their problem-solving routines to deal with messy, real-world problems. The Documented Problem Solutions technique prompts students to keep track of the steps they take in solving a problem — to "show and tell" how they worked it out. By analyzing these detailed protocols — in which each solution step is briefly explained in writing — teachers can gain valuable information on their students' problem-solving skills.

PURPOSE

Documented Problem Solutions have two main aims: (1) to assess how students solve problems and (2) to assess how well students understand and can describe their problem-solving methods. Therefore, the primary emphasis of the technique is on documenting the specific steps that students take in attempting to solve representative problems — rather than on whether the answers are correct or not. As they respond to the assessment, students benefit by gaining more awareness of and control over their problem-solving routines. Understanding and using effective problem-solving procedures is, after all, a critical component of mastery in most disciplines.

RELATED TEACHING GOALS

Develop ability to apply principles and generalizations already learned to new problems and situations (TGI Goal 1)
Develop problem-solving skills (TGI Goal 3)
Develop appropriate study skills, strategies, and habits (TGI Goal 16)
Improve mathematical skills (TGI Goal 17)
Prepare for transfer or graduate study (TGI Goal 22)
Learn techniques and methods used to gain new knowledge in this subject (TGI Goal 23)

Learn to evaluate methods and materials in this subject (TGI Goal 24)
Develop a commitment to accurate work (TGI Goal 39)
Develop ability to perform skillfully (TGI Goal 43)

SUGGESTIONS FOR USE   The Documented Problem Solutions technique is especially useful for assessing problem solving in highly quantitative courses, such as accounting, algebra, calculus, computer programming, engineering, microeconomics, physics, and statistics. It can also be used in other fields that teach structured approaches to problem solving, fields such as logic, tort law, organic chemistry, transformational grammar, and music theory.

EXAMPLES

From Algebra I (Mathematics)

> Before moving on to the next topic, an Algebra I instructor wanted to assess her students' approaches to solving quadratic equations. She assigned three problems as a Documented Problem Solution assessment, promising to give students homework credit for complete responses. She directed her students to spend no more than one hour working out the problems and documenting the solutions. After reading the responses she realized that there were three groups in the class: those who answered at least two problems correctly and documented their solutions well; those who answered at least two problems correctly but documented their steps poorly; and those who clearly misunderstood the solution process and got most or all answers wrong. These responses convinced her of the need to spend another session on quadratic equations, focusing on making the solution process explicit.

From Transformational Syntax (Linguistics)

> Students in this first-year linguistics course spend a great deal of time and effort learning to analyze and diagram sentences according to the Chomskyan transformational grammar approach. To gain insights into their problem-solving skills, the professor gave them a rather difficult sentence—one chock-full of embedded relative clauses and adverbial phrases—to diagram. He asked them to fold a piece of paper in half. On the left half of the page, they were to draw each step in the diagramming process; on the right half, they were to write a brief note explaining and justifying each step. The results of this Documented Problem Solution were surprising: although several students followed many of the same steps, they often gave very different reasons for their moves. His summary of these differences led to an in-depth class discussion of what constitutes legitimate and reasonable explanation.

STEP-BY-STEP PROCEDURE   1. Select one, two, or three representative problems from among the problems students have studied during the previous few weeks. If you decide to assign three problems, for example, try to select at least one that all the students can solve, another that most of the class can solve, and a third that will challenge most of your students.

2. Solve the problems yourself, and write down all the steps you take in solving them. Note how long it takes you and how many steps each problem solution required.

3. If you find any of the problems too time-consuming or too complicated, replace or revise them.

4. Once you have good problems that you can solve and document in less than thirty minutes, write them up for the students. Assume that it will take students at least twice as long as it took you to document the solutions. Make your directions very explicit.

5. Hand out and explain the assessment problem(s), making clear to the students that it is not a test or a quiz. It is more important for students to explain how they try to solve the problems than to get the right answers. Having well-documented steps is even more important if they fail to get a correct answer, since they can then diagnose where and how they went wrong. If you assign the assessment problem as homework, let students know the maximum amount of time they should spend on it.

TURNING THE DATA YOU COLLECT INTO USEFUL INFORMATION

If you are teaching more than a handful of students, select a few responses to analyze. After skimming quickly through all of them, pick three responses in which the answers are correct and the solutions well documented. Pick another set of three that contain well-documented solutions but incorrect answers. Compare the solutions within and across sets. Make notes on solution paths that led to successful outcomes and those that led to mistakes. Try to locate general zones, or the exact spots, in the solution processes that determined correct or incorrect results. For example, were the results incorrect because the students skipped steps? After completing your analysis, write down three or four main insights and/or suggestions to share with students. If time allows, prepare an overhead transparency or a handout detailing one or two particularly elegant solutions.

IDEAS FOR ADAPTING AND EXTENDING THIS CAT

Use this device as a diagnostic pre-assessment by giving the class two problems—one of low and the other of medium difficulty—to work through before they study the material. Use the results to gauge the best level at which to begin instruction.

Divide the class into small groups and ask the students with elegant, well-documented responses to explain their solution processes step by step to those who had difficulties.

Ask one or two students who documented their (successful) solutions especially well to lead the class through one of their responses, step by step.

Use this assessment as a regular part of homework assignments. For example, you might ask students to document one problem in each homework set, or one problem on each quiz or test. Students can be given credit for doing a thorough job of documenting, without receiving a grade.

PROS

The Documented Problem Solution technique helps teachers and students look "behind" specific answers to glimpse the students' thinking processes and problem-solving strategies. In other words, it focuses more attention on the process than on the product.

It allows the teacher and the students to become aware of a range of possible successful—and unsuccessful—approaches to problem solving.

By prompting students to make each step manifest and explicit, this CAT promotes the development of discipline-specific metacognitive skills—in this case, awareness of and control over problem-solving processes.

CONS

At first, many students may find it quite difficult to explain how they solve problems, even when their answers demonstrate that they do know how to solve them.

Even the faculty may not always be able to figure out and explain why a given set of steps worked or failed to work.

When students take different solution paths or are working at a wide variety of levels, it may not be useful or even possible to give general feedback on their responses.

CAVEATS

Don't expect students to write good step-by-step solutions the first or even the second time they try. Most students have little or no experience in reflecting on their own problem-solving processes. If you want students to develop this skill, you—or someone else—may have to help them learn how.

Documented Problem Solutions can be difficult and time-consuming to carry out. To get thoughtful and thorough responses, you may need to give students credit for completing the assessment.

Don't feel bound to analyze more data than you can comfortably handle, but make sure that students at all levels get some useful feedback.

REFERENCES AND RESOURCES

In her widely influential book *Errors and Expectations* (1977), the late Mina Shaughnessy provided a comprehensive description and discussion of her experiences as she attempted to develop error-analysis techniques to help her make sense of the bewildering writing of underprepared college students. Although it deals only with writing instruction, *Errors and Expectations* remains the most thoughtful and inspiring argument we know of for the use of error analysis to improve learning.

C L A S S R O O M
A S S E S S M E N T
T E C H N I Q U E

22

Audio- and Videotaped Protocols

Estimated Levels of Time and Energy Required for:

Faculty to prepare to use this CAT	**HIGH**
Students to respond to the assessment	**HIGH**
Faculty to analyze the data collected	**HIGH**

DESCRIPTION Audio- and Videotaped Protocols (A/V Protocols) are Classroom Assessment Techniques that edge over into Classroom Research. Indeed, protocols of this sort are commonly used in formal educational and psychological research on problem solving and metacognition. Even the simplest application of this technique is likely to be more time-consuming and complicated than any other in this handbook; however, it can provide a wealth of useful information to teacher and student alike. By studying an audio or video recording of a student talking and working through the process of solving a problem, teachers and students can get very close to an "inside view" of the problem-solving process.

PURPOSE On the simplest level, Audio- and Videotaped Protocols allow faculty to assess in detail how and how well students solve problems. But the real advantage of this technique is that it allows faculty to assess how students understand their problem-solving processes and how they explain those processes to themselves. Therefore, the main purpose of A/V Protocols is to assess metacognition—the learner's awareness of and control of his or her own thinking.

RELATED TEACHING GOALS Develop ability to apply principles and generalizations already learned to new problems and situations (TGI Goal 1)
Develop problem-solving skills (TGI Goal 3)
Develop appropriate study skills, strategies, and habits (TGI Goal 16)
Improve mathematical skills (TGI Goal 17)
Prepare for transfer or graduate study (TGI Goal 22)
Learn techniques and methods used to gain new knowledge in this subject (TGI Goal 23)
Learn to evaluate methods and materials in this subject (TGI Goal 24)
Develop a commitment to accurate work (TGI Goal 39)
Develop ability to perform skillfully (TGI Goal 43)

SUGGESTIONS FOR USE Because the process of recording students as they solve problems is complicated and time-consuming, this technique is feasible only with very small numbers of students. Consequently, A/V Protocols can be used in classes of average size if the instructor selects and reviews only a handful of student protocols. These protocols can be valuable in any course where students must learn complex procedures in order to solve problems. For example, students can be video- or audiotaped as they work through problems in courses in mathematics, physical sciences, engineering, statistics, or any other quantitative field. This technique can also be used to capture students solving "problems" in clinical nursing and allied health courses, in other vocational and technical areas, and in the performing arts. Even apprentice teachers can be assessed as they solve instructional "problems."

EXAMPLES

From Automotive Technology (Vocational and Technical Education)

The ten students in this course were given the task of diagnosing and fixing problems in new and highly sophisticated electronic carburetors. Working in pairs, students took turns videotaping each other as they quickly worked through a diagnostic routine, explaining each step. Each student was given fifteen minutes to diagnose the problem—which had been "caused" by the instructor—and to make the necessary adjustments. The instructor later viewed the videos and critiqued them by means of a checklist he had developed. He chose two videos for the whole class to view.

From Calculus for Secondary Teachers (Mathematics/Education)

To help her graduate students develop effective ways to teach the limit concept, this professor gave each of them a typical problem to solve. She asked them to prepare a ten-minute teaching demonstration of the steps in the problem solution and explained that the demonstration would be videotaped. The graduate students made appointments with the university's audiovisual department to be videotaped, prepared their own videotapes, and turned them in to the department secretary.

The instructor chose five students, more or less at random, whose tapes she reviewed and wrote comments about. She met with those students outside of class to give them feedback on their tapes and to prepare them to help her lead the next class. In the next class meeting, the class was divided into groups of five, and each group had a videotape playback unit. Using a few minutes from each of the videotapes she had watched, the instructor showed the students what to look for and how to provide useful feedback. She then allowed the small groups, each led by one of the students she had critiqued, to watch and give feedback on each other's videotapes. During the third hour of the class, all the students worked together to develop protocols for solving the limit problem and for teaching students to solve it.

From Introduction to Programming (Computer Science)

In this introductory course, students were asked to audiotape themselves as they solved a simple programming problem at the workstations. They were asked to talk into the microphones as if they were explaining each step over the telephone to classmates who could not see their screens. They were then asked to transcribe the first five minutes of their protocols into print via word processor and to hand in those transcriptions. Their instructor read through all the protocols quickly and then carefully assessed two very good ones and two very poor ones, comparing the steps each student had taken. Later, she gave students general feedback on their solutions to the programming problem, as well as detailed suggestions based on the close analysis.

STEP-BY-STEP PROCEDURE

1. Choose a problem that clearly requires the application of a several-step solution protocol, which students have already been taught or can be expected to know. Make sure the problem lends itself to "talking through" on audiotape or to "showing and telling" on videotape, and that it can be solved in a few minutes by most students.

2. Determine whether the problem protocol can be audiotaped and transcribed by students or should be videotaped. Videotape is obviously more complex and cannot be usefully transcribed by students without training.

3. Figure out in advance what you will look for in their responses and how you will analyze and respond to the protocols.

4. Make sure that the necessary facilities and equipment are readily available to students.

5. Draw up a problem statement and detailed directions for recording the solution protocol. Give students clear time limits for their recordings and/or length limits for the transcriptions.

6. Let students know what you are looking for in their recordings. Be prepared to give examples and to demonstrate what you would like them to do. Explain also what they are supposed to learn from this assessment exercise.

7. Make clear to students what kind and how much feedback they can expect to receive on their protocols from you and/or from each other.

TURNING THE DATA YOU COLLECT INTO USEFUL INFORMATION

Unless you have only a handful of student protocols to listen to, read, or watch, you will need to limit the number of points you focus on. Begin by creating a protocol of your own, listing the elements or steps of the problem solution that you expect to find in the students' responses. In many cases, you can create a checklist to use when reviewing students' protocols and then summarize several of those checklists to give feedback to the class. Or you can give each student a copy of the individual checklist you prepared on his or her work, thereby providing all the students with more detailed feedback on their own performance and allowing them to compare and connect your responses to their work with your overall response to the group.

Ask students to videotape and view each other as they work through the problem. Working in pairs or triads, students can take turns behind the camera.

Create a checklist for viewing and suggestions for giving feedback and have students view and comment on each other's tapes.

PROS

Recording a problem-solving protocol makes it available to faculty and other students who might not have been able to see the original procedure, and it allows repeated review and study.

Unlike the original demonstrations, the recordings can be stopped, rewound, and replayed at will.

This CAT requires the teacher and students to work closely together to understand the problem-solving process. This focused collaboration almost invariably benefits learning.

Teachers gain insights into how students process what they are learning from the class and from the course materials, allowing them to direct students' attention to critical points.

Students have opportunities to make their usually implicit problem-solving routines explicit and, thereby, to gain more control over those routines.

CONS

A/V Protocols require students and instructors to expend a considerable amount of time and energy.

There is, of course, virtually no way for students using this technique to remain anonymous. Therefore, some students may be inhibited from trying, because they are afraid that they will do a poor job in working through the protocol.

Unless you are working in a field where there is only one accepted way of solving a given type of problem, students' protocols are likely to be diverse and difficult or impossible to compare directly.

Some students who are relatively good problem solvers are relatively poor at demonstrating what they know. This is a difficult skill for many to develop.

CAVEATS

In many cases, the time and effort required for A/V Protocols cannot be justified unless students need to develop the ability to explain and demonstrate problem-solving skills in order to prepare for further education or employment.

Students will expect and probably should receive course credit for carrying out this CAT completely and well.

Instructors who use this CAT need to be open-minded about the variety of problem-solving approaches they are likely to see, and ready to respond to them in helpful ways.

REFERENCES AND RESOURCES See Nakaji (1991, pp. 81–84) for a detailed description of a Classroom Research project in which students were videotaped as they solved problems in physics. Nakaji's use of videotaping, though much more complex than this Classroom Assessment Technique, contributed much to its development.

Assessing Skill in Application and Performance

In a very real sense, the most lasting and important skills and knowledge that students learn in college are those they somehow learn to apply. As noted earlier, educational theorists and researchers commonly refer to the learning of facts and principles as "declarative learning," and to the learning of skills as "procedural learning." Learning the appropriate conditions—the when and where—for applying what one has learned is called "conditional knowledge." The five assessment techniques in this section assess students' conditional knowledge in five different ways.

Directed Paraphrasing requires that students translate something they have learned into language and concepts that a particular audience will understand; in other words, it assesses their skill at applying declarative knowledge to a new context. Applications Cards prompt students to come up with their own examples of possible applications of the material they are studying. Student-Generated Test Questions require students to review, evaluate, and apply what they have learned. The Human Tableau or Class Modeling technique assesses performance by engaging students in physically acting out their applications of knowledge. Finally, the Paper or Project Prospectus requires that students plan future applications and performance of knowledge.

In one way or another, these CATs encourage students to show what they know and demonstrate how well they can use it. As such, they all provide students with valuable practice in conditional learning and faculty with useful information for enhancing that learning.

Directed Paraphrasing

Estimated Levels of Time and Energy Required for:

Faculty to prepare to use this CAT	**LOW**
Students to respond to the assessment	**MEDIUM**
Faculty to analyze the data collected	**MEDIUM**

DESCRIPTION In many fields, particularly in the professions and the service sector, success depends on one's ability to translate highly specialized information into language that clients or customers will understand. Directed Paraphrasing is an assessment technique designed to assess and help develop that valuable skill. In this CAT, students are directed to paraphrase part of a lesson for a specific audience and purpose, using their own words.

PURPOSE On the simplest level, Directed Paraphrasing provides feedback on students' ability to summarize and restate important information or concepts in their own words; it therefore allows faculty to assess how well students have understood and internalized that learning. At the same time, this technique assesses the students' ability to translate that learning into a form that someone outside the classroom can understand. The fact that the paraphrase is "directed," aimed at a specific audience for a specific reason, makes the paraphrasing task more demanding and more useful than simple paraphrasing, for students and faculty alike.

RELATED TEACHING GOALS Develop ability to apply principles and generalizations already learned to new problems and situations (TGI Goal 1)
Improve writing skills (TGI Goal 15)
Develop appropriate study skills, strategies, and habits (TGI Goal 16)
Learn concepts and theories in this subject (TGI Goal 19)
Develop management skills (TGI Goal 37)
Develop ability to perform skillfully (TGI Goal 43)

SUGGESTIONS FOR USE Directed Paraphrasing is particularly useful for assessing the students' understanding of important topics or concepts that they will later be expected to explain to others. For example, in fields such as marketing, social work, public health, education, law, and criminal justice, much of a student's eventual success depends on his or her ability to internalize specialized and often complex information and then to communicate it effectively to the public.

In preprofessional courses, specifying the audiences for the paraphrases can be particularly useful, since students then can practice paraphrasing for their likely future clients. In more general college courses, especially in the humanities and social sciences, the audience might be other students in the class or students in related, lower-level courses. Basically, the more authentic the audience, the more useful the Directed Paraphrase.

EXAMPLES   The following are examples of Directed Paraphrasing prompts from several different disciplines.

From Gerontological Nursing (Nursing)

In one or two sentences, paraphrase what you have learned about hospice care to inform a dying, but still lucid, patient of its possible advantages over hospital or home care.

From Database Systems (Computer Science)

In plain language and in less than five minutes, paraphrase what you have read about computer viruses—such as the Michelangelo virus— for a vice president of a large insurance firm who is ultimately responsible for database security. Your aim is to convince her to spend time and money "revaccinating" thousands of workstations.

From Science in the Secondary Schools (Education)

First, in no more than two or three sentences, paraphrase the "punctuated equilibrium" theory of evolution advanced by Niles Eldredge and Stephen Jay Gould. Direct your paraphrase to a veteran science teacher who has taught the "modern synthesis" view for years and has never heard of this more recent theory. Next, write a paraphrase of the same theory but for a very different audience. Paraphrase "punctuated equilibrium" in two or three sentences for a bright seventh grader who knows a lot about dinosaurs but little about evolutionary theory.

From Managing Community Relations (Criminal Justice)

Imagine that you are the city's deputy police commissioner in charge of community relations and public affairs. For a two-minute presentation at a meeting of the police officers' union, paraphrase the arguments in favor of creating a civilian review board. Then, for an equally short statement at the next public meeting of the city council, paraphrase the arguments against creating a civilian review board.

From Small-Business Finance (Business/Management)

Imagine that you have just been invited to give a talk to a group of local small-business owners on specific ways in which proposed changes in the state tax code may affect them. Paraphrase, in one or two sentences, the proposed changes that are most likely to affect this audience.

1. Select an important theory, concept, or argument that students have studied in some depth. This should be a topic with some implications outside the classroom.

2. Determine who would be a realistic yet challenging audience for a paraphrase of this topic, what the purpose of such a paraphrase should be, and how long—in number of written words or amount of speaking time—the Directed Paraphrase should be. If your students are well prepared in the material and/or experienced in the field, direct them to paraphrase the same topic for two very different audiences.

3. Try responding to the Directed Paraphrase yourself, to see how realistic the assignment is. Can you write an effective paraphrase within the limits given?

4. Direct the students to prepare a paraphrase of the chosen topic. Tell them who the intended audience is, what the purpose is, and what the limits are on speaking time or on number of words or sentences. Let students know how much time they will have to respond to the assessment. (Unless you plan to review video- or audiotapes, have the students write out their Directed Paraphrases, even though in real life many of them would be spoken.)

**TURNING THE DATA YOU
COLLECT INTO USEFUL
INFORMATON**

If you have collected written feedback, you can begin by separating the responses into four piles, which might be labeled "confused," "minimal," "adequate," and "excellent." Then assess the responses by comparing them within and across categories. Pay particular attention to three characteristics of the response: the accuracy of the paraphrase, its suitability for the intended audience, and its effectiveness in fulfilling the assigned purpose. Another approach is simply to circle the clearest and muddiest points in each paraphrase, using different-colored pens or pencils, and then to look for common patterns of clarity and confusion.

**IDEAS FOR ADAPTING
AND EXTENDING
THIS CAT**

Direct students to paraphrase the same topic for two very different audiences, and then to explain in detail the differences between the two paraphrases.

Ask students to keep a journal of paraphrases as a summary of important topics in the course.

Have different students paraphrase different reading assignments or lectures and then ask them to share those paraphrases with the other members of their study groups or with the rest of the class.

Get an appropriate outside "expert" to comment on and assess some or all of the paraphrases and give authentic feedback to the students. Or have the students themselves role-play the parts of the expert readers.

Provide handouts with examples of particularly successful paraphrases.

Give each student a checklist of the strong and weak points of his or her response.

PROS

Directed Paraphrasing builds on and builds up the students' skills in actively and purposefully comprehending and communicating information learned in a course.

This technique allows the teacher to find out quickly and in some detail how well students have understood a given lesson, lecture, or segment of the course. This information can provide direction for instruction, as well as for syllabus revision.

It forces teachers and students to consider the wider relevance of the subject being studied and the importance of considering the needs and interests of the audience being addressed.

CONS

Unless strict length limits are enforced, Directed Paraphrases can take considerable time and effort to assess adequately.

It is difficult to establish qualitative criteria for a good paraphrase and also to make those criteria explicit to students.

The paraphrasing skills of some students will not improve appreciably unless the instructor provides some focused, individualized feedback. Once again, this is a rather time-intensive technique.

CAVEATS

If a Directed Paraphrasing exercise is to be a meaningful assessment and learning task, it must be well structured and planned. The choices of audience(s) and purpose are particularly important.

Students' first efforts are likely not to look much like their own words; after all, most students have had many years of practice in not writing in their own words.

This CAT must be used more than once during the course if students, as well as the instructor, are to learn from the process.

CLASSROOM
ASSESSMENT
TECHNIQUE
24

Applications Cards

Estimated Levels of Time and Energy Required for:

Faculty to prepare to use this CAT	**LOW**
Students to respond to the assessment	**LOW to MEDIUM**
Faculty to analyze the data collected	**LOW to MEDIUM**

DESCRIPTION

After students have heard or read about an important principle, generalization, theory, or procedure, the instructor hands out an index card and asks them to write down at least one possible, real-world application for what they have just learned. In a nutshell, that is the Applications Card technique.

PURPOSE

Applications Cards let faculty know in a flash how well students understand the possible applications of what they have learned. This technique prompts students to think about possible applications and, as a consequence, to connect newly learned concepts with prior knowledge. As they respond to the technique, students also see more clearly the possible relevance of what they are learning.

RELATED TEACHING GOALS

Develop ability to apply principles and generalizations already learned to new problems and situations (TGI Goal 1)

Develop ability to draw reasonable inferences from observation (TGI Goal 4)

Develop ability to think creatively (TGI Goal 7)

Develop appropriate study skills, strategies, and habits (TGI Goal 16)

Learn concepts and theories in this subject (TGI Goal 19)

Develop an appreciation of the liberal arts and sciences (TGI Goal 26)

Develop a capacity to think for oneself (TGI Goal 51)

SUGGESTIONS FOR USE

Since there are few, if any, disciplines with no possible applications, this CAT can be used in almost any course. It is often used in the social sciences, preprofessional studies, and vocational and technical education. Thanks to its simplicity, the Applications Card can be adapted to a wide variety of class types and sizes.

EXAMPLES   The following are examples of Applications Card prompts used by faculty in several disciplines to assess learning.

From Principles of Microeconomics (Economics)

> Gresham's law basically states that "good money drives out bad." Give at least one contemporary application of Gresham's law to something other than money.

From Statistics for Health Professionals (Statistics)

> After the class had studied statistical significance testing, the professor asked her students to provide "three possible applications of statistical significance testing to public health issues currently in the news."

From Introduction to the U.S. Political System (Political Science)

> "All politics is local" is an oft-repeated saying in American political life. Suggest two practical applications of this generalization to the politics of presidential campaigning. (Imagine that you are giving advice to a candidate.)

From Educational Psychology (Psychology)

> Psychologists have long noted the effects of "primacy" and "recency" on recall of information. These effects have some implications for classroom teaching and learning. Suggest one or two applications of these implications for teachers using the lecture method.

From Foundations of Physics (Physics)

> In his *Principia*, Sir Isaac Newton set forth—among many other important ideas—his Third Law, the heart of which is "To every action there is always opposed an equal reaction." Give three applications of Newton's Third Law to everyday life around the house.

From Human Resources Management (Business/Management)

> Having read and discussed several articles on total quality management (TQM), students in this course were asked to provide at least two feasible, low-cost applications of TQM to their own companies, the business school, or other organizations with which they were very familiar.

STEP-BY-STEP PROCEDURE

1. Identify an important—and clearly applicable—principle, theory, generalization, or procedure that your students are studying or have just studied.

2. Decide how many applications you will ask for and how much time you will allow for the assessment. One is often enough, and we suggest asking for no more than three applications. Three to five minutes is usually enough time. Before class starts, figure out exactly how you will word the assessment prompt.

3. Announce what you are going to do; then hand out small index cards or slips of paper. Remind students that the point is to come up with their own "fresh" applications, not to repeat applications they have heard in class or read in the text.

4. Collect the Applications Cards and let students know when they will get feedback.

TURNING THE DATA YOU COLLECT INTO USEFUL INFORMATION

Usually you will be able to tell right away (1) whether the applications are accurate (whether they are appropriate for the theory, procedure, or principle under discussion) and (2) how reasonable, useful, or creative the applications are. Quickly read once through the Applications Cards, marking the individual applications with symbols such as G, A, M, or N, for example — to stand for "great," "acceptable," "marginal," or "not acceptable" examples. If each Applications Card contains only one application, you can easily sort the cards into piles, according to their quality and correctness. Pick out three to five of the best applications — choose as broad a range of examples as possible — and one or two marginal or unacceptable responses to share with the class. If you plan to use the latter in class, change them just enough to disguise them from their originators.

IDEAS FOR ADAPTING AND EXTENDING THIS CAT

If applications are particularly difficult to generate, let students work in pairs or small groups to respond to the assessment.

Alternately, allow students to complete their Applications Cards as part of their homework assignment.

Encourage students to keep an "applications journal" in their class notebooks. Suggest that they devote two minutes at the end of every class session, or at any other appropriate time during class, to writing possible applications of what they are studying at that point.

Not all applications are equally desirable; some may be dangerous, unethical, or immoral. Therefore, in some courses, you may want to use Applications Card responses as a starting point for discussions of the possible consequences of various applications.

PROS

The Applications Card is an extremely simple and quick way to get students thinking about the potential uses of what they are learning, and to assess their skill and sophistication at doing so.

To come up with applications, students have to link what they are trying to apply with what they already know, thereby strengthening learning.

The realization that theories and principles presented in the classroom have real-world applications can increase student interest and motivation to learn.

When students get feedback on their Applications Cards, they benefit from hearing the best examples. Many times, students learn more from each other's examples of applications than from the teacher's or the textbook's examples.

Faculty benefit as well, by having a new, renewable source of example applications — thanks to feedback from the Applications Cards.

CONS

Prompting students to think about applications can shift the focus of the class to a more specific and concrete level than the instructor intends.

While most students are interested in applications, a few are not. Those who are not interested find this CAT beside the point.

Not all fields have easily identifiable applications to everyday life; so students in introductory-level courses may have more difficulty responding.

CAVEATS

Students who come up with poor or incorrect applications are likely to remember and learn those bad examples unless they receive feedback and examples of good applications. Follow-up is critical.

Students often want to discuss their applications beyond the few minutes that instructors have allotted for feedback. While teachers have generally reported that these discussions were lively and valuable, they did leave less time for other elements of the lesson.

Student-Generated
Test Questions

Estimated Levels of Time and Energy Required for:

Faculty to prepare to use this CAT	**MEDIUM**
Students to respond to the assessment	**MEDIUM to HIGH**
Faculty to analyze the data collected	**MEDIUM to HIGH**

DESCRIPTION

Most faculty discover early—often as graduate teaching assistants—that one of the best ways to find out how well they themselves understand the material they are teaching is to prepare test questions and model answers. This technique gives students the benefit of that experience—early on and in small doses.

PURPOSE

Student-Generated Test Questions allow faculty to assess at least three aspects of student learning. In these questions, teachers see what their students consider the most important or memorable content, what they understand as fair and useful test questions, and how well they can answer the questions they have posed. This information not only provides direction for teaching but can also alert the teacher when students have inaccurate expectations about upcoming tests. Responding to this CAT helps students assess how well they know the material, and receiving feedback can refocus their studying.

RELATED TEACHING GOALS

Develop ability to apply principles and generalizations already learned to new problems and situations (TGI Goal 1)
Develop appropriate study skills, strategies, and habits (TGI Goal 16)
Learn terms and facts of this subject (TGI Goal 18)
Learn concepts and theories in this subject (TGI Goal 19)
Learn to evaluate methods and materials in this subject (TGI Goal 24)
Develop a commitment to accurate work (TGI Goal 39)
Develop ability to perform skillfully (TGI Goal 43)

SUGGESTIONS FOR USE

Student-Generated Test Questions can be used in any course in which students take tests—if the instructor is willing to include (revised) student questions in the tests or at least to let students know what kinds of questions will be included. This assessment is best administered two or three weeks before a major test, such as a midterm or final examination, to allow time for feedback and for appropriate adjustments in teaching and studying. Be sure to let students know in advance whether the test will make any use of the questions they generate. If the test does not draw directly on student questions, students need feedback on how closely their questions parallel the kinds of questions they will see on the exam. With careful planning, this CAT can be used to generate questions that students can use in reviewing for tests and that faculty can modify to include in the test.

EXAMPLES

From Principles of Thermodynamics (Engineering)

To get a better sense of his students' level of sophistication, this engineering professor asked the students in his thermodynamics class to turn in three questions they expected to see on the first midterm exam, along with the correct answers to those questions. To his disappointment, most of the students handed in questions that tested knowledge of facts, terms, and principles or very simple problem-solving skills. The professor had much more challenging questions planned for the test; so he decided to give some examples of likely test questions when he gave feedback on their CAT responses. He prepared a handout containing five "prototypical" questions for the first midterm. Although the students were relieved to have this information in advance, they were also quick to let the professor know that they had not yet had any practice in solving these more difficult problems. Their homework and quizzes had all focused on what he had just referred to as "lower-level stuff." Just as he was about to react somewhat angrily to their assertions, he realized that the students were right. That realization led him to revise their subsequent homework assignments to stress "higher-level stuff" and to postpone the first midterm for a week.

From Kierkegaard and Nietzsche (Philosophy)

The requirements for this senior-level course included five short papers and midterm and final exams. Both exams consisted entirely of essay questions. The instructor decided to use this CAT to assess how deeply students were reading the two nineteenth-century philosophers and, specifically, to see what questions the students were asking themselves about the works they read. To that end, she asked the two dozen students each to prepare three potential final exam essay questions and accompanying A + responses. One question was to address a point of comparison between Kierkegaard and Nietzsche; another, to explore a point of clear contrast; and the third, to deal with the influence of both philosophers on contemporary thought.

Since generating and responding to these essay questions required a great deal of work, she decided to substitute this assignment for one of the five papers. The assessment was counted as equal to the other four papers. Students were given either full, half, or no credit for their responses to the assessment, but no grades.

The philosophy professor was impressed by the overall quality of the questions and answers she received, although many students had trouble either locating a point of comparison or posing a good question on it. In response, she paid special attention to the "comparison" questions in her feedback. Afterward, she selected the four best "contrast" and "influence" questions and one "comparison" question, made some revisions, and added three "comparison" questions of her own. She then gave these twelve to the students as review questions for the final examination. The students were told that the final exam would consist of six questions: two questions out of the four in each of the three categories. She urged them to study in groups to make sure they could answer all twelve of the possible questions.

STEP-BY-STEP PROCEDURE

1. Focus on a test or exam that is at least three weeks to a month away. Decide what types of questions on what specific topics you want students to generate. Imagine that you are writing specifications to yourself about the kinds of questions you want students to create, and write those directions down for your students. If you have already written the test questions, frame your directions so that students will write similar ones.

2. Decide how many questions you want students to generate. One or two questions of any type are usually enough, especially if you want students to supply answers.

3. Explain what you want the students to do, why you want them to do it, how their questions will be used, when they will get feedback, and how writing questions and getting feedback will help them perform better on the test.

TURNING THE DATA YOU COLLECT INTO USEFUL INFORMATION

First, make a rough tally of the types of questions the students propose. How many require only a knowledge of facts and principles? How many require paraphrasing or summarizing? How many require synthesis or analysis? Next, take a quick look at the range of topics the questions span. Are some important topics left out? Are others overrepresented? Then look for questions that are particularly well or poorly written. You may want to create a form or checklist to accomplish the above. On the checklist, you can quickly note the level of the question, relevance of the topic, difficulty, and clarity. As you read, extract a few questions to use as examples in giving feedback. If there are questions that students would benefit from reviewing, read and revise them as necessary and share them with the class.

IDEAS FOR ADAPTING AND EXTENDING THIS CAT

Many students, particularly those in introductory courses, may find it easier to generate test questions if they work in pairs or small groups.

In a large class, you may want to assign specific topics or units to certain groups of students. For example, you might ask students whose last names begin with the letters A–G to write questions on topics covered in the first three weeks of the course.

Prepare a handout of Student-Generated Test Questions for test review and offer suggestions on how best to prepare.

If you are working with students who are planning to become teachers, give them more feedback on the way they asked the questions and the kinds of questions they asked. Engage them in critiquing and revising the questions. Help students see what makes some test questions better than others for promoting learning.

PROS

By generating test questions students can learn what aspects of the course they understand and what aspects they do not understand.

When students suggest test questions and try to predict the actual test questions, they are — in effect — beginning to prepare, in useful ways, for the upcoming test.

Along with its other benefits, this CAT can help avoid unpleasant surprises. When faculty read student questions, they gain information on the class's expectations. As students get feedback on questions they have written, their instructor's plans for the test become clearer.

CONS

Many students will have had no experience in writing test questions. As a result, their efforts may be quite poor. The less experienced the students, the more direction and feedback they will need.

Given the opportunity, a small percentage of students may try to influence the instructor to include easy questions on the test.

Some students will be disappointed not to see their questions represented on the test, or at least on the review sheet.

CAVEATS

Since you cannot predict the quality or level of student questions, do not promise categorically to include them on the test.

Unless students clearly understand the advantages they can gain by creating their own test questions, they may regard this assignment as a thinly veiled attempt to get them to do the instructor's work.

Because this is likely to be a very demanding assessment, you may need to offer students some course credit for completing it. This is the kind of CAT that can reasonably substitute for a homework assignment.

Human Tableau or Class Modeling

Estimated Levels of Time and Energy Required for:

Faculty to prepare to use this CAT	**MEDIUM to HIGH**
Students to respond to the assessment	**HIGH**
Faculty to analyze the data collected	**HIGH**

DESCRIPTION

This technique is quite a departure from the norm. Unlike most of the CATs in this handbook, which elicit paper-and-pencil responses, students repond to the Human Tableau or Class Modeling techniques with their minds and their bodies. Groups of students create "living" scenes or model processes to show what they know. For example, students might pose as the figures in a painting, reenact a Druid ritual at Stonehenge, or model the operation of the fuel system in an automobile engine.

PURPOSE

This CAT allows students to demonstrate their ability to apply what they know by performing it—not just by writing or saying it. Just as some students learn more effectively by watching than by listening, others learn more effectively through movement. Some ideas and skills can best be learned—or at least reinforced—and assessed through movement, as well. This technique works especially well for assessing "kinesthetic" learners and learning.

RELATED TEACHING GOALS

Develop ability to apply principles and generalizations already learned to new problems and situations (TGI Goal 1)

Develop ability to synthesize and integrate information and ideas (TGI Goal 5)

Develop ability to think creatively (TGI Goal 7)

Develop aesthetic appreciations (TGI Goal 31)

Develop an informed historical perspective (TGI Goal 32)

Develop ability to work productively with others (TGI Goal 36)

Develop ability to perform skillfully (TGI Goal 43)

SUGGESTIONS FOR USE

The Human Tableau or Class Modeling technique is an interesting change-of-pace assessment. Because of its relative complexity, it usually can be carried out only once a term. It is a group assessment and therefore requires a course in which group work is encouraged. Because students must perform the assessments, this CAT works best in relatively small classes. The Human Tableau can be used in history and geography, art history and art appreciation, and any other field that relies on maps or visual compositions. Class Modeling works well in disciplines such as physics (classical mechanics), anatomy and physiology, and many vocational and technical fields, where students learn about relatively straightforward physical processes.

EXAMPLES

From Introduction to Neurophysiology (Biology/Nursing)

In past semesters, this instructor had experimented with various methods of teaching students about the human visual system—how the eyes, the nerves, and the brain work together to produce vision. Although students usually mastered the names and locations of the component parts, they rarely seemed to develop an appreciation for the dynamic nature of the system. To focus attention on the process of vision and the system, she broke the class into five groups of about eight students each and assigned them the task of "acting out" how the visual system works. She gave each group a checklist of elements that their Class Modeling had to represent and include. The most important point to the instructor was that the models demonstrate, in broad strokes, how visual images are created, transmitted, and stored by the eyes, the nervous system, and the brain, respectively.

The groups were given two weeks to prepare, and each group was to have five minutes of performing time. The groups were told that the assessment exercise was worth the same credit as a weekly quiz— about 5 percent of the total grade. Furthermore, all members of a group would get the same credit—either full credit or no credit. The instructor arranged to have the performances videotaped for later viewing and brought extra copies of the checklist for the students to fill out as they watched the other groups. Each of the "human models" of vision was quite different from the others, and all were at least adequate. Two groups used simple costumes and makeshift props—with members in "rod" and "cone" hats, for example—and received much applause. The groups took their performances very seriously, but they also clearly had fun.

After all the groups had performed, the teacher made some comments on strengths and weaknesses and encouraged class members to join in the critique. Many students had questions and comments based on their attempts to represent the process. She noticed that these students were discussing vision in much greater depth and detail than had been typical in past classes. The class seemed to her to have gotten "into" the topic very deeply. Later, on the midterm, the class scored higher on questions about vision than on any other topic, reinforcing the instructor's earlier estimate of the assessment's teaching and learning value.

From Aspects and Concepts of Art (Fine Arts)

To assess students' understanding of the development of perspective in European painting, this instructor assigned small groups of students the task of "posing" the same scene—the Madonna and child surrounded by the three "Wise Men"—as Human Tableaus. (A doll was used as the child.) Each group was asked to demonstrate the differences in perspective used by artists during the Late Roman, Late Byzantine, and Quattrocento periods. The instructor took instant photographs of each tableau and also made quick notes on the tableaus. The photos were transferred to slides, and she and the class critiqued each group's live "rendering" of these diverse solutions to the problem of perspective. On the whole, the groups came up with interesting and creative ways of portraying the "distorted" perspectives of the two earlier periods; but many students, to their surprise, had difficulty in posing the Renaissance tableaus.

STEP-BY-STEP PROCEDURE

1. Select a process or an image that has particular teaching and learning importance.

2. Ask yourself what your students could learn and demonstrate about their learning by physically representing this image or by modeling this process. In other words, what could you and the students learn from this demonstration that you could not learn from a more traditional type of assessment?

3. Ask yourself whether your students can, in a relatively short time and without props, create a Human Tableau or Class Model on this topic.

4. Ask yourself when and how you will make time to view and assess these "performances."

5. If you are still convinced that this learning and assessment project is worthwhile, write a direction sheet that explains the purpose, the procedure, and the points students should make through their tableaus or models. Since no tableau or model can fully represent the "real thing," be very clear about what students should highlight in their responses.

6. Divide the class into groups, explain the task, hand out the direction sheet, and elicit questions. Make sure the students understand what they are to do, how, and when.

TURNING THE DATA YOU COLLECT INTO USEFUL INFORMATION

This is a particularly challenging assessment to document and analyze. At the very least, you will want to create a checklist of important points that the tableaus or models should include. With such a checklist, you can more easily note the presence or absence of these points, and the effectiveness and creativity with which they are represented. You may want to share your checklist with class members who are serving as an audience at any given moment and enlist them in helping you document and assess the performances. If the performances are short, and in most cases they should be, consider having them videotaped. Although the videotaped assessment cannot take the place of your "live" notes, it can allow you and the students to study the group performances more carefully.

You should give the groups feedback on what, if anything, they left out or got wrong in their tableaus or models. At the same time, they need to know what was especially instructive and clever about their responses to this assessment technique. Throughout, be sure to help students see connections between their group representations and the objects or processes they are representing.

IDEAS FOR ADAPTING AND EXTENDING THIS CAT

If it is not feasible to have students act out their responses, consider having the groups write short but detailed scripts, explaining what they would do.

Have the groups document and write up their experiences as a graded, follow-up assignment. This assignment will allow them to incorporate feedback from the instructor and fellow students.

PROS

When students work in small groups to plan their Human Tableau or Class Modeling response, they must transform and apply what they have learned from reading and listening into doing. This process inevitably takes a lot of explaining, clarifying, planning, and negotiating—all focused on the task of clearly representing what they know.

This can be a very entertaining assessment project that can raise interest and motivation for learning.

As a side benefit, students will come to know one another better through the group work.

Some students who are not particularly adept at verbal or written expression shine in tasks such as this.

CONS

The Human Tableau or Class Modeling technique is so different from most students' classroom experience that they may not take it seriously; they may even refuse to participate.

Because of the public nature of this CAT, there can be no anonymity in responses. Students who find it threatening should be given an alternate written assessment activity.

Everything about this assessment is time-consuming and labor-intensive. It can have significant payoffs, but only after significant investments.

CAVEATS

The Human Tableau or Class Modeling technique is the kind of CAT that can easily take on a "life" of its own. Remember, its primary purposes are to assess learning and to enhance learning. You may need to downplay the dramatic (performance) aspects of the assessment and stress the didactic (instructional) ones.

Unless the class has a high level of group-work skill overall, the groups will need very detailed and explicit directions.

CLASSROOM
ASSESSMENT
TECHNIQUE

27

Paper or Project Prospectus

Estimated Levels of Time and Energy Required for:

Faculty to prepare to use this CAT	**MEDIUM**
Students to respond to the assessment	**HIGH**
Faculty to analyze the data collected	**HIGH**

DESCRIPTION

In this context, a prospectus is a brief, structured first-draft plan for a term paper or term project. The Paper Prospectus prompts students to think through elements of the assignment, such as the topic, purpose, intended audience, major questions to be answered, basic organization, and time and resources required. The Project Prospectus, on the other hand, may focus on tasks to be accomplished, skills to be improved, and products to be developed.

PURPOSE

The Paper or Project Prospectus assesses students' skill at synthesizing what they have already learned about a topic or field as they plan their own learning projects. In addition, this technique can give the instructor valuable information about the students' understanding of both the assignment and the topic—as well as their planning skills—before it is too late to make suggestions and shape direction. Students benefit from writing a prospectus because they thereby receive feedback before they begin substantive work on the papers or projects they have been assigned. This early feedback makes it less likely that the instructor or the students will be disappointed by the finished product.

RELATED TEACHING GOALS

Develop ability to apply principles and generalizations already learned to new problems and situations (TGI Goal 1)

Develop ability to synthesize and integrate information and ideas (TGI Goal 5)

Improve writing skills (TGI Goal 15)

Develop appropriate study skills, strategies, and habits (TGI Goal 16)

Develop management skills (TGI Goal 37)

SUGGESTIONS FOR USE

This assessment technique is appropriate for any course that requires students to write term papers or to carry out substantial projects. In social sciences and humanities courses, it can be used to give students feedback on their planned term papers. In fields such as social work, education, counseling psychology, and recreation, instructors can employ the prospectus to help students plan internship and fieldwork projects.

The Paper or Project Prospectus is most helpful to students and instructors when it is used several weeks before the assignment is due. In fact, it is best to use this CAT immediately after the paper or project is assigned, so that there will be adequate time for analysis and feedback. In large courses, if it is not feasible to read and comment on every prospectus, the instructor may give general feedback and suggestions to the class after a careful reading of a sample of the prospectuses. With some direction, the students can give each other more detailed feedback by working in small groups.

EXAMPLES   Exhibit 7.6 is a simple format that can be adapted for almost any term paper or other major writing assignment. Exhibit 7.7 is a format for fieldwork or internship projects.

Exhibit 7.6. Term Paper Prospectus.

Directions: The prompts listed below are meant to help you get started on your term paper. Respond to each of the prompts with a very brief, well-thought-out answer. Remember that this prospectus is only a plan. You will almost certainly change part of your plan, and you may even change all of it, before you complete this term paper. So make your best predictions and plans as you answer, but don't be surprised or concerned if you alter them somewhat as you proceed.

Proposed title:

Purpose (What will this paper do for the reader? For you?):

Major question(s) you hope to answer:

Work calendar (How will you spread the work out? When will you do it?):

Proposed table of contents/list of major sections:

Help/resources needed (What do you need in order to do an excellent job?):

Your biggest concern(s) or question(s) about the paper:

Exhibit 7.7. Term Project Prospectus.

Directions: The prompts listed below are meant to help you plan your term project. Respond to each prompt with a very brief, well-thought-out answer. Remember that this prospectus is just a plan. You will almost certainly change part of your plan, and you may even change all of it, before you complete your project. So make your best predictions and plans, but don't be surprised or concerned if you decide to alter them later.

Brief project description (What do you plan to do?):

Project site/setting (Where and with whom will you work?):

Major question(s) you hope to answer/goal(s) you hope to achieve:

Products/results (What will be the measurable outcomes of your project?):

Resources needed (What do you need in order to do an excellent job?):

Calendar of component tasks (When will you complete each part of the project?):

Your biggest concern(s) or question(s) about the project:

STEP-BY-STEP PROCEDURE

1. Determine the general outline of the term paper or project assignment for which students will write the prospectus. Write a clear and informative first-draft assignment sheet for students. These general directions should tell students how much freedom they have in determining the topic, form, content, purpose, audience, and the like. The assignment sheet should also tell students what criteria you will use to evaluate their final products. Try to keep it under one page in length.

2. Decide which elements of the assignment are most critical to the learning task and predict which are least likely to be handled successfully by the students. Make a checklist of qualities or elements you will

look for in the final product and rank them in the order of their importance. Then rank those same elements again, this time in the order of their difficulty for the students. For example, will the organization of the paper pose serious problems, or is choosing an appropriate topic a bigger challenge?

3. Revise the assignment sheet to reflect your priorities as expressed in the ranked list mentioned above. Check again to make sure you have left some room within the structure of the assignment for independent and creative responses.

4. Decide on the focus of the prospectus. Keep in mind both what you consider most important and what you suspect the students will find most difficult or least clear about the assignment. Compose three to seven questions or prompts to elicit information about those central and problematic elements. These are the questions that students should answer for you through the prospectus. Make sure to include a prompt that invites students to indicate their questions and concerns about the assignment. These are the questions that students should ask you through the prospectus.

5. Give out the assignment sheet first, and then the specific directions for the prospectus. Ask students not to begin substantive work on the assignment until they have received feedback on their prospectuses. Give them a brief but adequate amount of time to complete the prospectus—from two days to two weeks, depending on the nature of the assignment and the course meeting times.

6. Since the prospectus is the first step in a longer, graded assignment, there is no sense in making it anonymous. Although the prospectus should not be graded, it is wise to require completion of this CAT and to offer students a small amount of credit for a job well done.

TURNING THE DATA YOU COLLECT INTO USEFUL INFORMATION

Skim rapidly through the responses, or a sample of them, to get an idea of strengths and weaknesses. Circle or check points that catch your attention. In reading the prospectuses a second time, you might try to answer the following questions: Overall, which prompts received the clearest responses? Which the muddiest? What questions or confusions came up repeatedly and therefore should be clarified for the whole class? Which need individual responses? Are there groups of students who are working on similar projects and may therefore benefit from discussing and comparing their plans?

Note the range of topics and approaches that the students propose. Are the students following your instructions? Do you need to rethink your criteria for evaluating, or do you merely need to explain the criteria again more clearly to the students? Also note how, and to what degree, the prospectuses are related to the content and skills on which the course is focused. Make a short summary list of suggestions you can offer to the class as a whole, including suggestions about strengths they can build on and elements that need work.

Limit the amount of information you collect even further. For example, ask only for the title, purpose, and major questions to be answered.

Ask students to meet in small groups to present, discuss, and critically review each other's prospectuses before they hand them in.

For major assignments, such as theses or dissertations, use the prospectus to assess the students' readiness to produce detailed outlines. Once the prospectus has been cleared, the student can move on to detailed planning.

Have students write prospectuses for "dream" projects in your discipline that they would like to realize in the future, but that are too ambitious or time-consuming to carry out in your course.

PROS

The Paper or Project Prospectus is a device that finds its own level. It can be as simple or as elaborate as the assigned project requires.

It has immediate relevance to the students' work, concerns, and questions about the course. At the same time, it provides practice in a valuable and transferable skill.

This technique gives teachers both a preview of the students' interests and ideas and a forewarning of their problems and questions, allowing for timely and helpful feedback. This preview of the final products also makes it easier for teachers to evaluate them effectively when they are completed.

The prospectus reduces the likelihood that any students will totally miss the mark on the assignment, since the teacher can check on their understanding early in the process.

By requiring thoughtful planning, the prospectus improves the quality of the final product and enhances student learning. Time and energy invested in assessment at the front end of the process can have payoffs later.

CONS

The prospectus can tempt teachers to be too critical or directive too early in the assignment, increasing the risk that students will write more to please the instructor than to inform and instruct themselves.

This technique requires a significant amount of planning and work by the instructor, including reading, analyzing, and commenting on the prospectuses.

Some students find it difficult to plan major assignments in detail and may need coaching or instruction to produce prospectuses.

CAVEATS

Because of the time and work involved in carrying out this technique, it should be reserved for major term assignments. One prospectus per term is probably sufficient.

You may make the assignment as open or as structured as you wish; but clearly, if you hope students will respond creatively to the assignment, you must allow for and encourage creativity in at least some areas. Don't predetermine every aspect of the assignment.

The directions should make it clear that a prospectus is a plan, a forecast, and so may be discussed, adjusted, significantly reworked, or even totally scrapped. Encourage students to take some risks, to propose something they really are excited about doing.

Remember that many students have little or no experience in systematically planning their work. A poor prospectus, especially the first time through the technique, may not be a sign of poor ideas or lack of effort. Rather it may be an indication that the student needs work developing the skills required by the Paper or Project Prospectus.

Techniques for Assessing Learner Attitudes, Values, and Self-Awareness

College students need to be actively involved in their own learning. That was the general message of an influential report by the Study Group on the Conditions of Excellence in American Higher Education (1984): "There is now a good deal of research evidence to suggest that the more time and effort students invest in the learning process and the more intensely they engage in their own education, the greater will be their satisfaction with their educational experiences, and their persistence in college, and the more likely they are to continue their learning" (p. 17). Active engagement in higher learning implies and requires self-awareness and self-direction. *Metacognition* is the term used by cognitive psychologists to describe students' awareness and understanding of their own learning skills, performance, and habits. Although the emphasis of various researchers differs enough to make metacognition a somewhat fuzzy concept (Brown, Bransford, Ferrara, and Campione, 1983), the term *metacognition* usually refers to two different but related aspects: (1) awareness and knowledge of self-as-learner and (2) conscious self-control and self-regulation of cognition.

Research suggests that good learners engage in more metacognitive activities than poor learners do. Therefore, educators have been considering how to explicitly teach students metacognition. At the University of Texas, for example, an undergraduate course has been designed by Claire Weinstein to help students learn how to learn. Weinstein and Mayer (1986) emphasize four activities that will help students become more efficient and effective learners: comprehension monitoring, knowledge acquisition, active study skills, and support strategies.

Comprehension monitoring includes four types of knowledge plus some techniques or strategies for monitoring understanding. The types of knowledge are (1) self-knowledge, including an understanding of one's own learning preferences, abilities, and cognitive style; (2) knowledge of the learning task—what is required (for example, what type of test) and what needs to be learned; (3) knowledge of prior understandings; and (4) knowledge of strategies useful in the learning task. The techniques and strategies include self-questioning, paraphrasing and summarizing, and transforming knowledge from the form in which it was presented to another type of organization. All these monitoring activities help make students more active participants in their own learning and give them more control over their learning.

Several of the techniques in Chapter Seven call for the use of various kinds of knowledge and monitoring strategies. The Memory Matrix (CAT 5), for example, is a technique for transforming and reorganizing information; the One-Sentence Summary (CAT 13) is a technique for paraphrasing and summarizing. In this chapter, Punctuated Lectures help students stop and monitor whether and how well they are attending to learning.

Knowledge acquisition, the second category used by Weinstein and Mayer, includes two strategies whereby students make knowledge their own, instead of passively absorbing information: the strategies of elaboration and organization. Elaboration refers to activities that students might use to make the knowledge meaningful and therefore memorable. The use of analogy, for example, transforms new learning into something familiar. The paragraphs under "Ideas for Adapting and Extending" in each CAT description are examples of elaboration that deepen and extend knowledge about the assessment technique presented. The concept of organization refers to the student's ability to "chunk" materials into units that contain similar elements. Such organization makes the acquisition and manipulation of knowledge easier.

Weinstein and Mayer's third category, active study skills, includes skills such as planning, monitoring, and transforming knowledge—activities designed to give students more control over their learning and to make them more active participants. There are also, however, certain skills that are basic to most learning—how to find the main idea in readings or lectures, for example, and how to relate ideas. Some of the techniques in this chapter—for example, Process Analysis and Diagnostic Learning Logs—assess whether students possess certain active study skills. Other techniques—Interest/Knowledge/Skills Checklists, Goal Ranking and Matching, and Self-Assessment of Ways of Learning—assess whether students are aware of how they carry out the learning task and whether they can accurately assess their own learning skills.

Support strategies, Weinstein and Mayer's fourth category, are strategies that students need to develop in order to create and maintain a climate—both physical and emotional—that is conducive to learning. Some students, for example, engage in negative self-talk ("I'll never be able to do it," "I'm just too slow to finish the test," "I'm too old, too dumb, or too far behind"). Weinstein and Mayer believe that students can be taught to take control of their learning environments through monitoring, anxiety reduction, self-regulation, and similar strategies. Several CATs in this chapter are designed to assess monitoring and self-regulation.

Assessing Students' Awareness of Their Attitudes and Values

Although the development of knowledge and skills—higher-order thinking skills in particular—is a central goal of most college teachers, other important dimensions of higher learning also merit our attention. In introductory survey courses, for example, some teachers encourage students to explore their attitudes about the content of the course, about the discipline itself, or about social issues that relate to but transcend the classroom. Other instructors structure course work to help students develop skill in expressing their opinions and also in analyzing and examining those opinions. And in many courses, particularly in the humanities and liberal arts, faculty encourage students to develop the types of self-awareness traditionally associated with "the examined life."

The five CATs in this cluster are designed to help teachers better understand and more effectively promote the development of attitudes, opinions, values, and self-awareness that takes place while students are in their courses.

Classroom Opinion Polls

Estimated Levels of Time and Energy Required for:

Faculty to prepare to use this CAT	**LOW to MEDIUM**
Students to respond to the assessment	**LOW**
Faculty to analyze the data collected	**LOW**

DESCRIPTION   Many faculty already use de facto opinion polling in their classes when they ask students to raise their hands to indicate agreement or disagreement with a particular statement. This simple technique builds on that kind of informal polling, providing more anonymity for students and more honest and accurate data for faculty.

PURPOSE   Classroom Opinion Polling helps faculty discover student opinions about course-related issues. Students often have preexisting opinions about the material that they will encounter in courses, and those opinions—when they are unsupported by evidence—can distort or block the instructional message. The fact that many opinions are half-formed and unarticulated, and sometimes even unrecognized by the learners holding them, only intensifies their power to interfere with learning. By uncovering student opinions on specific issues, faculty can better gauge where and how to begin teaching about those issues—and what the roadblocks are likely to be. This CAT can sensitize faculty to potentially divisive questions and can provide a forewarning of likely conflicts. In addition, Classroom Opinion Polling encourages students to discover their own opinions about issues, to compare their opinions with those of their classmates, and to test their opinions against evidence and expert opinion.

RELATED TEACHING GOALS   Learn to understand perspectives and values of this subject (TGI Goal 21)

Develop an openness to new ideas (TGI Goal 27)

Develop an informed concern about contemporary social issues (TGI Goal 28)

Develop capacity to make informed ethical choices (TGI Goal 35)

Develop leadership skills (TGI Goal 38)

Develop a commitment to one's own values (TGI Goal 46)

Develop respect for others (TGI Goal 47)
Develop capacity to make wise decisions (TGI Goal 52)

SUGGESTIONS FOR USE   Teachers can use Classroom Opinion Polls to prepare students to discuss a controversial issue or to assess their opinions after they have studied the material. Polling can also be used as a pre- and post-assessment device, to determine whether and how students' opinions have changed in response to class discussions and assignments. Because students are more likely to have opinions on some matters than on others, and because opinions play a larger role in some disciplines than in others, Classroom Opinion Polls are most often used in social sciences, humanities, and professional studies courses. Thanks to its simplicity, this CAT can be adapted to almost any class, regardless of size. In fact, the data from a Classroom Opinion Poll taken at the beginning of a class session can often be tallied and presented well before the end of the same class.

EXAMPLES

From Native American Cultures in North America (Native American Studies/Anthropology)

The anthropology professor teaching this course, herself a member of the Navajo nation, polled her students' opinions on the following statement at the beginning and near the end of the course:

Native Americans who stay on the reservation are better off than those who leave.

(Circle the one answer that best captures your view.)

Strongly Disagree   Disagree   Don't Know   Agree   Strongly Agree

From Introduction to the U.S. Criminal Justice System (Criminal Justice/ Sociology)

To find out students' opinions of mandatory sentencing guidelines, this criminal justice instructor polled them on the following statements before they had read and discussed the relevant material. Later, they compared their answers with the research findings.

Directions: Circle A if you agree or D if you disagree with the statement:

Overall, mandatory sentencing guidelines have resulted in:

Greater public safety	A	D
Lower violent crime rates	A	D
More prison time served by repeat offenders	A	D
Less race- and class-biased sentencing	A	D

From a History of Modern France (History)

The upper-division history majors in this course were asked to respond to the following prompt:

> European civilization and the people of Europe would have advanced farther and more quickly if Napoleon Bonaparte had avoided war with Russia and Britain and instead had consolidated his power in the rest of Europe.
>
> (Circle the one answer that best captures your view.)
>
> Strongly Disagree   Disagree   Agree   Strongly Agree

From Energy and the Environment (Environmental Studies)

This professor used the following statements to assess her students' views on nuclear energy before they began reading and discussing that energy source:

> If I found a great house at a great price, close to work and near good schools, that was within five miles of a nuclear power plant, I would (circle only one):
>
> a. Be absolutely willing to consider buying it, and not worried about the plant
>
> b. Be somewhat willing to consider buying it, but concerned about the plant
>
> c. Be very skeptical about buying it, and worried about the plant
>
> d. Be absolutely unwilling to consider it because of the plant
>
> Assuming that I had a choice, if changes in my life-style would help make the construction of more nuclear power plants unnecessary, I would (circle only one):
>
> a. Not be willing to use less electrical energy or pay more for it
>
> b. Be willing to use much less electrical energy but not pay more for it
>
> c. Use the same amount of energy but be willing to pay a higher price for it
>
> d. Be willing to use much less electrical energy and pay a higher price for it

STEP-BY-STEP PROCEDURE

1. Preview the material that you plan to teach, looking for questions or issues about which students may have opinions that could affect their learning.

2. Choose one or two issues for your Classroom Opinion Poll and draw up the question or prompt and the response choices. Decide whether the question or prompt requires a binary response choice, such as "yes" or "no"; a scalar response with several choices ranging along a continuum, such as the scale running from "strongly disagree" to "strongly agree"; or a multiple-choice response.

3. After trying out the question and responses on a colleague and making any necessary revisions, create a polling form to duplicate or an overhead projector transparency.

4. Explain the exercise to students, remind them not to put names on the responses, and give them a couple of minutes to respond to the Classroom Opinion Poll.

TURNING THE DATA YOU COLLECT INTO USEFUL INFORMATION

To summarize responses to the Classroom Opinion Poll, all you have to do is count and tally. You may be able to tally the response in class while students are working independently or in groups, or a teaching assistant or student might tally the responses while you are teaching.

IDEAS FOR ADAPTING AND EXTENDING THIS CAT

After students have had some practice with this technique, ask them to explain or justify the opinions they express.

As a follow-up assignment, direct students to respond to an opinion very different from their own. Ask them first to critique the opinion and explain why they disagree; then have them write a rebuttal and justification from the point of view of someone holding the opinion they disagree with.

Encourage the class, or a Classroom Assessment Quality Circle group, to come up with informative, enlightening Classroom Opinion Polling questions.

PROS

Polling and reporting on opinions are familiar and inclusive activities that engage all the students—even the quietest and most reticent—in discovering and expressing their opinions.

Sharing the result of Classroom Opinion Polls helps students see, firsthand, the diversity of opinions among their own classmates, and can help them learn to accept and work with that range of opinions in a democratic spirit.

Teachers quickly gain information that can help them adjust their teaching approaches and prepare them to deal with a range of student opinions.

CONS

Faculty sometimes find that students' opinions are diametrically opposed to the evidence, to expert opinion, and/or to their own personal opinions. This outcome, though to be expected, can still come as an unpleasant surprise.

Some students find it difficult to commit themselves to a response, even though that response is anonymous.

CAVEATS   Polling students on their opinions implies that there will be discussion of the relevant issues. Be prepared.

In using Classroom Opinion Polls, as in using all other CATs that concern opinions, attitudes, or values, remember that student anonymity must be maintained and that feedback must be given carefully, to model respect and open-mindedness.

You may prefer not to tally and respond to the polls immediately. If you are disappointed, shocked, or offended by the class's answers, you may need time to prepare your response in private.

Double-Entry Journals

Estimated Levels of Time and Energy Required for:

Faculty to prepare to use this CAT	**MEDIUM**
Students to respond to the assessment	**HIGH**
Faculty to analyze the data collected	**HIGH**

DESCRIPTION   Students begin Double-Entry Journals by noting the ideas, assertions, and arguments in their assigned course readings that they find most meaningful and/or most controversial. These notes on the text are the first half of the Double-Entry Journal. The second entry in the Double-Entry Journal explains the personal significance of the passage selected and responds to that passage. In this way, students engage in a dialogue with the text, exploring their reactions to the reading.

PURPOSE   This technique provides detailed feedback on how students read, analyze, and respond to assigned texts. Faculty get a sense of what their students notice and value in those texts from the passages they choose to comment on in the first journal entries. Then, from the second journal entries, faculty learn why students value those passages. By analyzing students' responses to texts, faculty gain insights into student interests, concerns, and values — and into ways to help students connect the readings to their lives. Students, for their part, develop clearer understanding of how they read and why they respond to certain texts.

RELATED TEACHING GOALS   Improve reading skills (TGI Goal 14)

Develop appropriate study skills, strategies, and habits (TGI Goal 16)

Learn to understand perspectives and values of this subject (TGI Goal 21)

Prepare for transfer or graduate study (TGI Goal 22)

Develop an appreciation of the liberal arts and sciences (TGI Goal 26)

Develop an openness to new ideas (TGI Goal 27)

Develop a commitment to one's own values (TGI Goal 46)

Develop respect for others (TGI Goal 47)

Develop capacity to think for oneself (TGI Goal 51)

Double-Entry Journals are particularly useful in fields where close study of texts is critical—fields such as history, philosophy, political science, sociology, literature, ethnic studies, women's studies, theology, and law. To provide for some commonality among responses, teachers probably should apply this technique to a very short text or to a few pages of a longer text. In addition, because it is a time- and labor-intensive assessment technique, the Double-Entry Journal can be used only with small classes or small groups of students. To get the most useful feedback from this CAT, teachers may need to administer it more than once before students become adept at the process of writing notes to respond to notes.

EXAMPLES

From Masterpieces of Twentieth-Century Theater (Drama/Theater Arts)

Students in this course read and attend performances of influential plays written by European and North American authors in this century. To get a sense of his students' attitudes toward the modern theatrical aesthetic, the instructor asked them to write a Double-Entry Journal on the first act of Anton Chekhov's play *The Seagull*. Students were asked to copy three short passages of dialogue that, in their opinion, reflected the modernist aesthetic—or at least Chekhov's view of it—and, second, to respond by agreeing, disagreeing, or arguing with that passage. He urged them to choose three passages that provoked strong reactions.

As the instructor read through the completed Double-Entry Journal responses, he was able to divide the students into three groups: those who chose a relevant passage and responded thoughtfully and well, those who did only one of the two well, and those who neither chose well nor responded well. Soon after, he let the students know which passages were most often chosen and why, and gave them examples of excellent responses as well as weak ones.

From Contemporary Asian-American Literature (Asian-American Studies)

After assigning her students Maxine Hong Kingston's novel *The Woman Warrior*, this professor directed them to carry out a Double-Entry Journal exercise. The students were asked to select at least three personally significant, short passages in any five-page segment of the book, and then to explain the significance of each passage. The professor tallied and categorized the explanations that students gave for endowing certain passages with personal significance and then reported these reasons to the class. The reasons became the basis for a class discussion on the role of literature in ethnic minority communities.

STEP-BY-STEP PROCEDURE

1. Select an important text or part of a text from the course readings. The text or passage should be challenging and provocative, but also relatively short and self-contained.

2. Ask students to divide a few pieces of notepaper in half lengthwise by drawing a line down the middle from top to bottom—or provide a form. Let the students know before they start that you will collect and read the notes and give feedback on them, but that you won't grade them.

3. On the left half of the divided notepaper, students should copy a few lines or short passages from the text (three to five excerpts) that they find particularly meaningful.

4. On the right half of the page, students should explain why they chose each specific excerpt and then should write their reactions to those excerpts — their agreements, disagreements, questions, and the like. Suggest that they think of their Double-Entry Journals as a dialogue — a conversation with the text.

TURNING THE DATA YOU COLLECT INTO USEFUL INFORMATION

After making your own Double-Entry Journal on the selected text, you can easily determine what you consider the key points. Check the left side of the students' notes to see how many of your key points are included. Look also for other points that students have mentioned. Then analyze the right side of the journal — their explanations for their choices and responses to the excerpts they chose. Try to categorize the responses that students make, and then count the instances of each type of response.

IDEAS FOR ADAPTING AND EXTENDING THIS CAT

Ask students to write Double-Entry Journals on a lecture, rather than on a text. Make an audio- or videotape of the lecture for students who need or wish to review it.

If students initially have difficulties selecting passages on which to focus, you may wish to select a few key passages and ask all students to respond to them. The students can then be asked to select three more excerpts on their own and to respond to those as well.

Make this a first, ungraded step in a graded writing assignment. As the next step, after receiving feedback, students could write coherent essays based on their Double-Entry Journals.

Once students are familiar with and skillful in using this CAT, direct them to look back through their own Double-Entry Journals for patterns in the kinds of passages they chose to respond to and in the types of responses they wrote.

PROS

Double-Entry Journals give teachers something akin to a reading protocol, a record of students' careful reading of and reactions to a text. This information can help the teacher understand how students read: what they focus on and why.

This CAT encourages students to look for personal meaning in what they read, and to engage with the texts. It promotes self-reflective learning at the same time that it provides feedback on reading.

CONS

There is some danger that students will censor themselves or will try to write what they think the teacher wants to read, rather than writing candid personal responses.

Students often find this type of explicit response to reading unfamiliar and difficult. Consequently, their first efforts may be so poor that both they and the teacher become discouraged and dispirited.

This device requires skills that may be underdeveloped in many students. It's important to distinguish between a lack of skill in responding to a text and a lack of self-awareness.

Your students may need to be trained in this technique before you can productively assess their awareness of their own values and opinions.

REFERENCES AND RESOURCES This CAT is adapted from a technique discussed in Ann Berthoff's *Forming, Thinking, Writing* (1988, pp. 26–34). Berthoff refers to her approach as a "dialectical notebook."

30

Profiles of Admirable Individuals

Estimated Levels of Time and Energy Required for:

Faculty to prepare to use this CAT	**LOW**
Students to respond to the assessment	**HIGH**
Faculty to analyze the data collected	**HIGH**

DESCRIPTION This straightforward technique requires that students write a brief, focused profile of an individual—in a field related to the course—whose values, skills, or actions they greatly admire. For example, each student in a social work course might be asked to write a one-page profile of a social worker whom that student particularly admires.

PURPOSE This technique assesses what students value by asking them (1) to select and profile an individual in the field whose values and behavior they admire and (2) to explain what they find admirable about that individual and why. This information can help faculty understand the images and values students associate with the best practice and practitioners in the discipline under study. Profiles of Admirable Individuals also force students to assess their own values. And feedback on the responses of other students helps them realize that, in any classroom, there will be several different sets of values in play.

RELATED TEACHING GOALS

Learn to understand perspectives and values of this subject (TGI Goal 21)

Learn to appreciate important contributions to this subject (TGI Goal 25)

Develop an informed historical perspective (TGI Goal 32)

Develop capacity to make informed ethical choices (TGI Goal 35)

Develop leadership skills (TGI Goal 38)

Develop a commitment to one's own values (TGI Goal 46)

Develop respect for others (TGI Goal 47)

Develop capacity to make wise decisions (TGI Goal 52)

SUGGESTIONS FOR USE Profiles of Admirable Individuals are useful in courses where students are expected to explore their values and/or the values of the discipline in systematic ways. As a result, this CAT is particularly appropriate for ethics courses and in preprofessional training. Since this CAT provides a collage of information on students' values and their level of sophistication in expressing them, it is best used early in the course, to help instructors plan later assignments in which students are asked to confront or analyze their values in more direct and systematic ways.

EXAMPLES

From Ethics in Business (Business/Management)

The instructor in this course wanted to find out early whom her students regarded as models of ethical behavior in the business and corporate world. She also wanted information on the specific characteristics that students particularly admired. To elicit such information, she asked the students to prepare one-page profiles of individuals whom they considered particularly admirable—as businesspeople and as ethical role models. She asked students not to write their names on the profiles but to hand them in to her graduate assistant, so that, on a separate list, he could check off the names of those who completed the assessment.

Since this was a new and somewhat controversial required course—and the responses were anonymous—the instructor was not surprised to receive a few cynical responses. For the most part, however, students gave sincere, if quickly written, answers. She noted that the "admirable businesspeople" tended to be admired either because they had donated a great deal of money to good causes or because they headed "clean" companies, enterprises specializing in environmentally or socially benevolent practices or products. The instructor's definition of "ethical role models" was both broader and more demanding than either of these common responses. However, she was able to use these responses as the basis for the first serious class discussion.

From a History of Women in the United States (History/Women's Studies)

To get an idea of her students' knowledge, interests, and values, this history professor asked students in her course to write a one-page profile of an admirable woman in U.S. history. Students were directed to select a woman whom they found particularly admirable and to explain briefly which particular qualities or actions had earned their admiration. She offered students a small amount of course credit for completing the assessment.

The women that her students selected were almost all from the nineteenth or early twentieth century, and most of them were abolitionists and suffragists. The students cited the courage and altruism of these women as their most admirable qualities. The professor summarized these responses and reported them to the students, noting the common threads mentioned above. She left them with two questions: Who are the most admirable women in recent U.S. History? Are the same positive qualities still important?

STEP-BY-STEP PROCEDURE

1. Begin by trying the technique yourself. Can you think of one or more truly admirable individuals in your field? Can you explain and give examples of how and why each of these individuals is admirable? What admirable qualities do those individuals exhibit?

2. If you can think of a few admirable individuals and are confident that your students can as well, decide what criteria you will use in assessing their profiles. Those criteria should focus on such qualities as the clarity, completeness, and persuasiveness of the profiles, rather than on the identity of the individuals chosen.

3. Draw up clear directions for the profiles, defining the population from which the admirable individuals are to be selected. Let students know how long their profiles should be. One or two pages are usually sufficient.

TURNING THE DATA YOU COLLECT INTO USEFUL INFORMATION

The most useful information these profiles can yield is on the qualities and characteristics—what students cite as most admirable—of the individuals that students select. Although the identities of those profiled are relatively unimportant, the values they represent to the students are critical. Therefore, one easy way to analyze the results is to tally the number of times that particular characteristics or values—such as honesty, hard work, courage, enthusiasm, and love of learning—are mentioned in the profiles. This tally can provide a kind of straw poll of the values that students in your class most admire.

IDEAS FOR ADAPTING AND EXTENDING THIS CAT

Provide students with a list of possible subjects: individuals who are widely regarded as admirable and about whom the students can write profiles if they have no candidates of their own.

Direct students to reread their profiles and to rank, in order of importance, the characteristics and values their subjects embody.

Ask students to write second, parallel profiles of individuals who are distinctly not admirable and to explain what accounts for their negative appraisals.

Have students work in small groups, with each member reading the profiles written by others. Ask each group to draw up a composite list of qualitites that characterize admirable individuals in your field.

PROS

Writing a Profile of an Admirable Individual requires each student to consider his or her own values and to select an individual on the basis of that valuing.

This technique can provide faculty with clear information about the role models that have influenced students during their adolescence and early adulthood.

CONS

Discussing or writing about values makes some students uncomfortable.

Without doing some research, many students will not be able to identify admirable individuals in the disciplines they are studying.

Specifying the admirable characteristics of the individuals profiled is often a challenge.

The less explicit students are about their values, the more time teachers must spend reading the profiles — and, often, reading between the lines.

CAVEATS   Make certain to ensure students' anonymity in responding to questions about values.

Many students may be unable, at least at first, to come up with individuals within the field to profile. Or they may limit their profiles to telling the life stories of the individuals, rather than focusing explicitly on their characteristics as individuals. To avoid these problems, be sure to give students explicit guidelines and, if necessary, instruction in how to write well-focused profiles.

Some students may choose to write about individuals whom you have never heard of or do not find admirable. In either case, keep in mind that the identity of the individual the student chooses is much less important than the student's explanation of that individual's admirable qualities.

31

Everyday Ethical Dilemmas

Estimated Levels of Time and Energy Required for:

Faculty to prepare to use this CAT	**MEDIUM**
Students to respond to the assessment	**MEDIUM**
Faculty to analyze the data collected	**HIGH**

DESCRIPTION   Developmental psychologists, such as Lawrence Kohlberg and Carol Gilligan, have long explored and evaluated young people's responses to ethical dilemmas in order to understand their moral and ethical decision making and development. Everyday Ethical Dilemmas bring that inquiry into the college classroom, albeit on a very limited scale. In this CAT, students are presented with an abbreviated case study that poses an ethical problem related to the discipline or profession they are studying. Students respond briefly and anonymously to these cases, and faculty analyze the responses in order to understand the students' values.

PURPOSE   Everyday Ethical Dilemmas prompt students to identify, clarify, and connect their values by responding to course-related issues and problems that they are likely to encounter. As they respond to this CAT, students learn more about their values—and their classmates' values—and the ways in which these values affect their everyday decisions. Faculty get honest reactions and information on what students' values are and how they apply them, at least hypothetically, to realistic dilemmas.

RELATED TEACHING GOALS   Learn to understand perspectives and values of this subject (TGI Goal 21)
Learn to appreciate important contributions to this subject (TGI Goal 25)
Develop an informed historical perspective (TGI Goal 32)
Develop capacity to make informed ethical choices (TGI Goal 35)
Develop leadership skills (TGI Goal 38)
Develop a commitment to one's own values (TGI Goal 46)
Develop respect for others (TGI Goal 47)
Develop capacity to make wise decisions (TGI Goal 52)

Although ethical questions can and do arise in every field, ethical dilemmas are most often topics of classroom discussions in preprofessional and professional education—law, medicine, social work, education, engineering, and management—and in traditional liberal arts courses, especially philosophy and theology.

EXAMPLES

From Freshman Seminar (Study Skills/Personal Development)

This interdisciplinary course serves several aims—among them, introducing first-year college students to the values and standards of the academic community. To get a sense of her students' views on academic integrity, this psychology instructor prepared an Everyday Ethical Dilemma. The half-page case she wrote and distributed to the class concerned a college student, Anne, and her roommate, Barbara. Barbara told Anne that she was planning to take her boyfriend's final exam for him in a required science class, a class that Anne was also taking. The assessment asked the Freshman Seminar students to respond anonymously, in less than half a page, to the following two questions: (1) What, if anything, should Anne do about the plans Barbara and her boyfriend have for cheating on the final exam? (2) Depending on your answer to question 1, why should or shouldn't Anne do something?

The instructor allowed students ten minutes of class time to respond to the dilemma; she then collected the cases. When she read them after class, she was somewhat surprised to find that nearly 60 percent of the students thought that Anne should not do anything about the planned cheating. The reasons they gave were varied, but most centered around Anne's relationship to her roommate. Another quarter of the students thought that Anne should confront Barbara and try to talk her out of it, and a few favored notifying some campus authority. The instructor shared these results with the class and asked them to uncover the values behind various answers. A lively discussion of academic integrity ensued.

From Health Care Management (Public Health/Management)

Students in this graduate course were given the following Everyday Ethical Dilemma to respond to:

Imagine that you are the chief operating officer (COO) of a large city hospital. Faced with skyrocketing costs, you must decide either to make drastic reductions in services for the indigent and uninsured working poor in your community or to cover those costs by passing them along to insured customers. Briefly explain what you would do and how you would justify your decision to the hospital's governing board.

STEP-BY-STEP PROCEDURE

1. Decide on one specific ethical issue or question to focus on.

2. Locate or create a short case that poses the essential dilemma realistically in a few lines.

3. Write two or three questions that require students to take a position on the dilemma and to explain or justify that position.

4. Ask students to write short, honest, anonymous responses.

5. Allow enough class time for students to write responses, or make this a take-home assessment exercise.

TURNING THE DATA YOU COLLECT INTO USEFUL INFORMATION

First, read quickly through student responses to tally the number of students who have taken various positions on the Everyday Ethical Dilemma. Separate the responses according to these positions or answers; then read each group again quickly, to analyze the explanations or justifications given. Separate those justifications into the smallest possible number of meaningful categories. Let students know what the most common responses were and what the various justifications were for each of those responses.

IDEAS FOR ADAPTING AND EXTENDING THIS CAT

After students have written their individual responses to the Everyday Ethical Dilemma, organize a structured, small-group discussion of the issues. Then repeat the assessment and compare responses from the first and second administration of the CAT.

Classify responses according to a framework or schema that is relevant to your course and discipline, or one that is relevant to your own favorite theory of ethical development. For example, students' responses might be categorized according to Perry's (1970) "forms of intellectual and moral development."

Ask students to write responses to Everyday Ethical Dilemmas from two very different viewpoints.

Assign students the task of creating Everyday Ethical Dilemma cases and questions to be used in the class.

PROS

Everyday Ethical Dilemmas allow students to try out various ethical positions, to practice their ethical reasoning skills on hypothetical but realistic problems, and to get feedback on their responses. These experiences can help them better prepare to face similar dilemmas later, when stakes are much higher.

When faculty learn what students' values are in relation to important ethical questions, they are better able to help students explore and rethink those issues and develop ethical reasoning skills.

CONS

Some students resist and resent discussions of ethics and values in the classroom, or they believe that no amount of discussion can change their own or their classmates' minds. For these students, Everyday Ethical Dilemmas may be an intrusion or simply a waste of time.

Students' values may not be what the instructor hopes or expects them to be; as a result, the teacher may lose respect for or interest in his or her students.

CAVEATS   To assess and respond to students' values and ethical reasoning in a constructive manner, you will need a great deal of patience, skill, and self-knowledge. You may want to begin by using this CAT to focus on minor dilemmas and gradually work up to more critical and interesting ones. This procedure will allow you and your students to build trust, confidence, and skill.

**CLASSROOM
ASSESSMENT
TECHNIQUE**

32

Course-Related
Self-Confidence Surveys

Estimated Levels of Time and Energy Required for:

Faculty to prepare to use this CAT	**MEDIUM**
Students to respond to the assessment	**LOW**
Faculty to analyze the data collected	**LOW**

DESCRIPTION   In many instances, individuals who are generally self-confident may lack confidence in their abilities or skills in a specific context — for example, in their quantitative skills or their ability to speak in public. It is this type of domain- and even course-specific self-confidence that these surveys assess. Course-Related Self-Confidence Surveys, then, consist of a few simple questions aimed at getting a rough measure of the students' self-confidence in relation to a specific skill or ability.

PURPOSE   Course-Related Self-Confidence Surveys help faculty assess their students' levels of confidence in their ability to learn the relevant skills and material. When teachers know the students' level of confidence, and what affects that confidence, they can more effectively structure assignments that will build confidence and enhance motivation and learning. Once students are aware of their self-confidence in relation to specific tasks, they can focus their attention on controlling and improving their performance and self-confidence in tandem — setting up a "virtuous" cycle of success.

**RELATED TEACHING
GOALS**
Develop a lifelong love of learning (TGI Goal 30)
Develop (self-) management skills (TGI Goal 37)
Develop leadership skills (TGI Goal 38)
Develop a commitment to personal achievement (TGI Goal 42)
Improve self-esteem/self-confidence (TGI Goal 45)
Develop a commitment to one's own values (TGI Goal 46)
Cultivate emotional health and well-being (TGI Goal 48)
Cultivate physical health and well-being (TGI Goal 49)

SUGGESTIONS FOR USE   Course-Related Self-Confidence Surveys are useful in courses where students are trying to learn new and unfamiliar skills, or familiar skills that they failed to learn in previous attempts. Some examples would be introductory courses in mathematics, public speaking, and natural sciences. These surveys are best used before the skills in question are introduced, and again after students are likely to have made significant progress toward mastering them. Once the survey form has been created, the CAT is easy to administer and score and can be used even in very large classes.

EXAMPLES

From Fitness and Strength Training (Physical Education)

The instructor in this course knew from experience that many of the adult students in her classes, especially the women, initially lacked self-confidence in their ability to succeed in mastering physical skills and becoming fit. To help students become more aware of their self-confidence in relation to the course, to help them evaluate how realistic their levels of self-confidence were, and to help them recognize the relationship between their level of self-confidence and their likely success, she used the Self-Confidence Survey (see Exhibit 8.1). Of course, at the same time as the survey provided the students with information about themselves and about the class as a whole, it informed the instructor's approach to teaching them.

Exhibit 8.1. Sample Self-Confidence Survey Form.

Now that you've read the syllabus, how confident do you feel that you'll be able to do the following by the end of this course? (Circle the most accurate response.)

How Confident Do You Feel? (circle one)

1. Feel comfortable working out in a gym and/or running in public	Very	Somewhat	Not Very	Not at All
2. Run three miles in thirty minutes	Very	Somewhat	Not Very	Not at All
3. Do a hundred sit-ups without stopping	Very	Somewhat	Not Very	Not at All
4. Lift at least 50 percent more on each weight machine than you can now	Very	Somewhat	Not Very	Not at All
5. Maintain your own exercise program for a year after the class has ended	Very	Somewhat	Not Very	Not at All
6. Enjoy exercising regularly for the rest of your life	Very	Somewhat	Not Very	Not at All

7. If you circled "not very" or "not at all" in response to any items above, please briefly explain below why you don't feel confident.

In tallying and analyzing the responses, the instructor noticed an important discrepancy. Most students were confident that they could reach the short-term, physical goals—represented by questions 2, 3, and 4. At the same time, most of them had little confidence in their ability to feel comfortable exercising in public (question 1) or in maintaining and enjoying exercise (questions 5 and 6). Those who lacked confidence in reaching the longer-term goals most often explained that they had tried and failed before, or that they had very little willpower.

The instructor praised the students for their candor and their realistic self-appraisals, but she also pointed out the importance of building self-confidence, step by step, through achievement. She told students that they would work on building long-term self-confidence and motivation in three ways: by setting lifelong fitness goals along with "reachable" short-term objectives; by celebrating and savoring small successes; and by building positive, enjoyable exercise and health habits into their daily routines.

College Algebra (Mathematics/Developmental Education)

Most of the students taking this first-year course had histories of failure in mathematics and were taking the course only to fulfill a graduation requirement—two conditions that made the class especially difficult to teach. The instructor, who was familiar with the work of Sheila Tobias and others on math anxiety, believed that low self-confidence could impede the learning of mathematics. On the second day of class, to understand and help improve her students' self-confidence, she administered a survey form (see Exhibit 8.2). The instructor's form also included an example or two of each type of problem, to ensure that students knew what she was referring to. Those examples are not reproduced here.

Exhibit 8.2. Sample Survey: Self-Confidence in Mathematics.

This survey is to help both of us understand your level of confidence in your math skills. Rather than thinking about your mathematical self-confidence in general terms, please indicate how confident you feel about your ability to do the various kinds of problems listed below. (Circle the most accurate response for each.)

Kinds of Problems	*Self-Confidence in Your Ability to Do Them*			
1. Addition and subtraction problems	None	Low	Medium	High
2. Multiplication problems	None	Low	Medium	High
3. Division problems	None	Low	Medium	High
4. Problems involving fractions	None	Low	Medium	High
5. Problems involving decimals	None	Low	Medium	High
6. Graphing problems	None	Low	Medium	High
7. Square or cube root problems	None	Low	Medium	High
8. Word problems	None	Low	Medium	High
9. Equations using letters, not numbers	None	Low	Medium	High

The class's responses were somewhat predictable; the mean confidence level was highest for items at the beginning of the form, lowest for those at the end. The mathematics instructor noticed, however, that some students rated their self-confidence low across the board, while others rated consistently high. She reported the survey results to the class and asked students to help her interpret them. Specifically, the instructor asked students for suggestions on ways that she and they could raise everyone's performance and self-confidence in the algebra class. Students suggested working in small study groups, holding review sessions before tests, working with tutors, and using the available computer courseware for more practice and feedback.

STEP-BY-STEP PROCEDURE

1. Focus on skills or abilities that are important to success in the course.

2. Make up questions to assess students' self-confidence in relation to these skills or abilities. Be as specific as possible in your questions.

3. Create a simple survey form for gathering the data.

4. Allow students a few minutes in class to respond to the survey. Be sure to tell them that their survey responses are to be anonymous.

TURNING THE DATA YOU COLLECT INTO USEFUL INFORMATION

If data are collected with a survey form, then summarizing the data requires little more than tallying responses to the various possible responses.

IDEAS FOR ADAPTING AND EXTENDING THIS CAT

Break the class into small groups. Ask students to discuss and compare their responses with each other and to come up with practical suggestions for building competence and confidence.

Ask follow-up questions to find out which variables—especially which classroom variables—affect students' self-confidence most directly and how those variables might be manipulated to improve self-confidence.

PROS

Self-Confidence Surveys provide information on students' self-confidence—and, indirectly, on their anxieties—about specific and often controllable elements of the course, rather than about very general and amorphous concerns.

The simple act of publicly acknowledging that students may have low levels of self-confidence in certain areas—and that there may be some things they can do to remedy that situation—offers relief to many students, who believe they are the only ones to feel as they do.

This CAT helps students learn that a certain minimum level of confidence is necessary to learning.

CONS

Just as some students have unrealistically low levels of self-confidence, others have unjustifiably high self-confidence levels. In some ways, these overconfident students may be the most difficult ones to teach.

The discovery that a sizable number of students have low self-confidence can be depressing to faculty and students alike.

CAVEATS   Students need to understand that self-confidence should be based on demonstrated potential and performance, and that the best way for them to improve self-confidence—all things being equal—is to demonstrate to themselves that they perform well.

Obviously, some students have serious problems with self-confidence and self-esteem, and those problems may not be appreciably improved by course-specific efforts in one class.

Assessing Students' Self-Awareness as Learners

33. Focused Autobiographical Sketches

34. Interest/Knowledge/Skills Checklists

35. Goal Ranking and Matching

36. Self-Assessment of Ways of Learning

Students' assessments of the learning and growth they experience through participating in courses depend to a great extent on their images of their own starting points, skills, and capabilities, regardless of the accuracy of those images. These assessments also are influenced by the students' individual goals. All too often, the instructional goals of courses seem to be based on one of the following assumptions: that students' goals are identical to those of the course, that students' goals are irrelevant to those of the course, or that students have no goals. We suggest that most students do have learning goals, although they may not always be able to articulate them, and that information about students' goals can be very useful to teachers in planning, teaching, assessing, and revising their courses.

In any course, students are likely to learn more if they are capable of clearly articulating their goals and self-concepts and of making connections between those goals and self-concepts and the goals and requirements of the course. Self-awareness is crucial to involvement in learning. Each of the techniques in this section focuses on students' awareness of goals, interests, or ways of learning as they relate to the classroom. The Focused Autobiographical Sketch assesses students' self-awareness as learners in a specific field. Through Interest/Knowledge/Skills Checklists, students make explicit their level of interest in the various topics dealt with in a given course and assess their knowledge and experience in skills central to success in mastering those topics. Goal Ranking and Matching enables students to make their learning goals explicit and to rank them in order of their importance and achievability. The fourth technique, Self-Assessment of Ways of Learning, can be used to find out, in a very global sense, how students prefer to learn.

Focused Autobiographical Sketches

Estimated Levels of Time and Energy Required for:

Faculty to prepare to use this CAT	**MEDIUM**
Students to respond to the assessment	**HIGH**
Faculty to analyze the data collected	**MEDIUM to HIGH**

DESCRIPTION At one time or another, most college students have been asked to write personal statements or autobiographical essays. Such written self-portraits are often a required part of applications for admission and for scholarships, for example. College admissions and scholarship selection committees routinely assess these statements to make decisions about their authors. The Focused Autobiographical Sketch is simply a shorter, more specific version of these familiar tasks. In this technique, students are directed to write a one- or two-page autobiographical sketch focused on a single successful learning experience in their past — an experience relevant to learning in the particular course in which the assessment technique is used.

PURPOSE The Focused Autobiographical Sketch provides information on the students' self-concept and self-awareness as learners within a specific field. It gives the teacher a composite portrait of the range and diversity of levels of self-awareness and reflectiveness among students in the class. This information can help teachers determine "where the students are," so that they can more effectively gauge the appropriate level of instruction and set realistic course objectives. These sketches can also provide "starting-line" information against which to assess learning over the course of the semester.

RELATED TEACHING GOALS
Develop a lifelong love of learning (TGI Goal 30)
Develop leadership skills (TGI Goal 38)
Develop a commitment to personal achievement (TGI Goal 42)
Improve self-esteem/self-confidence (TGI Goal 45)
Develop a commitment to one's own values (TGI Goal 46)
Develop respect for others (TGI Goal 47)
Cultivate emotional health and well-being (TGI Goal 48)
Develop capacity to make wise decisions (TGI Goal 52)

SUGGESTIONS FOR USE The familiar autobiographical statements referred to in the "Description" section are used primarily for selection and gatekeeping — for summative evaluation of candidates. Focused Autobiographical Sketches, on the other hand, should be used only for diagnostic and formative evaluation. Therefore, this technique is appropriate for any course that aims at helping students develop their self-confidence, self-awareness, and skill at self-assessment. It is particularly useful in introductory courses, especially those that are likely to cause high levels of student anxiety. Mathematics, statistics, the natural sciences, and public speaking are examples of "high-anxiety" courses for many students. Underprepared learners and adult students returning to college seem to find this CAT especially helpful. Focused Autobiographical Sketches are most effective at the beginning of courses or units, and should only be used once a term in most cases. Because they are time-consuming to write and to analyze, they are best adapted to very small classes.

EXAMPLES

From Leadership (Public Administration)

In a graduate course on leadership skills for mid-career public administrators, the instructor's central goals were to help her students become more explicitly and critically aware of their preconceptions about leadership. In an attempt to determine an appropriate starting point for the class, as well as to collect "pretest" data for later comparison, she asked each student, during the first week of class, to write a one- or two-page Focused Autobiographical Sketch. The specific assignment was as follows:

> Write one or two pages—not more—relating and discussing a recent experience in which you exercised leadership in a public context and learned something significant about leadership from your success. Focus not only on what you learned but also on how and why you learned about leadership from that particular experience. What does it suggest about learning how to lead?

During the next class meeting, after she had analyzed and summarized their responses in general terms, the public administration professor divided the large class into prearranged small groups, which she had structured. Each group of five contained individuals with quite different leadership experiences. The members of each small group were to recount their stories very briefly and then extract any common, general principles for learning leadership skills.

From Speaking for Success (Speech Communication)

Students in this required course were often reluctant and sometimes even afraid to speak in public. In an attempt to help students realize that they (probably) did have some relevant, successful experience at public speaking—and to find out what that experience was—this speech professor adapted the Focused Autobiographical Sketch technique. Students were given the following prompt:

> In less than a page, and in less than fifteen minutes, describe one experience you have had in the past few years in which you

successfully spoke in public. ("In public" in this case could mean in front of three people you didn't previously know.) Why was it a success? What lesson(s) can you take from that experience that might help you in this class?

STEP-BY-STEP PROCEDURE

1. Determine what element or elements of the students' learning experiences you want to focus the autobiographical sketch on. Clearly limit the focus and make sure it is directly related to the course goals and objectives.

2. Limit the sketch still further by determining what period or periods in the students' lives and what specific areas of their lives — for example, professional, academic, or interpersonal — the sketch should cover.

3. Consider what scale, if any, or criteria you will use to assess the sketches. Then reconsider your focus in the light of your assessment criteria. Does it still make sense? Will you be able to analyze students' responses?

4. If the answer to both of the above questions is "yes," construct very explicit directions for the students to follow in writing the Focused Autobiographical Sketch. Since these sketches must be short, keep the field of concern as limited as possible.

TURNING THE DATA YOU COLLECT INTO USEFUL INFORMATION

Since the aim of this technique is to gather well-focused information on certain relevant learning experiences, the analysis of data should be limited to categorizing and counting those experiences in ways that will help you better focus the class. You may simply categorize the types of experiences recounted as relevant or not relevant to the course content, and then further break down the "relevant" category into subcategories, such as directly, indirectly, or tangentially relevant. Another approach is to assess the quality or intensity of the experiences recounted. A third option is to assess the level of self-awareness or critical reflection displayed in the sketches.

IDEAS FOR ADAPTING AND EXTENDING THIS CAT

As a follow-up, ask students to explain the criteria they applied in judging the experiences they chose to write about. For example, ask them to write about how and why they judged the experiences to be successful or meaningful.

Once trust has been built within the class, direct students to write a Focused Autobiographical Sketch about a lesson they learned from failure.

Direct students to focus on the same experience from the point of view of another person who was involved, or one who might have been.

PROS

Focused Autobiographical Sketches allow teachers to assess only those dimensions of the students' experiences likely to be relevant to the course content and goals, a much more effective approach than reading general personal statements.

This technique provides information on the range and diversity of past experience and level of self-awareness within a class. The information it yields can be used for setting instructional goals appropriate to the particular mix of students.

CONS
There are no simple, widely accepted guidelines on how to judge the quality or intensity or value of individual learning experiences; so this technique requires that teachers develop their own.

Reading such sketches, even very brief ones, requires a lot of time and attention, as does responding to them in even the simplest ways.

CAVEATS
Many students are relatively proficient at narrating their past experience, but unskilled at critically assessing it. Such students may need instruction and guidance in writing critical, reflective prose, and especially in focusing their writing, before their Autobiographical Sketches will yield much useful information.

Some students balk at revealing any information about themselves, even when that information is revealed anonymously. Although you will want to explain the purpose of this assessment and to encourage students to take part, do not force anyone to participate.

34

Interest / Knowledge / Skills Checklists

Estimated Levels of Time and Energy Required for:

Faculty to prepare to use this CAT	**MEDIUM**
Students to respond to the assessment	**LOW**
Faculty to analyze the data collected	**LOW to MEDIUM**

DESCRIPTION Course-specific Interest/Knowledge/Skills Checklists are brief, teacher-made versions of the commercial interest and skills inventories long used by guidance and career counselors. Teachers create checklists of topics covered in their courses and skills strengthened by or required for succeeding in those courses. Students rate their interest in the various topics, and assess their levels of skill or knowledge in those topics, by indicating the appropriate responses on the checklist.

PURPOSE These checklists inform teachers of their students' level of interest in course topics and their assessment of the skills and knowledge needed for and/or developed through the course. With such information, teachers can better plan and adjust their teaching agendas. They can plan how to approach topics about which students indicated particularly high or low interest. They can also adjust their syllabi to take into account the students' knowledge and skill levels. This CAT helps learners more realistically assess their interest in and preparation for the course. These twofold responses can provide teachers and learners with more useful insights than a more general interest inventory might.

RELATED TEACHING GOALS Prepare for transfer or graduate study (TGI Goal 22)
Develop a commitment to personal achievement (TGI Goal 42)
Cultivate a sense of responsibility for one's own behavior (TGI Goal 44)
Develop a commitment to one's own values (TGI Goal 46)
Develop capacity to make wise decisions (TGI Goal 52)

SUGGESTIONS FOR USE Interest/Knowledge/Skills Checklists are most useful in courses with flexible syllabi. For example, this kind of feedback can be helpful to those teaching upper-level electives, capstone courses, graduate seminars, adult education courses, and professional and personal development courses. Like

Goal Ranking and Matching (CAT 35), this technique works best if used at or just before the beginning of the course. It can then be readministered midway through, and again near the end of the course, to provide information on changes in students' assessments of their interests, knowledge, and skills.

EXAMPLES

From Senior Capstone Seminar (Psychology)

> The purpose of this capstone course was to help students integrate and evaluate what they had learned in the previous three and a half years of course work in psychology, and to help them prepare to use what they had learned after college. Because the students in this small seminar had a variety of interests, skills, and postbaccalaureate plans, the faculty leaders could not easily find common threads. In an attempt to remedy that problem, this professor made up an Interest/Knowledge/Skills Checklist before the semester began. Seniors planning to take the Capstone Seminar were required to turn in the completed checklist before they enrolled in the seminar. Their responses shaped her course planning, allowing her to put together a very specific reading list and to set up three working groups within the seminar. As a result, the seminar got off to a much faster and more productive start than it had in previous years.

From Improving Student Learning (Higher Education)

> The sample Interest/Knowledge/Skills Checklist shown as Exhibit 8.3 was used in an in-service professional development course for community college faculty. Because the course was intended to meet the needs and interests of these college teachers, and because their participation in the course was voluntary, the course leader wanted to use their responses to shape the course. The instructor shared the outcomes of the assessment with the faculty participants and explained how the elements of the course were designed to respond to their feedback. Their checklist responses showed clearly that most participants were interested more in practical applications than in theory. He also found that collecting, using, and giving faculty feedback on their responses encouraged interest and investment in the course.

STEP-BY-STEP PROCEDURE

1. Divide a piece of paper in half lengthwise and make two parallel lists. On one side, list the main topics your course will or could deal with. On the other side, list the related skills and/or knowledge required of students and/or to be acquired by students through your course.

2. Come up with a simple, useful, and appropriate way to code student responses. (For some teachers, the codes in the checklist above may serve as models.)

3. Make a draft checklist that contains the edited contents of both lists and the related coding schemes. Try the draft version out yourself; then revise it as required. Make up a final version of the checklist that is both easy to use and easy to code.

Exhibit 8.3. A Sample Interest/Knowledge/Skills Checklist.

Please respond to this checklist honestly and accurately. Do not write your name on it.

Part I: Interest in Possible Course Topics

Directions: Please circle the number after each item below that best represents your level of interest in that topic. The numbers stand for the following responses:

      0 = No interest in the topic
      1 = Interested in an overview of the topic
      2 = Interested in reading about and discussing this topic
      3 = Interested in learning how to apply ideas about this topic this semester

Possible Course Topics

1. Theories/research on college learning	0	1	2	3
2. Theories/research on college teaching	0	1	2	3
3. Teaching practices that promote effective learning	0	1	2	3
4. Clarifying teaching goals/creating better syllabi	0	1	2	3
5. Structuring more effective assignments	0	1	2	3
6. Understanding/responding to learning styles	0	1	2	3
7. Constructing better tests and quizzes	0	1	2	3
8. Helping students improve study and learning skills	0	1	2	3
9. Getting and giving feedback for improvement	0	1	2	3
10. Responding to diversity in student preparation	0	1	2	3

Part II: Self-Assessment of Related Skills and Knowledge

Directions: Please circle the letter after each item below that best represents your level of skill or knowledge in relation to that topic. The letters stand for the following responses:

      N = No skills, no knowledge
      B = Basic skills and knowledge
      F = Functionally adequate skills and knowledge
      A = Advanced level of skills and knowledge

Areas of Skill and/or Knowledge
(numbers in parentheses refer to course topics listed in Part I)

Current psychological and cognitive science theories and research on college student and adult learning (1)	N	B	F	A
Research on effective college teaching (2 & 3)	N	B	F	A
Syllabus construction (4)	N	B	F	A
Research/practice on skill development (5 & 8)	N	B	F	A
Analyzing learning styles (6)	N	B	F	A
Classroom test construction (7)	N	B	F	A
Research on learning/study strategies and skills (8 & 5)	N	B	F	A
Writing teaching and learning goals and objectives (9 & 4)	N	B	F	A
Classroom Assessment Techniques (10 & 9)	N	B	F	A

4. Let students know why you are asking them to assess their interests, skills, and knowledge. Make sure they understand how much and in what ways this information is likely to affect the syllabus and your teaching approach. Direct them not to write their names on the responses.

TURNING THE DATA YOU COLLECT INTO USEFUL INFORMATION

By tallying the responses for each item, you can easily see which items received significant numbers of very low or very high ratings. Then cluster the interests and skills into related groups and plot their values on a graph. Plotting parallel bar graphs to indicate interest levels for topic X and self-assessed skill/knowledge ratings for X can be informative to both teachers and students. You can show the class, for example, that some topics they have expressed great interest in learning will require them to work especially hard to develop their skill and knowledge; and you can point out topics on which you expect the class to perform well, given their self-ratings.

IDEAS FOR ADAPTING AND EXTENDING THIS CAT

Ask students to comment on the two or three topics they are most—or least—interested in and to explain in detail why they are, or are not, interested in these topics. Have students explain their lowest and highest knowledge and skills ratings as well.

Show students how they can analyze their own responses to discover mismatches and good fits between their interests and their skills and experiences. Ask them to take their checklists home, analyze them, and comment on one mismatch and how they intend to develop it into a good fit.

Use a graphic display to show the areas of overlap and fit between student interests and skills and the course topics and requirements.

PROS

By providing teachers with detailed, specific information on their students' interests and self-assessments of their skills and knowledge, the checklist makes course planning and instruction more focused and effective.

The teacher also can compare the students' assessments with his or her own assessment of their competence.

If students see that their interests and level of preparation are being taken into account by the teacher, they are likely to invest more effort in the course.

By requiring students to consider their interests and skills in explicit relation to the course at hand, this technique promotes self-assessment and awareness in the students who use it.

CONS

Preparing a checklist can be rather time-consuming. This "front-end" investment is offset by the fact that the checklist takes very little time to administer or code.

The interests, knowledge, and skill levels that students report may not fit well with the teacher's hopes and plans. In such instances, the teacher must either ignore the checklist results or redesign elements of the course.

CAVEATS   Although students may not express interest in a given topic, they might develop interest in that topic through the course. Often, as the saying goes, "Knowledge breeds enthusiasm."

In many courses, especially those at the introductory or beginning levels, students' assessments of knowledge and skills may provide more accurate and useful information about their self-confidence than about their prior learning.

35

Goal Ranking and Matching

Estimated Levels of Time and Energy Required for:

Faculty to prepare to use this CAT	**MEDIUM**
Students to respond to the assessment	**LOW**
Faculty to analyze the data collected	**LOW to MEDIUM**

DESCRIPTION Goal Ranking and Matching is a simple procedure that many faculty have adapted to use in the first or second day of class. It takes only a few minutes for students to list a few learning goals they hope to achieve through the course and to rank the relative importance of those goals. If time and interest allow, students can also estimate the relative difficulty of achieving their learning goals. The instructor then collects student lists and matches them against his or her own course goals.

PURPOSE The primary purpose of Goal Ranking and Matching is to assess the "degree of fit" (1) between students' personal learning goals and teachers' course-specific instructional goals and (2) between teachers' and students' rankings of the relative importance and difficulty of the goals. This CAT also enables teachers to create shared class goals. Faculty can use the information this technique provides to increase student motivation by helping students make connections between their personal goals and course goals, and—where appropriate—by incorporating student goals into the syllabus. Finally, this technique helps students learn to identify and clarify their own learning goals—an important lifelong learning skill.

RELATED TEACHING GOALS Learn to understand perspectives and values of this subject (TGI Goal 21)
Develop ability to work productively with others (TGI Goal 36)
Develop a commitment to personal achievement (TGI Goal 42)
Cultivate a sense of responsibility for one's own behavior (TGI Goal 44)
Develop a commitment to one's own values (TGI Goal 46)

SUGGESTIONS FOR USE Goal Ranking and Matching can be useful to any teachers who are interested in knowing what their students hope to get from their classes. The technique should be used in the first week of class. Students in elective courses and upper-division courses in their majors can usually respond to this CAT at the end of the first class meeting. Students in introductory, required courses may respond more adequately on the second day of class — after they have had a chance to learn what the course is about.

EXAMPLES

From Critical Reading and Writing (English)

In reading through his students' responses to the Goal Ranking and Matching technique, this English instructor found that most of them had more than one goal related to improving their writing, but that only one or two had mentioned reading. When he discussed his goals and theirs during the next class meeting, he took great care to point out his reading-related goals and the reasons for them.

From Repairing Electronic Systems (Automobile Technology)

In responding to feedback on the Goal Ranking and Matching technique, this vocational education instructor praised the class for listing many specific, practical learning goals related to understanding and repairing the complex electronic systems common in newer cars. He assured them that they could accomplish almost all of those "technical" goals through his course. At the same time, he pointed out two goals that he had included but that none of them had: (1) to learn how to stay current in skills and knowledge in this fast-evolving area and (2) to develop skill and confidence in clearly explaining diagnoses and planned repairs to customers. He invited class members to explain why these last two were also important goals, and several did so. The instructor then previewed some of the class activities and assignments that would address learning goals they and he had raised.

From Writers of the Harlem Renaissance (African-American Studies)

This instructor found that some of the students in her upper-division course were taking the course primarily to fulfill major requirements; others, to prepare for graduate work in African-American studies or English; and a third group, to prepare themselves for careers as professional writers. She put this information to use by creating three working groups within the class, each with somewhat different—but comparable—writing assignments. The whole class continued to read and discuss the same authors and texts in common while realizing some of their diverse writing goals through the "customized" assignments.

An Example from Classroom Assessment

Exhibit 8.4 is a Goal Ranking and Matching list that we made in relation to this handbook. Its main purpose is to illustrate how simple this CAT format can be (1 = the most important goal). You may want to look at our predictions of readers' goal rankings to see whether you agree with them.

Exhibit 8.4. Sample Goal-Ranking and Matching List.

Goals for This Book	Importance to the Authors	Predicted Importance to Readers
That it stimulate college teachers to experiment actively in assessing their students' learning and encourage them to come up with their own techniques.	1	2
That the assessment techniques and examples it contains be easily and immediately adaptable to and useful in a variety of disciplines.	2	1
That it interest and motivate faculty to begin practicing Classroom Research — systematic, long-term inquiry aimed at understanding student learning.	3	4
That it make explicit the connections between important current research on college teaching and learning and Classroom Assessment practices.	4	3

STEP-BY-STEP PROCEDURE

1. Before you begin, make sure that you have clearly articulated your instructional goals for the class. If you have not, go through this exercise yourself before trying it with your students.

2. Decide what, if anything, is negotiable — and to what extent. In other words, if you find that students' goals differ widely from yours, is there anything you are willing to substitute or alter to accommodate their interests? If there is absolutely nothing you can or will change, it may not be wise to use this CAT.

3. Either hand out a simple form or have students take out a piece of paper and list three to five goals they hope to achieve by taking your course. Explain that by "goals" you mean specific things they hope to learn. If you are teaching a required course, you may suggest that "to complete the requirement" and "to do well in the course" are general goals that everyone shares; therefore, the students don't have to repeat these goals but can write much more specific answers about what they hope to learn instead. Make sure the students understand that they are not to write names on their responses. This goal-writing step should take no more than three to five minutes.

4. Direct the students to rank the goals on their lists in the order of their importance in their lives. One way to explain this step is to say, "For example, if you could choose only one goal to accomplish, which would it be? That's number 1. If you could choose a second, which would it be? That's number 2." You may find it helpful to draw an example on the board. Ask them to write those rankings to the left of the goals on the list. This step may take another two or three minutes.

5. Collect the responses, remind students what you will use the data for, and let them know when you will discuss the results.

TURNING THE DATA YOU COLLECT INTO USEFUL INFORMATION

The most basic step in analyzing the data is to look for patterns in students' goals and categorize them accordingly. Since students are likely to have many of the same or similar goals, the challenge is to recognize those similarities despite superficial differences in individual expression. At the same time, you need to be alert for goals that are truly different or unique and categorize them as such.

Once you have divided the goal statements into a few categories and tallied the number of "votes" in each, compare those categories with your instructional goals. How well do they match, overall? For example, are there categories of student goals that don't overlap with course goals? For those categories that do match or overlap, are the students' rank orderings of importance in line with yours? Are students' goals much broader or narrower than yours? Do the students' estimates of difficulty fit with yours?

As you prepare to give students feedback on their responses, decide whether you can incorporate any of the students' goals into the course goals or connect them in any way. For example, can students realize some of their very specific goals by pursuing them in term papers or projects? If a number of students have goals that you cannot address in any way, prepare to tell them so in a positive but honest way. If possible, be ready to suggest other courses or programs that might address those goals.

IDEAS FOR ADAPTING AND EXTENDING THIS CAT

Ask students to rank the goals on their lists a second time — this time, in order of their difficulty to achieve. Ask them to use Roman numerals for this ranking, with I being most difficult, II next most difficult, and so on. Ask students to write these rankings to the right of the goals. This step will probably take another two minutes or so.

Ask students to rank their goal lists a third time — in order of the amount of time they will need to realize each goal. Have them then create a composite "level-of-challenge" rank ordering that reflects both time and difficulty rankings.

Break the class into small groups and direct the students in each group to come up with a mutually acceptable group response to the Goal Ranking and Matching.

Do a follow-up at midterm and near the end of the course. Look for changes in students' goals. Have they become more focused and realistic? More like the course goals, or more different from them? How well are the stated goals being achieved?

PROS

Goal Ranking and Matching raises students' awareness of their own learning goals, or their own lack of identifiable goals, in relation to a specific course. They begin to recognize their own investment in and responsibility for learning.

It allows faculty to determine whether and to what extent students' learning goals overlap their teaching goals — information that is critical to gauging the students' level of investment in and motivation for learning in that course.

This CAT gets students involved right from the start in a dialogue about the course's direction and aims. It therefore encourages active involvement and communication.

Students get immediate feedback on the match between their goals and the instructor's. When students know what to expect, they can make more informed choices about staying in the class or dropping out and can more effectively focus their energies if they stay.

CONS

Many students are accustomed to accepting faculty goals uncritically and will find it difficult to articulate their own. Their first attempts may result in general, vague statements that are difficult to interpret or respond to.

By finding out immediately that their goals and the teacher's do not match, some students may drop out who would otherwise have stayed in for at least a few more sessions. If you are under pressure to keep enrollments up, you may not want to take this risk.

CAVEATS

Remember that this skill, like any other, requires practice.

Don't ask if you don't want to know! Asking students to write down their goals implies that you are planning to read them and respond in a meaningful way.

Don't be hesitant to tell students about any differences between their goals and your goals for the course. If they express goals that you cannot or will not address, they should know that from the start.

Make an effort to respond to student goals in some way—particularly goals that are expressed by many students. You may, for instance, make changes in course content or allow some alternative assignments or suggest additional readings.

36

Self-Assessment of Ways of Learning

Estimated Levels of Time and Energy Required for:

Faculty to prepare to use this CAT	**MEDIUM to HIGH**
Students to respond to the assessment	**LOW to MEDIUM**
Faculty to analyze the data collected	**LOW to MEDIUM**

DESCRIPTION
Self-Assessment of Ways of Learning is one of the few Classroom Assessment Techniques in this collection that require the faculty who use them to adopt specific theoretical frameworks for learning. Self-Assessment of Ways of Learning prompts students to describe their general approaches to learning, or their learning styles, by comparing themselves with several different profiles and choosing those that, in their opinion, most closely resemble them. Since there are a number of ways to describe learning styles and ways of learning, faculty have to choose their own sets of profiles to use in assessing students.

PURPOSE
This technique provides teachers with a simple way to assess students' learning styles or preferences for ways of learning. By finding out whether students consider themselves primarily "visual learners," "aural learners," or "tactile learners," for example, faculty can choose among instructional approaches. In another schema, one might use this CAT to assess whether students learn more effectively through empathetic or adversarial approaches to discussion. This technique requires students to self-assess and therefore prompts them to realize their own learning preferences, strengths, or styles.

RELATED TEACHING GOALS
Learn to understand perspectives and values of this subject (TGI Goal 21)

Learn techniques and methods used to gain new knowledge in this subject (TGI Goal 23)

Develop a lifelong love of learning (TGI Goal 30)

Develop (self-) management skills (TGI Goal 37)

Develop a commitment to personal achievement (TGI Goal 42)

Cultivate a sense of responsibility for one's own behavior (TGI Goal 44)

Develop a commitment to one's own values (TGI Goal 46)

Develop capacity to think for oneself (TGI Goal 51)

SUGGESTIONS FOR USE   Since the Self-Assessment of Ways of Learning focuses on helping students understand how they best or most comfortably learn, this is a useful technique in first-year courses—especially in developmental education or personal development courses. Adult and returning students may also benefit from this assessment. It can be carried out in classes of any size, provided there are opportunities to discuss the results and their implications in manageable groups.

EXAMPLES

From Oral Interpretation (Speech/Drama)

> The instructor in this course aimed to help students understand that different people have different approaches to learning speeches or dialogue. To illustrate these differences in ways of learning, he wrote three extremely brief profiles of different speakers memorizing the same speech. Speaker A simply repeated the lines to himself over and over again, committing them to memory by rote. Speaker B developed a mental map of the speech, with visual images and cues that reminded her of the text to keep her on track. Speaker C had to choreograph the speech, associated various gestures and movements with different parts of the text. Following these three profiles were two related assessment questions:
>
> 1. Which one of these speakers most resembles you?   A B C (circle one)
>
> 2. Which one of the other two speakers has a way of learning speeches that you'd like to be able to use as well?   A B C
>
> The speech instructor learned, upon reading the responses, that most of his students felt they were most like Speaker A, using the rote-learned method, and that most wished they could develop a visual method of memorizing speeches. After receiving this feedback, he adjusted the course content so that it placed more emphasis on ways to improve memorization and visualization skills.

STEP-BY-STEP PROCEDURE

1. Select a framework for describing learning styles or preferences and determine what the main categories or types are within that framework.

2. Create profiles of learners to represent each of the categories or types. These profiles can be brief descriptions of how X, Y, and Z types of learners approach the same problem. For example, students might be given three very short profiles, describing a visual learner, an aural learner, and a tactile learner all trying to master the same material.

3. Develop two or three questions that will assess students' affinity for these various types of learners. The questions should require students to choose the types they most resemble or least resemble.

4. If possible, edit all of this material down to less than one page and create a handout containing the profiles and assessment question(s).

5. Try out your Self-Assessment of Ways of Learning on yourself and on a colleague before you use it in class. This trial run will likely lead to a few revisions.

6. Once the form is clear and unambiguous, duplicate and administer the assessment.

TURNING THE DATA YOU COLLECT INTO USEFUL INFORMATION

This is another "front-loaded" CAT; it is relatively difficult to construct but easy to analyze. Students are basically selecting the learning types that most resemble them, and so the first step is to tally the number of students who choose each of the types represented. Then tally the answers to any related questions and summarize the responses to the class. Be prepared to discuss and answer questions about the implications of the results for students and for instruction in the class.

IDEAS FOR ADAPTING AND EXTENDING THIS CAT

Organize class debates or discussions by dividing the students into groups of individuals with the same or similar self-selected ways of learning.

Ask students to identify the "pros" and "cons" of their particular styles or preferences.

Once students have identified their primary "styles" or "types," ask them to describe how someone who fits in another category would approach a learning task.

Organize study groups specifically to mix students with different preferences or styles.

PROS

Self-Assessment of Ways of Learning requires students to think carefully about how they learn and to realize that there are different valid approaches to the same material.

Once students realize that there are options in the ways one can approach learning, they may be encouraged to experiment with some other approaches.

Faculty can quickly gain insight into the learning styles or preferences of a class without resorting to complex commercial instruments and inventories.

CONS

In normal circumstances, students bring a mixture of styles and preferences to bear on their learning tasks. Any quick technique for categorizing those styles or preferences will, of necessity, lead to simplification and could lead to self-stereotyping.

CAVEATS

Learning styles or ways of knowing are best understood as tendencies or preferences, rather than as absolute characterizations of learners.

Individuals can and do display different styles or preferences in different settings.

Faced with a choice between a representation of one "pure" learning style or preference and another, most students will respond that they are like both in certain ways — or like neither. For this CAT to work, students have to be able to choose between shades of gray, rather than between black and white. Not all students may be able to make these relative choices.

REFERENCES AND RESOURCES   This CAT is only slightly adapted from an exercise presented by Blythe McVicker Clinchy, coauthor of *Women's Ways of Knowing* (Belenky, Clinchy, Goldberger, and Tarule, 1986), at the 1990 Lilly Conference on College Teaching at Miami University, Oxford, Ohio. See Clinchy's (1990) article, "Issues of Gender in Teaching and Learning" for an in-depth discussion of gender and ways of knowing in the classroom.

Assessing Course-Related Learning and Study Skills, Strategies, and Behaviors

The four Classroom Assessment Techniques in this cluster focus student and faculty attention on the ways students carry out their work, the actual behaviors they engage in as they try to learn inside and outside the classroom. These CATs focus on metacognitive skills as well as behaviors, however, since they require and presuppose conscious awareness of mental activity, monitoring, and control.

The amount of time students spend studying and the quality of that study time are important factors in determining student learning success. Productive Study-Time Logs allow faculty and students to pinpoint and analyze how and how much study time is being used. Punctuated Lectures focus students' attention on what they are doing in the classroom during lectures or presentations and how that behavior is helping or hindering their learning. Process Analysis uncovers the steps students take in carrying out homework assignments—once again assessing the "how" of learning. And Diagnostic Learning Logs provide faculty with insights into students' awareness of their own course-specific academic strengths and weaknesses. In various ways, each of these CATs promotes the development of sophisticated self-assessment skills.

37

Productive Study-Time Logs

Estimated Levels of Time and Energy Required for:

Faculty to prepare to use this CAT	**MEDIUM**
Students to respond to the assessment	**MEDIUM to HIGH**
Faculty to analyze the data collected	**HIGH**

DESCRIPTION   Productive Study-Time Logs (PSTLs) are simply thumbnail records that students keep on how much time they spend studying for a particular class, when they study, and how productively they study at various times of the day or night.

PURPOSE   This technique helps students discover how much they study for a particular course, how well they spend their study time, and at what times studying reaps the greatest returns. Once they have this information, students can make better decisions about when, where, and how to use their study time. Productive Study-Time Logs also allow faculty to assess the amount and quality of out-of-class time all their students are spending preparing for class, and to share that information with students. By comparing the results of their Study Logs with those of their classmates, students can determine whether their level of commitment is in line with their goals and expectations.

RELATED TEACHING GOALS   Develop ability to draw reasonable inferences from observations (TGI Goal 4)
Develop appropriate study skills, strategies, and habits (TGI Goal 16)
Prepare for transfer or graduate study (TGI Goal 22)
Develop (self-) management skills (TGI Goal 37)
Improve ability to organize and use time effectively (TGI Goal 41)
Cultivate a sense of responsibility for one's own behavior (TGI Goal 44)
Cultivate emotional health and well-being (TGI Goal 48)
Develop capacity to make wise decisions (TGI Goal 52)

SUGGESTIONS FOR USE   Productive Study-Time Logs can be used in courses where students consistently complain about the amount of time they are investing in studying. This CAT can help you find out whether they have a legitimate complaint. It is also useful in classes where you suspect that some students may be doing poorly primarily because they don't realize that the students who are doing well are (1) studying *more* than they are and (2) studying *more effectively* than they are. One summary of feedback from the class's PSTLs is often more convincing than any number of teacherly admonitions. For greatest positive effect, this technique should be used at the beginning of the semester in first-year courses.

EXAMPLES   See Chapter Five, Example 10, for a Productive Study-Time Log used in a statistics course. That example also provides a sample PSTL form.

STEP-BY-STEP PROCEDURE

1. Decide what you most want to know, and what you most want students to notice, about their use of study time. For example, is it enough to know how many hours they study overall? Do you want to know on what days they study? At what times of day? Are you interested in the relative quality or productivity of their studying? What about where they study, and the relation of location to productivity?

2. Make up the simplest log sheet possible for capturing the information you need. Try it out yourself for a few days to make sure it is clear and adequate.

3. Decide how many days the Productive Study-Time Logs are to cover, and have enough copies made up.

4. Explain the process and go over the forms. Make sure to have a couple of examples of completed sheets to show students.

5. To ensure that you get the right kind and amount of feedback, let students know exactly what to include—and what not to—in their PSTLs.

6. Make sure students know when the PSTLs are due and when they can expect to hear a summary of the data. Allow yourself enough time to complete the analysis before your report date.

TURNING THE DATA YOU COLLECT INTO USEFUL INFORMATION

If you have created a well-organized PSTL form, it should be easy for you to sum up totals and calculate averages for the amount of time studied. Summarizing the overall productivity of study time, and the amount of study time at various levels of productivity, is a bit more complex. The most important aspect of this CAT is not the specific number of hours but the general trends that the summary numbers illustrate. Look for days of the week and times of day when most studying occurs—and when the most productive studying occurs. In the same way, look for patterns linking study in certain locations with higher or lower productivity in studying.

IDEAS FOR ADAPTING AND EXTENDING THIS CAT

Results from this CAT can generate useful small-group and whole-class discussions on studying, in which students can share ideas and experiences.

In statistics, mathematics, or psychology courses, the analysis of data from the PSTL technique can be done by students as a course assignment.

PROS

By completing a simple PSTL form every day for a week, students gain valuable information on their own study habits. Armed with this information, they have a better chance of making productive changes in their routines.

By collecting and summarizing these forms, instructors get a picture of the level and quality of their students' out-of-class investment in learning.

In the process of comparing their study habits with those of their classmates, some students will realize that they are not studying enough or well enough or both—and will be motivated to do something about it.

This kind of information can help faculty revise their syllabi to increase, decrease, or better distribute the student work load.

CONS

Since this CAT cannot be done in the classroom under more or less controlled circumstances, some students are bound to forget to fill in their logs on some of the days, and some will wait until the last minute to complete the whole thing.

Those students who are putting in many hours but doing poorly are likely to be further discouraged by the results of the PSTL.

Even the simplest forms generate a great deal of information. Summarizing and analyzing the data can be time-consuming.

CAVEATS

If students strongly believe that you will adjust the work load downward in response to their PSTLs, they may be tempted to exaggerate in their time logging. Don't even hint that you might change the work load in response to the logs. If you decide to do so after you have seen the results, your decision will be based on better data.

Finding out the average amount of time your students study may come as an unwelcome surprise. Think through your response before you report back to the class.

38

Punctuated Lectures

Estimated Levels of Time and Energy Required for:

Faculty to prepare to use this CAT	**LOW**
Students to respond to the assessment	**LOW**
Faculty to analyze the data collected	**LOW**

DESCRIPTION

This technique requires students and teachers to go through five steps: listen, stop, reflect, write, and give feedback. Students begin by listening to a lecture or demonstration. Then, after a portion of the presentation has been completed, the teacher stops the action. For a quiet moment, the students reflect on what they were doing during the presentation and how their behavior while listening may have helped or hindered their understanding of that information. They then write down any insights they have gained. Finally, they give feedback to the teacher in the form of short, anonymous notes.

PURPOSE

The Punctuated Lecture technique is designed to provide immediate, on-the-spot feedback on how students are learning from a lecture or demonstration. It focuses students' attention on how they are processing, or failing to process, the information being presented and on how their behavior is influencing that processing. This feedback lets teachers and students know what may be distracting. More important, it encourages students to become self-monitoring listeners and, in the process, more aware and more effective learners.

RELATED TEACHING GOALS

Improve skill at paying attention (TGI Goal 9)
Develop ability to concentrate (TGI Goal 10)
Improve listening skills (TGI Goal 12)
Develop appropriate study skills, strategies, and habits (TGI Goal 16)
Cultivate a sense of responsibility for one's own behavior (TGI Goal 44)

SUGGESTIONS FOR USE

As the title suggests, the Punctuated Lecture technique is designed for use in classes where lectures or lecture-demonstrations are a primary method of instruction. A particularly valuable time to use this technique is during lectures that introduce difficult concepts or complex procedures.

From Methods and Materials of Secondary Education (Education)

After giving a basic definition and description of Classroom Research, the instructor in a teacher education course stopped and asked the students to recall what they were doing during the previous ten minutes while she was talking. She directed them to reconstruct a history of their behaviors—both mental and physical—during that period. She gave them two minutes in which to recall their behaviors and then asked them to reflect on how those behaviors may have helped or hindered their understanding and learning of the information presented. To make this large question easier to grasp, she asked the students to consider these specific subquestions:

1. How fully and consistently were you concentrating on the lecture during those few minutes? Did you get distracted at any point? If so, how did you bring your attention back into focus?

2. What were you doing to record the information you were receiving? How successful were you?

3. What were you doing to make connections between this "new" information and what you already know?

4. What did you expect to come next in the lecture and why?

After another minute or two of silence, she directed the students to write brief answers to each of the questions, describing how they were processing the lecture and assessing how well their strategies were working. She allowed a few minutes for students to write but did not collect their responses.

She stopped again after about twenty minutes of lecturing and quickly ran through the five steps of the technique, this time collecting their written self-assessments.

STEP-BY-STEP PROCEDURE

1. Choose a lecture that introduces new material and that can be effectively divided into ten- or twenty-minute segments. Decide in advance on the two spots where you will "punctuate" the lecture and schedule enough time during the session to work through the technique.

2. Don't forewarn students about the first "punctuation," but once you do stop, explain that the point is to give them an opportunity to reflect on their own learning behaviors.

3. Direct the students to take the two next steps in the process; that is, to reflect and write. Set time limits for each. Give them a minute or two to reflect and approximately the same amount of time to write.

4. After the first run-through, collect the written feedback.

TURNING THE DATA YOU COLLECT INTO USEFUL INFORMATION

Analyze the students' comments with the goal of helping them develop their skills at actively and effectively monitoring their own listening. Look at what students say they do and how they think what they are doing affects their learning. But look also at how specific and precise the language is that students use to describe what they are doing and thinking in class. Their descriptions can indicate how well they are paying attention and how carefully they are monitoring their learning. Look for points in the listening process where you can help them by directing their attention, suggesting strategies, or simply stopping to let the students reflect.

<table>
<tr><td>IDEAS FOR ADAPTING
AND EXTENDING
THIS CAT</td><td>Go through the exercise two or three times in as many weeks, stopping after progressively longer segments of the lectures.</td></tr>
<tr><td></td><td>Ask students to save their written reflections in folders. After they have gone through the exercise a few times, direct them to analyze their responses, looking carefully for patterns and changes over time.</td></tr>
<tr><td></td><td>Share particularly acute and detailed student reflections with the whole class as examples of effective self-analysis.</td></tr>
<tr><td></td><td>Direct students to develop "processing plans" and to try them out in your class. In other words, once students have realized that they actually are doing things while they are listening and that they can choose to engage in behaviors that will be more supportive of learning, encourage them to experiment at modifying their listening behaviors in an effort to improve their learning.</td></tr>
<tr><td>PROS</td><td>The Punctuated Lecture technique allows students and teachers to assess the information-processing behavior students engage in while listening to a lecture. In other words, it provides a window on how students learn.</td></tr>
<tr><td></td><td>It promotes active listening and self-reflective learning skills that are transferable to many contexts.</td></tr>
<tr><td></td><td>It focuses attention squarely on self-monitoring, an important component of metacognition.</td></tr>
<tr><td>CONS</td><td>At first, many students will find it very difficult to recall and explain what they do while they are listening to a lecture and thus may find the exercise initially frustrating.</td></tr>
<tr><td></td><td>Most students and teachers have not developed a precise and flexible vocabulary for talking about how they learn or about what behaviors they are engaging in as they learn. It will take time for a class to build up a meaningful, shared vocabulary with which to consider these issues.</td></tr>
<tr><td>CAVEATS</td><td>Don't expect immediate results from the technique. Trying to get an idea of how students process information while they are listening is a very challenging task.</td></tr>
<tr><td></td><td>Since many people still believe that the mind is a "black box," be prepared to face skepticism and a certain amount of resistance to the</td></tr>
</table>

suggestion that explicit control over one's information processing is possible or desirable.

REFERENCES AND RESOURCES   We owe the idea for this technique to John Boehrer, director of the Pew Project on Case Studies in International Relations and faculty development specialist at Harvard University's John F. Kennedy School of Government.

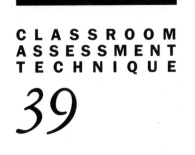

CLASSROOM
ASSESSMENT
TECHNIQUE

39

Process Analysis

Estimated Levels of Time and Energy Required for:

Faculty to prepare to use this CAT	**MEDIUM**
Students to respond to the assessment	**HIGH**
Faculty to analyze the data collected	**HIGH**

DESCRIPTION Whereas Productive Study-Time Logs (CAT 37) focus on how much time students spend in doing academic work, this technique focuses students' attention on the process—on how they do their academic work. Process Analysis requires that students keep records of the actual steps they take in carrying out a representative assignment and asks them to comment on the conclusions they draw about their approaches to that assignment.

PURPOSE This technique gives students and teachers explicit, detailed information on the ways in which students carry out a representative assignment. This diagnostic information can be used to help students pinpoint problems in their methods of working and, ultimately, improve them. Specific information on students' ways of doing homework also shows faculty which elements of the process are most difficult for students and, consequently, where teachers need to offer more instruction and direction.

RELATED TEACHING GOALS Develop appropriate study skills, strategies, and habits (TGI Goal 16)
Improve mathematical skills (TGI Goal 17)
Develop skill in using materials, tools, and/or technology central to this subject (TGI Goal 20)
Develop a commitment to accurate work (TGI Goal 39)
Develop ability to perform skillfully (TGI Goal 43)

SUGGESTIONS FOR USE This is an especially useful technique for courses in which students carry out the same types of assignment several times during the term—assignments such as homework problem sets, essays, lab reports, and projects. This CAT can also be used to assess learning in courses that require the mastery of physical procedures—courses such as music, dance, physical education, medical and nursing education, and other vocational fields.

From Master Class in Piano (Music)

After the first few weeks of class, this music professor and pianist decided to find out how his students were preparing the pieces he assigned. As part of one assignment, he asked students to write down each step they took in working up a Chopin nocturne. He asked them to note what they did first, second, and so on, from the time they began working on the piece until they were ready to perform. The instructor suggested that they write no more than a sentence on each step in the process. He collected the Process Analysis responses on the day his ten students performed the nocturne in class. Because their feedback was not anonymous, he could informally correlate the quality of each in-class performance—which he recorded—with the Process Analysis. As a result, he and the students saw evidence that those who had first analyzed the piece—and then spent most of their time working systematically on the most difficult passages—were more successful in shaping and playing the whole nocturne well than students who had played the entire piece through time and time again. Although these results did not surprise the instructor, they offered proof to the class that the analytic approach he was suggesting could lead to more correct and more musical playing.

From College Writing Workshop (English)

Before she committed class time to teaching various approaches to the writing process, an instructor in a developmental writing course wanted to find out how her students were writing. Specifically, she wanted to know whether they were using prewriting strategies such as "free writing," "self-questioning," and "brainstorming" and whether they were writing more than one draft of their weekly assignments. Therefore, she asked her students to do a Process Analysis on their first weekly essay. She directed them to keep a simple record of the steps they took in preparing the essay and, after they had finished, to comment briefly on how useful each step had been in getting the assignment done.

Several of her students seemed totally baffled by the idea that there might be a writing process. They simply wrote their essays in one sitting: no steps, no drafts, no revision. A few students mentioned that they made notes or outlines before writing, but they did not regard those steps as very useful. And a handful said that they had written a first draft. Not surprisingly, most of their essays read like first drafts to the instructor. This feedback showed the composition teacher two things: that most of her students did need instruction in the writing process, and that it would be even more difficult to convince them of the value of that approach than she had anticipated. She realized that she would need first to explain her criteria for good essay writing and then to demonstrate how the writing-as-a-process approach could help them meet those criteria.

STEP-BY-STEP PROCEDURE

1. Choose an assignment that meets the following three criteria: (a) You are genuinely interested in how students work through it. (b) Your students are likely to benefit from focusing on it and will have other opportunities to use what they learn from your feedback. (c) The assignment is complex enough to provide an interesting Process Analysis.

2. Let students know from the outset, before you give the focus assignment itself, that they will be required to keep a record of their work processes — what steps they took, how much time each step took — and to describe those processes as an assessment technique.

3. Give instructions and examples of how to keep records of their processes, what to include, and how long the final product should be.

4. Ask students to hand in the Process Analysis along with the assignment or immediately after they have handed in the assignment.

TURNING THE DATA YOU COLLECT INTO USEFUL INFORMATION

Read and grade the assignments themselves first — without looking at the Process Analyses. Then read the Process Analyses and assess the overall work schemes for clarity and explicitness, the number of steps taken, the effectiveness of each step, and so on. Look for similarities and differences among students' analyses in the number, content, and order of the steps. See whether there are any common patterns in the processes students report.

IDEAS FOR ADAPTING AND EXTENDING THIS CAT

To make the assessment less burdensome, stagger the Process Analysis exercise so that only a few students are responding to the CAT at any given time.

Have students read each other's Process Analyses and compare notes on how they worked.

Direct students to focus on only one stage of the process, such as the beginning, the end, or a particularly difficult part.

Ask students to focus on one step that they would like to improve. Then direct them to redesign their processes so that they can accomplish that change.

PROS

Process Analysis focuses student and teacher attention on the most transferable elements of the lesson by focusing on process rather than on products.

By explicitly breaking down the work process into distinct steps, Process Analysis allows students and teachers to tinker with and improve those steps and, consequently, to make the whole process more effective.

Process Analysis allows teachers to compare the steps the students actually go through in completing an assignment with the steps they taught them to take.

This technique may help uncover generally productive strategies. These productive strategies can be shared among the students and incorporated into the teachers' repertoires.

CONS

Students may resist keeping a process record or, even if they are willing, find it time-consuming and difficult.

Teachers may discover that their evaluations of the quality of students' assignments are not highly correlated with the approaches that the students took.

These self-analyses are challenging and time-consuming to analyze.

CAVEATS   Don't make the Process Analysis so complex and demanding that it overwhelms the assignment it is based on. Ask students to outline the process they have gone through—not to narrate it.

Some students will find it difficult to articulate their work processes, simply because they have never been asked to do so. They may need several examples of informative responses before they carry out the assessment themselves.

Those students who could most benefit from analyzing their own work may be the least motivated to do so. Consider offering a reward for the difficult work involved in responding to this technique. That reward might be a small, fixed number of points added to the assignment grade for those who carefully complete the analysis.

CLASSROOM ASSESSMENT TECHNIQUE

40

Diagnostic Learning Logs

Estimated Levels of Time and Energy Required for:

Faculty to prepare to use this CAT	**MEDIUM**
Students to respond to the assessment	**HIGH**
Faculty to analyze the data collected	**HIGH**

DESCRIPTION   Diagnostic Learning Logs are essentially limited, tightly focused versions of the academic journals many teachers already use. In these logs, students keep records of each class or assignment. When responding to class sessions, students write one list of the main points covered that they understood and a second list of points that were unclear. For assignments, students record problems encountered or errors made, as well as excellent and successful responses. At regular intervals, the students reflect on, analyze, and summarize the information they have collected on their own learning. They then diagnose their strengths and weaknesses as learners and generate possible remedies for problems.

PURPOSE   Diagnostic Learning Logs provide faculty with information and insight into their students' awareness of and skill at identifying their own strengths and weaknesses as learners. Specifically, this technique assesses students' skills at recognizing, documenting, diagnosing, and suggesting remedies for their own learning difficulties in specific classes. At the same time, it informs the teacher about the students' ability to use those skills to assess their strengths and successes.

Much as good medical doctors question patients carefully to inform their diagnoses, a college teacher can use information gained through this technique to make more effective instructional diagnoses. Diagnostic Learning Logs provide teachers with opportunities for comparing their diagnoses and prescriptions for instructional "treatments" with those of informed and reflective students. They also provide students with practice in skills necessary to becoming independent, self-directed learners.

RELATED TEACHING GOALS   Develop analytic skills (TGI Goal 2)
Develop problem-solving skills (TGI Goal 3)
Develop appropriate study skills, strategies, and habits (TGI Goal 16)
Prepare for transfer or graduate study (TGI Goal 22)

Develop a commitment to accurate work (TGI Goal 39)
Develop a commitment to personal achievement (TGI Goal 42)
Develop ability to perform skillfully (TGI Goal 43)
Cultivate a sense of responsibility for one's own behavior (TGI Goal 44)

SUGGESTIONS FOR USE   Diagnostic Learning Logs are most useful in courses where students work on similar assignments or tasks and get frequent feedback on their performance—courses such as mathematics, writing, foreign languages, music, lab sciences, accounting, computer programming, dance, and athletics. Because keeping a learning log demands a commitment to self-improvement and achievement, this technique often works well in upper-level courses in the student's major field. At the same time, the return on time invested in this CAT is sometimes greatest with underprepared beginning students.

The first time students try this technique, the logs should be collected and assessed after one or two entries. Giving students feedback on their first learning log entries will prevent them from missing the point and wasting time documenting and commenting on irrelevant issues.

EXAMPLES   Exhibit 8.5 is a format that might be given to students as an example of what to include in a learning log.

Exhibit 8.5. Sample Diagnostic Learning Log Entry Form.

Course: Date:

Entry focuses on (circle one): class session, homework assignment, test, quiz

I. Class Session Entry

   1. List the main points you learned from this session. Give examples if possible.

   2. List points from this session that are unclear to you. Give examples if possible.

   3. Write a few questions that you need answers to before you can understand the points listed in 2.

II. Homework Assignment or Test Entry

1. Briefly describe the assignment or test. What was it about?

2. Give one or two examples of your most successful responses. Try to explain what things you did that made them successful.

3. Give one or two examples, if relevant, of errors or less successful responses. What did you do wrong or fail to do in each case?

4. The next time you confront a similar situation, what, if anything, could you do differently to increase your learning?

STEP-BY-STEP PROCEDURE

1. Let students know that you will be asking them to keep records of what they learned from class sessions, assignments, tests, and quizzes. Explain also that they will be assessing their own learning — their successes and their failures. Tell them why you are asking them to keep these records, explaining the benefits that both you and they should derive from the technique.

2. Provide them with a sample format, such as the one in Exhibit 8.5. Work through the technique in class, modeling and explaining as necessary.

3. Help students focus by pointing out strengths and weaknesses, successes and failures, correct responses and errors in their work. Be selective, however, and limit your comments to a few important points.

4. Ask students to make copies of their logs and hand in those copies at set intervals. Your first deadline should be after one or two weeks, just to check whether students understand the process. After you are sure they get it, you might ask for submissions monthly or at natural breaks in the course schedule.

TURNING THE DATA YOU COLLECT INTO USEFUL INFORMATION

The main point of assessing these logs is to compare your sense of what the class is and is not understanding, and why, with the students' self-reports and self-analyses. Assess the logs to discover the range and kinds of responses students make to their own learning. Keep a record of the kinds of questions students raise and the types of problems they identify.

One simple way to categorize responses follows:

(0) Doesn't identify successful or unsuccessful responses

(1) Identifies but doesn't diagnose causes of successful or unsuccessful responses

(2) Identifies and diagnoses, but doesn't offer solutions

(3) Identifies, diagnoses, and offers solutions

As you repeat this technique, you will also be able to assess what impact the steps you have taken in response to the students' logs have had. Repeat analyses will show whether there are changes in students' skills at identifying, diagnosing, and prescribing solutions to their own learning problems.

IDEAS FOR ADAPTING AND EXTENDING THIS CAT

Read and assess logs from a different subgroup of students each week as a way of spreading out the work.

Ask students to focus their log entries on their learning of specific information, concepts, theories, or skills.

Limit the amount of data you collect by including fewer questions in your format or by asking students to indicate those sections of their logs they want you to assess.

PROS

Diagnostic Learning Logs encourage students to become more self-reflective, active, and independent learners.

The technique introduces students to a self-assessment protocol that can be transferred to virtually any learning situation.

It provides the teacher with organized, classifiable, and assessable data on students' metacognitive skills—their skills at observing, evaluating, and criticizing their own learning.

The learning logs can provide teachers with valuable insight and suggestions from students for improving learning.

CONS

Learning logs are essentially another ongoing assignment that requires time and effort from students and teachers.

Unless a continuing attempt is made to focus on strengths and successes, this technique can leave students demoralized from paying too much attention to their weaknesses and failures.

CAVEATS

Most students probably will have had little previous experience at this type of structured self-assessment. Don't give up if their first efforts show weak self-critical skills. Instead, teach students, through coaching, examples, and illustrations, how to carry out the technique.

Resist the temptation to focus only on what the students don't understand and can't do. Try to give almost as much attention to skills and knowledge they can build on in positive ways. Encourage them to capitalize on their strengths as they improve their weaknesses.

Don't try to read too many logs at any one time, and don't feel bound to read every word.

REFERENCES AND RESOURCES

In the last decade, much has been written about the uses of journal writing as a learning tool — particularly, though not exclusively, by composition teachers. Selfe and Arbabi (1986) and Selfe, Petersen, and Nahrgang (1986) describe experiments in focused academic journal writing in engineering and mathematics courses, respectively.

Techniques for Assessing Learner Reactions to Instruction

Research on the ability of college students to evaluate teachers and courses has had mixed reviews, particularly from faculty. Despite several decades of concentrated work, some controversy remains over the quality of the research, the consistency of the findings, and, especially, the usefulness of student evaluations. Much of the controversy over student evaluations of teaching concerns their use in making promotion and tenure decisions—an issue that will not be addressed here, since our interest is in helping teachers design, collect, and use student reactions to improve their own teaching.

Some advantages in using students as evaluators are inescapable: students have ample opportunity to see teachers in action on good days and bad; they are the audience for whom the teaching is intended; and they are in a good position to evaluate the impact of the teaching on their own learning. But are the reactions of students reliable, valid, and useful for the purpose of improving teaching, course materials, assignments and activities, and—consequently—useful for improving learning?

The first part of this question—whether students are reliable judges of teaching effectiveness—is easier to answer than the other two parts (whether their reactions are valid and useful). Although there are plenty of tales about alumni who, in their maturity, have found virtues in professors whom they did not respect when they were in college, research shows that students and former students remain quite consistent over the years in their judgments about the effectiveness of teachers and courses (Drucker and Remmers, 1950; Centra, 1973a, 1973b; Gleason, 1986). The standard instruments that have been used to collect student judgments show reliabilities in the .70s to .90s, and it is now generally agreed that "the responses of individual students to commonly used rating forms is both internally consistent and fairly stable over time" (Kulik and McKeachie, 1975, p. 223). Although reliability coefficients are lower when the ratings for any given teacher come from students in different courses or even in different sections of the same course taught by that instructor, the reliability and consistency of student judgments suggest that students are generally reliable in their evaluations of teachers and courses; they tend not to change their opinions over the ups and downs of the semester or even over the years.

The question of the validity of student judgments is more difficult and controversial. Here the question is, "Are students really good judges of effective teaching?" The answer is probably that students are the best evaluators a teacher can get on some matters and not very credible judges on others. The validity question most frequently asked by researchers is "Do students rate highest those teachers from whom they learn the most?" Although the best present answer seems to be a qualified "yes" (Gleason, 1986), the answers are complicated because the criteria for determining how much a student has learned are complex. Scores on final examinations, for example, may give a better evaluation of the textbook than of the teacher, since many teachers, in a desire to be "fair" in grading, base examination questions on the required readings rather than on in-class activities. Consequently, if students desiring good grades overcompensate for poor teaching by increased out-of-class effort, those studying with poor teachers may actually score higher on text-based finals than students who experienced good teaching (Dubin and Taveggia, 1968; McKeachie, Pintrich, Lin, and Smith, 1986). That is one reason for our classification of the assessment techniques in this chapter into two separate focus categories—teaching-related and course-related. Another way of seeking answers to the validity question is to investigate the extent of agreement between students and other presumably qualified judges. Here again, the general answer is that there is reasonable agreement among students, faculty colleagues, and administrators, both on what constitutes good teaching and on who the effective teachers are (Blackburn and Clark, 1975; Gleason, 1986). The research suggests that teachers held in high regard by students are generally held in high regard as teachers by colleagues and deans.

A substantial body of research now exists on what students consider important factors in effective teaching. Feldman (1976) reviewed a group of studies in which students were asked to describe "good" or "ideal" or "best" teachers. He found eight characteristics that were usually ranked high in all studies: concern for students, knowledge of subject matter, stimulation of interest, availability, encouragement of discussion, ability to explain clearly, enthusiasm, and preparation. Factor analytic studies of student rating forms show rather similar clusters of characteristics. After reviewing nearly sixty factor analytic studies, Feldman concluded that there were three major clusters in effective teaching: the instructor's ability to present the material, to encourage students to learn, and to regulate and deal fairly with students. Kulik and McKeachie (1975) reviewed eleven factor analytic studies of teacher-rating scales and found similar factors, which they labeled as follows: "skill"—the ability to communicate in an interesting way, to stimulate intellectual curiosity, and to explain clearly; "rapport"—empathy, interaction with and concern for students; "structure"—organization and presentation of course material; and "overload"—the work load and instructor demands.

Whereas the research indicates that good teachers have certain characteristics in common and that these characteristics can be reliably identified by students, the research on the usefulness of these evaluations to teachers is less optimistic. Student evaluations of teachers and courses have become well accepted by faculty members and are now used on most college campuses for evaluation purposes (Seldin, 1984); but there is, as yet, little evidence that teachers change their behaviors as a result of such feedback alone (Centra, 1973a; Blackburn and others, 1986). Teachers may not regard the evaluations as useful because they themselves were not involved in the design of the evaluations and because student evaluations are rarely designed so that they explicitly help teachers improve their teaching. As Riegle and Rhodes (1986) point out, the information generated from most faculty evaluation procedures is used for multiple purposes: to appoint, to award tenure, to inform salary and promotion decisions, to terminate, and to help teachers improve. It is the last purpose that interests us here, and in that context Riegle and Rhodes suggest that the metaphor of "critiquing" is more appropriate than the usual metaphors of rating, assessing, appraising, or judging. If evaluations encouraged students to "critique" rather than "judge" teaching and course material, the results might be more useful.

We believe that it is possible to effect significant improvement in teaching through obtaining feedback from students, especially—perhaps only—if individual teachers are able to design the types of feedback that will be most useful and most acceptable to them. The purpose of the assessment suggestions given in the sections on teaching methods and on course materials is to help faculty think about new ways to collect data that shed light on the questions they have about their own teaching, about the organization of their syllabi, and about the materials they are using.

Assessing Learner
Reactions to
Teachers and Teaching

As already noted, many departments, programs, and colleges use teacher evaluation forms — whether in-house or commercial products — as a source of information for tenuring, reappointing, and promoting faculty members. However, few such evaluations are designed to help those same faculty directly improve teaching and learning in their classrooms. Even when the results are shared with the teachers who have been evaluated, they cannot readily draw useful, specific conclusions about how to improve their teaching from such information.

All the techniques in this cluster are designed to provide context- and teacher-specific feedback that can be used to improve teaching. They all emphasize the important role students can play as observers and assessors of teaching. At the same time, these CATs provide ways to improve students' skills at constructively carrying out those roles. These five CATs differ primarily in ease of use and level of organizational complexity. Chain Notes provide the teacher with information on how students are reacting while the class is in progress — with immediate, spontaneous reactions rather than post hoc, considered reflections. Electronic Mail Feedback also makes very limited demands but allows for more response time and more feedback. Teacher-Designed Feedback Forms combine the ease of administration and analysis inherent in traditional, structured teacher-evaluation questionnaires with the utility of course-specific questions posed by the individual classroom teacher. The Group Instructional Feedback Technique (GIFT) and Classroom Assessment Quality Circles both capitalize on the ability of groups to give more comprehensive and useful feedback than individuals can. The GIFT is a one-time assessment that involves the whole class, while Quality Circles usually involve small groups of students over the whole semester.

CLASSROOM
ASSESSMENT
TECHNIQUE

41

Chain Notes

Estimated Levels of Time and Energy Required for:

Faculty to prepare to use this CAT	**LOW**
Students to respond to the assessment	**LOW**
Faculty to analyze the data collected	**LOW**

DESCRIPTION

To respond to Chain Notes, students in a lecture course pass around a large envelope on which the teacher has written one question about the class. The students have all been given index cards beforehand. When the envelope reaches a student, he or she spends less than a minute writing a response to the question, then drops the card in the envelope and passes it on. This CAT results in a rich, composite record of each individual student's reactions to the class in action. In this way, Chain Notes allow teachers a view of their class through all their students' eyes.

PURPOSE

The purpose of Chain Notes is to elicit a very limited amount of written feedback from each student on what he or she noticed about the teaching and learning occurring at a given moment during the class session. This feedback can give the teacher a "sounding" of the students' level of engagement and involvement. It also lets the teacher know what students are really attending to during the course of the class. When the Chain Note reaches a student, it prompts that individual to self-assess for a moment—to ask, "What am I paying attention to?" and "What am I learning right now?" Prompting students to think about what they are doing in class can help them gain control over that behavior.

RELATED TEACHING GOALS

Improve skill at paying attention (TGI Goal 9)
Develop ability to concentrate (TGI Goal 10)
Improve listening skills (TGI Goal 12)
Develop appropriate study skills, strategies, and habits (TGI Goal 16)
Improve ability to organize and use time effectively (TGI Goal 41)
Cultivate a sense of responsibility for one's own behavior (TGI Goal 44)

SUGGESTIONS FOR USE

Chain Notes are most useful in large lecture or lecture-discussion classes where many students have little direct contact with the teacher. The Chain

Note question to which students are responding can be quite open-ended or rather specific, depending on the directions the students receive. In general, the more specific the question, the more useful and informative the responses.

From Introduction to Psychology (Psychology)

To assess how students were reacting to the lectures in his large introductory course, the instructor decided to make use of the Chain Notes technique. He wrote across the front of a large manila envelope: "Immediately before this reached you, what exactly were you paying attention to?" He handed out 3-by-5-inch index cards at the beginning of the next class and directed the students to answer the question only at the moment the envelope reached them, to drop their cards in the envelope, and then to pass it on.

As the psychology instructor read through the Chain Note responses later in the day, he noticed that only about half of the students mentioned anything related to his lecture or their notes. Approximately a quarter of the students were paying attention to other students, and almost as many indicated they were not paying attention to anything, or were lost in daydreams. He prepared a one-page summary handout on the results, which contained no evaluative comments. Even though he was disappointed by the results, he realized that admonishing the students for being honest would probably doom subsequent efforts to get useful feedback. So, biting his tongue, he simply passed out the handout and gave students two minutes to read it.

After the students had read the summary of Chain Note results, the instructor invited them to comment on their reactions. Once again, he avoided making evaluative comments. Several students said that they were relieved to find they were not the only ones who sometimes failed to pay attention, but that they wanted to do better. Since the students had been studying conditioning, he asked them to comment on ways he and they could increase attention during the lectures. Students suggested that he move around more, draw and write more on the board, use more examples, tell a few jokes, and allow them a two-minute stretch break in the middle of the class. At the same time, students suggested tactics they could employ, such as keeping cards on their desks, in view at all times, with "Pay Attention!" written on them, or writing messages to themselves in their class notes whenever they felt attention starting to wane. As an outcome of discussing Chain Note feedback, both the instructor and his students decided to try some new techniques for maintaining attention.

From Composing with Computers (English)

This section of what was essentially a first-year composition course was held in the college's computer lab, and students learned to use word-processing software to assist them in prewriting, composing, revising, and editing. Having noticed that most students spent quite a bit of their time staring at the screen, the instructor decided to try to find out what students were doing as they sat there. She wrote the following Chain

Techniques for Assessing Learner Reactions to Instruction **323**

Note question on a large manila envelope: "What exactly were you doing during the minute or so before this reached you?" At the beginning of the next lab session, she handed out slips of paper and explained the process. She let students know that she was gathering data to get a better understanding of how they worked, so that she might be better able to help them. Then she started the envelope on its way and let the class get to work. As they worked, the instructor circulated, stopping to assist students who requested her help.

Most of the students seemed to forget about the Chain Note envelope until it reached them. Then they wrote for a few seconds, deposited their slips, and returned to whatever they had been doing. In reading the responses later, the instructor noted three groups of similar responses. A number of students were just waiting for her to come by their stations, so that they could ask for help. Other students were thinking about alternate ways of writing something. A third group of students were thinking about how frustrated or uncomfortable they felt trying to write their drafts in a noisy, public space. There were also several other responses that were not categorizable.

The composition instructor made up a handout in order to share the Chain Note results with her students. She then asked students to suggest ways they might use their computer lab time more effectively, given their responses.

STEP-BY-STEP PROCEDURE

1. Compose a question that will help you—and your students—capture a moment of their mental activity during the class session. Your Chain Note question might ask students what they are focusing attention on, or how well.

2. Make sure the question can be answered quickly by every student, regardless of the moment during the class when the Chain Note reaches him or her. Have someone else read the question before you use it, to make sure it is focused and unambiguous.

3. On a large envelope, print the question and directions for responding, and find enough blank index cards or slips of paper for your class.

4. At the beginning of class, announce what you are doing and why, and go over the directions for responding to the Chain Note. Emphasize the importance of not writing before the envelope arrives, and of writing a quick, honest, and anonymous response when it does. Pass out cards or slips of paper.

5. After you are sure that the students understand the process, start the Chain Note envelope on its rounds.

TURNING THE DATA YOU COLLECT INTO USEFUL INFORMATION

You can make a first cut at the data by categorizing reactions in any of the following ways: engaged/not engaged, focus on self/focus on teacher/focus on other students/focus on content, question/praise/neutral comment/complaint, or on target/off target/can't tell. Whatever criteria you use for categorizing the data, the point should be to detect patterns in responses. Discussing these patterns in the feedback with students can often lead to suggestions for more effective teaching and learning.

Make a videotape recording of the class in which students are writing Chain Notes. Ask students to indicate the exact time they finish writing their Chain Notes before dropping them in the envelope. Before you read the students' reactions, play the videotape and write your own Chain Notes in reaction to it. Then compare your notes to the students' responses and look for patterns in attention that might be related to what you see on the videotape.

Use Chain Notes two or three times over a four- to six-week period and note any changes you observe in the sophistication, content, and tone of the notes.

PROS

The Chain Notes technique can elicit feedback from every member of the class.

It encourages students to be reflective, evaluative, and active observers and requires that they monitor what they are taking in.

The responses tend to be very spontaneous and honest, because of the spontaneity of the CAT itself and the guarantee of anonymity.

The reactions are more concrete and specific than those written at the end of a session.

The technique generates a collage of "snapshots" of the class dynamic. It helps the teacher spot positive and negative trends in the class. This early-warning device can help teachers build on the former and ameliorate the latter.

CONS

The act of writing the note can distract the student from whatever is going on in the class at that moment. Some students resent being asked to divide their attention.

By their very nature, Chain Notes are episodic and fragmentary and so may be difficult to interpret.

Some students, particularly those in small classes, may hesitate to respond honestly for fear that the teacher will recognize their handwriting.

Other students may focus on "fixed" variables—qualities of the classroom environment or the teacher that cannot be changed. For example, one student's Chain Note comment was that the instructor's slight but unfortunate resemblance to a murderer in a play distracted her.

CAVEATS

This is not a device for the thin-skinned or for those teachers who are convinced that they command their students' absolute attention at all times.

Techniques for Assessing Learner Reactions to Instruction **325**

Remember that the parts of a Chain Note don't necessarily sum up to any coherent whole.

Do not base major changes in a course or in your teaching on the reactions in one Chain Note. While this is a good exploratory technique, it is not a valid confirmatory one. Follow up on ideas suggested by the technique by using other, more focused, less hurried assessment techniques.

42

Electronic Mail Feedback

Estimated Levels of Time and Energy Required for:

Faculty to prepare to use this CAT	**LOW**
Students to respond to the assessment	**LOW**
Faculty to analyze the data collected	**LOW to MEDIUM**

DESCRIPTION

As the use of computers grows on campuses, so does electronic networking. In courses where every student has access to electronic mail—also known as E-mail—this technology offers faculty a good alternative to the usual paper-and-pencil CATs. The instructor poses a question to the class, via electronic mail, about his or her teaching, and invites student responses. Students respond to the E-mail question with a personal, though anonymous, message sent to the teacher's electronic mailbox.

PURPOSE

The purpose of Electronic Mail Feedback is to provide a simple, immediate channel through which faculty can pose questions about the class and students can respond to them.

RELATED TEACHING GOALS

Develop skill in using materials, tools, and/or technology central to this subject (TGI Goal 20)
Learn to evaluate methods and materials in this subject (TGI Goal 24)
Develop ability to work effectively with others (TGI Goal 36)
Develop management skills (TGI Goal 37)

SUGGESTIONS FOR USE

Electronic Mail Feedback is easiest to implement in courses where students are already using computers for other purposes. Examples of such courses are statistics, composition, economics, and many business courses. This technique can be used on a regular basis, but it is particularly useful whenever the teacher feels there may be a problem in the class that has not surfaced, or before or after high-stress periods such as exams or holidays.

EXAMPLES

From Principles of Computer Science (Computer Science)

The instructor in this large introductory course asked students to respond to her Electronic Mail Feedback question between the end of class on Thursday and Sunday noon. Her question was "What is one specific, small change I could make that would help you learn more effectively in this course?" On Sunday afternoon she read her E-mail, analyzed the feedback, and wrote an E-mail response to the class, letting them know which suggestions she would act on, which she would not, and why. In class the next Tuesday, she asked the students how many had read her response; about one-third had. She informed the rest of the class that her response would be accessible on E-mail for two more days if they wished to read it.

From Office Technology (Vocational and Technical Education)

Students in this community college course were learning advanced word-processing applications and various office software packages. In part to give students practice in using E-mail, and in part to get feedback on her teaching, the instructor decided to use Electronic Mail Feedback. She asked students to write a few brief sentences in answer to the following question: "If you were the teacher of this class, what would you do to make computer lab assignments more useful?"

STEP-BY-STEP PROCEDURE

1. Make sure that electronic mail is available to students and that they know how to use it.

2. Write one or two questions in which you ask for students' reactions to some aspect of your teaching. Make sure that the questions are about teaching behaviors you can—and may be willing to—change.

3. Write an E-mail message to the students. Tell them what you want to know and why. Give them clear instructions on the length and type of response you are seeking and on the deadline for responding.

4. Send it to their electronic mailboxes or to an electronic class bulletin board.

TURNING THE DATA YOU COLLECT INTO USEFUL INFORMATION

The analysis of responses to Electronic Mail Feedback questions is usually very simple. Note and summarize answers to your questions and categorize them according to types or themes if possible. Keep a record, as well, of concerns and comments that are not direct responses to your questions. These "off-the-wall" responses may be expressions of important and highly charged feelings and opinions about your teaching.

IDEAS FOR ADAPTING AND EXTENDING THIS CAT

Since electronic mail is more a technology than a technique, many of the CATs in this handbook can be adapted for use in E-mail.

If you can avail yourself of a trusted peer or faculty development consultant, have the students actually write to that person about your class. Ask your colleague or the consultant to summarize the contents of the E-mail messages and report back to you. This is another way to encourage honesty and openness.

If you don't have electronic mail, or your students don't have access, you can achieve some of the same effects with telephone voicemail or an answering machine.

PROS   Electronic Mail Feedback can do double duty. While you are eliciting information on your teaching, you can familiarize students with the use of electronic mail, a valuable skill in many fields.

The electronic mail format is not tied directly to the classroom or the class schedule. Students can respond to E-mail messages whenever they wish from any workstation that is linked. Faculty who have electronic mail access can read student responses anytime.

This CAT encourages honest, informal, and open-ended responses to questions teachers pose. When students give faculty handwritten feedback, they may worry that their handwriting will give their identities away. E-mail responses can be more securely anonymous.

CONS   Precisely because it is easy to respond, students may write longer responses than you hope for or have time to read.

But because there is no set time or place for responding, fewer students may take the time to do so.

On many bulletin board systems, anyone who has access can read all the other messages. Not all faculty will be comfortable with the fact that others can read student comments on their classes.

If others do have access, some students may make provocative, rude, or humorous statements just because they know they have an audience.

CAVEATS   Don't use this technique if there are students in your class who have no access to electronic mail.

Don't ask questions about areas of your teaching that you cannot or will not change.

Assuming your classroom is equipped with networked computers or terminals, if you want everyone to respond to your question, give students class or lab time to do so.

If students' comments can be accessed and read by others, make sure to let them know this ahead of time.

REFERENCES AND RESOURCES   Although some of its technical details are now out of date, Heinz Dreher's (1984) article provides a simple and clear argument for the use of electronic mail in the classroom.

CLASSROOM
ASSESSMENT
TECHNIQUE

43

Teacher-Designed Feedback Forms

Estimated Levels of Time and Energy Required for:

Faculty to prepare to use this CAT	**MEDIUM**
Students to respond to the assessment	**LOW**
Faculty to analyze the data collected	**LOW to MEDIUM**

DESCRIPTION   Standardized teacher evaluation forms are widely used, in part because they are easily administered and because they yield data that are easily coded and analyzed. In addition, the information from various administrations of the same evaluation form can be compared over time. The questions on standardized forms, however, are often too general to provide the detailed information that faculty need for improving their teaching. And it often takes months to find out the results. Faculty can benefit from the advantages of evaluation forms and collect the specific information they need by preparing short, simple, course-specific evaluation forms. These feedback forms contain anywhere from three to seven questions in multiple-choice, Likert-scale, or short fill-in answer formats.

PURPOSE   Teacher-Designed Feedback Forms elicit limited, focused responses to very specific questions posed by the instructor. Faculty can quickly and easily analyze data from Feedback Forms and use the results to make informed and timely adjustments in their teaching. Students profit by providing detailed feedback on teaching early enough to benefit from its use. By giving students a summary of the class's feedback and discussing the adjustments they and students can make to improve learning, faculty demonstrate their concern with student progress and their willingness to respond to reasonable suggestions. Since students evaluate teachers, in part at least, on their awareness of and responsiveness to the class's learning level and needs, these forms can help faculty get the student evaluations they deserve.

RELATED TEACHING GOALS   Develop ability to draw reasonable inferences from observations (TGI Goal 4)

Learn to evaluate methods and materials in this subject (TGI Goal 24)

Cultivate an active commitment to honesty (TGI Goal 50)

SUGGESTIONS FOR USE   Very simple Teacher-Designed Feedback Forms can be used to good effect in almost any course, except perhaps the smallest seminars. To get information early enough to make necessary adjustments and to track changes over time, teachers should introduce the forms in the first or second week of class and administer them a few times, at regular intervals, during the term. These forms are best administered during the last five to ten minutes of the class and, if possible, during the last class meeting of the week. This procedure avoids derailing other learning activities and allows teachers more time to analyze and summarize feedback before the next class session.

EXAMPLES   Exhibit 9.1 is a sample feedback form that one of the authors has developed and adapted for use in several undergraduate and graduate courses.

Exhibit 9.1. Sample Teacher-Designed Feedback Form.

Directions: Please respond honestly and constructively to the questions below by circling the responses you most agree with and writing brief comments.

1. On the scale below, please rate the *clarity* of today's session.

1	2	3	4	5
totally unclear	somewhat unclear	mostly clear	very clear	extremely clear

2. Overall, how *interesting* did you find today's session?

1	2	3	4	5
totally boring	mostly boring	somewhat interesting	very interesting	extremely interesting

3. Overall, how *useful* was today's session in helping you learn the material?

1	2	3	4	5
useless	not very useful	somewhat useful	very useful	extremely useful

4. What did you find most helpful about today's class? (Please list one or two specific examples.)

5. How could the class have been improved? (Please give one or two specific suggestions.)

STEP-BY-STEP PROCEDURE

1. Write three to five specific questions about your teaching that you would like students to respond to. Make sure that those questions relate directly to your instructional goals for the class.

2. Develop appropriate coded responses, either multiple-choice or scaled, for those questions.

3. Make up a one-page, carefully worded form to collect focused, constructive responses.

4. To protect anonymity, ask students to turn in forms to a teaching fellow or secretary, or to leave them in an envelope pinned to your office door.

5. After you have analyzed the feedback forms, summarize the results to the class and outline the specific action(s) you intend to take in response to student reactions.

In analyzing student responses to these feedback forms, give more attention to the direction, intensity, and consistency of the responses than to their actual numerical values or means. The precoded responses make it easy to see patterns in the responses across the whole class. For example, if you simply tally the number of students who circled 1, 2, 3, and so on, for each question, you can quickly see areas of disagreement, agreement, or polarization within the class. The comments, though less easily compared, often provide teachers with the most useful feedback for improving their teaching.

IDEAS FOR ADAPTING AND EXTENDING THIS CAT

After you have gone through this process once or twice, ask students to come up with questions they would like to see on the next feedback form. They can devise these questions individually or produce them as the result of a structured group exercise.

Focus the assessment, and thus students' attention, on longer instructional periods, such as on several classes devoted to dealing with one unit, experiment, chapter, or book.

If you have a Classroom Assessment Quality Circle, give its members the task of collecting and summarizing the data.

Use electronic mail to collect responses.

PROS

By explicitly assessing your teaching to find out how well you are achieving your instructional goals, you publicly demonstrate your commitment to those goals, your respect for students' assessments, and your professional integrity.

If you construct the questions carefully, the students' responses should provide context-specific, focused feedback that will help you make adjustments in your teaching.

In carrying out this technique and following up with related adjustments, you provide a role model for students of a professional who is sufficiently self-assured to listen to and learn from his or her students' criticisms, opinions, and insights.

Teaching students, by personal example, the value of inviting and welcoming evaluation by others is one of the most important outcomes of this technique. Since evaluation is a constant in student life and a critical factor in many jobs, students who learn to make constructive use of it — rather than fearing or resenting the process — will gain distinct advantages.

CONS

Because of their own fear of criticism or dislike of evaluation, some students may view your use of the feedback forms as an admission that something is wrong or as a sign of weakness.

Good feedback forms take a lot of thought to construct. When you have constructed a useful one, though, you may be able to use it in other, similar courses.

Some students, in their responses, may not answer the questions you asked, or they may fail to respond to them constructively.

CAVEATS   Don't overuse the feedback form technique. Two or perhaps three administrations over the course of a semester are enough to indicate your sincere interest and provide useful information without risking overkill.

Ask questions about alterable variables, those elements of your teaching behavior you can and are willing to change.

Don't promise any changes that you may not be able to deliver, and always promise somewhat less than you are confident you can achieve.

Group Instructional Feedback Technique

Estimated Levels of Time and Energy Required for:

Faculty to prepare to use this CAT	**MEDIUM**
Students to respond to the assessment	**MEDIUM**
Faculty to analyze the data collected	**MEDIUM to HIGH**

DESCRIPTION   This technique has many names and many variations, but they all center on getting student responses to three questions related to their learning in the class. However they are worded, these three questions basically ask, "What works? What doesn't? What can be done to improve it?" In an ideal administration of the Group Instructional Feedback Technique (GIFT), someone other than the teacher quickly polls students on these questions, determines which are the most frequent responses, summarizes them, and then reports back to the instructor.

This feedback is a GIFT in two senses. First, it is already at least partially summarized and analyzed by the time it reaches the instructor. And second, it allows the instructor to see his or her course through the eyes of a detached but sympathetic observer. If no outside "information gatherer" is available, instructors can collect useful data from their own classes by giving students more responsibility in the process and adopting a few safeguards.

PURPOSE   The Group Instructional Feedback Technique (GIFT) is designed to provide instructors with a quick, rough summary of the most frequent responses to three questions: (1) What do students think is helping them learn? (2) What is hindering their learning? (3) What specific suggestions do they have for improving learning in the classroom? This process gives students a chance to compare their responses with those of their classmates.

RELATED TEACHING GOALS   Develop ability to draw reasonable inferences from observations (TGI Goal 4)

Learn to evaluate methods and materials in this subject (TGI Goal 24)

Develop ability to work productively with others (TGI Goal 36)

Cultivate an active commitment to honesty (TGI Goal 50)

SUGGESTIONS FOR USE The GIFT works most effectively in classes of twenty-five to one hundred students. Since this technique can provide helpful feedback when there are problems in a class, it should be used before the problems become serious — preferably, well before the middle of the term.

EXAMPLES

From Organic Chemistry (Chemistry)

> The veteran chemistry professor who taught the more than 150 students in this first-year course heard about the Group Instructional Feedback Technique from a friend who had used it in a first-year physics course. The chemistry professor agreed to try it only after he had convinced his colleague from physics to act as the "visiting assessor." The two of them worked out the details over lunch in the faculty club. These were the prompts they agreed on:
>
> 1. Give one or two examples of specific things your instructor does that really *help you learn* organic chemistry.
>
> 2. Give one or two examples of specific things your instructor does that *make it more difficult* for you to learn organic chemistry.
>
> 3. Suggest one or two *specific, practical changes* your instructor could make that would help you improve your learning in this class.
>
> They agreed to do the assessment during the fourth week of their fourteen-week semester. The chemistry professor told the students what was going to happen and asked them to cooperate fully with his colleague. He assured them that their responses would remain anonymous, and he urged them to give honest, thoughtful feedback. Twenty minutes before the end of the next class, the physics professor arrived, and the chemistry professor introduced him and left.
> 　　The "visiting assessor" quickly explained what he was doing and why, and how the process would work. He asked students to take about five minutes to write answers to all three questions on index cards and then to take five more minutes to discuss their answers in a small group of at least three other students. He then asked the groups to share only those reponses that they had heard from several members. He quickly listed common responses to the first two questions and then asked the students to indicate whether they agreed with each response by raising their hands. The physics professor simply estimated the percentages of students raising their hands each time and wrote that rough estimate on the board. In this way, the whole class saw how much agreement there was on a few common "helpful" and "not helpful" points. At the end of the exercise, he collected the index cards so that he could report back more accurately on responses to the first two questions and so that he could summarize the students' suggestions for improvement.
> 　　What follows is a list of rough percentages of the class agreeing with common responses. The physics professor summarized this information and shared it with the chemistry professor, along with a list of a few illustrative comments he had transcribed from the index cards.

Specific things the instructor does that really *help you learn* organic chemistry:

Previews what will be on the tests	90%
Connects lectures to the textbook	80%
Uses good examples	70%
Elicits and answers questions	50%
Uses visuals to illustrate	40%

Specific things the instructor does that *make it more difficult* for you to learn organic chemistry:

Talks too fast	95%
Doesn't give enough small tests	75%
Lectures at too advanced a level	60%

Specific, practical changes that would help you improve your learning in organic chemistry:

Talk slower	90%
Give more frequent, smaller tests	75%
Provide an outline or study guide	50%

The chemistry professor was relieved to see and hear the results and grateful to his colleague for collecting, summarizing, and explaining the results. He decided to let his chemistry students know that he would try to talk more slowly and that he would make a few adjustments where he could in response to their other requests.

STEP-BY-STEP PROCEDURE

1. Decide exactly how you want the GIFT questions worded, how much class time you will allow for the process, and whether you are willing to invite someone else in to conduct the assessment. (If you choose to collect the data yourself, skip to Step 4.)

2. Invite a trusted colleague, teaching fellow, or faculty development consultant to visit your class to conduct the GIFT assessment. Schedule a mutually convenient date and ask the "visiting assessor" to come during the last fifteen or twenty minutes of class. Make sure that your visitor knows the questions you want asked and that the two of you agree on the assessment procedure and the follow-up steps.

3. Prepare the students for the visit by letting them know who is coming, when, and why. Stress that your purpose is to find out how you can help them improve the quality of their learning.

Instructions for the person who collects the data:

4. Introduce yourself and remind students of the purpose of your visit. Review the assessment procedure and write the questions on the board—or display them on an overhead projector to save time.

5. Allow students three or four minutes to write answers, and another three or four minutes to compare their answers with those of two or three students nearby.

6. If you are leading this assessment with your own students, this is the time to collect written feedback. If you are visiting someone else's class, you may ask students to volunteer common responses. Write those common responses on the chalkboard or overhead.

7. If you are visiting, and if time allows, ask students to raise their hands to indicate agreement with common responses. Count or estimate the percentage of the students agreeing each time.

TURNING THE DATA YOU COLLECT INTO USEFUL INFORMATION

If you have polled the students and obtained rough percentages of agreement on certain items, you will gain details by reading written responses. Tally the most common written responses, particularly the suggestions, for the teacher you are assisting or for yourself. List the comments if possible. You may want to give students feedback on only the three most common responses to each question.

IDEAS FOR ADAPTING AND EXTENDING THIS CAT

Skip the small-group step and collect individual written responses to these questions from your own students. Take precautions to safeguard their anonymity.

Ask members of a Classroom Assessment Quality Circle to collect the responses and perhaps to lead the assessment.

Collect feedback on only one question. The most useful of the three questions may be the one that elicits suggestions for improvement.

PROS

When a third party collects the feedback, the GIFT procedure allows students more freedom to respond and gives the teacher an opportunity to see the class through the eyes of another observer.

The technique focuses students' attention on what helps and what hinders their learning, not on what they like or don't about you or the class.

Students have a chance to hear each other's comments and suggestions and to indicate whether or not they agree with them.

CONS

When a visitor carries out the technique, the regular instructor gives up time and some control over the course.

Some articulate students with complaints may negatively influence others through the group discussion and polling process.

The "visiting assessor" may see and hear things that reflect badly on you and the class.

CAVEATS

If at all possible, trade visits—one for one—with a colleague. This procedure builds trust and makes honest assessment more likely.

When arranging to have a colleague visit your class, make sure to schedule the feedback session as well.

Lacking detailed knowledge of the context and the students, the visitor may not be able to understand and summarize the class's responses. To avoid this possibility, you may need to invite a visitor from your own specialty or, at the least, prepare that person to understand what he or she will experience in your class.

REFERENCES AND RESOURCES   This CAT is an adaptation of small-group instructional diagnosis (SGID), a widely used approach to eliciting focused student reactions to a class. Redmond and Clark (1982) and Bennett (1987) discuss various ways to use SGID and provide sample questions. Weimer (1990, pp. 107–108) succinctly summarizes the pros and cons of SGID.

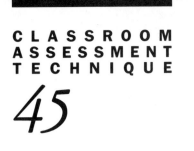

CLASSROOM
ASSESSMENT
TECHNIQUE
45

Classroom Assessment
Quality Circles

Estimated Levels of Time and Energy Required for:

Faculty to prepare to use this CAT	**HIGH**
Students to respond to the assessment	**HIGH**
Faculty to analyze the data collected	**MEDIUM to HIGH**

DESCRIPTION Quality Control Circles, originally a Japanese management technique for involving teams of workers and managers more directly in industrial planning and problem solving, have been modified and applied to a variety of organizations in the United States during the past fifteen years. Impressed by the effectiveness of the Quality Circle approaches used in many U.S. companies and government agencies, a number of college instructors have recently begun experimenting with classroom applications. This Classroom Assessment Technique draws inspiration most directly from educational adaptations of Quality Control Circles. In this application of the approach, however, the focus is on involving groups of students in structured and ongoing assessment of course materials, activities, and assignments.

PURPOSE Classroom Assessment Quality Circles have two complementary purposes. The first is to provide a vehicle for regularly collecting thoughtful responses from students on their assessments of class sessions, readings, exams, and major assignments. The second, equally important, purpose is to offer students a structured, positive way to become more actively involved in their classroom learning. Involvement in Quality Circles gives students practice in working together to assess their classroom experiences and to suggest ways to improve the group's learning.

RELATED TEACHING GOALS Develop ability to draw reasonable inferences from observations (TGI Goal 4)

Develop ability to distinguish between fact and opinion (TGI Goal 8)

Learn to evaluate methods and materials in this subject (TGI Goal 24)

Develop ability to work productively with others (TGI Goal 36)

Develop management skills (TGI Goal 37)

Develop respect for others (TGI Goal 47)

Cultivate an active commitment to honesty (TGI Goal 50)

SUGGESTIONS FOR USE
Classroom Assessment Quality Circles are an especially powerful way to engage and involve students in large-enrollment courses. This technique will work, however, only if the instructor is flexible and open to student observations, opinions, and suggestions. Allowing the Quality Circle to function means giving students some of the power in the classroom, even if that power is only advisory.

EXAMPLES

From History of Western Civilization (History)

Faced with an enrollment of nearly two hundred students in his History of Western Civilization course, the professor asked for volunteers who would be interested in forming Classroom Assessment Quality Circles to help him monitor and improve teaching and learning in the class. Thirty students volunteered initially, but only twenty decided to commit to the Quality Circles after learning what they would entail. He split the twenty volunteers into three more or less even groups and asked each group to join him once every three weeks for a scheduled, hour-long meeting to give him feedback on learning in the class.

After an initial training session with all twenty students, the instructor began meeting with the groups on a rotating basis and saw each group four times in the course of the semester. Each of the twenty Quality Circle members was responsible for contacting, polling, or meeting with a group of nine fellow students to elicit their reactions to the class and pass on information from the Quality Circles. The instructor told the rest of the students in the class that these three Quality Circle groups would help him monitor and improve the quality of teaching and learning in the class. He urged students to take their comments, positive and negative, and concerns to the Quality Circle members. The instructor agreed never to ask the Quality Circles who had said what.

The history professor encouraged the members of the Quality Circles to come up with their own ways of collecting information, but he asked them to keep the focus on learning quality. He suggested that, in one way or another, they pursue the following three basic questions in gathering data: What is helping students learn? What is making learning more difficult? What specific, practical steps could he and the class take to improve learning?

Each week, the instructor met with one of the groups in the department's conference room. Coffee and tea were provided, and the discussions were usually lively and constructive—even on weeks when the groups reported frustration and confusion. From them, he gained a wealth of information, some of which he used to adjust his teaching. The twenty students got a chance to meet regularly, in small groups, with their professor to discuss the course—and they received credit worth two homework assignments.

STEP-BY-STEP PROCEDURE
1. Consider seriously whether you want to meet regularly with one or more small groups of students to get their feedback on the course. If you do, decide which specific elements of the class you will ask these groups to focus their attention on.

2. Ask for volunteers or appoint one or more groups of five to eight students to serve as Classroom Assessment Quality Circles. Make sure to offer the students some compensation for their time and energies. You might grant them credit for one or more assignments or give them a certain number of points toward their final grades for participating:

3. Set up an agenda for the first meeting and give the students a few simple guidelines on how to work effectively in a Quality Circle group. Basically, they must make sure that everyone is heard and that everyone, including the instructor, listens actively and constructively.

4. Make very clear to the members of the Quality Circles which aspects of the course they can expect to affect. If certain areas of the course are not open to discussion, let them know that also.

5. Arrange to meet with the Quality Circles on a regular basis, so that you have ongoing feedback and they have opportunities to practice their assessment and group-work skills.

6. Introduce the members of the Classroom Assessment Quality Circles to the rest of the class and encourage class members to seek them out and offer suggestions or criticisms to be discussed at the Quality Circle meetings.

7. Make sure to respond to the Quality Circles about their suggestions and to respond to the class as a whole, as appropriate, so that the rest of the students know they are being well represented.

TURNING THE DATA YOU COLLECT INTO USEFUL INFORMATION

When meeting with the Quality Circles, listen carefully, ask a few good questions, and talk very little. Take careful notes on their reports. Ask the members, in a nonconfrontational way, how many students mentioned a particular question or concern. Continuously check with other members of the group, to evaluate the degree to which perceptions are shared. Look for patterns over time in the kinds of issues that the Quality Circles bring to your attention.

IDEAS FOR ADAPTING AND EXTENDING THIS CAT

If you have a very large class with several teaching fellows, train them to lead Classroom Assessment Quality Circle groups. The teaching fellows can then form an "inner" Quality Circle to inform and advise you.

Ask members of the Quality Circles to meet before their meetings with you and to draw up proposed agendas for your meetings.

Give the Quality Circles some class time occasionally, to report to their fellow students.

PROS

Having direct, personal, and purposeful contact with the teacher in a large class can motivate Quality Circle members to take their participation in the course much more seriously.

The instructor gains the advantage of access to several pairs of ears and eyes, and to several approaches to problem solving.

Those in the Quality Circles can serve both as advocates for their fellow students and as liaisons between instructor and students. In large classes, the use of representatives can make communication more efficient and effective.

By setting up and cooperating with the Quality Circles, instructors actively demonstrate their commitment to listening to student feedback on courses. This clear commitment sends the message to members of the Quality Circles and to the rest of the class that their assessments do matter. This message encourages students to assess the course more thoughtfully and responsibly.

CONS

Classroom Assessment Quality Circles take extra time and preparation on the part of teachers and students. While the students can be compensated with credit toward the grade, the instructor probably will not be compensated with anything other than the information and satisfaction the technique provides.

Unless the process is explained clearly and used regularly, members of the class are not likely to take it seriously.

Some students who volunteer for the Quality Circles will not yet have developed group-work skills needed to use this CAT productively. Therefore, the instructor often must provide training in the process itself in order for the Quality Circles to work effectively.

CAVEATS

Perhaps the worst outcome occurs when the teacher starts a Quality Circle and then discontinues or loses interest in it. Think hard about the pros and cons before extending an invitation to students to form the Quality Circles. Think carefully about how you can productively lead the groups, and ask yourself whether you are ready to take students' suggestions seriously.

Since students in the Quality Circles may not know how to collect feedback or what questions to ask of their classmates, you may need to provide them with some examples. Help them gather information from a wide variety of students, not just the most vocal ones.

To work well with a Quality Circle, you will need to be both thick-skinned and tolerant. When the message is not welcome, it is all the more important to welcome the messengers.

The students in the Quality Circle need to receive some extrinsic reward for participating. More important, they need to be shown the value of their work and praised when they do it well.

REFERENCES AND RESOURCES

Useful applications of the Quality Circle technique to college teaching are discussed in Hirshfield (1984), Kogut (1984), and Zeiders and Sivak (1985). The first two articles contain reports on the authors' experiences with the technique. In *Early Lessons*, Cottell (1991, pp. 43–54) describes his use of this CAT in a large accounting course.

Assessing Learner Reactions to Class Activities, Assignments, and Materials

The techniques in this section are designed to give teachers information that will help them improve their course materials and assignments. At the same time, these five CATs require students to think more carefully about the course work and its relationship to their learning. The RSQC2 technique (Recall, Summarize, Question, Comment, and Connect) is a highly structured modular technique that assesses student recall, reaction, and evaluation of classroom activities. Group-Work Evaluations help teachers and students understand and improve the effectiveness of study and project groups. Reading Rating Sheets elicit student reactions to course readings, and Assignment Assessments do the same for homework assignments. Finally, given the almost universal use of tests and exams, Exam Evaluations should be applicable to a great many college classrooms.

CLASSROOM
ASSESSMENT
TECHNIQUE

46

RSQC2
(Recall, Summarize, Question, Connect, and Comment)

Estimated Levels of Time and Energy Required for:

Faculty to prepare to use this CAT	**LOW**
Students to respond to the assessment	**LOW to MEDIUM**
Faculty to analyze the data collected	**MEDIUM**

DESCRIPTION

RSQC2 is a modular Classroom Assessment Technique. Teachers can use the whole thing or select individual components to administer. When the whole RSQC2 is used, this five-step protocol guides students quickly through simple recall, summary, analysis, evaluation, and synthesis exercises focusing on a previous class session.

PURPOSE

RSQC2 allows instructors to compare detailed information on the students' recall, understanding, and evaluations of a class session against their own. It also informs teachers of students' questions and comments that need timely responses. This technique provides students with a comprehensive framework for recalling and reviewing class sessions.

RELATED TEACHING GOALS

Develop ability to synthesize and integrate information and ideas (TGI Goal 5)
Improve skill at paying attention (TGI Goal 9)
Improve memory skills (TGI Goal 11)
Develop appropriate study skills, strategies, and habits (TGI Goal 16)
Develop (self-) management skills (TGI Goal 37)

SUGGESTIONS FOR USE

RSQC2 is particularly useful to students who lack preparation in the relevant discipline and to those who lack sophisticated learning and study skills. This technique is best used at regular intervals, at least at first. If classes meet only once or twice a week, it can profitably be used to begin each class. If classes meet every day, or three times a week, consider using it to end — or begin and end — the week. You need not go through all the steps in the procedure to benefit from the technique; many faculty omit the "Comment" step, for instance, and others work through only one or two different steps at a time.

From Mathematical Concepts (Mathematics/Developmental Education)

Many students in this remedial mathematics course had great trouble connecting each class session with the classes that came before and after. To help students better recall and connect the material, their instructor decided to use the RSQC2 technique. At the beginning of the fourth class meeting of the semester, this developmental math instructor asked students to take two minutes to recall and list the most important ideas from the previous class. She then asked them to write a sentence summarizing as many of those important points as possible. The summary step took about three minutes. Next, she asked them to write one question about the material from the previous class that they wanted answered. Fourth, she asked them to make one connection between what they had learned in the previous class and any of the classes before that. And last, she asked them to comment on how confident they had felt, during the last class, in their ability to do the homework. All in all, the RSQC2 assessment took about ten minutes, after which she asked students to hand in their reponses.

When the math instructor looked through the RSQC2 feedback, she was initially disheartened. Although nearly everyone had come up with a recall list, very few students had written coherent sentences summarizing their lists of points, and only a few had made reasonable connections. There were a few good questions, but many students had come up with no questions at all. Most of them reported that they had felt very uncomfortable during the previous class. All in all, the feedback showed that her students were not doing well in the class and were not feeling happy about their performance.

In response to the feedback, the developmental instructor decided to do two things. First, she decided to share her summary of the responses, but to accentuate the positive. So she gave examples of good, complete summaries, questions, and connections, and a few articulate comments. After responding to some questions, she praised the students for a good first attempt. She then told them that they would be using the technique at the beginning of the next class—but only the Recall, Summarize, and Question steps—and asked them to try to be ready. Their next responses, though still weak, were much improved, and the instructor focused the class's attention on writing useful summary sentences.

From Conversational German (German/Foreign Languages)

To assess what students were learning and to give them more practice using German, this instructor taught his students the RSQC2 technique and then used it during the first five minutes of each class period. Students would quickly write their responses to the five prompts; then the instructor would ask them to volunteer their answers, in German, to one prompt. For example, on one day the German instructor would solicit the recalled information from the class, writing summary words and phrases on the board as students called them out. He would then invite students to add any missing points to their lists and hand them in. At the next class session, he would move to another step, going over summary sentences or connections or comments before collecting the written feedback. One RSQC2 step was discussed at each class, however: the students' questions in German about German. For each class, the instructor gave only three brief pieces of feedback on the RSQC2 responses. Over a few weeks, students became very fluent in using the CAT, and their responses grew more sophisticated.

STEP-BY-STEP PROCEDURE

Note: It is always a good idea to write your own responses to the RSQC2 before you ask students to do so.

1. Recall: At the beginning of class, ask students to make a list—in words or simple phrases—of what they recall as the most important, useful, or meaningful points from the previous class. Allow one or two minutes for them to write the list. Then ask each student to choose, from his or her list, three to five main points and rank them in order of importance. This step should take another one or two minutes at most.

2. Summarize: Direct them to summarize as many of the most important points as they can into one summary sentence that captures the essence of the previous class. Give them one or two minutes to write a summary sentence.

3. Question: Ask them to jot down one or two questions that remained unanswered after the previous class. Allow one or two minutes again.

4. Connect: Ask students to explain—in one or two sentences written in as many minutes—the connection(s) between the main point(s) of the previous class and the major goal(s) of the entire course.

5. Comment: Invite the students to write an evaluative comment or two about the class. Here are a few possible comment stems you can suggest as starting points: "What I enjoyed most/least was..." or "What I found most/least useful was..." or "During most of the class, I felt..." This step also requires a couple of minutes.

6. Collect the RSQC2 feedback, letting students know what kind of feedback they can expect to receive and when they will receive it.

TURNING THE DATA YOU COLLECT INTO USEFUL INFORMATION

Before you begin to analyze the data, decide which set of responses you are going to work with: questions, connections, summaries, or comments. Unless you have a very small class or a great deal of time to spare, don't try to analyze all of them. If you have already written your own RSQC2 responses, you can compare them with those of your students. Note whether or not you and they got the same basic points in your "Recall" lists. When you compare their responses with yours, note omissions, additions, and errors in the students' "Recall" lists and summaries. Assess the degree of "fit" between your summary of the class and the students': How close are they? Look for patterns in the questions and comments. Do several students mention the same topics or concerns? Share with students the information you obtained on one of the prompts.

IDEAS FOR ADAPTING AND EXTENDING THIS CAT

Encourage students to share the items on their "Recall" lists with each other. Elicit responses and create a class "Recall" list, and perhaps a class summary.

After the process is clearly understood, let students take over the teacher's role. A different student or pair of students can be responsible for each RSQC2 session.

To save class time, let the Classroom Assessment Quality Circle or a graduate assistant carry out steps 1 to 3 or 1 to 4—before class starts each day—and share the results.

Use this technique at the end of very long classes, rather than at the beginning.

If students have difficulty responding, let them work in pairs or small groups and submit group responses.

PROS

RSQC2 gives the teacher immediate feedback on what students recall and value and on what they have questions about, as well as on the connections they see.

It gives students a highly structured opportunity to recall, summarize, and evaluate material presented in a previous class and to compare or share their recall, understanding, and evaluation with fellow students and the teacher.

By stressing connections, it provides an explicit cognitive "bridge" between "old" and "new" information and ideas.

RSQC2 forces participants continually to review, recycle, reorganize, reconsider, and integrate the major points of the course.

CONS

RSQC2 is a relatively time-consuming activity, especially the first few times it is attempted.

It can seem to be or become a waste of time unless everyone participates actively and effectively. As is true for most of these techniques, if it is overused or used poorly, it can easily become a mindless, pro forma activity.

Because this CAT usually generates more data than can be analyzed, students who want some feedback on each element of the assessment can become frustrated.

CAVEATS

Decide before you use the technique whether you want all, part, or none of the data it generates, and let students know before they start.

Be prepared for the process to go slowly the first couple of times. Make sure to schedule enough time to work through the steps you plan to use. You may need to model your responses, in order to help students see how you carry out each of the steps.

Don't ask students to write down questions or comments about the class unless you are willing to respond to them in a thoughtful manner.

If you allow students to think carefully about their responses, any of the steps in the protocol could take up to fifteen minutes. By announcing and observing time limits, you can encourage students to work quickly.

Group-Work Evaluations

Estimated Levels of Time and Energy Required for:

Faculty to prepare to use this CAT	**MEDIUM**
Students to respond to the assessment	**LOW**
Faculty to analyze the data collected	**LOW**

DESCRIPTION Group-Work Evaluation forms are simple questionnaires used to collect feedback on students' reactions to cooperative learning (where students work in structured groups toward an agreed-upon learning goal) and study groups.

PURPOSE As more and more faculty experiment with cooperative and collaborative learning techniques, there is more need for and interest in assessing group work. Group-Work Evaluations can help students and teachers see what is going well and what is not going well in learning groups, so that potentially destructive conflicts in groups can be discovered and defused. At the same time, this CAT can be used by faculty and students to gain insights into the group process.

RELATED TEACHING GOALS Develop appropriate study skills, strategies, and habits (TGI Goal 16)
Develop ability to work productively with others (TGI Goal 36)
Develop (self-) management skills (TGI Goal 37)
Develop leadership skills (TGI Goal 38)
Develop respect for others (TGI Goal 47)
Cultivate an active commitment to honesty (TGI Goal 50)

SUGGESTIONS FOR USE Group-Work Evaluations are most helpful in classes where students regularly work in small groups, such as courses taught by the case method. The assessments can be done whenever the groups meet, and whether they meet in class or out. As is the case with many other CATs this technique should be introduced soon after the groups begin working together, since it provides feedback that can inform their development and improve their effectiveness.

EXAMPLES

From English Composition (English)

Early in the term, this composition instructor organized her twenty-five students into five groups of five each. Students were to remain in these groups for half the term and then would be reassigned. The instructor used the groups in class for prewriting and revising exercises, and encouraged students to meet and study together outside of class time. For several years, she had noticed that some groups worked well and others were a disaster, but she could not account for the differences and did not know how to prevent the disasters. In an attempt to improve her understanding of the group dynamic, she decided to use the Group-Work Evaluation technique.

At the next class meeting, she handed out a questionnaire (see Exhibit 9.2) and asked students to respond only after their half-hour group-work sessions had ended. Each student was asked to write his or her group's number—I through V—on the sheets, but not to write names.

Exhibit 9.2. Sample Group-Work Evaluation Form.

1. Overall, how effectively did your group work together on this assignment?

       Poorly   Adequately   Well   Extremely well

2. Out of the five group members, how many participated actively most of the time?

       None   One   Two   Three   Four   All five

3. Out of the five group members, how many were fully prepared for the activity?

       None   One   Two   Three   Four   All five

4. Give one specific example of <u>something you learned from the group</u> that you probably wouldn't have learned working alone.

5. Give one specific example of <u>something the other group members learned from you</u> that they probably wouldn't have learned otherwise.

6. Suggest one change the group could make to improve its performance.

She sorted the responses into their respective groups and then quickly read and tallied each group's responses. Not too surprisingly, the groups that rated their effectiveness highest also indicated a higher level of participation and preparation. The members of the more effective groups were also more likely to give complete answers to questions 4, 5, and 6. In the less effective groups, however, several individuals had thoughtful suggestions for improving performance.

At the next class meeting, the composition instructor shared a summary of the responses and let the students draw their own conclusions—which were not very different from hers. She then shared the suggestions and asked the groups to come up with a few simple, practical guidelines for more effective functioning.

STEP-BY-STEP PROCEDURE

1. Decide what you want to know about the group work and what you most want students to notice about it, and compose a few questions to get at that information.

2. Choose the most important questions, no more than four or five, and create a simple Group-Work Evaluation Form for collecting feedback.

3. Before handing out the forms, explain the purpose of the assessment and the process to students. If you want to analyze responses by groups, make sure that the students somehow indicate the groups they belong to, without giving away their individual identities.

TURNING THE DATA YOU COLLECT INTO USEFUL INFORMATION

If possible, tally the fixed-response answers and summarize the comments within working groups first; then aggregate the results across groups. Scrutinize the feedback for indications that some groups are working particularly well or poorly. Responses from these "outlier" groups may provide clues on how to improve performance in all the groups.

IDEAS FOR ADAPTING AND EXTENDING THIS CAT

Ask the groups themselves to come up with questions they would like to assess through the Group-Work Evaluation process.

Have groups suggest solutions to the concerns raised through the assessment.

PROS

Conflicts are virtually inevitable in small groups. This CAT provides a simple means for detecting conflicts early, before they permanently damage the group dynamic.

At the same time, this process can allow the instructor and the students to find out early what is working well, how, and why — and to profit from that information.

From the instructor's summary of the feedback, students in all groups learn that there are some common advantages and disadvantages to group work.

CONS

Giving students a chance to express concerns with group work may raise expectations that you or they can quickly resolve them.

Some students simply dislike working in groups and may use this assessment exercise as an opportunity to sabotage the process.

Some students will almost surely resent the focus on "process" that this CAT requires, preferring to expend their efforts solely on the creation of "products" or "outcomes."

CAVEATS

The social dynamic of small groups often works against candor when things are not going well. Make it clear that you expect and want honest answers, and find a way to ensure that neither you nor other students can identify individual respondents.

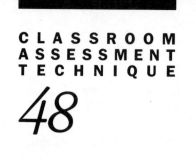

CLASSROOM
ASSESSMENT
TECHNIQUE
48

Reading
Rating Sheets

Estimated Levels of Time and Energy Required for:

Faculty to prepare to use this CAT	**LOW**
Students to respond to the assessment	**LOW**
Faculty to analyze the data collected	**LOW**

DESCRIPTION   Reading Rating Sheets are short, simple assessment forms that students fill out in response to their assigned course readings.

PURPOSE   The purpose of Reading Rating Sheets is to provide faculty with feedback on students' evaluations of their course readings. Faculty use this CAT to find out how interesting, motivating, clear, and useful their assigned readings are from the students' point of view. This information can help teachers adjust the way they teach those texts in the short run and rethink the selection of course readings over the longer term.

RELATED TEACHING   Improve reading skills (TGI Goal 14)
GOALS   Develop appropriate study skills, strategies, and habits (TGI Goal 16)
Learn to evaluate methods and materials in this subject (TGI Goal 24)
Cultivate an active commitment to honesty (TGI Goal 50)
Develop capacity to think for oneself (TGI Goal 51)

SUGGESTIONS FOR USE   Reading Rating Sheets are useful assessments in courses where there are several different assigned readings and faculty have some choice in assigning readings. It is a good technique to use when students seem to be having trouble with particular readings or to be resisting them. Conversely, Reading Rating Sheets can help instructors find out, first, why students find some reading assignments more helpful than others and, second, why they appreciate and enjoy some readings more than others.

EXAMPLES

From Philosophy of the Person (Philosophy)

The philosophy professor teaching this introductory general education course held one large lecture each week and then broke the class into three groups for weekly section meetings. All the students were assigned supplementary readings. The instructor required students to fill out Reading Rating Sheets on the supplementary readings and compared the responses each week.

Largely in response to student feedback, the philosophy professor selected the supplementary readings that students had rated as most helpful and clear and used them for all sections the following semester. One of the unintended benefits of using this CAT was that more students seemed to come to section better prepared for the discussions. When she asked them why they were better prepared, several students said that the Reading Rating Sheets, and her feedback on them to the class, encouraged them to do the class reading more often and more carefully. Exhibit 9.3 is a typical example of the Reading Rating Sheets she used to collect anonymous reactions.

Exhibit 9.3. Sample Reading Rating Sheet from Philosophy of the Person.

Title of the supplementary reading: _____

1. How well did you read this assignment? (Circle only one response.)
   A. Completely and carefully
   B. Completely, but not carefully
   C. Only partially, but carefully
   D. Not completely or carefully

2. How useful was this reading assignment in helping you understand the topic?
   A. Very useful
   B. Useful
   C. Not very useful
   D. Useless

3. How clear and understandable was the reading?
   A. Very
   B. Adequately
   C. Not very
   D. Not at all

4. Having read this assignment, do you think I should assign it again next term?
   Yes   No

5. Please explain your answer to question 4 in a sentence or two below.
   _____
   _____
   _____

From Academic Reading Skills (English as a Second Language/ Developmental Education)

The instructor in this course for ESL students used Reading Rating Sheets both as a way to gather information on the usefulness of the various essays, articles, and short stories he assigned and as a way to build common ground for class discussions of the readings. His Reading Rating Sheet contained the following prompts:

1. Title of the reading

2. How useful was it to you in improving your vocabulary and reading skill?

3. How interesting was the reading to you?

4. Would you recommend it to a friend? Why or why not?

5. What did you learn from it that you want to make sure to remember?

1. Determine why you want students to rate the course readings. To make decisions about which readings to include in future syllabi? To focus student attention on specific aspects of the texts? Your reason for using the technique should inform your choice of questions.

2. Write a few questions, no more than four or five. Provide most of them with "yes/no" or multiple-choice responses, followed up with one or two short-answer questions to prompt reasons and explanations.

3. Make sure to include a question that assesses how thoroughly students have read the material being rated.

4. Try answering these questions yourself after reviewing the assigned reading, and then revise as necessary.

5. Create the simplest Reading Response Sheet form possible. Ask students to complete it out of class, as soon as they finish a reading, or at the beginning of the next class.

TURNING THE DATA YOU COLLECT INTO USEFUL INFORMATION

Consider setting aside any responses from students who have not read the material thoroughly. Tally answers to the multiple-choice and "yes/no" questions and look for patterns in the comments that will allow you to group them into meaningful clusters. In giving students feedback, focus most attention on responses that rate the learning value of the reading.

IDEAS FOR ADAPTING AND EXTENDING THIS CAT

Give individual students or groups of students responsibility for tallying and summarizing the material.

Use the same basic format to assess student reactions to other course materials, such as videotapes, films, and courseware.

Provide class time for students to compare and discuss their Reading Rating Sheet responses in small groups. Ask each group to suggest ways to learn more from reading assignments.

PROS

Reading Rating Sheets focus students' attention on evaluating assigned readings as learning aids, a perspective new to many learners. If reading is a lifelong learning skill worth promoting, this is one way of drawing students' attention to its value.

This technique recognizes that students can make valid judgments about the readings they are assigned—especially on the usefulness and clarity of those readings to them as learners.

It gives teachers feedback on how and how well students read the assignments.

CONS   Some students are prone to dislike any assigned reading that is dense and/or difficult, and therefore may give low ratings to any challenging assignments.

If most students fail to do the readings, or do them haphazardly, the assessment will yield few useful data.

CAVEATS   It makes little sense to take Reading Rating Sheets seriously when students have not done the required readings. For this reason, you may want to include a question on the sheet that separates those who have read the material from those who have not.

Don't ask questions that imply that you will change reading assignments unless you are really willing to do so.

Don't give students the impression that Reading Rating Sheets are a popularity contest. Remind them that they are to rate the readings on their clarity and usefulness in advancing their learning and— most of the time, at least—not on how much fun or how easy the readings are.

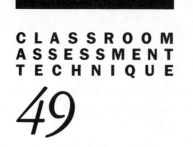

CLASSROOM
ASSESSMENT
TECHNIQUE
49

Assignment Assessments

Estimated Levels of Time and Energy Required for:

Faculty to prepare to use this CAT	**LOW**
Students to respond to the assessment	**LOW**
Faculty to analyze the data collected	**LOW to MEDIUM**

DESCRIPTION   Course assignments, from daily homework to term papers, provide students with the practice that allows them to learn and apply the material presented in class. Other CATs in this handbook focus students' attention on *how* they carry out course assignments. Assignment Assessments ask students to consider the value of these assignments to them as learners.

PURPOSE   Assignment Assessments help faculty see their assignments through students' eyes, giving them feedback on the learning value of the homework, papers, and projects they assign. This CAT, like Reading Rating Sheets, prompts students to think about and evaluate their assignments as learning tools.

RELATED TEACHING GOALS   Develop appropriate study skills, strategies, and habits (TGI Goal 16)
Learn to evaluate methods and materials in this subject (TGI Goal 24)
Cultivate an active commitment to honesty (TGI Goal 50)
Develop capacity to think for oneself (TGI Goal 51)

SUGGESTIONS FOR USE   Although they can be used in introductory courses, Assignment Assessments often yield the most useful data from students in intermediate and advanced classes and from adult learners, because these groups have some experience and perspective to bring to their assessments of the assignments. When this CAT is used in introductory courses, it should not be applied to the first or second assignment of the term. The simplicity of this CAT makes it adaptable to most disciplines.

EXAMPLES

From Principles of Financial Accounting (Accounting/Business)

The instructor in this required first-year class simply asked her students to answer the following two questions about their weekly problem sets:

(1) What part or aspect of the problem sets contributes the most to your learning? (2) What specific, practical change would you suggest to improve the problem sets as learning exercises?

Reading quickly through the index cards on which students had written their responses, the accounting teacher saw that most students valued the variety of problems she included in the homework; the fact that they were realistic, "real-world" problems; and the care with which she went over them in class. Many students suggested, however, that it would be more effective to assign one or two fewer problems and expect a higher quality of answers.

From Seminar in Physical Anthropology (Anthropology)

Each week, this professor gave his small, upper-division class a drawing or photograph of human remains and three possible reconstructions based on that evidence. The weekly assignment was for students to select the one reconstruction they found most compelling, to explain why, and to critique the other two reconstructions. Put another way, in two pages or so, students were to evaluate the reconstructions in view of the evidence presented in the pictures and drawings.

After a few weeks, the instructor asked students to assess how this assignment contributed or failed to contribute to their learning. They were asked to list positives, negatives, and suggestions for improvement. Students came up with many positives in common, but only two negatives. First, most students could not decipher the comments scrawled all over the papers returned to them. Second, many felt that the two-page limit was too limiting, since they had three reconstructions to comment on.

The anthropology professor, who spent hours each week writing comments on the papers, was shocked to find out that students couldn't read them. One student suggested that he type his comments directly into a portable computer as he read the papers. The professor decided to try it. In response to the second negative, the instructor decided to cut back the number of reconstructions presented to two, rather than increase the amount of writing he would have to read.

STEP-BY-STEP PROCEDURE

1. Choose an assignment to assess, preferably one that is repeated or ongoing.

2. Write two or three questions that will assess the value of the assignment to students' learning.

3. Make up a simple Assignment Assessment form — especially if you want students to do the assessment outside of class — or write the questions on an overhead transparency or on the chalkboard to be copied.

TURNING THE DATA YOU COLLECT INTO USEFUL INFORMATION

Since most instructors who use Assignment Assessments ask open-ended questions, they must read through the responses first and then sort them into categories. In addition to quantifying the feedback, pick out a few exemplary comments to share with the class when you summarize the data.

IDEAS FOR ADAPTING AND EXTENDING THIS CAT

Allow ten minutes or so of class time and have students do the Assignment Assessment in small groups. Ask each group to come up with composite answers to the assessment questions.

Have students assess assignments for their relevance to the jobs or careers they are preparing for.

PROS

Knowing that they will have an opportunity to assess assignments gives some students more motivation to actually do the assignments.

Students are in the best position to assess how much assignments contribute to their learning. This CAT recognizes and takes advantage of their perspective.

This kind of feedback, over time, can help faculty significantly improve their assignments and courses.

CONS

As they may with other assessment techniques in this cluster, some students may respond to the Assignment Assessments in ways designed to convince faculty to lower the work load.

You may receive useful feedback too late to benefit the students who provided it.

CAVEATS

To avoid raising student expectations and causing disappointment and frustration, don't ask students to assess assignments that you are unwilling to consider changing.

Use the assessment questions to focus the students' attention on whether and how much they learned from the assignments, not on how much they enjoy the assignments or how difficult they are.

50

Exam Evaluations

Estimated Levels of Time and Energy Required for:

Faculty to prepare to use this CAT	**LOW**
Students to respond to the assessment	**LOW to MEDIUM**
Faculty to analyze the data collected	**MEDIUM**

DESCRIPTION   Students view tests and examinations as critical indicators of faculty expectations; as a result, faculty can use tests and exams to direct student learning.
All too often, however, the learning function of testing is overlooked. This
simple technique allows teachers to examine both what students think they
are learning from exams and tests and students' evaluations of the fairness,
appropriateness, usefulness, and quality of tests or exams.

PURPOSE   The overriding purpose of Exam Evaluations is to provide teachers with
specific student reactions to tests and exams, so that they can make the exams
more effective as learning and assessment devices.

RELATED TEACHING   Develop appropriate study skills, strategies, and habits (TGI Goal 16)
GOALS   Learn to evaluate methods and materials in this subject (TGI Goal 24)
Cultivate an active commitment to honesty (TGI Goal 50)
Develop capacity to think for oneself (TGI Goal 51)

SUGGESTIONS FOR USE   Exam Evaluations can be profitably used to get feedback on any substantial
quiz, test, or exam. To ensure that the memory of the test is still fresh in
students' minds, you may want to include the Exam Evaluation within the
exam itself, as the final section; or you might hand out the Exam Evaluation
form soon after the students have completed the exam.

EXAMPLES

From Development in Early Childhood (Child Development)

For this instructor in early childhood development, the writing, giving,
and grading of tests was one of the most difficult and time-consuming
parts of teaching. Nonetheless, she was convinced that weekly mini-
tests were the most appropriate evaluations for her course and stu-

dents. She did wonder, however, whether it would make any difference to student learning and satisfaction if she switched from short-answer, fill-in tests to multiple-choice tests. If not, then she planned to switch to multiple-choice tests because they would be quicker and easier for her to score.

She decided to experiment with the two testing formats. She created two weekly tests and then translated the content of both into the two formats. She divided the class in half, giving one half the multiple-choice test and the other the short-answer test. The following week, she reversed the groups. After the second week's test, she handed out a short Exam Evaluation sheet (see Exhibit 9.4).

Exhibit 9.4. Sample Exam Evaluation Form.

In the past two weeks, you have taken two different types of weekly tests—one multiple-choice and one fill-in, short-answer type. Please answer the following questions about those tests as specifically as possible.

1. Did you feel that one type of test was a fairer assessment of your learning than the other? If so, please explain.

2. Did you enjoy doing one test more than the other? If so, why? (N.B.: I particularly want to know whether it was the content or the form that you enjoyed.)

3. Did you learn more from one type of test than from the other? If so, what is it about the test that accounts for that?

4. Which type of test would you prefer as your weekly test during the rest of the semester? Why?

STEP-BY-STEP PROCEDURE

1. Focus on a type of test or exam that you are likely to give more than once during the course. Write down one or two questions you would like to ask your students that may help you improve the test.

2. Choose the most important questions, no more than four or five, and decide whether to add them to the test or exam itself or to make up a separate, follow-up evaluation.

3. Whether you incorporate the Exam Evaluation into the test or use it as a follow-up, make sure to build in the extra time that students will need to respond to the assessment questions.

TURNING THE DATA YOU COLLECT INTO USEFUL INFORMATION

The central focus of the analysis ought to be on finding out what the students are or are not learning from the test—a task that requires careful attention to the content of student comments. Try to distinguish comments that address the fairness of your grading from those that address the fairness of the instrument as a learning assessment. If you have asked students to express their preferences, tabulate those results but link them to the reasons that students give for those preferences. Some reasons are more serious and relevant than others.

IDEAS FOR ADAPTING AND EXTENDING THIS CAT	Ask students to submit questions that they would have included in the test or exam.
	Provide class time for students to compare and discuss their answers in groups. Ask each group to come up with two or three suggestions for improving the test as a learning experience.
PROS	Exam Evaluations focus on exams and tests as learning exercises.
	The technique shows respect for students' judgments of their own learning and recognizes their investment in the process.
	It gives teachers feedback on an element of the course that fundamentally affects student learning and satisfaction.
CONS	Students may raise questions about tests and exams and grading that teachers may not want to address.
CAVEATS	At first, students may find it difficult to determine or express what they have learned from a test. You will probably get better answers if you ask quite specific questions about learning.
	Don't ask questions about elements of the exam that you are not willing to consider changing. If you do ask such questions, you are likely to raise students' expectations and cause disappointment.
	Before you use this technique, consider how you might respond to students' objections to the tests — not only how you can defend the tests but also how you might change them.
	While you may wish to evaluate a test that will not be given again to the same students — a final exam, for example — the results will not benefit the present students, and thus their motivation to respond may be lower.
REFERENCES AND RESOURCES	For a more complete discussion of the use of exams to promote learning, see the article by McMullen-Pastrick and Gleason (1986).

PART

THREE

Building on
What We
Have Learned

Lessons and Insights from Six Years of Use

In the course of almost six years of work with Classroom Research, we have learned a great deal about classrooms, college teachers, and teaching and learning. That learning has come from three sources: our own research on the Teaching Goals Inventory (TGI); reports by faculty on their experiences with Classroom Assessment and Classroom Research; and our surveys and observations of groups of college teachers participating in the Classroom Research Project. The purpose of this chapter is to pull together insights gained and lessons learned from these three sources, synthesizing and consolidating them to lay the groundwork for Chapter Eleven, which takes a fresh look at future directions for Classroom Research.

LESSONS LEARNED FROM OUR OWN RESEARCH ON THE TGI

We gained many important insights from analyzing the responses of thousands of college faculty to the Teaching Goals Inventory (TGI). In fact, we made our first important discovery just as we were beginning to construct the TGI six years ago. In reviewing the literature, we found that researchers rarely asked college faculty about their teaching. Over the years, college teachers have been asked almost every conceivable question on surveys except what they are trying to accomplish in their classrooms. So we decided to ask just that via the Teaching Goals Inventory, a questionnaire consisting of fifty-two teaching goals and related questions. In responding to the TGI, faculty are asked to select one course they are currently teaching, and to rate each goal's importance for that particular course.

The results reported here are from an administration of the TGI in the spring of 1990. The respondents were more than 2,800 faculty members from fifteen community colleges and seventeen private four-year colleges spread widely across the United States (see Chapter Two for details of the administration.) Our sample is frankly biased in the direction of faculty who consider teaching their first priority. All the colleges in our sample are, first and foremost, teaching institutions. One mission these thirty-two diverse colleges have in common is the education of undergraduates.

In analyzing the TGI responses from 2,824 college teachers, we found a high degree of consensus on the teaching goals considered most essential. Faculty at both community colleges and four-year colleges listed the following four goals among their top five: to develop the ability to apply principles and generalizations already learned to new problems and situations, to develop the capacity to think for oneself, to develop analytic skills, and to learn the terms and facts of the subject matter. Those four goals express widely accepted functions of higher education, endorsed by educators as well as by the general public.

A second finding came to light when we grouped all fifty-two goals from the TGI into six statistically derived clusters. We found that the two clusters rated highest were those containing goals that emphasize higher-order thinking skills and discipline-specific knowledge. There is nothing particularly surprising in that. Walk into any undergraduate psychology class in any college, for instance, and you will probably find an instructor teaching students something about psychology as a field of study and, at the same time, helping them strengthen higher-order thinking skills such as analysis and synthesis.

Colleagues in higher education and nonacademics alike should take comfort in these findings, since they confirm the assumption that most college teachers agree on the importance of helping students master a body of knowledge and develop the ability to think clearly. But that about wraps up what we found predictable. The rest of the findings are not ones we would have predicted—at least not to the extent they occurred.

One important finding, which emerged without equivocation from all of our work with the TGI, is that faculty teaching priorities are related more to academic discipline than to any other factor. Teachers of a given discipline—whether male or female, full-time or part-time, experienced or inexperienced, teaching in a public community college or a private four-year college—share a value system with respect to teaching goals that is distinctively discipline-related and significantly different from that of colleagues in other disciplines. Furthermore, the greater the difference between the subjects taught, the greater the difference in teaching priorities. That is, the priorities of college math teachers differ more from those of English faculty than from those of science instructors.

While we did find some *statistically* significant differences on other variables, differences attributable to gender, age, or other demographic variables do not appear to be *educationally* significant. For example, the differences noted between men's and women's teaching goals are probably attributable more to the teacher's choice of discipline—which is gender-related—than to personal values. Thus, our tentative conclusion is that math instructors, for example, are likely to share a common set of teaching priorities more because they teach math than because they are predominantly men.

Disciplinary differences are also clearly revealed in responses to a question we asked at the end of the TGI. The question was "In general, how do you see your primary role as a teacher?" The results are shown in Table 10.1. The first column includes the total sample, comprised of teachers from all disciplines in community and four-year colleges. And, in the

Table 10.1. Primary Teaching Role as Perceived by College Teachers, by Discipline.

Primary Teaching Role	Percent Rating Goal "Essential"									
	All	Hum.	Eng.	Basic Skills	Soc. Sci.	Bus.	Med.	Sci.	Math	Arts
Higher-order thinking skills	28	32	47	13	44	26	17	28	35	20
Facts and principles	28	31	17	8	35	28	18	55	44	24
Jobs/careers	17	2	3	7	4	32	44	10	2	11
Student development	17	24	19	20	14	12	12	3	7	37
Basic learning skills	7	6	15	51	2	1	1	3	9	3
Role model	3	5	2	2	3	1	8	2	3	5

aggregate results, we once again see a familiar pattern. The two winning role preferences are "Developing higher-order thinking skills" and "Teaching the facts and principles of the subject matter." However, each of these familiar roles got only 28 percent of the total votes. "Preparing students for jobs/careers" and "Fostering student development and personal growth" are not far behind, with each endorsed as the primary role by 17 percent of all faculty respondents. The two remaining roles, "Helping students develop basic learning skills" and "Providing a role model for students," trailed far behind, splitting the remaining 10 percent of the votes between them.

The patterns of faculty role preferences that emerge when we consider the primary teaching role most frequently chosen by faculty in each disciplinary grouping are of considerable interest. Reading across the top row of Table 10.1, we see that 32 percent of the humanities faculty, 47 percent of the English teachers, and 44 percent of the social science instructors regarded their primary role as the development of higher-order thinking skills. Math and science faculty are more concerned with teaching the facts and principles of their disciplines (44 and 55 percent, respectively). Faculty in the two preprofessional fields of business and medicine (mostly nursing and allied health at the undergraduate level) are most interested in preparing students for jobs and careers (32 and 44 percent of these faculty). Teachers of the arts (37 percent) were most likely to view their primary role as "Fostering student development and personal growth," perhaps because personal expression lies at the heart of the fine and performing arts. And while "Helping students develop basic learning skills," the most specific of all the faculty roles, attracted 51 percent of the basic skills instructors, only 7 percent of the faculty overall considered it primary. Finally, perhaps because college teachers are modest about their potential influence on undergraduates, only 3 percent of the respondents chose "Providing a role model for students" as their primary role. Despite all the talk about the importance of women and minorities serving as role models for students, we found no evidence that minority and women faculty were significantly more likely than white males to perceive themselves as role models.

Table 10.2 offers another way of looking at disciplinary differences. In this table, the three TGI goals rated highest by each disciplinary group are shown. Goal 1, for example, "Develop ability to apply principles and generalizations already learned to new problems and situations," was rated "essential" by a majority of all teachers in the basic skills, social sciences, business, medicine, and science. Of special interest in these data is the difference between the orientations of faculty in qualitative and quantitative disciplines. The set of high "essential" ratings given to Goal 1 comes primarily from faculty in the sciences and preprofessional fields, while the humanities group shows its highest values in the row of figures for Goal 51, "Develop capacity to think for oneself." Notice that social science and basic skills teachers identify with both the quantitative and the qualitative groups. These "split loyalties" can probably be explained, on the one hand, by the fact that groups of basic skills faculty include math teachers as well as English teachers and, on the other hand, by differences among social scientists, whose orientations range from heavily quantitative to predominantly qualitative.

Not shown in Table 10.2, but of particular significance in view of today's emphasis on the development of writing skills, is the surprisingly low endorsement of Goal 15, "Improve writing skills," by faculty outside the field of English. Despite two decades of discussion about "writing across the curriculum," most English teachers—and, it turns out, most faculty in other disciplines—apparently still regard the improvement of writing as the responsibility of English departments. Even in the humanities, social sciences, and business—fields with ample opportunity for writing—the improvement of student writing skills was considered "essential" by only 27, 21, and 14 percent of respondents, respectively. Similarly, math teachers accept the lion's share of the responsibility for improving mathematical skills (Goal 17), with 84 percent rating this goal as "essential." And, like their English counterparts, mathematics instructors don't get much support. Only 17 percent of their colleagues in the sciences rate the improvement of mathematical skills as "essential" to their teaching.

Table 10.2. Three Top-Priority Teaching Goals, by Discipline.

TGI Goal No.	Teaching Goal	Percent Rating Goal "Essential"								
		Arts	Hum.	Eng.	Basic Skills	Soc. Sci.	Bus.	Med.	Sci.	Math
1	Apply principles				59	57	69	73	61	
17	Math skills									84
18	Terms and facts						61		60	
52	Wise decisions							70		
2	Analytic skills			66						73
45	Self-esteem				63					
51	Think for self	66	59	75	65	50				
44	Responsible for self							68		
21	Value of subject		56			52				
19	Concepts and theories								71	
7	Creativity	69								
15	Writing skills			84						
31	Aesthetic appreciation	78								
27	Openness to ideas		56							
3	Problem solving						57			84

Table 10.3. The Clusters of the TGI.

Mean Cluster Ratings (M) and Percent (%) "Essential" Ratings

	TGI Cluster	Four-Year Colleges		Community Colleges	
		M	%	M	%
I	Higher-order thinking	3.05	43	3.09	45
III	Discipline-specific	2.86	37	2.83	36
VI	Personal development	2.28	25	2.41	28
V	Work and career	2.27	21	2.50	26
IV	Liberal arts	2.16	21	2.02	18
II	Basic skills	2.12	18	2.29	22

Therefore, one of our most compelling findings is that *what* you teach has a good deal to do with how you teach—or at least with what your teaching priorities are and how you perceive your primary role as a teacher. *What* you teach is also a better predictor of your teaching goals and role than *where* you teach.

We expected more and greater differences than we found between the teaching goals of instructors in public, open-admissions community colleges and those of faculty teaching in private, four-year liberal arts colleges. The missions of these two types of colleges appear quite distinctive, and certainly the student bodies are different—although the private four-year colleges in our sample are only moderately selective. Table 10.3 shows very little difference in the teaching goals of faculty in these two types of institutions. Table 10.3 presents the mean cluster scores—that is, the average rating given to the eight to ten items in each cluster—for the six empirically derived TGI clusters. It also shows the percentage of teachers in each type of college rating the items in the cluster "essential" to their teaching, averaged across all items in the cluster.

The small differences that do exist are in predictable directions and are probably attributable more to the nature of the curriculum than to the preferences of individuals. In other words, because the community college curriculum has more vocational and basic skills courses, we find more community college faculty expressing priorities that are characteristic of those fields. Similarly, because four-year colleges offer more courses in the humanities, we find more four-year faculty expressing the priorities of the liberal arts. The slightly higher endorsement of personal development goals by community college teachers is moderately surprising, given the greater emphasis on the arts in the curriculum of small liberal arts colleges and their traditional interest in student development. Community college teachers, however, frequently emphasize the personal attention given to students, and they work with a student population that is often perceived as short on self-confidence. These concerns may be showing through in their priorities.

We found a great range of individual teaching priorities. We had expected more agreement among teachers on the highest- and lowest-priority goals, but every single one of the fifty-two items on the TGI received the full range of responses. In other words, goals that some teachers found "essential" to their teaching were deemed "not applicable" or "unimportant" by others. In the abstract, it is hard to imagine a college teacher saying, for example, that developing "the capacity to think for oneself" is unimportant. Yet, in our data, 9 college mathematics teachers were not concerned with accomplishing that particular goal (130 of their colleagues in mathematics, however, considered it essential). At the same time, not one of the math teachers rated the "development of problem-solving skills" unimportant. However, 53 of their colleagues in the humanities did consider problem-solving skills "not applicable" or "unimportant" in the particular classes they chose to describe for the TGI.

LESSONS LEARNED FROM REPORTS BY FACULTY PARTICIPANTS

The self-scorable version of the Teaching Goals Inventory has proved useful to faculty interested in identifying and clarifying what they are trying to achieve. Once teaching goals are clear, though, the most important task in Classroom Assessment lies in developing individualized, context-specific Classroom Assessment Techniques that will provide teachers with good information on how well they are achieving those goals.

From the reports of teachers who have been adapting and applying Classroom Assessment, we were able to draw conclusions about their various approaches. In addition, we gained information about the effects of Classroom Assessment on students.

Observations About Teachers' Use of Classroom Assessment

One of the most valuable lessons we learned from working with faculty on Classroom Research is just how resourceful and innovative they are at devising assessment techniques to gather useful information about the impact of their teaching on student learning. We also learned that there are differences in what teachers do with the feedback from Classroom Assessments.

Faculty Adapt Classroom Assessment Techniques in Creative Ways. To no one's surprise, the simpler Classroom Assessment Techniques (CATs) have been used far more than those that are more complex. The Minute Paper (CAT 6), for example, is easy to explain, easy to use, and flexible enough to fit any class, any time. Perhaps because of its widespread use, the Minute Paper has been modified through experience more often than any other Classroom Assessment Technique. In the next few paragraphs, we focus on several modifications of the Minute Paper as examples of the creative ways in which teachers adapt CATs to fit their diverse goals, needs, students, and circumstances.

One influential modification of the Minute Paper was developed by Frederick Mosteller (1989), the distinguished Harvard professor of statistics. Professor Mosteller typically writes the key points of his lectures on the chalkboard at the beginning of each class session. When, at the end of the class, he would ask students to write the most important thing they had learned, they often simply repeated those same key points. Moreover, their answers to the second Minute Paper prompt—"What question remains uppermost in your mind?"—were often no more than simple requests for amplifications of the key points. As a result of his experience with the "off-the-shelf" Minute Paper, Mosteller decided to ask just one question: "What was the muddiest point in the lecture?" Although it seems, at first blush, a simple abbreviation of a Classroom Assessment Technique, Mosteller's "Muddiest Point" is actually an excellent example of a discipline-based modification. If the lesson of the day in a statistics class, for instance, is on multiple regression, most students are probably going to say that the most important thing they learned was something about the techniques or uses of multiple regression. To an experienced statistics teacher, the additional questions that students will have are probably equally predictable. Thus, as Mosteller discovered, he was not gaining much information from the use of the conventionally worded Minute paper. What he really wanted to know was what students did not understand about multiple regression. So he modified the Minute Paper to ask students what they found unclear or "muddy" in his lectures.

In contrast, in a course on the American novel, the teaching goal is not so much mastery of the subject matter as it is interpretation and appreciation of that subject matter. The important feedback sought by teachers of literature is not usually what students fail to understand—which would, in the case of a novel, be difficult for students to articulate—but, rather, what meaning or significance the students find in the text. As a result, teachers of literature have adapted the Minute Paper to ask questions such as "What was the most meaningful insight you gained from this novel?" and "What important question did the novel make you ask of yourself?"

A different kind of discipline-based adaptation of the Minute Paper is presented by Melissa Kort (1991), a teacher of writing at Santa Rosa Junior College. Since teachers of writing normally do get frequent written feedback from students, they can monitor progress more effectively than most of us in other disciplines. For Kort, therefore, the question was not so much what students were learning as which class activities they found most helpful. As a result, her adaptation of the Minute Paper consisted of asking students to comment on the value of various kinds of writing exercises. In her own words, she learned from their responses that her personal "preference for open-ended techniques like freewriting and clustering contradicted the students' need for more structured approaches" (p. 37).

The main lesson we learned from these and many other reports is that teachers need to develop assessment techniques that provide feedback appropriate to their academic disciplines, their individual teaching goals, and their students. Consequently, all the CATs presented in this handbook are starting points, ideas meant to stimulate faculty to design their own assessment techniques. The lessons we learned about the need to fit assessment techniques to specific classes is summed up in a maxim we use in Classroom Research workshops: "Adapt; don't adopt."

Classroom Assessment Feedback Challenges Teachers' Assumptions. Another lesson we learned from faculty is that student responses to Classroom Assessment Techniques frequently surprise them, often challenging their unexamined assumptions. Sometimes faculty are pleasantly surprised because feedback shows that things are actually better than they thought. At other times, however, teachers find out that things have not gone as well as they had assumed. And, once in a while, Classroom Researchers discover that the assumptions on which they base their syllabi are simply not valid. In our own teaching, Classroom Assessments have surprised us as well. Sometimes the surprises are dismaying; but at other times, the unexpected feedback is heartening. As the teachers' reports make clear, the feedback that directly challenges faculty assumptions often turns out to be the most valuable information for improving teaching and learning.

Teachers Respond to Feedback in Various Ways. Nearly all successful Classroom Researchers share the results of their assessments with students, but they do so in many different ways. Some teachers reserve a few minutes at the beginning of class to summarize the results of the most recent Classroom Assessment exercise. Others write brief summaries of the results on the chalkboard or on overhead transparencies. Still other teachers prepare handouts on results. However they respond, the point is that faculty do let students know what they learned from the feedback and what they and the students need to do next, in order to improve learning.

Most faculty also say that they change—some dramatically, others slightly—what they do as teachers. Mosteller, for example, prepared handouts or scheduled class time to revisit topics in statistics that many students identified as "muddy points." As a result of the feedback she received, Kort gave more structure to her writing assignments. Other faculty have incorporated new instructional methods, such as cooperative learning and computer-assisted instruction, into their courses as a result of lessons learned from Classroom Assessment. In these and many other ways, faculty capitalize on data gathered with even the simplest CATs to stimulate and guide them as they adjust their teaching to improve learning.

Effects of Classroom Assessment on Students

Even as it prompts faculty to rethink and redesign their teaching, feedback from Classroom Assessments normally changes more than just teachers' behavior. When students respond to Classroom Assessment Techniques and receive feedback on their responses, their attitudes and behaviors also change. Faculty often report the following four observable, interrelated, positive effects of Classroom Assessment on their students: more active involvement and participation; greater interest in learning, self-awareness as learners, and metacognitive skill; higher levels of cooperation within the classroom "learning community"; and greater student satisfaction.

Classroom Assessment Increases Active Involvement in Learning. Virtually all the teachers we have worked with report that using Classroom Assessment increases student participation and involvement in the classroom, especially among students who previously avoided asking questions and taking part in discussions. For example, discussing a Classroom Assessment Project carried out with advanced calculus students, Ronald Shelton (1991, p. 62) writes: "Some students who hesitate to speak up in class will write good thought-provoking questions and comments." This participation is critical because, as education research consistently demonstrates, active student "involvement in learning" is fundamental to learning success (Study Group on the

Conditions of Excellence in American Higher Education, 1984; Gamson and Chickering, 1987).

Many faculty also remark on positive "spillover" effects of Classroom Assessment, such as increased use of office hours. John Olmsted's comments on changes in office-hour use by students in his large, introductory chemistry class are typical: "Before [I introduced] Classroom Research techniques, no more than 10 percent of lower-division students took advantage of my office hours, despite repeated exhortations. . . . During the first half of the semester [in which he began using CATs and kept a log of office-hour visits], over 50 percent of the students enrolled in the course had made at least one office-hour visit, a fivefold increase" (Olmsted, 1991, p. 63). This is also a promising finding because student-faculty interaction is, in general, positively related to learning.

Classroom Assessment Promotes Metacognitive Development. A second change that most Classroom Researchers have observed is that when they inform their classes about the results of Classroom Assessment, students become more actively interested in the process of learning itself. Kort (1991, p. 40) found that sharing results with her writing students "helped establish learning as an important topic for discussion." David Nakaji, a physics teacher, reported that one of the major outcomes of his involvement in Classroom Research for his students is an "increased awareness and appreciation of themselves as learners and individuals" (Nakaji, 1991, p. 86). Philip Cottell, an accounting instructor, also found that Classroom Assessment improved metacognition among his students:

> First, as students get used to the idea that they must express things about which they are unclear, they focus more on their own learning processes. I find evidence of focusing on learning in the fact that the quality of questions I receive [on Minute Papers] improves as the semester progresses. That is, the later questions pertain more to accounting techniques or important concepts and less to "right answers" than the earlier questions did. Thus, students, through self-assessment of learning in progress, appear to gain maturity in their learning of accounting [Cottell, 1991, p. 51].

The three Classroom Researchers quoted above are describing the development of metacognition, defined as the learner's awareness, understanding, and control of his or her own learning process. As faculty use Classroom Assessment, they typically promote metacognition in three ways: by explicitly teaching students to use CATs that require self-assessment, by providing guided practice in using those CATs, and by giving feedback on and encouraging discussion of student responses. Once again, as with active involvement and faculty-student interaction, there is strong evidence from education research that explicit instruction in metacognitive skills and strategies is related to more and better learning — especially when students learn a variety of discipline-specific skills and strategies.

Classroom Assessment Increases Cooperation and a Sense of the Classroom as a "Learning Community." Faculty often report that Classroom Assessment is helpful in "lowering barriers" and in raising levels of trust and comfort in the classroom. Charles Walker, a psychology professor, found that Classroom Assessment helped his students realize that both he and they were after the same basic goal, successful learning: "Instead of engaging in confrontation, students and I found ourselves cooperating, trying to identify the most troublesome topics and exploring ways to understand *and* teach that which had not yet been learned or taught" (Walker, 1991, p. 77; emphasis in original). In a similar vein, Nakaji (1991, p. 86) notes that "the intense nature of the assessments, the increased personal contact, and the overall tone and philosophy of Classroom Research as a tool to benefit students [have] strengthened and improved the bond between students and myself." And Cottell (1991, p. 51) believes that Classroom Assessment improves student-teacher cooperation because "the level of trust in the class increases as students express their questions and doubts without suffering any negative repercussions."

As students listen to their instructor's responses to Classroom Assessments, they learn about themselves and their classmates. As faculty summarize data collected with simple Classroom Assessment Techniques, they give a voice to ideas and viewpoints of learners who are otherwise silent in the classroom. These students are often reassured to find that their peers have similar questions, confusions, or opinions. At other times, they are taken aback by feedback that highlights the diversity of learning styles and viewpoints within a class. Kort (1991, p. 40) expresses the experience of many Classroom Researchers: "What students begin to learn through Classroom Assessment about themselves in relation to their classmates also improves their collaboration and cooperation in class." And, in reviewing student responses from a multicampus program that combines elements of Classroom Assessment, cooperative learning, and multicultural education, Susan Obler and her colleagues report: "They [students] describe benefits they gain from getting feedback from a variety of people from cultures other than their own" (Obler, Arnold, Sigala, and Umbdenstock, 1991, p. 114).

When faculty demonstrate their commitment to assessment and self-assessment on the day-to-day level, they send a powerful signal to students about the importance of listening carefully to the ideas and opinions of others. And, as teachers provide their classes with feedback on responses to these assessments, they confront learners with perhaps the most startling dimension of human diversity — individual intellectual diversity — and model positive ways of dealing with differences. By creating an environment in which asking questions and voicing confusions are not only safe but valued — and by explicitly focusing students' attention on the shared task of improving learning — faculty can use Classroom Assessment to help create meaningful communities of learners in their classrooms.

Classroom Assessment Increases Student Satisfaction. Most teachers who use this approach receive formal student feedback about Classroom Assessment on student evaluations and informal feedback when their students volunteer comments during the term. Many teachers use Classroom Assessment Techniques to discover their students' opinions about Classroom Assessment. From almost all reports, the news is positive. Most students appreciate and enjoy assessing learning and getting feedback. Students see the use of Classroom Assessment as evidence that faculty are aware of their learning levels and progress and care about their opinions and ideas. Many students also comment that these techniques give them practical ways to find out about their progress or lack of it early enough for them to make any necessary changes.

Students whose instructors use Classroom Assessment tend to believe they are learning more and are convinced that their teachers are sincerely committed to improving learning. Therefore, it should come as no surprise that faculty often experience improvements in their student evaluation ratings when they begin to use this approach. For example, three professors in three very different fields — Cottell (1991, p. 53), Olmsted (1991, p. 62), and Walker (1991, p. 75–76) — all document improvements in their student evaluations as a result of Classroom Assessment.

Classroom Assessment May Improve Course Completion Rates. Student retention and course completion rates are important indicators of success in higher education, particularly for community colleges. Although many external factors can influence student decisions to stay in or drop out of a given course, what teachers do in the classroom can also make a difference. In a major study focused on student retention, the American College Testing (ACT) Program and the National Center for Higher Education Management Systems (NCHEMS) found that the two campus characteristics most powerfully related to high retention were a caring attitude by faculty and staff and high-quality teaching (Beal and Noel, 1980). More recently, Vincent Tinto, a noted researcher in this field, asserted that "the secret of effective retention lies in the development of effective educational communities which actively involve students in the learning process" (Tinto, 1990, as cited in Kelly, 1991, p. 7).

Given the positive relationship among active involvement in learning, a caring faculty, and higher student retention, we expected to see higher retention in courses taught by Classroom Researchers. Indeed, many faculty who use Classroom Assessment report improved attendance and higher course completion rates as collateral benefits. Although we have no reason to doubt these individual reports, the evidence from two carefully done assessments of campus programs is equivocal. In the first study — carried out with faculty at the College of Marin in Kentfield, California — Nancy Stetson compared overall class grades and retention rates in "Classroom Research courses with [those in] other courses taught by the same instructor in which this approach was not used, with the same courses taught during the same semester the year before, at the same time of day, and the like" (Stetson, 1991, p. 123–124). She failed to find statistically significant differences, overall, between the paired-comparison groups. In the second study, however, Diana Kelly did find statistically significant improvements in course completion rates, though not in grades. Using a similar paired-comparison research design, Kelly studied the effects of Classroom Research on the retention of adult learners in courses taught by part-time faculty at Fullerton College, a community college in Fullerton, California. "From Spring 1990 to Fall 1990, the completion rate of the Classroom Research Group classes went up by 3.6%, while the college evening class completion rate went up

.3% and the overall college completion rate went up .8%" (Kelly, 1991, p. 131).

How can we account for this difference in results? First, faculty in the Marin study were primarily full-time tenured instructors teaching the usual mixture of community college students in daytime classes. Faculty in the Fullerton study were part-time, nontenured instructors teaching mostly part-time, adult students. As Kelly suggests, at least part of the difference in findings may be explained by the fact that "Classroom Assessment is particularly powerful with adult learners who are underprepared for college-level work" (p. 13). Faculty characteristics also may contribute to the difference in results. Most of the faculty in the College of Marin study were experienced instructors, highly rated by their students and quick to become involved in innovative programs to improve teaching and learning. These instructors already may have been doing nearly all that could be done to encourage retention before they began using Classroom Assessment. Our as yet untested hypothesis is that less experienced faculty may realize more dramatic results—more improvement in retention rates at least—than their seasoned colleagues do.

Further comparative research will be required to "break the tie," as well as to determine whether Classroom Assessment benefits less experienced students and faculty more than their better-prepared counterparts. It is consistent with many findings in education research, however, to suggest that those students and faculty who have the most to gain are likely to gain the most from Classroom Research.

But Does Classroom Assessment Increase Student Learning? The jury is still out on this question. Most faculty who regularly use Classroom Assessment do so because they are convinced that it improves student learning. These teachers can explain why they believe students are learning better, and they usually have several anecdotes to share in support of their convictions. Some Classroom Researchers, using test scores and grades as indicators, have indeed found evidence of increased student learning in classes where they have used Classroom Assessment (Walker, 1991, pp. 74–75; Shelton, 1991, p. 51). But other Classroom Researchers have failed to document learning improvement with such indicators (Olmsted, 1991, p. 64; Stetson, 1991, pp. 123–124; Kelly, 1991, p. 11).

How can we account for the gap between faculty and student perceptions of improved learning and the equivocal evidence? After years of working with faculty, we can suggest several possible reasons for this disparity. One possibility, of course, is that Classroom Assessment really does not improve student learning. It may be that faculty, impressed by the sudden wealth of detailed feedback they receive from Classroom Assessment, are simply getting a clearer look at what was going on unseen all along. A crude analogy would be to biologists imagining that the number of microscopic life forms has drastically increased because of the invention of the microscope. The idea that Classroom Assessment simply reveals what already exists is a possible explanation, but not, we think, the most likely one.

There are three other possible explanations for the disparity between convictions and quantifiable evidence. First, students may be learning more, but grades may not be sensitive to that improvement. Average class grades are problematic indicators of improved learning. We have found that faculty tend to "curve" class grades, consciously or unconsciously, keeping them within a fairly narrow range and damping semester-to-semester variation. Some departments also have implicit or explicit grading policies that limit the percentage of students who can receive A's or F's, or that suggest acceptable average grades for classes; therefore, even if some overall learning improvement occurs, it is likely to be "washed out" in the calculation of test scores and final grades. Second, students may actually be learning more, but not more of what they are being tested on. Many faculty use Classroom Assessment Techniques to assess and promote teaching goals related to higher-order thinking skills, personal development, or attitudes and values. But those same teachers often continue to test and grade students in relation to other goals—usually content mastery. This mismatch between assessment and testing can occur because faculty do not feel confident testing other kinds of learning, or do not believe that such testing is appropriate. Third, Classroom Assessment may not help students learn more of the material, but it may help them learn it better. Students' understanding and long-term retention could well be improving without having any necessary effect on their performance on tests requiring immediate recall of facts and principles. In our experience, classroom tests rarely focus on long-term recall or depth of understanding.

Determining whether the use of Classroom Asssessment really improves student learning will require carefully planned and well-controlled experiments or quasi-experiments. To date, we know of no one who has had the resources or time to carry out this type of confirmatory research, but we hope that someone soon will. Our prediction is that the results of such research, like the results of most social science research, will not be clear-cut. Rather, the researchers are likely to find that Classroom Assessment does help students improve their learning in some cases and does not in others, the difference depending largely on what they and their teachers do in response to the feedback.

In summary, many faculty have reported anecdotal evidence that their use of Classroom Assessment has improved student learning. Some teachers have gone a step further, documenting their assertions with evidence in the form of higher grades and scores. But other teachers, equally dedicated to the use of Classroom Assessment, have found no such differences in their students' performance. Therefore, there is not enough evidence at this point to prove conclusively that the use of Classroom Assessment will improve student learning or grades. At the same time, we have not seen or heard any evidence to suggest that Classroom Assessment causes students to learn less, score lower on tests, or get poorer grades. The same can be said about the effects of Classroom Assessment on student course completion rates.

This "no bad news" news is more significant than it may seem at first glance. When faculty introduce Classroom Assessment into their classes, they are spending some class time on new activities. However limited, this is time that they and the students previously spent in other ways. As a result, faculty may be cutting lectures a bit short, or working through fewer problems on the board, in order to free a few minutes up to use a CAT. There has been no evidence to date, however, that taking time for Classroom Assessment has diminished student learning of the content that is taught. Nor have faculty who practice this approach noted higher dropout rates or increased absenteeism.

We believe that using Classroom Assessment provides many benefits to learners and no significant risks to their learning of content. As we noted above, there is agreement among practitioners—and evidence from surveys of faculty and students—that using this approach increases participation and involvement, promotes metacognitive development, improves classroom cooperation, and enhances satisfaction. In other words, Classroom Assessment, when used well, appears to do much good and no harm.

FACULTY VIEWS ON COSTS AND BENEFITS OF CLASSROOM ASSESSMENT

After two years of working closely with groups of faculty on several college campuses, we surveyed experienced participants in the Classroom Research Project to explore their views on the costs and benefits to teachers of using Classroom Assessment. The three most frequently mentioned "costs" were, respectively, time required, sacrifice of some content coverage, and frustration when closure is not reached.

Classroom Assessment takes faculty time. No matter how simple the Classroom Assessment Technique used, some out-of-class faculty time is required to plan the assessment, analyze feedback, and prepare a response. It also takes time, when teachers are collaborating, to discuss Classroom Assessment experiences with colleagues. And it takes time in class to administer the CAT, collect feedback, and respond to student feedback. Time is the faculty's most precious resource, so any time required is a cost.

Many faculty also felt that they were able to "cover less content" as a result of using Classroom Assessment—primarily because the assessments had convinced them of the need to review, revisit, or reteach important material not learned well enough. Before using CATs, most faculty said, they would simply have gone on; but faced with feedback indicating inadequate learning, they chose to respond. Even when faculty felt sure that they had taught somewhat less but taught it better, they still regretted the loss of content "coverage."

The third cost is related to the fact that Classroom Assessments often raise more questions about student learning than they answer. Teachers sometimes commented that they could have spent a week pondering their students' responses to a single assessment question because the data were so rich. But time and the pressure to cover material kept them moving. Student responses are sometimes puzzling, or even opaque. One Classroom Assessment question has a tendency to lead to another. And a response that works well for one class may not work at all the following semester, even in the same course. Faculty noted this paucity of final answers, or lack of closure, as the third major cost of participating in Classroom Research.

By far the most frequently mentioned benefit of Classroom Assessment was collegiality, followed by positive student response and intellectual excitement. We were fascinated to observe that the benefits faculty ascribed to Classroom Assessment were, in many ways, mirror images of the costs. For example, although faculty often complained that meeting with their fellow Classroom Researchers cost them time, those same teachers overwhelmingly endorsed their interaction with colleagues as the most important benefit. The benefits of finding time to talk about their projects outweighed the costs, but the costs were still real. The second benefit, students' responses to the CATs and their active engagement in the process, often convinced faculty to trade off some breadth of coverage for more depth in learning. To complete the ironic parallelism, the flip side of the ultimately unfinishable and unpredictable nature of Classroom Assessment that sometimes frustrated faculty is the open-ended, dynamic quality that they valued as a source of intellectual excitement.

SUMMARY OF LESSONS LEARNED FROM FACULTY PARTICIPANTS

In addition to discovering what faculty see as the main costs and benefits of Classroom Assessment, we learned two important, related lessons from observing faculty during the Classroom Research Project. First and most important, we found that most teachers participating in organized Classroom Research programs were convinced that the benefits of Classroom Assessment outweighed the costs—even though they were quite aware of the costs. We also discovered that the teachers who were most satisfied and most likely to continue using Classroom Assessment shared four characteristics. First, they dedicated modest amounts of time to Classroom Assessment, both in and out of class. Second, they spent some of that time discussing their projects with other interested teachers. Third, when it became necessary to trade breadth for depth, they cut as little course content as possible and made sure that only peripheral material was sacrificed. Fourth, the most successful Classroom Researchers pursued assessment questions that, though challenging, were focused and limited enough to provide them with useful feedback.

Some of the original conceptualization of Classroom Research turns out, in hindsight, to have been right on target. The major premise of Classroom Research—that discipline-based faculty can become able, creative, and highly motivated Classroom Researchers—has proved itself beyond our wildest expectations. Faculty members teaching anthropology through zoology in colleges from Miami to Anchorage have taken Classroom Research into their classrooms and have developed imaginative and useful assessments of students' learning.

Originally, we proposed this model of Classroom Research because it seemed to combine the best features of professional development and teacher evaluation, both of which are central concerns of the assessment movement. Classroom Research is a promising approach to professional development because its emphasis on carefully observing students in the process of learning, combined with collecting data and reflecting on its implications for teaching, adds to faculty knowledge about teaching and learning in the specific disciplines. Indeed, given the enormous variety of disciplines, students, classrooms, and instructors that characterize U.S. higher education, we think it is imperative that faculty generate their own knowledge about the relationships between teaching and learning in their fields of study. We see Classroom Research, therefore, as one useful approach to the professionalization of college teaching.

With the growing emphasis on teacher evaluation, we also saw Classroom Research as a way for teachers to grab the teacher evaluation "bull by the horns" and conduct their own self-evaluations. Given the value that faculty place on academic freedom and individual autonomy, we suspect that self-evaluation has a better chance of improving teaching and learning than evaluation imposed from outside. We have seen our twin goals of developing Classroom Research and Classroom Assessment as modes of professional development and as approaches to faculty self-evaluation amply fulfilled.

Taking the Next Steps in Classroom Assessment and Research

When we first introduced the concept of Classroom Research, we had certain purposes and rationales clearly in mind. Our basic premise was that teachers could learn a great deal about how students learn by carefully and systematically observing the students in their classrooms in the act of learning. Although all of us have spent a considerable portion of our lives in classrooms, both as students and as teachers, most of us are not very astute observers of what goes on there. We teach pretty much as we were taught, despite occasional clear recollections that some forms of teaching that we now use did not work very well for us or our classmates when we were students. So our original purpose was to introduce the idea that classrooms can be used as laboratories to observe and study students in the process of learning, and then to modify teaching to make it more effective.

In our first practical venture into the world of Classroom Research, we devised certain tools that were flexible enough for use by any college teacher in any classroom and would provide useful feedback for both teachers and students about the progress of learning in that classroom. These tools were christened Classroom Assessment Techniques (CATs) and were a bit like recipes for lab experiments that could be tried in the classroom and evaluated for the quality of useful feedback they provided. Teachers could modify and adapt CATs to meet their particular tastes and needs, taking into account the amount of time they were willing to spend and the precision of information needed.

In part because Classroom Research was born at a time when sharp criticism of education, specifically of the quality of students' learning, was merging into constructive action in the form of the assessment movement, Classroom Research began with Classroom Assessment. Indeed, almost everything we have done in Classroom Research to date has really been Classroom Assessment. We have followed traditional assessment procedures to a "T." State your goals (that is, what you want to accomplish), devise appropriate measures to see whether you are accomplishing those goals, collect the data, feed back the results, modify the treatment, and reevaluate. This is the basic feedback loop of classical assessment.

Although Classroom Assessment is only part of Classroom Research, there are reasons why it has been the predominant element and why this handbook contains the most comprehensive set of Classroom Assessment Techniques we know how to provide. In the first place, if classrooms are to serve as laboratories for teachers' study of learning, the laboratories have to be equipped with good tools. Prior to the development of a wide variety of CATs, tools for Classroom Research were quite primitive. The major, and sometimes only, tools most faculty had for measuring learning were classroom tests—usually used for grading purposes at the end of a learning unit—and class participation, a notoriously unreliable measure of learning. Clearly, if the goal of Classroom Research is to study learning with the intention of improving it, the first step is to provide adequate tools for assessment. Second, we discovered early that most college teachers, whose background and training usually include little or no information about learning, need some experience with practical measures of student learning before they can delve productively into the complexities of Classroom Research.

Throughout this handbook, we have summarized what practicing Classroom Asssessors and our own research have taught us; but two major lessons were largely unanticipated, and they hold special significance for new directions for Classroom Research.

First, we did not fully anticipate the highly distinctive profiles of the teaching goals espoused within the academic disciplines. Second, we did not foresee that Classroom Assessment would turn out to be a highly social, collaborative learning experience for teachers. Initially, we saw Classroom Assessment as something faculty could do to improve teaching in their own classrooms without the necessity of grants, administrative approval, or committee meetings. So, in the early years, we talked about the need for confidentiality and warned administrators not to ask faculty how their Classroom Assessments turned out. We took this position largely because we wanted Classroom Assessors to feel free to risk searching for the bad news as well as the good news about their teaching. Meanwhile, Classroom Researchers were talking about their results—the bad news as well as the good—to anyone who would listen.

It appears that once teachers begin to raise questions about their own teaching and to collect data about its impact on learning, there is a self-generated pressure to raise questions and discuss findings with colleagues. We feel this pressure constantly in requests to help teachers build networks and establish channels of communication. As mentioned in the Preface, much has been done to facilitate communication among practicing Classroom Researchers via publications, conferences, videotapes, teleconferences, and newsletters. It is also clear that individual teachers have managed to meet their needs for discussion and interaction through the formation of dyads, triads, and occasionally larger seminars and discussion groups on campus. But there is a missing element that people still seem to be seeking.

What is missing, we believe, is the creation of more formal, institutionally recognized groups that are engaged in continuing intellectual exploration of research on teaching and its application in the classroom. Our finding that teaching goals are clearly associated with the discipline taught suggests a natural solution. The ready-made disciplinary group that occupies a place of formal recognition and authority within colleges is the department or division. Organizationally, the department is the link between the classroom and the college. It is also the first level of "community" for college faculty members, connecting them with others who share their disciplinary interests and also with the disciplinary world represented by professional academic associations, such as the American Psychological Association. Departments and professional associations are the logical "homes" for next steps in Classroom Research and Classroom Assessment. They offer a unique solution to the two issues that stand out as most prominent in our experience with Classroom Assessment. They give teachers a collaborative group experience with colleagues who are likely to share a common set of teaching goals.

This emphasis on disciplinary affiliations, incidentally, is not meant to discourage or negate in any way the important work of interdisciplinary studies and general education programs. Indeed, we would regard these programs as exceptionally important "disciplinary" groups, sharing common values and teaching goals and as eager as any department to evaluate how well students are learning what they think it is important to teach.

DEPARTMENTAL ENGAGEMENT IN CLASSROOM RESEARCH

We offer the following suggestions for a departmental program in Classroom Research. A natural first step would be the administration of the Teaching Goals Inventory (TGI) to all members of the department, part-time as well as full-time teachers. Faculty members will certainly be interested in knowing, for example, whether, as a department, they espouse a fairly narrow range of goals and have relatively high agreement on priorities or whether they show a wide range of goals and priorities. We would expect departments to differ on TGI profiles. Departments with a wide scope of responsibility, ranging from qualitative to quantitative methodologies, such as sociology, will probably show considerable diversity of teaching goals. Those with a tighter focus, such as mathematics, may show high agreement focused around a smaller number of priority goals.

Whatever the departmental profile, the next step is for the faculty to discuss whether they like the teaching profile they have generated as a group. If, for example, no one is teaching certain TGI goals that are regarded as important by the department or division, how should that oversight or lack of emphasis be addressed? For example, should new courses be added, or should faculty assume more responsibilitiy for addressing those goals in existing courses? If the profile turns out to be too narrow, what might be done to give students a broader educational experience? Obviously, there is no right or wrong TGI departmental profile. The compilation of a teaching-goals profile by the department simply provides information, which may then be used to determine whether students are exposed to the learning options that are important to the faculty.

A next step is to select, adapt, or create Classroom Assessment Techniques that faculty might use in their classrooms to see how well they are accomplishing their goals. Some faculty members with common goals might wish to form dyads or triads to develop assessment techniques that are especially appropriate to their teaching goals, to try them out in class, and to compare results. It might be interesting, for example, to have all faculty members use a common CAT on a specified day in the semester, just to see what a day of student learning in the department looks like. Ultimately, the department may wish to form task forces to devise some Departmental Assessment Techniques (DATs) that assess whether the department as a whole is accomplishing its goals.

Some of the professional disciplinary groups also might take on a project of devising appropriate assessment techniques for faculty in their disciplines. Working task forces could be small and local, involving teachers from two or three campuses. Or the national association could involve a number of teachers in special-interest groups, with the assignment to develop CATs that can be made available to teachers nationwide. Professional journals on the teaching of psychology, English, nursing, and the like are natural outlets for publication of the work of such task forces.

Basically, the suggestions we have made so far speak to the need for Classroom Assessors to collaborate with other faculty in their disciplinary groups in assessing the accomplishment of common teaching goals. This is really an extension of Classroom Assessment, from the already well-developed individual work that is emphasized in this handbook to the development of formally recognized group work. This extension offers a number of advantages to institutions. It involves faculty in a meaningful way in the assessment process, heightening awareness of what to look for and providing some consensus about departmental missions and their relationship to overall college missions.

Collaborative Classroom Assessment, including both inter- and intra-departmental activities, also engages faculty intellectually in thinking directly about the purposes and missions of undergraduate education. Where do students learn what is promised or implied in college mission statements and recruitment materials? Are there large gaps between departmental goals and institutional missions—teaching goals that somehow fall between the cracks of departmental structures?

VENTURES INTO LEARNING THEORY

While much of the work in departments, colleges, and professional associations will continue the well-formulated pattern of Classroom Assessment, we note the continuing hunger for deeper understanding of the complexities of learning. This need is recognized in the implied promise of the name "Classroom Research." The expectation is that research conducted in the classroom will advance knowledge about learning. Without question, Classroom Assessment can advance knowledge about a particular situation. A good Classroom Assessor can tell, subjectively at least, whether a given teaching technique works, to what extent it works, and for which students. What Classroom Assessment does not tell us is *why* it works. For that, we need to establish relationships between learning theory and teaching practice.

We use the term *theory* instead of *research* quite deliberately here. "Research into practice" is the more familiar concept. The perpetual hope is that practitioners will use the results of research to improve practice. That has not happened to any great extent in education. Research with the necessary controls to make it "scientific" is not readily transferable to the classroom, with its wide array of uncontrollable variables. The kind of empirical research that has predominated in education often tells us what happened but not why. For that we need theory.

If teaching is to become a true profession, teachers need to be able to launch hypotheses about why students respond the way they do. They need to deepen their understanding of the learning process, and they need to be able to explain how teaching affects learning. At present, there is a small group of Classroom Researchers, most of them in the social sciences, who seek further challenges and want to move beyond Classroom Assessment to Classroom Research. They are usually trained in the empirical methods and statistics of education and the social sciences, and understandably see some variation on traditional educational research as the next logical step for Classroom Research.

While we laud their desire to seek the next challenge, we do not think that the future of Classroom Research—and here we are using the "brand name," capital C and capital R—lies in conducting traditional educational research in college classrooms. Most faculty members have neither the desire nor the time to turn themselves into educational researchers. Nor do we think that such a direction would maximize the contributions of Classroom Research. There is already an army of social scientists who are skilled and interested in experimental design, pre- and post-measures of learning, statistical treatment of data, and the newer qualitative methods. It is not our desire to turn a dedicated chemistry teacher into an educational researcher who conducts research on learning in chemistry classrooms—although we staunchly defend and applaud her desire to do so if she wishes. Rather, we advocate a future for Classroom Research that would capitalize on everything a good chemistry teacher brings to her teaching: knowledge of chemistry, interest in teaching it to students, a daily opportunity to observe students closely, and a desire to know more about learning in order to improve her own teaching. Experienced teachers have been observing students in real-life settings for years, and they have some unarticulated theories, even subconscious theories, about how students learn in their disciplines. Their experience with Classroom Assessment makes them more systematic and sensitive observers of learning in the classroom, and the opportunity to discuss their observations with colleagues leads naturally to questions and tentative theories about teaching and learning. Theory is, after all, simply a way of organizing observations within a framework that suggests where to look for further observations that fit or, equally important, casts doubt on the theoretical framework by finding facts that do not fit.

A promising next step for advanced Classroom Assessors is to venture beyond Classroom Assessment into learning theory. We suggest the formation of year-long study seminars that are designed to relate teachers' personal theories about learning to formal theories that have been advanced through decades of research and theory building. For each seminar meeting, one or two people might be assigned to do some background reading and make a limited number of readings available to the members of the seminar. (See Menges and Svinicki, 1991, for some ideas and references to readings.) The primary purpose of the study group would be to relate the personal observations of classroom teachers—frequently uncovered or tested by means of Classroom Assessment—to the broader body of theory that is available.

Most teachers can come up with dozens of insights into something that really works for them. Making the connections between successful teaching approaches and searching for the underlying causes constitutes a personal theory of learning. Connecting one's own insights with those of colleagues and scholars in the formal study of learning leads to the gradual building of a framework that suggests new Classroom Research experiments for validation through Classroom Assessment.

Certain learning theories have particular relevance for certain teaching goals and for certain departments. For instance, teachers of remedial and developmental studies are frequently concerned about self-esteem and study habits; thus, they might be especially interested in theories of self-efficacy and metacognition. Teachers of science tend to espouse teaching goals that emphasize content mastery; thus, they may be interested in theories of cognition. Teachers of fine and performing arts may be interested in theories of creativity; teachers of business, in theories of leadership, application, and the like. Theories of motivation have implications for student retention, and theories about multiculturalism cut across departmental boundaries. Learning theory is not a singular concept. It consists of a wide variety of explanations that tie together the observations that can be made through the careful and systematic monitoring of students in the process of learning.

It is probably wise to select just one area for the study group to focus on during any given year, and we urge that the theory be kept as close as possible to the everyday experiences of teachers in order to capitalize on their unique real-life perspectives. The following description of a teaching experience happens to come from a well-known researcher, but it could just as easily have come from many teachers of developmental studies. Merlin C. Wittrock is a professor of education at UCLA whose research at the Army Research Institute was "intended to help enlisted men who had failed reading comprehension tests. . . learn how to read better" (Wittrock, 1988, p. 292). This is what he says about his experience:

> When we first worked with these young men, we learned that some of their motivations were quite different from what we expected. Many of them had given up on themselves. Because many of them had been told from childhood that they could not read, they believed that they were never going to learn how to read. When some of them came to class, they would quickly find reasons why they did not want to do what we had assigned them. They would say things such as, "This is too long a reading," or "We are not interested in this reading." We learned quickly that we had to know much about their attributional patterns, and their feelings of self-efficacy. . . .
>
> We also learned that their concepts of their ability to read were quite limited. We originally gave them a lengthy booklet of passages to read in 2 weeks, 1 hour per day. Many of them took one look at the booklet, put it down, and gave up. We quickly learned that attention to details, such as handing out reading material no more than 1 page long, was critical for motivation. Any material longer than that seemed beyond some of them. Many of them would not attempt to read it.
>
> These points may sound mundane, but they are neither mundane nor trivial [Wittrock, 1988, pp. 292–293].

Many developmental teachers will think that this noted researcher's points are, if not mundane, at least so familiar as to be quite unremarkable. But it is not the individual incidents recounted here that are noteworthy; rather, it is the explanatory rationale underlying the many small incidents in the behavior of these men. Today we talk about a theory of self-efficacy, which, briefly stated, is that people will not put forth the effort to do something, no matter how much help we give them, if they don't believe they can do it. Again, that may not seem an especially remarkable theory, but it has enormous implications for teaching, starting with casting doubt on the effectiveness of "drill and skill" assignments, which assume that it is lack of skill or lack of practice that plagues high-risk students. Modest Classroom Research experiments, designed by teachers to show developmental students that through their own efforts they can succeed, would help confirm the self-efficacy theory, while disconfirming a theory that held sway for many years—namely, the theory of the fixed IQ.

Another example of formal theory that has important implications for classroom teaching comes from the advances made in cognitive psychology in recent years. Theories of cognition suggest that the way in which students organize and store information is extremely important to learning. Learning in introductory courses, for example, is often more difficult than learning in advanced courses, because the knowledge framework that organizes the learning is sparse; therefore, students in these courses cannot easily relate new learning to old (Weinstein and Meyer, 1991). The more connections students can make between new learning and what they already know, the easier it is to process and retrieve the information. One implication of this theory is that teachers should make more and better use of analogies, examples, and metaphors.

A simple analogy illustrating cognitive theories about the importance of organization in retention and retrieval, for example, might be found in the closet organizers that we see advertised today. If there is no organization to your closet and you simply throw everything in a heap on the floor, you are obviously going to have trouble retrieving your yellow power tie when you need it, and you are also going to have to rely on memory alone to recall whether you even have a yellow tie. If, on the other hand, ties go in a particular place in your well-organized closet, you can store and retrieve it easily. At least, that is the theory of cognitive psychology and closet organizers.

Ultimately, we believe that the value of Classroom Research will be enhanced through the merging of teachers' personal theories with formal theories. We also hope that the more collaborative forms of Classroom Assessment and Classroom Research suggested in this chapter are responsive to the demands of experienced Classroom Assessors for more institutionally recognized forms of scholarship on teaching and learning.

In conclusion, we hope that this handbook, based on our growing understanding of the uses and potential contributions of Classroom Assessment and Classroom Research, will accomplish its original, and still primary, purpose of helping teachers understand the impact of their teaching on students' learning. We also hope that experienced Classroom Assessors will use their skills and understanding to advance the study of learning and improve the practice of college teaching.

RESOURCES

Colleges
Participating in
the 1990 Teaching
Goals Inventory
Survey

Community Colleges

    College of the Desert, California

    Collin County Community College, Texas

    Crowder Community College, Missouri

    Cuesta College, California

    De Anza College, California

    Diablo Valley College, California

    Howard Community College, Maryland

    Kellogg Community College, Michigan

    Los Medanos College, California

    Massachusetts Bay Community College, Massachusetts

    Metropolitan Technical Community College, Nebraska

    North Arkansas Community College, Arkansas

    St. Louis Community College, Missouri

    St. Petersburg Community College, Florida

    Santa Rosa Junior College, California

Four-Year Colleges

    Averett College, Virginia

    Bethel College, Kansas

    Centenary College, Louisiana

Clarke College, Iowa

Converse College, South Carolina

Drury College, Missouri

Lenoir-Rhyme College, North Carolina

Marietta College, Ohio

Marymount College, California

Milligan College, Tennessee

Monmouth College, Illinois

Mount Mercy College, Iowa

Roanoke College, Virginia

Rust College, Mississippi

St. Mary's College, Rhode Island

Trevecca Nazarene College, Tennessee

Wilberforce University, Ohio

Teaching Goals Inventory and Self-Scorable Worksheet

Purpose: The Teaching Goals Inventory (TGI) is a self-assessment of instructional goals. Its purpose is threefold: (1) to help college teachers become more aware of what they want to accomplish in individual courses; (2) to help faculty locate Classroom Assessment Techniques they can adapt and use to assess how well they are achieving their teaching and learning goals; (3) to provide a starting point for discussions of teaching and learning goals among colleagues.

Directions: Please select ONE course you are currently teaching. Respond to each item on the Inventory in relation to that particular course. (Your responses might be quite different if you were asked about your overall teaching and learning goals, for example, or the appropriate instructional goals for your discipline.)

Please print the title of the specific course you are focusing on:

_____

Please rate the importance of each of the fifty-two goals listed below to the specific course you have selected. Assess each goal's importance to what you deliberately aim to have your students accomplish, rather than the goal's general worthiness or overall importance to your institution's mission. There are no "right" or "wrong" answers, only personally more or less accurate ones.

For each goal, circle only one response on the 1-to-5 rating scale. You may want to read quickly through all fifty-two goals before rating their relative importance.

In relation to the course you are focusing on, indicate whether each goal you rate is:

(5) Essential   a goal you always/nearly always try to achieve
(4) Very important   a goal you often try to achieve
(3) Important   a goal you sometimes try to achieve
(2) Unimportant   a goal you rarely try to achieve
(1) Not applicable   a goal you never try to achieve

Rate the importance of each goal to what you aim to have students accomplish in your course.

	Essential	Very Important	Important	Unimportant	Not Applicable
1. Develop ability to apply principles and generalizations already learned to new problems and situations	5	4	3	2	1
2. Develop analytic skills	5	4	3	2	1
3. Develop problem-solving skills	5	4	3	2	1
4. Develop ability to draw reasonable inferences from observations	5	4	3	2	1
5. Develop ability to synthesize and integrate information and ideas	5	4	3	2	1
6. Develop ability to think holistically: to see the whole as well as the parts	5	4	3	2	1
7. Develop ability to think creatively	5	4	3	2	1
8. Develop ability to distinguish between fact and opinion	5	4	3	2	1
9. Improve skill at paying attention	5	4	3	2	1
10. Develop ability to concentrate	5	4	3	2	1
11. Improve memory skills	5	4	3	2	1
12. Improve listening skills	5	4	3	2	1
13. Improve speaking skills	5	4	3	2	1
14. Improve reading skills	5	4	3	2	1
15. Improve writing skills	5	4	3	2	1
16. Develop appropriate study skills, strategies, and habits	5	4	3	2	1
17. Improve mathematical skills	5	4	3	2	1
18. Learn terms and facts of this subject	5	4	3	2	1
19. Learn concepts and theories in this subject	5	4	3	2	1
20. Develop skill in using materials, tools, and/or technology central to this subject	5	4	3	2	1
21. Learn to understand perspectives and values of this subject	5	4	3	2	1
22. Prepare for transfer or graduate study	5	4	3	2	1
23. Learn techniques and methods used to gain new knowledge in this subject	5	4	3	2	1
24. Learn to evaluate methods and materials in this subject	5	4	3	2	1
25. Learn to appreciate important contributions to this subject	5	4	3	2	1

*Rate the importance of each goal to what you aim
to have students accomplish in your course.*

	Essential	Very Important	Important	Unimportant	Not Applicable
26. Develop an appreciation of the liberal arts and sciences	5	4	3	2	1
27. Develop an openness to new ideas	5	4	3	2	1
28. Develop an informed concern about contemporary social issues	5	4	3	2	1
29. Develop a commitment to exercise the rights and responsibilities of citizenship	5	4	3	2	1
30. Develop a lifelong love of learning	5	4	3	2	1
31. Develop aesthetic appreciations	5	4	3	2	1
32. Develop an informed historical perspective	5	4	3	2	1
33. Develop an informed understanding of the role of science and technology	5	4	3	2	1
34. Develop an informed appreciation of other cultures	5	4	3	2	1
35. Develop capacity to make informed ethical choices	5	4	3	2	1
36. Develop ability to work productively with others	5	4	3	2	1
37. Develop management skills	5	4	3	2	1
38. Develop leadership skills	5	4	3	2	1
39. Develop a commitment to accurate work	5	4	3	2	1
40. Improve ability to follow directions, instructions, and plans	5	4	3	2	1
41. Improve ability to organize and use time effectively	5	4	3	2	1
42. Develop a commitment to personal achievement	5	4	3	2	1
43. Develop ability to perform skillfully	5	4	3	2	1
44. Cultivate a sense of responsibility for one's own behavior	5	4	3	2	1
45. Improve self-esteem / self-confidence	5	4	3	2	1
46. Develop a commitment to one's own values	5	4	3	2	1
47. Develop respect for others	5	4	3	2	1
48. Cultivate emotional health and well-being	5	4	3	2	1
49. Cultivate physical health and well-being	5	4	3	2	1
50. Cultivate an active commitment to honesty	5	4	3	2	1
51. Develop capacity to think for oneself	5	4	3	2	1
52. Develop capacity to make wise decisions	5	4	3	2	1

53. In general, how do you see your primary role as a teacher? (Although more than one statement may apply, please circle only one.)

1 Teaching students facts and principles of the subject matter
2 Providing a role model for students
3 Helping students develop higher-order thinking skills
4 Preparing students for jobs/careers
5 Fostering student development and personal growth
6 Helping students develop basic learning skills

Source: Classroom Assessment Techniques, by Thomas A. Angelo and K. Patricia Cross. Copyright © 1993. Permission to reproduce is hereby granted.

Teaching Goals Inventory, Self-Scoring Worksheet

1. In all, how many of the fifty-two goals did you rate as "Essential"?
   _____

2. How many "Essential" goals did you have in each of the six clusters listed below?

Cluster Number and Name	Goals Included in Cluster	Total Number of "Essential" Goals in Each Cluster	Clusters Ranked— from 1st to 6th— by Number of "Essential" Goals
I Higher-Order Thinking Skills	1–8	_____	_____
II Basic Academic Success Skills	9–17	_____	_____
III Discipline-Specific Knowledge and Skills	18–25	_____	_____
IV Liberal Arts and Academic Values	26–35	_____	_____
V Work and Career Preparation	36–43	_____	_____
VI Personal Development	44–52	_____	_____

3. Compute your cluster scores (average item ratings by cluster) using the following worksheet.

A Cluster Number and Name	B Goals Included	C Sum of Ratings Given to Goals in That Cluster	D Divide C by This Number	E Your Cluster Scores
I Higher-Order Thinking Skills	1–8	_____	8	_____
II Basic Academic Success Skills	9–17	_____	9	_____
III Discipline-Specific Knowledge and Skills	18–25	_____	8	_____
IV Liberal Arts and Academic Values	26–35	_____	10	_____
V Work and Career Preparation	36–43	_____	8	_____
VI Personal Development	44–52	_____	9	_____

Source: Classroom Assessment Techniques, by Thomas A. Angelo and K. Patricia Cross. Copyright © 1993. Permission to reproduce is hereby granted.

1990 Comparative Data on the Teaching Goals Inventory in Community Colleges

The TGI was administered to 1,873 community college faculty members in the spring of 1990. Through the statistical procedure of cluster analysis, six clusters were identified. Shown below are the items in each cluster, item means (M) and standard deviations (SD), and the percent (%) of teachers rating the item "essential" to the teaching of a selected course. Cluster means and the average ratings for items in the cluster are also given for comparative purposes.

The data presented here represent a composite of faculty, including all disciplines and vocational/career specialties. As the analysis presented in Chapter Two (in the section entitled "Background: Development of the Teaching Goals Inventory") shows, the differences in teaching goals among teaching disciplines are highly significant. These comparative data are presented primarily for use by colleges in assessing the composite teaching priorities of their institutions.

	M	SD	%
Cluster I: Higher-Order Thinking Skills	*3.09*	*0.86*	*45*
1. Develop ability to apply principles and generalizations already learned to new problems and situations	3.49	0.75	62
2. Develop analytic skills	3.32	0.87	54
3. Develop problem-solving skills	3.19	1.03	51
4. Develop ability to draw reasonable inferences from observations	3.06	1.00	41
5. Develop ability to synthesize and integrate information and ideas	3.18	0.89	44

		M	SD	%
6.	Develop ability to think holistically: to see the whole as well as the parts	3.16	0.93	45
7.	Develop ability to think creatively	2.93	1.03	35
8.	Develop ability to distinguish between fact and opinion	2.39	1.37	27
Cluster II: Basic Academic Success Skills		*2.29*	*1.20*	*22*
9.	Improve skill at paying attention	2.71	1.06	27
10.	Develop ability to concentrate	2.67	1.08	27
11.	Improve memory skills	2.26	1.13	15
12.	Improve listening skills	2.74	1.03	27
13.	Improve speaking skills	1.58	1.29	12
14.	Improve reading skills	2.30	1.26	21
15.	Improve writing skills	2.21	1.35	24
16.	Develop appropriate study skills, strategies, and habits	2.72	1.05	27
17.	Improve mathematical skills	1.45	1.52	18
Cluster III: Discipline-Specific Knowledge and Skills		*2.83*	*1.06*	*36*
18.	Learn terms and facts of this subject	3.32	0.85	54
19.	Learn concepts and theories in this subject	3.21	0.93	48
20.	Develop skill in using materials, tools, and/or technology central to this subject	2.85	1.34	45
21.	Learn to understand perspectives and values of this subject	2.94	0.98	33
22.	Prepare for transfer or graduate study	2.06	1.33	18
23.	Learn techniques and methods used to gain new knowledge in this subject	3.06	0.98	40
24.	Learn to evaluate methods and materials in this subject	2.74	1.03	30
25.	Learn to appreciate important contributions to this subject	2.46	1.06	18
Cluster IV: Liberal Arts and Academic Values		*2.02*	*1.29*	*18*
26.	Develop an appreciation of the liberal arts and sciences	1.93	1.31	14
27.	Develop an openness to new ideas	2.89	1.09	36

	M	*SD*	*%*
28. Develop an informed concern about contemporary social issues	1.95	1.32	16
29. Develop a commitment to exercise the rights and responsibilities of citizenship	1.50	1.35	10
30. Develop a lifelong love of learning	2.73	1.10	30
31. Develop aesthetic appeciations	1.80	1.32	14
32. Develop an informed historical perspective	1.77	1.26	11
33. Develop an informed understanding of the role of science and technology	1.89	1.35	14
34. Develop an informed appreciation of other cultures	1.68	1.41	14
35. Develop capacity to make informed ethical choices	2.03	1.40	18
Cluster V: Work and Career Preparation	*2.50*	*1.00*	*26*
36. Develop ability to work productively with others	2.57	1.23	22
37. Develop management skills	1.53	1.29	09
38. Develop leadership skills	1.52	1.23	07
39. Develop a commitment to accurate work	3.06	1.00	42
40. Improve ability to follow directions, instructions, and plans	2.92	1.01	36
41. Improve ability to organize and use time effectively	2.59	1.11	24
42. Develop a commitment to personal achievement	2.77	1.03	29
43. Develop ability to perform skillfully	3.01	1.10	42
Cluster VI: Personal Development	*2.41*	*1.19*	*28*
44. Cultivate a sense of responsibility for one's own behavior	2.76	1.22	36
45. Improve self-esteem/self-confidence	2.77	1.07	31
46. Develop a commitment to one's own values	2.03	1.36	17
47. Develop respect for others	2.39	1.28	25
48. Cultivate emotional health and well-being	1.60	1.35	11
49. Cultivate physical health and well-being	1.14	1.35	09
50. Cultivate an active commitment to honesty	2.54	1.29	30

		M	*SD*	%
51.	Develop capacity to think for oneself	3.39	0.81	56
52.	Develop capacity to make wise decisions	3.03	1.01	40

53. In general, how do you see your primary role as a teacher? (Although more than one statement may apply, please circle only one.)

	%
Teaching students facts and principles of the subject matter	27.1
Providing a role model for students	1.9
Helping students develop higher-order thinking skills	26.3
Preparing students for jobs/careers	21.0
Fostering student development and personal growth	15.4
Helping students develop basic learning skills	8.3

1990 Comparative Data on the Teaching Goals Inventory in Four-Year Colleges

RESOURCE

D

The TGI was administered to 951 four-year college faculty members in the spring of 1990. Through the statistical procedure of cluster analysis, six clusters were identified. Shown below are the items in each cluster, item means (M) and standard deviations (SD), and the percent (%) of teachers rating the item "essential" to the teaching of a selected course. Cluster means and the average ratings for items in the cluster are also given for comparative purposes.

The data presented here represent a composite of faculty, including all disciplines and vocational/career specialties. As the analysis presented in Chapter Two (in the section entitled "Background: Development of the Teaching Goals Inventory") shows, the differences in teaching goals among teaching disciplines are highly significant. These comparative data are presented primarily for use by colleges in assessing the composite teaching priorities of their institutions.

	M	SD	%
Cluster I: Higher-Order Thinking Skills	3.05	1.02	43
1. Develop ability to apply principles and generalizations already learned to new problems and situations	3.37	0.88	59
2. Develop analytic skills	3.20	1.01	49
3. Develop problem-solving skills	2.89	1.19	40
4. Develop ability to draw reasonable inferences from observations	3.10	0.98	41
5. Develop ability to synthesize and integrate information and ideas	3.26	0.87	49

Resources **403**

	M	SD	%
6. Develop ability to think holistically: to see the whole as well as the parts	3.19	0.93	47
7. Develop ability to think creatively	2.88	1.05	34
8. Develop ability to distinguish between fact and opinion	2.51	1.26	26
Cluster II: Basic Academic Success Skills	*2.12*	*1.23*	*18*
9. Improve skill at paying attention	2.41	1.20	21
10. Develop ability to concentrate	2.44	1.20	23
11. Improve memory skills	2.01	1.20	13
12 Improve listening skills	2.52	1.15	22
13. Improve speaking skills	1.80	1.32	12
14. Improve reading skills	2.17	1.27	18
15. Improve writing skills	2.32	1.24	20
16. Develop appropriate study skills, strategies, and habits	2.41	1.15	19
17. Improve mathematical skills	0.99	1.34	10
Cluster III: Discipline-Specific Knowledge and Skills	*2.86*	*1.05*	*37*
18. Learn terms and facts of this subject	3.30	0.83	50
19. Learn concepts and theories in this subject	3.30	0.89	53
20. Develop skill in using materials, tools, and/or technology central to this subject	2.74	1.35	41
21. Learn to understand perspectives and values of this subject	3.15	0.88	41
22. Prepare for transfer or graduate study	1.85	1.34	14
23. Learn techniques and methods used to gain new knowledge in this subject	2.98	0.99	37
24. Learn to evaluate methods and materials in this subject	2.82	1.11	33
25. Learn to appreciate important contributions to this subject	2.75	1.01	26
Cluster IV: Liberal Arts and Academic Values	*2.16*	*1.30*	*21*
26. Develop an appreciation of the liberal arts and sciences	2.33	1.26	22
27. Develop an openness to new ideas	3.01	1.04	40

		M	*SD*	%
28.	Develop an informed concern about contemporary social issues	2.18	1.33	21
29.	Develop a commitment to exercise the rights and responsibilities of citizenship	1.48	1.37	10
30.	Develop a lifelong love of learning	2.80	1.10	33
31.	Develop aesthetic appreciations	1.87	1.44	19
32.	Develop an informed historical perspective	2.20	1.29	19
33.	Develop an informed understanding of the role of science and technology	1.73	1.37	13
34.	Develop an informed appreciation of other cultures	1.80	1.46	18
35.	Develop capacity to make informed ethical choices	2.18	1.36	19

Cluster V: Work and Career Preparation   *2.27*   *1.23*   *21*

		M	*SD*	%
36.	Develop ability to work productively with others	2.18	1.26	17
37.	Develop management skills	1.51	1.40	12
38.	Develop leadership skills	1.70	1.31	12
39.	Develop a commitment to accurate work	2.85	1.04	32
40.	Improve ability to follow directions, instructions, and plans	2.48	1.16	23
41.	Improve ability to organize and use time effectively	2.34	1.21	19
42.	Develop a commitment to personal achievement	2.46	1.18	22
43.	Develop ability to perform skillfully	2.63	1.30	32

Cluster VI: Personal Development   *2.28*   *1.22*   *25*

		M	*SD*	%
44.	Cultivate a sense of responsibility for one's own behavior	2.57	1.26	29
45.	Improve self-esteem/self-confidence	2.44	1.22	23
46.	Develop a commitment to one's own values	2.13	1.34	18
47.	Develop respect for others	2.32	1.33	24
48.	Cultivate emotional health and well-being	1.43	1.35	09
49.	Cultivate physical health and well-being	0.96	1.29	07
50.	Cultivate an active commitment to honesty	2.48	1.28	27

	M	SD	%
51. Develop capacity to think for oneself	3.33	.82	52
52. Develop capacity to make wise decisions	2.87	1.11	36

53. In general, how do you see your primary role as a teacher? (Although more than one statement may apply, please circle only one.)

	%
Teaching students facts and principles of the subject matter	29.0
Providing a role model for students	6.4
Helping students develop higher-order thinking skills	31.8
Preparing students for jobs/careers	11.2
Fostering student development and personal growth	18.3
Helping students develop basic learning skills	3.4

Bibliography of Resources on Classroom Research and Assessment

RESOURCE

E

PUBLICATIONS
Angelo, T. A. "Faculty Development for Learning: The Promise of Classroom Research." In S. Kahn (ed.), *To Improve the Academy*. Stillwater, Okla.: New Forums Press, 1989.

Angelo, T. A. (ed.). *Classroom Research: Early Lessons from Success*. New Directions for Teaching and Learning, no. 46. San Francisco: Jossey-Bass, 1991.

Angelo, T. A., and Cross, K. P. "Classroom Research for Teaching Assistants." In J. D. Nyquist, R. D. Abbott, and D. H. Wulff (eds.), *Teaching Assistant Training in the 1990s*. New Directions for Teaching and Learning, no. 39. San Francisco: Jossey-Bass, 1989.

Cross, K. P. "A Proposal to Improve Teaching." *AAHE Bulletin*, 1986, *39*(1), 9–15.

Cross, K. P. "The Adventures of Education in Wonderland: Implementing Educational Reform." *Phi Delta Kappan*, 1987, *68*(7), 496–502.

Cross, K. P. "Teaching for Learning." *AAHE Bulletin*, 1987, *39*(8), 3–7.

Cross, K. P. *Feedback in the Classroom: Making Assessment Matter*. Washington, D.C.: American Association for Higher Education, 1988.

Cross, K. P. "In Search of Zippers." *AAHE Bulletin*, 1988, *40*(10), 3–7.

Cross, K. P. "Classroom Research: Helping Professors Learn More About Teaching and Learning." In P. Seldin and Associates, *How Administrators Can Improve Teaching: Moving from Talk to Action in Higher Education*. San Francisco: Jossey-Bass, 1990.

Cross, K. P. *Streams of Thought About Assessment*. Washington, D.C.: American Association for Higher Education, Assessment Forum, 1990.

Cross, K. P. "Teaching to Improve Learning." *Journal of Excellence in College Teaching*, 1990, *1*, 9–22.

Cross, K. P. "College Teaching: What Do We Know About It?" *Innovative Higher Education*, 1991, *16*(1), 7–25.

Cross, K. P., and Angelo, T. A. *Classroom Assessment Techniques: A Handbook for Faculty*. Ann Arbor: National Center for Research to

Improve Postsecondary Teaching and Learning, University of Michigan, 1988.

Cross, K. P., and Angelo, T. A. "Faculty Members as Classroom Researchers: A Progress Report." *Community, Technical, and Junior College Journal*, 1989, *59*(5), 23–25.

Cross, K. P., and Fideler, E. F. "Assessment in the Classroom." *Community/Junior College Quarterly of Research and Practice*, 1988, *12*(4), 275–285.

Fideler, E. F. (ed.). *Educational Forum*. Wellesley Hills, Mass.: Windsor Press, 1991.

Goswami, D., and Stillman, P. R. (eds.). *Reclaiming the Classroom: Teacher Research as an Agency for Change*. Portsmouth, N.H.: Boynton/Cook, 1987.

Kelly, D. K. *The Effects of Classroom Research by Part-Time Faculty upon the Retention of Adult Learners*. Saratoga Springs, N.Y.: National Center upon Adult Learning, Empire State College, 1991.

Kort, M. S. "Classroom Research and Composition Classes." *Teaching English in the Two-Year College*, May 1991, pp. 98–102.

Light, R. J. *The Harvard Assessment Seminars: Explorations with Students and Faculty About Teaching, Learning, and Student Life*. First Report. Cambridge, Mass.: Harvard University, 1990.

Light, R. J. *The Harvard Assessment Seminars: Explorations with Students and Faculty About Teaching, Learning, and Student Life*. Second Report. Cambridge, Mass.: Harvard University, 1992.

Mosteller, F. "The 'Muddiest Point in the Lecture' as a Feedback Device." *On Teaching and Learning: The Journal of the Harvard-Danforth Center*, 1989, *3*, 10–21.

Weimer, M., Parrett, J. L., and Kerns, M-M. *How Am I Teaching? Forms and Activities for Acquiring Instructional Input*. Madison, Wis.: Magna Publications, 1988.

VIDEOTAPES *Classroom Research: Empowering Teachers*. 18 min. Catalogue no. 38022. University of California Extension Media Center, 2176 Shattuck Ave., Berkeley, Calif. 94704. Ph. (510) 642-0460. (Rental or purchase)

K. Patricia Cross on Classroom Research. 25 min. Catalogue no. 38023. University of California Extension Media Center, 2176 Shattuck Ave., Berkeley, Calif. 94704. Ph. (510) 642-0460. (Rental or purchase)

Teacher-Directed Classroom Research. 15 min. College of Marin. Order from Product Development and Distribution, Miami-Dade Community College, 11011 S.W. 104th St., Miami, Fla. 33176. Ph. (305) 347-2158. (Purchase)

References

Angelo, T. A. (ed.). *Classroom Research: Early Lessons from Success.* New Directions for Teaching and Learning, no. 46. San Francisco: Jossey-Bass, 1991.

Association of American Colleges. *Integrity in the College Curriculum: A Report to the Academic Community.* Washington, D.C.: Association of American Colleges, 1985.

Astin, A. W. *Four Critical Years: Effects of College on Beliefs, Attitudes, and Knowledge.* San Francisco: Jossey-Bass, 1977.

Astin, A. W. "The Measured Effects of Higher Education." *Annals of the American Academy of Political and Social Science.* Nov. 1982, pp. 1–20.

Astin, A. W. *Achieving Educational Excellence: A Critical Assessment of Priorities and Practices in Higher Education.* San Francisco: Jossey-Bass, 1985.

Astin, A. W., and Panos, R. *The Educational and Vocational Development of College Students.* Washington, D.C.: American Council on Education, 1969.

Ausubel, D. P. *Educational Psychology: A Cognitive View.* Troy, Mo.: Holt, Rinehart & Winston, 1968.

Bayer, A. E. "Faculty Composition, Institutional Structure, and Students' College Environment." *Journal of Higher Education*, 1975, 46(5), 549–565.

Beal, P. E., and Noel, L. *What Works in Student Retention: The Report of a Joint Project of the American College Testing Program and the National Center for Higher Education Management Systems.* Iowa City, Iowa: American College Testing Program, 1980.

Belenky, M. F., Clinchy, B. M., Goldberger, N. R., and Tarule, J. *Women's Ways of Knowing: The Development of Self, Voice, and Mind.* New York: Basic Books, 1986.

Bennett, W. E. "Small Group Instructional Diagnosis: A Dialogic Approach to Instructional Improvement for Tenured Faculty." *Journal of Staff, Program, and Organizational Development*, 1987, 5(3), 100–104.

Berthoff, A. E. *Forming/Thinking/Writing: The Composing Imagination*. Upper Montclair, N.H.: Boynton Cook, 1982.

Berthoff, A. E., with Stephens, J. *Forming/Thinking/Writing*. (2nd ed.) Portsmouth, N.H.: Boynton Cook, 1988.

Blackburn, R. T., and Clark, M. J. "An Assessment of Faculty Performance: Some Correlates Between Administrator, Colleague, Student, and Self Ratings." *Sociology of Education*, 1975, *48*, 242–256.

Blackburn, R. T., and others. *Faculty as a Key Resource: A Review of the Research Literature*. Ann Arbor: National Center for Research to Improve Postsecondary Teaching and Learning, University of Michigan, 1986.

Bloom, B. S., Hastings, J. T., and Madaus, G. F. *Handbook on Formative and Summative Evaluation of Student Learning*. New York: McGraw-Hill, 1971.

Bloom, B. S., and others. *Taxonomy of Educational Objectives*. Vol. 1: *Cognitive Domain*. New York: McKay, 1956.

Borgen, F. H., and Barnett, D. C. "Applying Cluster Analysis in Counseling Psychology Research." *Journal of Counseling Psychology*, 1987, *34*, 456–468.

Bowen, H. R. *Investment in Learning: The Individual and Social Value of American Higher Education*. San Francisco: Jossey-Bass, 1977.

Brown, A. L., Bransford, J. D., Ferrara, R. A., and Campione, J. C. "Learning, Remembering, and Understanding." In F. H. Flavell and E. M. Markman (eds.), *Handbook of Child Psychology*. Vol. 3: *Cognitive Development*. (4th ed.) New York: Wiley, 1983.

Center for Faculty Evaluation and Development in Higher Education. *IDEA Survey Form: Student Reactions to Instruction and Courses*. Manhattan: Center for Faculty Evaluation and Development in Higher Education, Kansas State University, 1975.

Centra, J. A. "Effectiveness of Student Feedback in Modifying College Instruction." *Journal of Educational Psychology*, 1973a, *65*(3), 395–401.

Centra, J. A. "The Student as Godfather? The Impact of Student Ratings on Academia." *Educational Researcher*, 1973b, *2*(10), 4–8.

Centra, J. A. "The How and Why of Evaluating Teaching." *New Directions for Higher Education*, 1977a, *17*, 93–106.

Centra, J. A. "Student Ratings of Instruction and Their Relationship to Student Learning." *American Educational Research Journal*, 1977b, *14*(1), 17–24.

Chickering, A. W. *Education and Identity*. San Francisco: Jossey-Bass, 1969.

Clinchy, B. M. "Issues of Gender in Teaching and Learning." *Journal of Excellence in College Teaching*. 1990, *1*, 52–67.

College Board. *What Students Need to Know and Be Able to Do*. New York: College Board, 1983.

Cottell, P. G., Jr. "Classroom Research in Accounting: Assessing for Learning." In T. A. Angelo (ed.), *Classroom Research: Early Lessons from Success*. New Directions for Teaching and Learning, no. 46. San Francisco: Jossey-Bass, 1991.

Cronbach, L. J. "Coefficient Alpha and the Internal Structure of Tests." *Psychometrika*, 1951, *16*, 297–334.

Cross, K. P. *Feedback in the Classroom: Making Assessment Matter*. Washington, D.C.: American Association for Higher Education, 1988.

Cross, K. P., and Angelo, T. A. *Classroom Assessment Techniques: A Handbook for Faculty*. Ann Arbor: National Center for Research to Improve Postsecondary Teaching and Learning, University of Michigan, 1988.

Cross, K. P., and Fideler, E. F. "Assessment in the Classroom." *Community/ Junior College Quarterly of Research and Practice*, 1988, *12*(4), 275–285.

Cunningham, P. M., and Cunningham, J. W. "Content Area Reading-Writing Lessons." *The Reading Teacher*, 1987, *40*, 506–512.

Davis, R. "A Plea for the Use of Student Dialogs." *Improving College and University Teaching*, 1981, *29*(4), 155–161.

Dreher, H. V. "Electronic Mail: An Example of Computer Use in Education." *Educational Technology*, 1984, *24*(8), 36–38.

Drucker, A. J., and Remmers, H. H. *Do Alumni and Students Differ in Their Attitude Toward Instructors?* Purdue University Studies in Higher Education, no. 70. West Lafayette, Ind.: Purdue University, 1950.

Dubin, R., and Taveggia, T. C. *The Teaching-Learning Paradox: A Comparative Analysis of College Teaching Methods*. Eugene: Center for the Advanced Study of Educational Administration, University of Oregon, 1968.

Feldman, K. A. "Grades and College Students' Evaluations of Their Courses and Teachers." *Research in Higher Education*, 1976, *4*, 69–111.

Feldman, K. A. "Consistency and Variability Among College Students in Rating Their Teachers and Courses: A Review and Analysis." *Research In Higher Education*, 1977, *6*, 223–274.

Feldman, K. A., and Newcomb, T. M. *The Impact of College on Students*. San Francisco: Jossey-Bass, 1969.

Fideler, E. F. (ed.). *Educational Forum*. Wellesley Hills, Mass.: Windsor Press, 1991.

Gaff, J. G., and Wilson, R. C. "The Teaching Environment." *American Association of University Professors Bulletin*, 1981, *67*, 475–493.

Gamson, Z., and Chickering, A. "Seven Principles for Good Practice in Undergraduate Education." *AAHE Bulletin*, 1987, *39*, 5–10.

Gleason, M. "Getting a Perspective on Student Evaluation." *AAHE Bulletin*, 1986, *38*, 10–13.

Henry, L. H. "Clustering: Writing (and Learning) About Economics." *College Teaching*, 1986, *34*(3), 89–93.

Hirshfield, C. "The Classroom Quality Circle: A Widening Role for Students." *Innovation Abstracts*, 1984, *6*(12), 1–2.

Kelly, D. K. *The Effects of Classroom Research by Part-Time Faculty upon the Retention of Adult Learners*. Saratoga Springs, N.Y.: National Center upon Adult Learning, Empire State College, 1991.

Kogut, L. S. "Quality Circles: A Japanese Management Technique for the Classroom." *Improving College and University Teaching*, 1984, *32*(2), 123–127.

Kohlberg, L. *The Psychology of Moral Development: The Nature and Validity of Moral Stages*. New York: HarperCollins, 1984.

Korn, H. A. *Psychological Models Explaining the Impact of College on Students*. Ann Arbor: National Center for Research to Improve Postsecondary Teaching and Learning, University of Michigan, 1986.

Kort, M. S. "Re-visioning Our Teaching: Classroom Research and Composition." In T. A. Angelo (ed.), *Classroom Research: Early Lessons from Success*. New Directions for Teaching and Learning, no. 46. San Francisco: Jossey-Bass, 1991.

Krathwohl, D. R., Bloom, B. S., and Masia, B. B. *Taxonomy of Educational Objectives: The Classification of Educational Goals*. Vol. 2: *Affective Domain*. New York: McKay, 1964.

Kulik, J. *Student Reactions to Instruction: Memo to the Faculty*. Ann Arbor: University of Michigan, 1976.

Kulik, J. A., and McKeachie, W. J. "The Evaluation of Teachers in Higher Education." In F. N. Kerlinger (ed.), *Preview of Research in Education*. Vol. 3. Itasca, Ill.: Peacock, 1975.

MacGregor, D. *The Human Side of Enterprise*. New York: McGraw-Hill, 1960.

McKeachie, W. J., Pintrich, P. R., Lin, Yi-Guang, and Smith, D.A.F. *Teaching and Learning in the College Classroom: A Review of the Research Literature*. Ann Arbor: National Center for Research to Improve Postsecondary Teaching and Learning, University of Michigan, 1986.

McMullen-Pastrick, M., and Gleason, M. "Examinations: Accentuating the Positive." *College Teaching*, 1986, *34*(4), 135–139.

Menges, R. J., and Svinicki, M. D. (eds.). *College Teaching: From Theory to Practice*. New Directions for Teaching and Learning, no. 45. San Francisco: Jossey-Bass, 1991.

Mosteller, F. "The 'Muddiest Point in the Lecture' as a Feedback Device." *On Teaching and Learning: The Journal of the Harvard-Danforth Center*, 1989, *3*, 10–21.

Mueller, D. J. *Measuring Social Attitudes: A Handbook for Researchers and Practitioners*. New York: Teachers College Press, 1986.

Nakaji, D. M. "Classroom Research in Physics: Gaining Insights in Visualization and Problem Solving." In T. A. Angelo (ed.), *Classroom Research: Early Lessons from Success*. New Directions for Teaching and Learning, no. 46. San Francisco: Jossey-Bass, 1991.

Norman, D. A., "What Goes On in the Mind of the Learner." In W. J. McKeachie (ed.), *Learning, Cognition, and College Teaching*. New Directions for Teaching and Learning, no. 2. San Francisco: Jossey-Bass, 1980.

Novak, J. D., and Gowin, D. B. *Learning How to Learn*. New York: Cambridge University Press, 1984.

Obler, S., Arnold, V., Sigala, C., and Umbdenstock, L. "Using Cooperative Learning and Classroom Research with Culturally Diverse Students." In T. A. Angelo (ed.), *Classroom Research: Early Lessons from Success*. New Directions for Teaching and Learning, no. 46. San Francisco: Jossey-Bass, 1991.

Olmsted, J., III. "Using Classroom Research in a Large Introductory Science Class." In T. A. Angelo (ed.), *Classroom Research: Early Lessons from*

Success. New Directions for Teaching and Learning, no. 46. San Francisco: Jossey-Bass, 1991.

Perry, W. G., Jr. *Forms of Intellectual and Ethical Development in the College Years: A Scheme*. Troy, Mo.: Holt, Rinehart & Winston, 1970.

Redmond, M. V., and Clark, D. J. "A Practical Approach to Improving Teaching." *AAHE Bulletin*, 1982, *1*, 9–10.

Riegle, R. P., and Rhodes, D. M. "Avoiding Mixed Metaphors of Faculty Evaluation." *College Teaching*, 1986, *34*(4), 123–128.

Roxbury Community College. *Teaching from Strengths Conference*. Boston: Roxbury Community College, 1986.

Schumacher, E. F. *Small Is Beautiful*. New York: HarperCollins, 1975.

Segal, J. W., Chipman, S. F., and Glaser, R. (eds.). *Thinking and Learning Skills*. Vol. 1: *Relating Instruction to Research*. Hillsdale, N.J.: Erlbaum, 1985.

Seldin, P. "Faculty Evaluation: Surveying Policy and Practices." *Change*, 1984, *16*(3), 28–33.

Selfe, C. L., and Arbabi, F. "Writing to Learn: Engineering Student Journals." In A. Young and T. Fulwiler (eds.), *Writing Across the Disciplines: Research into Practice*. Upper Montclair, N.J.: Boynton/Cook, 1986.

Selfe, C. L., Petersen, B. T., and Nahrgang, C. L. "Journal Writing in Mathematics." In A. Young and T. Fulwiler (eds.), *Writing Across the Disciplines: Research into Practice*. Upper Montclair, N.J.: Boynton/Cook, 1986.

Shaughnessy, M. P. *Errors and Expectations: A Guide for the Teacher of Basic Writing*. New York: Oxford University Press, 1977.

Shelton, R. "Classroom Research in Undergraduate Math Classes." *Educational Forum*. Vol. 2. Wellesley Hills, Mass.: Windsor Press, 1991.

Stetson, N. E. "Implementing and Maintaining a Classroom Research Program for Faculty." In T. A. Angelo (ed.), *Classroom Research: Early Lessons from Success*. New Directions for Teaching and Learning, no. 46. San Francisco: Jossey-Bass, 1991.

Study Group on the Conditions of Excellence in American Higher Education. *Involvement in Learning*. Washington, D.C.: National Institute of Education, 1984.

Tinto, V. "Education and the Principles of Effective Retention." A speech to the faculty and staff of Fullerton College, Fullerton, Calif., Aug. 17, 1990.

Tobias, S. *Overcoming Math Anxiety*. New York: Norton, 1978.

Walker, C. J. "Classroom Research in Psychology: Assessment Techniques to Enhance Teaching and Learning." In T. A. Angelo (ed.), *Classroom Research: Early Lessons from Success*. New Directions for Teaching and Learning, no. 46. San Francisco: Jossey-Bass, 1991.

Weaver, R. L., and Cotrell, H. W. "Mental Aerobics: The Half-Sheet Response." *Innovative Higher Education*, 1985, *10*, 23–31.

Weimer, M. *Improving College Teaching: Strategies for Developing Instructional Effectiveness*. San Francisco: Jossey-Bass, 1990.

Weinstein, C., and Mayer, R. "The Teaching of Learning Strategies." In M. C. Wittrock (ed.), *Handbook of Research on Teaching*. New York: Macmillan, 1986.

Weinstein, C. E., and Meyer, D. K. "Cognitive Learning Strategies and College Teaching." In R. J. Menges and M. D. Svinicki (eds.), *College Teaching: From Theory to Practice*. New Directions for Teaching and Learning, no 46. San Francisco: Jossey-Bass, 1991.

Wilson, R. C. "Improving Faculty Teaching: Effective Use of Student Evaluations and Consultants." *Journal of Higher Education*, 1986, *57*(2), 196–211.

Wilson, R. C., and Gaff, J. G. *College Professors and Their Impact on Students*. New York: Wiley, 1975.

Wittrock, M. C. "A Constructive Review of Research on Learning Strategies." In C. E. Weinstein, E. T. Goetz, and P. A. Alexander (eds.), *Learning and Study Strategies: Issues in Assessment, Instruction, and Evaluation*. San Diego, Calif.: Academic Press, 1988.

Zeiders, B. B., and Sivak, M. "Quality Circles from A to Z: King Arthur to Theory Z." *The Clearing House*, 1985, *59*(4), 123–124.

Index

Matrix for, 110, 143–144. *See also*
Fine arts
Asian-American studies, Double-Entry
Journals for, 110, 264
Assessable questions, in Classroom Assessment Project Cycle, 36, 40–45, 47
Assignment Assessments: applying, 109,
110, 112, 113, 114; described, 343,
356–358
Association of American Colleges, 14
Astin, A. W., 14
Astronomy: assessing categorizing skills
in, 65–67, 110; Classroom Assessment
Project in, 51; Misperception/Preconception Check for, 110, 134–135
Attention skills (Goal 9): Chain Notes
for, 322–326; Empty Outlines for,
138–141; Focused Listing for, 126–
131; Minute Paper for, 148–153; Muddiest Point for, 154–158; Punctuated
Lectures for, 303–306; RSQC2 for,
344–348
Attitudes and values, course-related, assessing, 75–79, 87–90, 257–279
Audio- and Videotaped Protocols: applying, 109, 110, 111, 112, 113; described, 213, 226–230
Ausubel, D. P., 117
Autobiography. *See* Focused Autobiographical Sketches
Automotive technology: Annotated Portfolios for, 210; Goal Ranking and
Matching for, 291

B

Background Knowledge Probe: in
anthropology, 63–65; applying, 109,
110, 111, 113; described, 119, 121–
125
Barnett, D. C., 16
Basic Academic Success Skills cluster, 17,
20, 113, 367, 369
Bayer, A. E., 14
Beal, P. E., 375
Belenky, M. F., 83, 298
Bennett, W. E., 338
Berthoff, A. E., 187
Biology: Categorizing Grid for, 110, 161;
Defining Features Matrix for, 110,
165; Human Tableau or Class
Modeling for, 110, 245; Memory
Matrix for, 144–145; Misperception/
Preconception Check for, 110, 134;
One-Sentence Summary for, 110,
184–185; Pro and Con Grid for, 110,
169
Blackburn, R. T., 318, 319
Bloom, B. S., 14, 106, 116, 181
Boehrer, J., 306
Borgen, F. H., 16
Bowen, H. R., 14, 15–16

Bradford College, Teaching Goals
Inventory at, 14
Bransford, J. D., 255
Brown, A. L., 255
Business and management: Application
Cards for, 110, 237; Assignment
Assessments for, 356–357;
Categorizing Grid for, 110, 161–162;
Directed Paraphrasing for, 110, 233–
234; Empty Outlines for, 110, 139–
140; goals in, 367–368; and learning
theory, 386; Pro and Con Grid for,
110, 169; Problem Recognition Tasks
for, 110, 215; Profiles of Admirable
Individuals for, 110, 268; What's the
Principle? for, 110, 219; Word Journal
for, 110, 189–190

C

Calculus: active learning in, 372; One-
Sentence Summary for, 110
California: Classroom Research in, 375–
376; Teaching Goals Inventory in, 15
California, Berkeley, University of,
research at, 10
Campione, J. C., 255
Categorizing, assessing skills in, 65–67
Categorizing Grid: applying, 109, 110,
112, 113; in astronomy, 65–67;
described, 159, 160–163
Center for Faculty Evaluation and
Development in Higher Education, 14
Centra, J. A., 107, 317, 319
Chain Notes: applying, 109, 111, 112,
113, 114; described, 320, 322–326
Chemistry: active learning in, 373; Exam
Evaluations for, 110; Group
Instructional Feedback Technique for,
110, 335–336; Misperception/
Preconception Check for, 137;
Muddiest Point for, 110, 156
Chickering, A. W., 14, 219, 373
Child development: Empty Outlines for,
110, 139; Exam Evaluations for, 359–
360
Chipman, S. E., 116
Citizenship (Goal 29), 21
Civil engineering, Pro and Con Grid for,
169
Clark, D. J., 338
Clark, M. J., 318
Class activities and materials, assessing
learner reactions to, 98–102, 343–361
Classroom Assessment: applying, 363–
387; assumptions of, 7–11;
background of, 381–382; beginning,
1–102; benefits of, 4–5, 26, 379;
characteristics of, 4–6; as context-
specific, 5–6; costs of, 378; described,
3–11; faculty use of, 4, 370–372;
feedback from, 6; as formative
approach, 5; future for, 381–387;

Group Instructional Feedback Technique (GIFT): applying, 109, 110, 114; described, 321, 334–338

Group-Work Evaluations: applying, 109, 111, 112, 114; described, 343, 349–351; in developmental education, 98–102

H

Half-Minute Papers, 152

Half-Sheet Response. *See* Minute Paper

Harvard University: faculty development at, 306; Graduate School of Education at, 14; Muddiest Point at, 158, 370–371; research at, 10; Seminars on Assessment at, 14

Hastings, J. T., 106, 116

HDWDWW, 187

Health. *See* Emotional health; Physical health; Public health

Health science, Misperception/Preconception Check for, 134

Henry, L. H., 202

Higher education: Interest/Knowledge/Skills Checklists for, 286–287; mission of, 3, 366

Higher-Order Thinking Skills cluster, 16, 17, 20, 113, 366, 367, 369

Hirshfield, C., 342

Historical perspective (Goal 32): in anthropology, 42, 63–65; Background Knowledge Probe for, 121–125; Everyday Ethical Dilemmas for, 271–274; Human Tableau or Class Modeling for, 244–247; Invented Dialogues for, 203–207; Profiles of Admirable Individuals for, 267–270

History: Classroom Assessment Quality Circles for, 111, 340; Classroom Opinion Polls for, 111, 260; Exam Evaluations for, 111; Focused Listing for, 131; Invented Dialogues for, 207; Minute Paper for, 111, 149–150; Misperception/Preconception Check for, 111, 133–134; Profiles of Admirable Individuals for, 111, 268

History of science, Concept Maps for, 111, 200

Holistic thinking (Goal 6): Concept Maps for, 197–202; Minute Paper for, 148–153; Word Journal for, 188–192

Honesty (Goal 50): Assignment Assessments for, 356–358; Classroom Assessment Quality Circles for, 339–342; Exam Evaluations for, 359–361; Group Instructional Feedback Technique for, 334–338; Group-Work Evaluations for, 349–351; Misperception/Preconception Check for, 132–137; Reading Rating Sheets for, 352–355; Teacher-Designed Feedback Forms for, 330–333

Human Tableau or Class Modeling: applying, 109, 110, 111, 113, 114; described, 231, 244–247

Humanities. *See* Art and humanities

I

Ideas. *See* Openness to ideas

Implementing: in Classroom Assessment Project Cycle, 34, 36, 49–54; of Classroom Assessment Techniques, 29–30

Inference drawing (Goal 4): Application Cards for, 236–239; Categorizing Grid for, 160–163; Classroom Assessment Quality Circles for, 339–342; Concept Maps for, 197–202; Defining Features Matrix for, 164–167; Group Instructional Feedback Technique for, 334–338; Invented Dialogues for, 203–207; Pro and Con Grid for, 168–171; Productive Study-Time Logs for, 300–302; Teacher-Designed Feedback Forms for, 330–333

Integrating. *See* Synthesizing and integrating

Interest/Knowledge/Skills Checklists: applying, 109, 111, 112, 114; described, 280, 285–289; and metacognition, 256

International relations, Muddiest Point for, 155

Interpretation, for responding, 54–56

Invented Dialogues: applying, 109, 111, 112, 113, 114; described, 181, 203–207

J

Jigsaw learning, with group memory, 65

Journalism, Minute Paper for, 111, 151

Journals. *See* Double-Entry Journals; Word Journal

K

Kelly, D. K., 375, 376

Knowledge. *See* Background knowledge Probe; Course-related knowledge and skills; Prior knowledge, recall, and understanding

Kogut, L. S., 342

Kohlberg, L., 56, 271

Kort, M. S., 371, 372, 373, 374

Kulik, J. A., 14, 107, 317, 318

L

Leadership skills (Goal 38): Analytic Memos for, 177–180; Classroom Opinion Polls for, 258–262; Course-Related Self-Confidence Surveys for, 275–279; Everyday Ethical Dilemmas

226–230; Background Knowledge Probe for, 121–125; Categorizing Grid for, 160–163; Chain Notes for, 322–326; Concept Maps for, 197–202; Content, Form, and Function Outlines for, 172–176; Defining Features Matrix for, 164–167; Diagnostic Learning Logs for, 311–315; Directed Paraphrasing for, 232–235; Documented Problem Solutions for, 222–225; Double-Entry Journals for, 263–266; Empty Outlines for, 138–141; Exam Evaluations for, 359–361; Focused Listing for, 126–131; Group-Work Evaluations for, 349–351; in math class, 40; Memory Matrix for, 142–147; Minute Paper for, 148–153; Muddiest Point for, 154–158; One-Sentence Summary for, 183–187; Paper or Project Prospectus for, 248–253; Problem Recognition Tasks for, 214–217; Process Analysis for, 307–310; Productive Study-Time Logs for, 300–302; Punctuated Lectures for, 303–306; Reading Rating Sheets for, 352–355; RSQC2 for, 344–348; Student-Generated Test Questions for, 240–243; What's the Principle? for, 218–221; Word Journal for, 188–192

Study skills, strategies, and behavior, assessing, 90–95, 299–315

Study skills and personal development, Everyday Ethical Dilemmas for, 112, 272

Study time. *See* Productive Study-Time Logs

Summary. *See* One-Sentence Summary

Svinicki, M. D., 385

Synthesis and creative thinking, assessing, 72–75, 181–212

Synthesizing and integration (Goal 5): Approximate Analogies for, 193–196; Concept Maps for, 197–202; Human Tableau or Class Modeling for, 244–247; Invented Dialogues for, 203–207; Minute Paper for, 148–153; One-Sentence Summary for, 183–187; Paper or Project Prospectus for, 248–253; in political science, 72–75; RSQC2 for, 344–348; Word Journal for, 188–192

T

Tableau. *See* Human Tableau or Class Modeling

Tarule, J., 83, 298

Taveggia, T. C., 318

Teacher-Designed Feedback Forms: applying, 109, 113, 114; described, 320–321, 330–333

Teachers and teaching, assessing learner reactions to, 95–98, 320–342. *See also* Faculty

Teaching Goals Inventory (TGI): administration of, 17–18, 27; applications for, 8; aspects of, 13–23; and Classroom Assessment Project Cycle, 36–45; Classroom Assessment Techniques by clusters of, 105, 107, 113–114; for Classroom Assessments, 19, 22–23; in departments, 383; development of, 13–18; goal clusters of, 15–17; lessons and insights from, 365–370; listing of goals in, 20–21; self-scoring, 18, 20–22, 370; scoring, 18–19. *See also for specific goals:* Goal 1, Principles, applying; Goal 2, Analytic skills; Goal 3, Problem solving; Goal 4, Inference drawing; Goal 5, Synthesizing and integrating; Goal 6, Holistic thinking; Goal 7, Creative thinking; Goal 8, Facts and opinions; Goal 9, Attention skills; Goal 10, Concentration; Goal 11, Memory; Goal 12, Listening skills; Goal 13, Speaking skills; Goal 14, Reading skills; Goal 15, Writing skills; Goal 16, Study skills; Goal 17, Math skills; Goal 18, Terms and facts; Goal 19, Concepts and theories; Goal 20, Materials and tools; Goal 21, Values of subject; Goal 22, Transfer or graduate study preparation; Goal 23, Techniques and methods; Goal 24, Evaluating subject materials; Goal 25, Contributions to subject; Goal 26, Appreciation of liberal arts and sciences; Goal 27, Openness to ideas; Goal 28, Concern for social issues; Goal 29, Citizenship; Goal 30, Lifelong learning; Goal 31, Aesthetic appreciation; Goal 32, Historical perspective; Goal 33, Science and technology understanding; Goal 34, Other cultures; Goal 35, Ethical choices; Goal 36, Working with others; Goal 37, Management skills; Goal 38, Leadership skills; Goal 39, Accurate work; Goal 40, Following directions; Goal 41, Time use; Goal 42, Personal achievement; Goal 43, Performance skills; Goal 44, Responsibility for self; Goal 45, Self-esteem; Goal 46, Values commitment; Goal 47, Respect for others; Goal 48, Emotional health; Goal 49, Physical health; Goal 50, Honesty; Goal 51, Thinking for self; Goal 52, Wise decisions

Teaching target lesson, in implementation, 49–50

Techniques and methods (Goal 23): Audio- and Videotaped Protocols for,

Skills Checklists for, 285–289; Pro and Con Grid for, 168–171; Productive Study-Time Logs for, 300–302; Profiles of Admirable Individuals for, 267–270

Wittrock, M. C., 386

Women's studies: Classroom Assessment Project in, 37–39; Concept Maps for, 112, 198, 200; Profiles of Admirable Individuals for, 112, 268

Word Journal: applying, 109, 110, 111, 112, 113; described, 181, 188–192

Work and Career Preparation cluster, 17, 21, 114, 367, 369

Working with others (Goal 36): Classroom Assessment Quality Circles for, 339–342; in developmental education, 98–102; Electronic Mail Feedback for, 327–329; Goal Ranking and Matching for, 290–294; Group Instructional Feedback Technique for, 334–338; Group-Work Evaluations for, 349–351; Human Tableau or Class Modeling for, 244–247; in speech communication, 82–87

Writing. *See* English and writing

Writing skills (Goal 15): Analytic Memos for, 177–180; Content, Form, and Function Outlines for, 172–176; Directed Paraphrasing for, 232–235; and disciplinary differences, 368; Paper or Project Prospectus for, 248–253

Z

Zeiders, B. B., 342

Zoology, Categorizing Grid for, 112, 161